Quiet Times

FOR PARENTS

H. Norman Wright

HARVEST HOUSE PUBLISHERS
Eugene, Oregon 97402

Cover design by Koechel Peterson & Associates, Minneapolis, Minnesota

QUIET TIMES FOR PARENTS

Copyright © 1995 Harvest House Publishers
Eugene, Oregon 97402

Wright, H. Norman.
    Quiet times for parents / H. Norman Wright.
        p. cm.
    ISBN 1-56507-357-6 (hardcover)
    ISBN 0-7369-0126-4 (softcover)
    1. Parents—Prayer-books and devotions—English. 2. Devotional
calendars. I. Title.
BV4529.W74 1995   95-44183
242'.645—dc20   CIP

Printed in the United States of America.

00 01 02 / BP / 10 9 8 7 6 5 4 3 2

Introduction

Perhaps you've read the initial book in this series, *Quiet Times for Couples*. The book was designed to assist couples in building their spiritual intimacy, and the response to it has been overwhelming.

This second volume is a brand-new concept—*Quiet Times for Parents*. Some people have asked, "Is there such a possibility? Parenthood is such a hurried, hassled experience!" Yes, quiet times can and do exist for parents. A few minutes a day, by yourself or with your partner, can bring you a sense of renewal for the calling and challenges of being a parent.

The thoughts and encouragements on these pages have been drawn from the wisdom and insight of many authors who have traveled the path that you are on right now. Built upon the Word of God, the pages are designed to give you inspiration, hope, and guidelines for specific situations. Based on biblical principles, these pages contain an encyclopedia of information ranging from theology and prayer to discipline and character formation. Because of the breadth of topics, I've included a topical index in case you are in need of immediate assistance in a particular area.

I hope that with the help of *Quiet Times for Parents*, your journey as a parent will be easier and more fulfilling and that you will gain a renewed vision of the full meaning of God's Word in your life.

—H. Norman Wright

January 1

Train up a child in the way he should go [and in keeping with his individual gift or bent], and when he is old he will not depart from it (Proverbs 22:6, AMP).

*H*ave you ever wondered as a parent, *What in the world am I doing?* Many parents have asked that, especially after a particularly stressful, unproductive, disastrous, exhausting day. One parent said, "There are days when I question whether I've accomplished anything. It seems like I follow one child for a while and then another, either trying to head off a pending disaster or trying to salvage the remnants of the most recent one. Is this what parenting is all about? Is this what I'm supposed to be accomplishing with my life? I feel like a janitor."

Another parent reflected, "Parenting is a lot different than I ever expected. Some days I think I'm more of a chauffeur and other days the enforcer of homework. Then there are the times when I'm a censor for TV programs and the chef of a fast-food diner! I wanted my life to count for something as a parent, but I wonder at times what it is. Have I lost sight of something? Am I putting my time and energy into the right areas or should I be focusing elsewhere?"

Sometimes the task of parenting seems survival more than anything else. It's so easy to become immersed in the tasks and activities of running the home, of putting out brush fires, instead of focusing on our calling as Christian parents.

In the past, there were times when God called His people back to their primary purpose. With today's hectic schedules, it may be helpful to refocus on our calling as parents. Consider these thoughts and read them out loud each day for a month. You won't lose sight of them if you do that!

> The primary goal of child rearing is to produce godly character in children so that God will be glorified. This perspective transforms the task of child rearing. Our goal is no longer merely to resolve family conflicts and find a little peace. Now we are participating in God's great program of the ages. We are shaping lives for eternity. We are helping to form each child's character so that he or she reflects God's glory.[1]

January 2

Yes, they shall sing of the ways of the Lord, and joyfully celebrate His mighty acts (Psalm 138:5, AMP).

*Y*ou've changed. You're different today than you were last year, five years, or ten years ago. We all change and that's good, for change means growth. Events in our lives impact us and cause us to make course corrections. Sometimes what affects us also irritates us, for it dislodges us from a comfortable niche.

Perhaps there were occasions when you wanted something different in your life and you got it. But you didn't realize how much what you received would alter the whole direction of your life. It was not all that you expected. And you couldn't go back to the way life had been before. It was a permanent change and you had to learn to live with it.

Life is full of events that change us or cause our lifestyle to be turned upside-down. Sometimes we don't recognize how much power or force some events or incidents contain until after they happen. Consider earthquakes. They rumble in unannounced and with a shattering force that rocks and sways the very mountains God created and the sturdiest buildings man has erected. They change the life and direction of not just a few people but sometimes an entire nation. God can use unusual natural events such as earthquakes, tornadoes, or hurricanes to capture a person's attention. Sometimes the people affected turn their thoughts to Him because of what they've experienced. But God may surprise us. What He chooses to use to change a life or the direction of mankind may not be what we expect. T.S. Sullivan describes it well:

> When God wants a great work done in the world or a great wrong righted, he goes about it in a very unusual way. He doesn't stir up his earthquakes or send for his thunderbolts.
> Instead he has a helpless baby born, perhaps in a simple home and of some obscure mother. And then God puts his idea into the mother's heart and she puts it into the baby's mind.
> And then God waits.
> The greatest forces in the world are not the earthquakes and the thunderbolts. The greatest forces in the world are babies.[2]

If you've had one, you know what he's talking about. By the way, how will your child impact the world for God in the future?

January 3

Trust in the LORD with all your heart and lean not on your own understanding (Proverbs 3:5).

*H*ave you ever wished for an instruction manual on how to parent? Most of us have. As one prospective parent said, "It seems overwhelming what's facing us. In a few months we will have the responsibility for a new life. How will we know what to do? It would be so much easier if we knew exactly what our child will need."

Now, that's a request that can be filled, for all children need the following:

> What do children need? And how well can parents meet their needs? Children need acceptance. They need praise and appreciation. They need to learn they can trust their parents not to deceive them or to break promises. They need consistency and fairness. They need to feel that their fears, their desires, their feelings, their inexplicable impulses, their frustrations, and their inabilities are understood by their parents. They need to know exactly where the limits are, what is permitted and what is prohibited. They need to know that home is a safe place, a place of refuge, a place where they have no need to be afraid. They need warm approval when they do well, and firm correction when they do wrong. They need to learn a sense of proportion. They need to know that their parents are stronger than they are, able to weather the storms and dangers of the outer world and also able to stand up to their (children's) rages and unreasonable demands. They need to feel their parents like them and can take time to listen. They need perceptive responses to their growing need for independence.[3]

As you reflect upon each one of these needs, how are they being fulfilled in your family? Can you think of ways they could be fulfilled even more? Knowing what you are accomplishing can help ease the pressure and stress you may be feeling. Oh, you won't succeed all the time, because all parents are amateurs to begin with. But focus more on when you are meeting your children's needs than when you aren't, and you will find yourself becoming even more competent.

January 4

Do not be anxious about anything, but in everything, by prayer and petition, with thanksgiving, present your requests to God (Philippians 4:6).

*I*t's been one of those days. Hectic, hurried, and hassled. You couldn't stop for a minute; you would have been run over. They were all right behind you waiting for you to stumble— deadlines, dishes, the dentist, duties waiting to devour you if you dallied just for a moment. It seemed that everyone and every- thing from the kids to the endless phone interruptions wanted a piece of you. When one task was completed (or just started) the next one raised its head demanding to be noticed. A spilled plate (full of food), the dog's dish overturned, the stopped-up toilet, and the forgotten child crying and waiting at school to be picked up and taken to practice all seemed to make your day... worse. In the midst of it all you wondered, *Will it ever end? Where will I find more time? What else can go wrong? How can I hurry more?*

But wait! Hold it. Hurrying isn't the answer. It won't help. It won't work. It will stress you out more and build a sense of panic. What you want to do is slow down. Yes, that's what I said: slow down. In fact, when your day is coming apart and you're running around in circles, stop. Hold everything. Sit down in a comfort- able chair, take a deep breath and . . . read the following prayer:

Steady my hurried pace with a vision of the eternal reach of time.

Give me, amid the confusion of the day, the calmness of the everlasting hills.

Break the tensions of my nerves and muscles with the soothing music of the singing streams that live in my memory.

Teach me the art of taking minute vacations—of slowing down to look at a flower, to chat with a friend, to pat a dog, to smile at a child, to read a few lines from a good book.

Slow me down, Lord, and inspire me to send my roots deep into the soil of life's enduring values, that I may grow toward my greater destiny.

Remind me each day that the race is not always to the swift; that there is more to life than increasing its speed.

Let me look upward to the towering oak and know that it grew great and strong because it grew slowly and well.[4]

January 5

A glad heart makes a cheerful countenance, but by sorrow of heart the spirit is broken. . . . All the days of the desponding and afflicted are made evil [by anxious thoughts and forebodings], but he who has a glad heart has a continual feast [regardless of circumstances] (Proverbs 15:13,15 AMP).

*L*augh a little. No, laugh a lot. Those are words of wisdom. Laughter is one of God's gifts. Life is filled with incidents that lend themselves to not just a snicker, but an uncontrolled siege of laughter.

What's the laughter level in your family? As a parent, your children will supply you with many opportunities to laugh. Some of the time you may wonder if you should be laughing or you wish you hadn't. Sometimes your kids misbehave in ways that are highly punctuated with something funny and you end up desperately trying to keep a straight face while you correct them. We've all been through that dilemma.

A sense of humor reflects a healthy atmosphere within the home. The Scripture says, "A joyful heart is good medicine, but a broken spirit dries up the bones" (Proverbs 17:22, NASB). Solomon tells us what happens when we lose our sense of humor. We will have a broken spirit, a lack of inner healing, and dried-up bones. When we lose our ability to enjoy life, something is wrong somewhere.

Humor relaxes. It relieves tension. It brings a balance into life. It gives you a respite from the heaviness of life's concerns and griefs. Those who don't laugh tend to shrivel up like a dried-out prune.

Who tells the jokes in your family? Parents, what are the humorous incidents that happened to you as a child? Have you shared those with your children? Some families end their meal time with the question, "What's the funniest thing you experienced or heard about today?"

When you laugh as a family, remember to laugh with one another rather than at one another. Look for the lighter side in the seriousness of life. It will help make parenthood a bit easier.

January 6

You are not your own for you have been bought with a price
(1 Corinthians 6:19,20).

*Y*ears ago a Christian publishing house came out with a ministry to help prospective parents. It was called "The Cradle Roll Program." This program provided written materials to assist parents who were preparing for their child. The title of the material was called "Loan of a Life," which reflected the fact that children don't really belong to us. They're not our possession. We've been entrusted with their care and, in the natural progression of life, they will be relinquished at a given point in time to form their own families. Actually, you will relinquish them in many different ways all through their lives as they progress toward maturity. Understanding what this process entails ahead of time makes it much easier to handle.

> To understand what relinquishment is we must first understand what God is like and what the essence of His relationship to us is. As He is to us, so must we (so far as possible) be to our children.
> God's attitude as a parent combines loving care and instruction with a refusal to force our obedience. He longs to bless us, yet He will not cram blessings down our throats. Our sins and rebellions cause Him grief, and in His grief He will do much to draw us back to Himself. Yet, if we persist in our wrongdoing He will let us find, by the pain of bitter experience, that it would have been better to obey Him.
> To relinquish your children does not mean to abandon them, however, but to give them back to God, and in so doing to take your own hands off them. It means neither to neglect your responsibilities toward them, nor to relinquish the authority you need to fulfill those responsibilities. It means to release those controls that arise from needless fears, or from selfish ambitions.[5]

How are you doing in your relinquishing? Is it difficult at times? Scary? It's not easy to take our hands off and let our children flounder or fend for themselves. They don't do things our way. They'll make some bad choices along with the good. But God knows all about that, doesn't He?

January 7

Blessing for a home: *O Lord God Almighty, bless this house. In it may there be health, chastity, victory over sin, strength, humility, goodness of heart and gentleness, full of observance of your law and gratefulness to God, the Father, and the Son, and the Holy Spirit.*[6]

Prayer of Faith for Our Home

Almighty God,
You have called us to the holy state of matrimony
and have shared with us your gift of creation.
We thank you for making our love fruitful.

May we be worthy representatives
of you, dear Lord,
in forming our children
in your knowledge and love.

May our children ever walk in
the ways of your commandments
and live according to
the teachings of your holy Church.

May our example, dear God,
be such as to inspire our children
to grow into the likeness
of your Son, Jesus Christ.

May we be firm but kind in discipline.
May we stand as one
united in authority
so as to be consistent.

May we never confuse
permissiveness with love.
May we teach our children
respect for your authority
in ourselves and
in all your representatives on earth.

May our home be as a Church,
for you, Lord Jesus Christ,
are present wherever two or three are gathered
together in your name.

May praises of God frequently
rise from the lips and hearts of our family
and may we all one day
be united in our eternal home. Amen.

Anonymous

January 8

I will do whatever you ask in my name, so that the Son may bring glory to the Father. You may ask me for anything in my name, and I will do it (John 14:13,14).

Thoughts from a Pastor

Dr. Lloyd John Ogilvie, former pastor of Hollywood Presbyterian Church and now chaplain of the U.S. Senate, concluded each page of his book *God's Best for My Life* with a thought for the day. Perhaps some of these will make your journey through this day easier.

"The Lord does not ridicule our fears; He comes to walk through them with us."

"Prayer is not to change, but to receive, the mind and will of God."

"Our problem is not to get God to answer our prayers, but to recognize the answers already given."

"When we recognize God's gifts in us or the people we love or the things we do, then there is a deep sense of gratitude which issues in creative pride."

"I will think, act, and react as a servant, doing whatever I can to serve others today. Through Christ, I know where I came from and where I'm going, and therefore I have nothing to lose and everything to give."

"We do not need to defend ourselves if the Lord is our ultimate security."

"Christ has given us as a gift to one another to express the love and forgiveness of the cross in our relationships. Today I will 'behold' each person in my life as a trust from the crucified Lord."

"Fear closes the doors of life. The resurrected Christ gives us the courage to open them."

"Discouragement is a warning signal that we need a renewed relationship with the Lord. Don't wait for the discouragement to end before you go to Him; go to Him to end the discouragement."

"Today I want God's will and His kingdom to come in my life in fullness of power."[7]

January 9

See how great a love the Father has bestowed upon us...
(1 John 3:1, NASB).

C hildren often come to their parents and ask, "Mommy, Daddy, do you love me?" You reply with "yes" and tell them how much you love them. They then go away satisfied. We all want to know that we're loved; we are like children in that regard.

One little girl went to her father and asked, "Daddy, what are the times when you don't love me?" He answered, "I love you all the time. There isn't a time that I don't love you. You should know that." This didn't satisfy her for she continued, "But Daddy, I've heard you say if you're not good and you don't obey, we won't love you." Her father said, "But I didn't mean that. I always love you. I just said that to get you to mind me. That's all."

She thought for a moment and said, "It makes me feel that you love me for the way I behave, not just for me." Her father gulped.

It's easy to convey the message to our children that they are loved based upon what they do. It comes across by what we say, what we don't say, how we say it, and how we look at our children. One father described his experience this way:

> Some time ago Denalyn was gone for a couple of days and left me alone with the girls. Though the time was not without the typical children's quarrels and occasional misbehavior, it went fine.
> "How were the girls?" Denalyn asked when she got home.
> "Good. No problem at all."
> Jenna overhead my response. "We weren't good, Daddy," she objected. "We fought once, we didn't do what you said once. We weren't good. How can you say we were good?"
> Jenna and I had different perceptions of what pleases a father. She thought it depended upon what she did. It didn't. We think the same about God. We think his love rises and falls with our performance. It doesn't. I don't love Jenna for what she does. I love her for whose she is. She is mine.
> God loves you for the same reason. He loves you for whose you are, you are his child. It was this love that pursued the Israelites. It was this love that sent the prophets. It was this love which wrapped itself in human flesh and descended the birth canal of Mary.[8]

Thank God He's given us a model for His love.

January 10

Fixing our eyes on Jesus, the author and perfecter of faith . . . (Hebrews 12:2, NASB).

A boy went into a pet shop, looking for a puppy. The store owner showed him a litter in a box. The boy looked at the puppies. He picked each one up, examined it, and put it back into the box.

After several minutes, he walked back to the owner and said, "I picked one out. How much will it cost?"

The man gave him the price, and the boy promised to be back in a few days with the money. "Don't take too long," the owner cautioned. "Puppies like these sell quickly."

The boy turned and smiled knowingly, "I'm not worried," he said. "Mine will still be here."

The boy went to work—weeding, washing windows, cleaning yards. He worked hard and saved his money. When he had enough for the puppy, he returned to the store.

He walked up to the counter and laid down a pocketful of wadded bills. The store owner sorted and counted the cash. After verifying the amount, he smiled at the boy and said, "All right, son, you can go get your puppy."

The boy reached into the back of the box, pulled out a skinny dog with a limp leg, and started to leave.

The owner stopped him.

"Don't take that puppy," he objected. "He's crippled. He can't play. He'll never run with you. He can't fetch. Get one of the healthy pups."

"No thank you, sir," the boy replied. "This is exactly the kind of dog I've been looking for."

As the boy turned to leave, the store owner started to speak but remained silent. Suddenly he understood. For extending from the bottom of the boy's trousers was a brace—a brace for his crippled leg.

Why did the boy want the dog? Because he knew how it felt. And he knew it was very special.

What did Jesus know that enabled him to do what he did? He knew how the people felt, and he knew that they were special.

I hope you never forget that.

Jesus knows how you feel.

You are precious to him. So precious that he became like you so that you would come to him.[9]

That's something to remember!

January 11

Train up a child in the way he should go [and in keeping with his individual gift or bent], and when he is old he will not depart from it (Proverbs 22:6, AMP).

*D*o you ever feel guilty over what your children do or the way they're turning out? Do you ever wonder what you've done wrong? Do you ever question your capabilities? If so, you're like most parents. Perhaps you've been taught some misinterpretations of Proverbs 22:6. Dr. James Kennedy says,

> Many parents feel guilty when they read Proverbs 22:6 because they hear it saying they can expect their children to be converted only if they're perfect parents. But that line of thinking ignores the biblical passages assuring them that if they try to live godly lives, God will bless them.
> God does not require or expect you to be perfect. He knows that's impossible. He asks only for your best effort.[10]

Some parents attempt to manipulate God to touch their children's lives. They stand up in church and say, "Father, I praise You because You have saved my child. I praise You because she is a believer in Your sight. Now, please manifest this truth in her life so I might praise You for that as well."

Other parents fall back upon the promises of infant baptism. They maintain, "I had my child baptized and made him a child of God. God never loses one of His children."[11]

But biblical faith is much more complicated than that. Our God is the personal Lord of the universe. He is working out His plan of redemption through Jesus Christ according to His perfect will. God is sovereign in our salvation, and He grants it according to His mercy upon whom He chooses (*see* Romans 9–11; Ephesians 1).

Our sovereign Lord can be touched by our prayers. He allows Himself to be influenced by them. But we can never force Him to act. We need to hope that He will act, yet always be ready to accept His decision with peace and submission.[12]

January 12

Train up a child in the way he should go [and in keeping with his individual gift or bent], and when he is old he will not depart from it (Proverbs 22:6, AMP).

*W*hat does Proverbs 22:6 tell us about parenting? It explains the parental responsibility to dedicate our children to God and train them in His ways.

In the original Hebrew text, the phrase "in the way that he should go" reflects the thought that parents need to consider the particular child's stage of development and unique personality. The Amplified Bible says, "In keeping with his individual gift or bent." Rather than teaching that we should respond to every child in the same way, this verse urges parents to train their child to love God and serve Him in light of the child's unique gifts and temperament.

Dr. Gleason Archer summarizes the parents' duties and their realistic expectations this way:

> This type of training implies a policy of treating children as even more important than one's own personal convenience or social life away from home. It means impressing on them that they are very important persons in their own right because they are loved by God, and because He has a wonderful and perfect plan for their lives. Parents who have faithfully followed these principles and practices in rearing their children may safely entrust them as adults to the keeping and guidance of God and feel no sense of personal guilt if the child later veers off course. They have done their best before God. The rest is put to each child himself.[13]

If you follow the advice in Proverbs 22:6, there's a good probability that your children will either remain true to this instruction all their lives or return to God's teachings as they mature. Remember, though, that this is only a probability, not a certainty. What's important is that you understand the uniqueness of each child's personality and adapt your responses to that uniqueness. When you do that, you'll find yourself relaxing and becoming less frustrated. And isn't that another good reason to adapt to your children!

January 13

If anyone does not provide for his relatives, and especially for his immediate family, he has denied the faith and is worse than an unbeliever (1 Timothy 5:8).

*M*uch is said about what we leave for our children through our wills and living trusts. At one time or another everyone has to consider what will be left to his or her children when he or she dies. But you will leave more than that. You have passed on your genes as well. There is a biological pattern that was transferred to each child. There is also an emotional pattern that is being passed on from you to them just as it was passed on to you. We call all of this your legacy.

You're making an impact—an imprint on your children's lives. Most parents want to leave a positive model for their children. If the legacy you received from your parents wasn't the best or you feel you were shortchanged, don't despair. This is your opportunity to be a transition person and break the linkage from the past. Focus on what and who you want to become and what you want to do. And above all, be there for your children. Be there, be present, be available, be approachable, be loving, and reflect Jesus' love in your life.

Talk over how you want to raise your children. What rare experiences could you create for your children that would not only be a terrific memory, but also change their life in some way? What are the times that your children really want you with them? What special event do all of you need to attend so the memory is complete? Do you know? Has your child told you? Have you asked?

January 14

I trust in you, O LORD; I say, "You are my God." My times are in your hands (Psalm 31:14).

I miss the early years with my children. I was so tied up in work at that time."

"The nest doesn't seem to empty as fast as I want. They're sure slow about moving out."

"I looked at that small chair and started to cry. It seemed like just yesterday my son was sitting in it."

"I'm sure I'll be glad when they leave. But won't I feel useless?"

"That room seemed so empty when he left."

"I'm looking forward to a new job—this time for pay!"

"Now that they're gone, we sit, we don't talk, don't look at each other. Nothing!"

"Parenting is hard work and I want to get out of this job."

"We married at 20 and had the first one at 22. The last one came at 34. He left when he turned 21. Why didn't someone tell us it would take 29 years until we were alone again as a couple!"

"We've adjusted to the children being gone. I hope none of them get a divorce or lose a job and have to move back. I like this step!"

"I don't want to build my happiness on when they call, write, or visit. I need my own life now."

"They left too soon, married too young, and had kids too soon. I hope they realize I'm not their babysitter. I already raised one family and I'm not going to raise another."

"I've done what I could. They're in the Lord's hands now. And I guess they always have been, come to think of it."

Perhaps your children have already left. Do you ever say any of the above statements? Who did you share those thoughts with? Or maybe you're in the midst of raising a tribe of young ones and don't have a minute to think about what you'll say then, let alone now!

Take a break and reflect for a moment. How will you feel when your children are gone? What would you like to say to them about them when they leave? What would your partner want to say? Let God guide your thoughts.

January 15

A good name is rather to be chosen than great riches, and loving favor rather than silver and gold (Proverbs 22:1, KJV).

A daughter wrote the following poem about her dad. It's a tribute that perhaps all dads would like to have said about them.

Dad

Dad, you gave me life,
   The family name to hold.
   You taught me humble pride,
   And purity, fine as gold.

Dad, you gave me love.
   You always held my hand.
   You gave me trusting faith,
   That in hard times will stand.

Dad, you gave me strength.
   You showed me how to smile.
   You were my constant friend,
   Down many a weary mile.

Dad, you gave to me a goal,
   To follow all my dreams,
   And gave me loving praise;
   Today, how much it means.

Dad, you are my tower;
   You hold a special place.
   When walking in your footsteps,
   There I see your noble face.

Dad, you were a godly man;
   You taught me how to pray,
   To love the Lord forever;
   His Word will light the way.

Dad, many years have passed away
   Since you said "good-bye" to me.

      I'll look for you in heaven,
      Where we'll spend eternity![14]

January 16

Consider it pure joy, my brothers, whenever you face trials of many kinds, because you know that the testing of your faith develops perseverance (James 1:2,3).

Shattered Dreams—A Personal Note

One of the struggles that we as parents may experience today is the shattering of the dreams we have for our children. When a child begins living a lifestyle that is not a reflection of our own, we may end up feeling devastated.

My wife and I have been there. I will never forget the day our daughter Sheryl walked into my office and calmly told me that she understood the values her mother and I had lived by and taught her, but she had decided to take a different direction for her own life. This wasn't an adolescent in the throes of an identity crisis, but a 21-year-old woman.

For the next four years, we experienced deep heartache as we watched our daughter live contrary to her own values as well as ours. Perhaps we hurt even more than others because our communication with her never faltered. Since we kept in close touch, we didn't have to wonder where she was and what was happening. Those were long and painful years.

Then one Sunday morning, the three of us were in the worship service at Hollywood Presbyterian Church, where we attend. At the conclusion, an invitation was given for salvation, rededication, praying for the sick, and the laying on of hands for healing. Sheryl turned to me and said, "Daddy, will you walk up there with me?" I tearfully escorted her to the altar and had the privilege of seeing my daughter rededicate her life to Jesus Christ. Afterward, my wife and I witnessed the changes that took place in Sheryl's life. Two years later, I had the joy of escorting her down another church aisle to be united in marriage to a strong Christian man.

We experienced the deep wounds, but we also had the tremendous joy of experiencing the return of a prodigal daughter. Whenever I hear or read about the prodigal son in Luke 15, I always remind myself that each and every one of us is a prodigal in some way. It's just that some detours in life are much more apparent than others.

January 17

Confess your sins to each other and pray for each other so that you may be healed. The prayer of a righteous man is powerful and effective (James 5:16).

*D*o you have any special family traditions? These can include what you do for the holidays, birthdays, vacations, at meal time, the way you greet one another, or the way you say good-night. For example, years ago the Walton family on television would say goodnight to each other loud enough from each of their rooms so everyone could hear and respond. And come to think of it, watching this program together each week was a family tradition for millions of families in this country. They wouldn't miss it.

Take a moment and respond to the following questions:

1. What were the family traditions that you experienced in your family while growing up?

2. Which family traditions did you bring with you into your current family?

3. What new family traditions have you created?

4. What family traditions did your spouse bring with him or her?

5. What are the purposes and values of your family traditions?

The Tremaines were a family of five. Sunday dinner was a family affair that usually involved guests or some of the children's friends. All the plates were placed face down on the table. When everyone was seated, they would turn them over. One of the plates was labeled, "You are special today." Since the plates were put on the table randomly—including one on the floor for their dog, a husky named Blackie—no one knew in advance who would be honored that day. It was usually a wild time when Blackie was the special pooch for the day!

What's a new tradition that you would like to create? Perhaps it's the selection of a Scripture for the week that you all commit yourselves to follow, or telling each family member, "I prayed for you today!"

January 18

You know that we dealt with each of you as a father deals with his own children (1 Thessalonians 2:11).

*C*harlie Shedd is such an open, honest person. He tells it like it is and shares the lessons he has learned about life and parenting. To his son, Peter, he writes about an experience with his son Philip:

> ... I promise you that I will never say "No" if I can possibly say, "Yes."

> We see it often. Babies raised in a positive atmosphere develop much better personalities than those who constantly hear the words, "No," "Stop," "Don't."

> Let me show you what I mean. This has to do with a dirty old bale of binder twine. When we moved from Nebraska to Oklahoma, we brought it along. I had used it there to tie sacks of feed and miscellaneous items. It cost something like $1.15. So I said, "Now, Philip, you see this binder twine? I want you to leave it alone." But it held a strange fascination for him and he began to use it any time he wanted. I would say, "Don't," "No," and, "You can't!" But to no avail.

> That went on for six or eight months. Then one day I came home, tired. There was the garage, looking like a no-man's land with binder twine across, back and forth, up and down. I had to cut my way through to get the car in. And was I provoked! I ground my teeth as I slashed at that binder twine. Suddenly, when I was halfway through the maze, a light dawned. I asked myself, "Why do you want this binder twine? What if Philip does use it?" So when I went in to supper that night, Philip was there and I began, "Say, about that binder twine!" He hung his head, and mumbled, "Yes, Daddy." Then I said, "Philip, I've changed my mind. You can use that old binder twine any time you want. What's more, all those tools out in the garage I've labeled 'No'—you go ahead and use them. I can buy new tools, but I can't buy new boys." There never was a sunrise like that smile. "Thanks, Daddy," he beamed. And guess what, Peter. He hasn't touched that binder twine since![15]

I guess sometimes we're not that much different from our children, are we?

January 19

. . . and how from infancy you have known the holy Scriptures, which are able to make you wise for salvation through faith in Christ Jesus (2 Timothy 3:15).

*I*sn't it ironic that the moment that dependent little child invades your life you start working with him or her to someday become independent from you! It seems that all of the time you spend with your child is to help him or her *not* need you. But that is your calling and your purpose. How do you do it?

Consider what one family did:

> As the children got older, we began studying Scripture together. . . . Then we started to talk about their quiet times and the things we were learning in our walks with the Lord. From our journals we shared what the Lord was teaching us. If we had a hard week, we felt free to talk about it and soak up the affirmation of our family. We took our concerns to the Lord in a spirit of oneness.
>
> We also helped Tanya and Todd develop goals for their own lives. We felt part of being independent is knowing where you are going. In 1983, we became familiar with MasterPlanning Associates, which helped us consider questions such as, "What are you dreaming of accomplishing five to twenty years from now?" Or, "What needs do you feel deeply burdened by and uniquely qualified to meet?" We helped our children assess the milestones they had already passed and the ideas they would like to see become reality. We talked about colleges and careers and our purpose in life. Together we were able to dream dreams, some of which have already come true.
>
> One of the most practical things we did during our family times was talk about events to come. Each week we got out the calendar, looked at the commitments, and then planned the rest of the week. When the children were little, they were most interested in free time for play; but little by little their activities began to match ours. Looking at the calendar together has helped us take an active interest in one another's lives and avoid the miscommunications which plague busy families. Therefore we were better able to pray for each other and to understand the pressures and opportunities we shared.[16]

What steps can you take this week to make Scripture a part of your children's daily lives?

January 20

My son, be attentive to my Wisdom [godly Wisdom learned by actual and costly experience], and incline your ear to my understanding [of what is becoming and prudent for you], that you may exercise proper discrimination and discretion and your lips may guard and keep knowledge and the wise answer [to temptation] (Proverbs 5:1-2, AMP).

*W*hat's a dad to do? That's the question many fathers ask not just in the early years of parenting but all the way through. Often it's a question asked quietly and silently inside their heart and mind. After all, not too many dads want to admit they don't know. Aren't they supposed to just *know* what to do? Well, perhaps. Then again, perhaps not. All mothers and fathers can use some help and guidance. Here are some guidelines worth considering. Having a road map makes it much easier to get to your destination.

The effective father recognizes that fatherhood is a mandate from God, and he accepts the responsibilities and privileges it brings. He makes a major investment of his time and energy in this calling. He knows also that the God who called him to this unique ministry will sustain him through it.

In his book *The Effective Father*, Gordon MacDonald uses the analogy of an orchestra conductor to describe the father's pacesetting role. In the analogy, the father is the conductor, his family is the orchestra, and God is the composer of the music. The father's task is to make sure the "orchestra" plays the music the way the "composer" wrote it. In other words, his job is to make sure the members of his family are living the way God intends for them to live.

How does the effective father set this kind of pace?

—By expecting obedience from his children and following through to make sure he gets it.

—By protecting his children from harmful influences and supervising their character development.

—By developing good habits in his children's lives.

—By dealing directly with sinful or immature behavior.

—By teaching God's standards for living, as found in the Bible (Deuteronomy 11:18-19).

—By living before his children the kind of life he wants them to live. (Joshua 24:14-15).

All this develops a pace of life that his children can learn to follow.[17]

January 21

I press on toward the goal to win the prize for which God has called me heavenward in Christ Jesus (Philippians 3:14).

*H*ave you ever had days when you wanted to resign from your family? Probably! Totally overwhelmed by the ongoing battle, you're tempted to just give up trying so hard. Children feel that way at times. So do parents . . . and spouses . . . and siblings . . . and even grandparents! When everything falls apart, we all have those fleeting thoughts—and sometimes lasting ones too! Sometimes we don't even *like* that other person, even though we still *love* them.

Recently I saw a book titled, *Where Does a Mother Go to Resign?* Many of you moms can identify with that title.

Think about your calling this way:

> Parenthood is like a marathon race. It's long, demanding, and exhausting. Few pursuits, though, give a greater sense of accomplishment or "high." To carry the analogy a little further, three quarters through the race, marathoners get to a point called "hitting the wall," when their body is screaming, "Stop, I'm out of gas," just prior to getting their second wind and moving on strong again.
>
> Parents, too, hit the wall—sometimes literally—most often about three quarters through the race, when they're raising teenagers, although it can happen at any time with any age child. You can reach the limits of your energy to cope raising a baby with colic, a two-year-old whose every third word is *no*, or a ten-year-old who has decided that schoolwork isn't for him. As we will soon see, strong parents, like strong runners, have found that if they can persevere past the point of near-exhaustion, a smoother going often follows. Stamina is a core quality of successful parenting.[18]

Other factors enter into running this marathon besides sheer stamina. Our efforts will not always be recognized, appreciated, or even liked. Parenting is definitely not a popularity contest. If it were, we would lose much of the time.

It's reassuring, though, to know that you don't have to be popular. You don't have to be a superparent. You don't have to compare yourself with other parents. Just be faithful . . . and rely upon the Lord.

January 22

The LORD GOD said, "It is not good for the man to be alone; I will make a helper suitable for him" (Genesis 2:18, NASB).

A Letter to a Child about to Be Married

From time to time, this volume will share messages for you to pass on to your child about his or her own future marriage. As you think about sharing these to prepare your child for a major event in his or her life, you may discover yourself reflecting on your own marriage. That's all right, because every marriage needs maintenance and renewal.

Marriage is risky business. And it's a lot more risky today than it was back then. That's why I admire your courage to commit your whole life to someone even when marriages look shaky.

Refuse to marry? That would be like standing at the Grand Canyon and keeping your eyes closed because you were afraid to look. Imagine a child who won't play in water because she might get wet. Marriage holds too much joy, too many hopes, too much happiness, too many laughs, too much life to shy away from it.

Marriage can have a dark side. There are too many broken hearts to pretend that marriage can't hurt. But those are just the stories that get our attention. We usually fail to notice the local newspaper announcements of fiftieth wedding anniversaries or the eighty-year-old neighbor who says she loves her husband more now than the day she married him.

The potential in marriage is enormous. It is like a treasure chest. Every year you open the lid more and more to discover rare jewels you wouldn't dare dream of. Pity the person who is afraid to even peek inside.

If you start to wonder what you're getting into, remember, that happens to most of us. Anxiety comes with the wedding vows. That's all right.

But your love for this person will not be deterred by the marriage flutters. Every worthwhile endeavor has its bumpy roads.

Celebrate! You have made a fantastic decision. Take each day as it comes. Don't get bogged down in yesterday or try to lead ahead into tomorrow. This is the day that God has given for your life together to begin. Live it courageously.[19]

January 23

He called a little child and had him stand among them. And he said: "I tell you the truth, unless you change and become like little children, you will never enter the kingdom of heaven" (Matthew 18:2,3).

C hildren teach us so much about life. They remind us of the simple pleasures and help us put things into perspective. Author Max Lucado tells of this experience with his three daughters.

Bedtime is a bad time for kids. No child understands the logic of going to bed while there is energy left in the body or hours left in the day.

My children are no exception. A few nights ago, after many objections and countless groans, the girls were finally in their gowns, in their beds, and on their pillows. I slipped into the room to give them a final kiss. Andrea, the five-year-old, was still awake, just barely, but awake. After I kissed her, she lifted her eyelids one final time and said, "I can't wait until I wake up."

Oh, for the attitude of a five-year-old! That simple uncluttered passion for living that can't wait for tomorrow. A philosophy of life that reads, "Play hard, laugh hard, and leave the worries to your father." A bottomless well of optimism flooded by a perpetual spring of faith. Is it any wonder Jesus said we must have the heart of a child before we can enter the kingdom of heaven?

I like the way J.B. Phillips renders Jesus' call to childlikeness: "Jesus called a little child to his side and set him on his feet in the middle of them all. 'Believe me,' he said, 'unless you change your whole outlook and become like little children you will never enter the kingdom of Heaven.' "[20]

That's an interesting thought . . . change your whole outlook. I wonder what there is about my outlook that needs to be changed? How about yours? Is there something we are missing out on as adults because we are too busy, too involved, too serious, too preoccupied, too calloused, too critical, too grown-up, too . . . adult?

There's an excitement about life that children maintain. There's an eagerness about welcoming the next day that lurks in the mind of children as they sleep. They can't wait to see what the new morning holds. And why not? They're not as encumbered by the cares and concerns of life. They don't have to worry about tomorrow. We do. Or do we? Didn't Jesus say something about not worrying about tomorrow? I wonder. Would that help us change our outlook?

January 24

"Honor your father and mother"—which is the first com-
mandment with a promise—"that it may go well with you and
that you may enjoy long life on the earth" (Ephesians 6:2,3).

Sarah sat alone. Her hands, freckled with age, rested in her lap.
She wore her finest dress. Her nursing home room spoke of spring-
time: daisies in the vase, a poinsettia blooming outside her window.

"Sundays are special, you know."

Her nursing home wall spoke of family: an enlargement of
grandson Jason hugging Brando the terrier; a framed portrait of
her son Jerry, the dentist, and his family in Phoenix; Sarah and her
late husband cutting their fortieth wedding anniversary cake. "It
would have been fifty years next May."

Sarah sat alone. "They came last Christmas," she said brightly
(as if defending her family).

A telegram and a birthday card were taped to the dresser mirror. A church group sang hymns down the hall. She had done her
best to make the small room look homey, but a person can only do
so much.

A thousand miles away a family played.

Sarah is not sick or ugly. She is not useless or decrepit. Sarah is
simply old. Sarah is not senile, though at times, she confesses, the
naivete of senility is tempting. She doesn't suffer from cancer or
arthritis. She hasn't had a stroke. No, her "disease" is much more
severe. She suffers from rejection.

Our society has little room for the aged. People like Sarah come
in scores. No one intentionally forgets them. Maybe that's why it is
so painful. If there were a reason: a fight, a mistake, a dispute. . . .
But usually it's unintentional. Unintentional rejection. It will kill
Sarah; she'll die of loneliness. It doesn't matter how nice the con-
valescent home is; nurses and old folks don't replace a grandbaby's
smile or son's kiss.

Spend all your love on her now.
Forget not the hands, though spotted,
The hair, though thinning,
The eyes, though dim.
For they are a part of you.
And when they are gone, a part of you is gone.[21]

Who needs your touch, your phone call, your visit . . . today?

January 25

My son, do not forget my teaching, but keep my commands in your heart (Proverbs 3:1).

*L*et's imagine that your child is about to go off to school for the first time and you want him or her to gain the most he or she can from these coming years of education. Or perhaps your child, now a young adult, has just received a diploma from the university and in a week begins a new career.

As a parent, you want your child to do his or her best. So . . . what advice would you give? Consider what this parent wrote:

Dear Child,

As you go off to this new venture, I know you want to be successful. I know you want to do the best you can and utilize all the gifts God has given to you. I have just a few thoughts to share with you. Always be willing to learn. Have the attitude of teachability. Be willing to learn and then relearn. Have the attitude that there's always something new that you can learn. How can you be a lifelong learner?

Learn with your eyes. Notice what is going on around you. Always ask yourself, "What don't I understand and how can I learn it?"

Take the attitude, "Even though this is working, there may be an even better way." In other words, stay flexible. When something is flexible, it doesn't break. It bends. Flexibility means staying power and growth. Always listen with your mind and your heart. Hear what others can't always put into words. Understand, absorb, think about, and practice James 1:19, "Be a ready listener." Learn from every person around you, those above and those below. Those who lead and those who follow. Those you agree with and those you don't. When you fail, and you will at times, fail forward. Failure is not a setback if you make it a learning experience so you can do something different the next time.

Finally, always believe in yourself as I believe in you and as God does. Remember who you are. You're not just my child, but a child of the King. Reflect that.

Your Loving Parent[22]

January 26

May God give you of heaven's dew and of earth's richness—an abundance of grain and new wine (Genesis 27:28).

*I*n the Old Testament you will find several occasions when fathers blessed their children. These blessings signified acceptance, which is foundational to building self-esteem. Blessing your child will bolster their self-image and help solidify their unique identity.

In their book, *The Blessing*, Gary Smalley and John Trent suggest five elements that constitute a blessing. The first is *meaningful touch*. Studies show that loving touches greatly enhance physical and emotional health. Hugging your child, placing your hand on his or her head, and gently squeezing his or her shoulder convey love and acceptance to your child and create a close bond between you.

Second, blessing may be bestowed through *spoken words*—words of love, affirmation, and acceptance. Bless your child with kind words each day. Watch closely for things to compliment your child about, especially things you tend to take for granted. Make a list of positive words you want to say.

The third element of a blessing is *expressing high value* to your child. Recognize your child as a special person and communicate this through your words. Let your child know you not only treasure him or her as a special gift but that you also believe in him or her.

The fourth element is *picturing a special future* for your child. Does your child feel hopeful or discouraged by your messages to him or her about what lies ahead? Not only did Isaac bless Jacob with hopeful words about his future, Jesus also has blessed us with words of promise concerning our future with Him (John 14:2-3).

The final element of a blessing is an active commitment from you as a parent to do everything you can to help your child fulfill his or her potential. This means giving time, resources, and yourself. It means disciplining yourself to grow and develop in order to be a more effective model and guide. How? By praying for your child each day and sharing God's Word through what you say and how you live your life. It means helping your child develop the uniqueness God has built into him or her. As you bless your children, you will discover a wonderful blessing for your own life as well.[23]

January 27

We have different gifts, according to the grace given us. If a man's gift is prophesying, let him use it in proportion to his faith (Romans 12:6).

*T*ake heart. There are many different styles of parenting. You don't have to be a replica of all the other parents you've known. God wants you to have the freedom to express your unique personality in your parenting (even if you're different from your partner) as well as your spiritual gifts.

Let's consider for a moment how your spiritual gifts may be reflected in your parenting style. Romans 12:6 says, "Having then gifts . . ." The word "gift," in the Greek text, is *charisma*. The root of this Greek word means "joy" or "gladness." The seven gifts described in Romans 12:6-8 are to be considered as gifts of joy. So if you are aware of your gift and you use it, the result is you will be a person bringing joy and gladness. And remember, your gift is just that . . . it's a gift from God. There are seven such gifts, so you can expect to find seven approaches to parenting.

The first gift mentioned is prophecy. It means to "speak out" or to "declare." It also has the connotation of proclaiming in a direct manner. A parent reflecting this gift is a person who is telling, declaring, or speaking out about something. Could this be your gift or one of your children's?

A person with the gift of prophecy doesn't waver. He speaks the truth without much hesitation. The prophetic person acts on whatever he believes is right, sometimes without concern over the consequences. Other people know where he stands and a child can trust his word because he doesn't waver. He is usually a person of action. He is persuasive and even competitive.

The person with the gift of prophecy attracts people. But if he is not careful, he can also push them away. He has strong convictions and the unusual capacity to stand alone.

Is this your gift? Someone else's in the family? If so, how can it be used in the most positive way to bring honor and glory to God? That's something to talk about.[24]

January 28

The grace of the Lord Jesus Christ, and the love of God, and the fellowship of the Holy Spirit, be with you all (2 Corinthians 13:14, NASB).

*A*t the conclusion of a church service just before you leave, the pastor usually starts speaking again—not to continue the sermon but to close with a few words we call the benediction.

Benedictions used to be passages of Scripture, although today you may hear just about anything. In addition to the benediction above, two of the more common ones are these:

> May the God of peace, who through the blood of the eternal covenant brought back from the dead our Lord Jesus, that great Shepherd of the sheep, equip you with everything good for doing his will, and may he work in us what is pleasing to him, through Jesus Christ, to whom be glory for ever and ever. Amen (Hebrews 13:20,21).

> To him who is able to keep you from falling and to present you before his glorious presence without fault and with great joy—to the only God our Savior be glory, majesty, power and authority, through Jesus Christ our Lord, before all ages, now and forevermore! Amen (Jude 24,25).

As you read these passages, you are reminded that you're not going to go through the week or even the day alone. Jesus Christ is going with you.

Why should these and other benedictions be limited to an expression at the conclusion of a church service? Couldn't these be daily expressions of our family life? What would happen if . . .

- ✦ you gave a silent or audible benediction to your children as they left for school, went to a friend's house for a slumber party, left for camp, went out on their first date, left for college, or walked down the aisle to be married?

- ✦ the entire family came together once or twice a week and one of the family members shared a personal benediction prepared for others?

Something new, but it's worth trying.

January 29

A wise man's heart guides his mouth, and his lips promote instruction. Pleasant words are a honeycomb, sweet to the soul and healing to the bones (Proverbs 16:23,24).

Our bodies are works of art (remember that beauty is in the eye of the beholder!). Each body has a vast array of different organs with varied purposes. One of them that we can't do without is our heart. Many people today suffer from heart problems. This is the era of angiograms; angioplasty; single, double, and triple bypasses; and even heart transplants.

How is your heart? Is it doing well? I'm not asking if you are free from pain, skipped beats, arrythmia, mitral valve prolapse, or defective valves. Rather, is your heart free from *trouble*? A troubled heart lacks peace and calm assurance. Some days it's reflected by unrest, uncertainty, discontentment, an inner churning.

Troubled hearts come in many forms:

The heavy heart. "An anxious heart weighs a man down, but a kind word cheers him up" (Proverbs 12:25).

The deceitful heart. "There is deceit in the hearts of those who plot evil, but joy for those who promote peace" (Proverbs 12:20).

The sorrowful heart. "Even in laughter the heart may ache, and joy may end in grief" (Proverbs 14:13).

The backsliding heart. "The faithless will be fully repaid for their ways, and the good man rewarded for his" (Proverbs 14:14).

The angry heart. "A man's own folly ruins his life, yet his heart rages against the LORD" (Proverbs 19:3).

Do you or your children ever experience a troubled heart? Do you know how you can detect these problems? Proverbs 20:11,12 tells us, "Even a child is known by his actions, by whether his conduct is pure and right."

Use your ears. Listen with your eyes, too. Let Him be the source of your thoughts, words, and actions. He can comfort and change the troubled heart.[25]

January 30

You will guard him and keep him in perfect and constant peace whose mind [both its inclination and its character] is stayed on You, because he commits himself to You, leans on You, and hopes confidently in You. So trust in the Lord (commit yourself to Him, lean on Him, hope confidently in Him) forever; for the Lord God is an everlasting rock [the Rock of Ages] (Isaiah 26:3,4, AMP).

Here is a prayer that all parents can relate to. Be sure to read this aloud as your own.

Loving Father:

Your words, "for the Lord of all shows no partiality," and your example of a father not partial to any of us, his children, taught me something very important about being a parent. As a mother of children who are individually unique, who have different gifts depending on the role you created them to play, who are as human as I am human and who will most likely hurt me as I have hurt you, I needed to learn that my root love for each of my children must be like yours—without preference. It was you who helped me do that and I will be forever grateful.

What saddens me though, dear God, is that I feel my children, especially my growing-up children, do not believe my love is impartial. When I scold one of them or demand obedience, they forget I did the same to their brothers and sisters. When I give time or attention to another, they don't remember when they were ill, or unhappy or in any way doing battle with life. That's when I see the hurt in their eyes—a feeling of being neglected or a longing for affection—and my heart aches. I lie in bed later wondering if any one of them had an equally or, worse yet, a more demanding need of which I was not aware. But, oh God, I have only two arms for hugging, only one lap for holding, only two hands for helping and only one demand-cluttered mind with which to make moment-to-moment decisions as to who or what must take priority. Regretfully too, I am often a weary parent, an uncertain parent, an impatient parent.

So again I come to you in prayer, asking that you help me be a better parent and help my beloved children to somehow understand that my heart, like all true parent's hearts, can only love in equal parts.[26]

January 31

Wait for the LORD; be strong and take heart and wait for the LORD (Psalm 27:14).

A favorite phrase of parents is, "Wait!" It comes in several formats: "Now you wait right there until I tell you to move" or, "Now just wait! It's too close to dinner time for you to snack"or, "Wait—wait—wait! You're doing that all wrong!"

You may feel as if your entire life is made up of waiting. You wait in line at the store, at the traffic signal, for the child or spouse who's late, for the delivery . . . isn't anyone on time anymore? You hurry to your doctor's appointment and you end up—you guessed it—waiting!

Waiting seems like such a waste of time. Sometimes it is, but there is one exception. Listen to David and what he says about waiting for the Lord in Psalm 27:14.

If you're a parent of prayer, you know that sometimes you need to wait on God for your prayers to be answered. When you're waiting for something to change in your life or for a child to turn away from the problems he or she is creating, your best resource is to wait upon the Lord. If you're in the midst of a difficult time in your life, wait upon God. Your strength will come from Him and it will come during the difficult time, not after.

The word "wait" in the original Hebrew text means "to twist or stretch." It's a verb, but the noun form means "line," "cord," or thread." Picture it this way: a strong rope or thread is made while you twist and weave yourself around the Lord so tightly that your weakness is replaced by His power and might. An exchange is occurring—your weakness for His strength. Wouldn't you like that? Wouldn't that help . . . especially when you're coming un-raveled?

God's Word promises this elsewhere, too. "Those who wait for the LORD will gain new strength" (Isaiah 40:31, NASB). "I have strength for all things in Christ Who empowers me [I am ready for anything and equal to anything through Him Who infuses inner strength into me; I am self-sufficient in Christ's sufficiency]" (Philippians 4:13, AMP).

Wait . . . wait . . . wait . . . upon the Lord.[27]

February 1

And he told them this parable: "The ground of a certain rich man produced a good crop. He thought to himself, 'What shall I do? I have no place to store my crops.' Then he said, "This is what I'll do. I will tear down my barns and build bigger ones, and there I will store all my grain and my goods . . .'" (Luke 12:16-18, NIV).

*P*ossessions—this is what life is all about for many people. We begin with a used Ford, graduate to a Mazda convertible and finally we have our BMW (along with the payments). The apartment is outgrown and a one-story fixer-upper is a joy until the new split-level in a gated community with five bedrooms and a pool becomes a must. Nothing wrong with any of these if you can afford them. But not just in terms of money, but the time it took you to accumulate the money to accumulate the . . . you know. Few people steal money to acquire goods. That's difficult. It's easier to steal time from relationships. Price tags should ask the questions, "Why is this necessary? Who wants it? What will you do with what you get now and thirty years hence? Or when you die?" Disturbing questions. Ken Gire helps us put all of this in perspective with his prayer.

Dear Teacher,

Teach me what life is all about.

Help me to learn that it does not consist of possessions, no matter how many, no matter how nice.

Help me to realize that the more things I selfishly accumulate, the more barns I will have to build to store them in. Help me to realize, too, that the storage fee on such things is subtracted from a life that could be rich toward you instead.

Teach me that life is more than the things necessary to sustain it. Help me to learn that if life is more than food, surely it is more important than how the dining room looks; it's more than clothes, certainly it is more important than whether there's enough closet space to hold them.[1]

February 2

The Lord gives skillful and godly Wisdom; from His mouth come knowledge and understanding (Proverbs 2:6, AMP).

*P*arenting is a job, a vocation, a calling, a profession, a career. Can you think of any other words to describe it? Even if you can't, that's enough to work with. Actually, parenting is all of the above!

To accomplish and fulfill all that those words entail, you need a plan—a simple workable plan. Let's borrow one from a parent by the name of Sheila West. Her plan is called MINI steps—Moving In Natural Increments. These steps are designed to keep you moving through all the confusion and chaos of employment, parenting, or both. Three key components will keep you on track.

The first one is *agility*. And this doesn't necessarily mean the ability to navigate the stairs with a load of wash, tiptoeing around the toys and shoes strewn in your way! Rather, it's the ability to respond in a productive way—quickly and resourcefully. It's the ability to look at what's going on around you, consider your options, and make a good decision. It includes keeping your thoughts straight and making wise decisions. Agility also involves praying that you see your options clearly and having an alert mind that draws from God's wisdom.

Anticipation is simply thinking in a futuristic way—ahead. It's not that you're controlled by the future. Rather, you're preparing for it even though you may not have all the information you need. It's saying, "All right, if this were to occur I would do this, or if this happened I would do that." When change occurs suddenly, you can shift direction. You're preparing for the unexpected.

Adaptability is the ability to flex and be versatile. You're capable of trying something different instead of entrenching yourself in the same old ruts. When one method of disciplining your child doesn't work, or other people don't seem to hear your concerns, you're willing to try something new.

A final question: To what extent are you using the three steps in Sheila's MINI plan? Is it time for a change?[2]

February 3

Get rid of all bitterness, rage and anger, brawling and slander,
along with every form of malice. Be kind and compassionate to
one another, forgiving each other, just as in Christ God forgave
you (Ephesians 4:31,32).

*I*n these verses we find a vocabulary test for parents. Please
take a moment to define the following words: bitterness, wrath,
anger, clamor, evil speaking, malice, kindness, tenderhearted, and
forgiveness. Better yet, why not ask your children (and your
spouse) for their definitions as well. Finished? Let's check your
answers.

Bitterness is a feeling of deep resentment and ill will toward another person. It comes from storing up hurt, disappointment, rejection, and conflict.

Wrath is an uncontrolled temper that rages like a violent wind-
storm tearing trees up by their roots.

Anger is a strong feeling of irritation. Sometimes it's healthy. But
it can also involve revenge. You know, payback time . . . usually
with interest.

Clamor is an interesting word. You may think of someone bang-
ing cymbals together, but it refers to a sense of unrestraint with no
regard for others.

Evil speaking. This can include verbal abuse or slander that
damages the reputation of other people, even family members. Be
careful what you say about your children and spouse, especially
to your parents or in-laws.

And then there's malice, which includes arrogance, violence,
malevolence, or even depraved desire.

None of these reflect the presence of Jesus Christ in the family.
All of them are banned by Scripture. They destroy people and
families.

Kindness. There are many ways to define it. The same is true
about tenderhearted. What about meeting the needs of other
people to build their life and sense of well-being? That's a start.

And forgiveness . . . well, this is taking an eraser and wiping
the slate so clean it's as though the infraction never—and I mean
never—occurred. Isn't that what God has done for us?

February 4

[He whose gift is] practical service, let him give himself to serving; he who teaches, to his teaching (Romans 12:7, AMP).

A person whose gift is serving is devoted to meeting the needs of others. In fact, some people who have this gift seem to anticipate and care for needs even before they are evident.

The word "practical" is a very rich and deep word, although you probably wouldn't know it today. It means "designed for us; utilitarian; concerned with the application of knowledge to useful ends; or concerned with, or dealing efficiently with everyday activities."[3]

This is actually the gift of practical service. It's true that all parents will reflect some aspect of this gift, but for some their entire life is devoted to this calling.

The most literal translation of "practical" is "service or ministering." Various Bible translations all convey the idea of "giving assistance or advantage to another person." And it is done with a sense of joy and delight, not begrudgingly.

A child raised by a parent who has this gift will see cheerfulness on display when his needs are met. This parent engages in a great amount of teaching that's usually done by showing and demonstrating rather than telling. The parent may verbalize his instruction, but *doing* is his forte.

All of us need to be givers in some way. This is the calling to everyone who claims Jesus as Lord of their life. But the spiritual gift of practical service is different.

Some parents say, "Neither my spouse nor I have this gift. We'd like our child to be influenced by someone with this gift. What do we do?"

Find a friend or relative who manifests this gift in a healthy, balanced way. There needs to be both a joy in giving as well as knowing how not to neglect one's own needs. Who do you know with this gift? If it's you, how can you use your gift for the glory of God?[4]

February 5

Let your tears run down like a river day and night...
(Lamentations 2:18, NASB).

*P*arents are guardians. They've been entrusted with the care, cultivation, and nurturing of a delicate creation called a child. The younger the child, the more fragile he or she is. And children are very impressionable. The emotions they experience are wild, untamed, not understood, and need to be guided and shaped.

God has given His children two precious but fragile gifts. Cupped within our emotions, these gifts bubble up or spill out as needed. Their names are laughter and tears. Both are wonderful friends to the poised person. They can be enjoyed privately or given as an investment in others.

But like everything else in life, they can be abused, squandered, or employed at the wrong time. Tears can be manipulative. Laughter can be deceptive. Both can be shaped into destructive weapons.

Loving parents realize that it is important to train children on the proper use of laughter and tears. They must help their children make these dimensions of their emotions friends rather than enemies.

I've watched macho dads mislead their boys by telling them tears are for women and sissies. They aren't stopping the boys' tears with that kind of irresponsible advice, they're merely changing the direction that the tears are falling. Instead of falling from a boy's eyes, those little drops of emotion will splash on the floor of his soul—compressed, denied, and spoiled.

Tears are friends. Allies. Like the valve on top of a pressure cooker, they relieve the soul. Like laughter, they can soothe and medicate a broken heart. Denying their expression is cruel.

We parents can be equally guilty of wiping joy from our children's faces. Placing stoic expectations on souls that were tailor-made for laughter is a crime. A loving home needs to be bathed in laughter, with parents setting the pace.[5]

That's right. You're the pacesetter. So let your tears flow when they need to, and laugh a lot.

February 6

Train up a child in the way he should go [and in keeping with his individual gift or bent], and when he is old he will not depart from it (Proverbs 22:6, AMP).

Whether you know it or not, you're a risk taker. Yes, you really are. Oh, you may think of yourself as hesitant, shy, tentative, reserved, cautious, and all that. But if you're a parent, you're a risk taker. Every day you face new changes and challenges. When you have a child your life changes forever. Most parents, however, don't know all the changes involved; or if they do, they don't adequately prepare for them.

One of the most frequently asked questions by parents is, "What do I do now?" Many parents creep along the path of uncertainty, never being quite sure that what they're doing is right but hoping and praying that it is.

In addition to the risk of change there is the possibility your children won't turn out the way you want or be all that you want them to be. What if they don't meet your expectations, achieve what you want, or fail to follow your Christian beliefs? God experienced that. Adam and Eve had the perfect environment, but they chose another way. Perhaps if God was willing to run that risk, so can we as parents.

There's another risk you face, too. It's the possibility that your children could turn out *just like you!* A replica. A spitting image! How do you feel about that? When you see yourself starting to emerge in the behavior, beliefs, and attitudes in your children, you may have mixed feelings. Some traits you want them to reproduce, some you don't.

Aside from heredity, how does such imitation happen? You know and I know—by what your children experience and see in the home. This, then, is an area of your children's lives you can do something about. Talk with your children. Be transparent. Share how you are attempting to grow and change. Use the Scripture together as your model for living. It will lower the risk factor.[6]

February 7

[Jesus] said: "I tell you the truth, unless you change and become like little children, you will never enter the kingdom of heaven" (Matthew 18:3).

*P*arents do a lot of teaching. It's a constant calling and challenge. And for some parents, the responsibility is intensified if they choose to home school their children.

Teaching can take place formally and informally, through telling, explaining, or by example. But teaching is also a two-way street. Not only are you going to teach your children, but you're also going to be taught . . . by your children. And in many ways.

Sometimes parents make the statement, "I wish I was a child again. Life was so simple then." It may seem that way to us as adults, but is life really all that simple to a child? That's a question to consider.

What can you learn from a child?

A child can teach you about the simple forgotten pleasures of life. He can show us how fascinating it is to look at the multiple colors reflected in the beating wings of a monarch butterfly. A child can teach you to reactivate your funny button as his or her laughter over silly things permeates the rooms of your house.

A child can teach you to be in awe over something that now has become commonplace in your life.

A child can teach you about faith and trust in Jesus as he or she prays for a sick puppy or for a friend to like him or her again.

A child can teach you the wonder of being inquisitive when he or she bombards you with question after question in the endless search to know.

A child can teach you how to love and express your love with no inhibitions or reservations about what others think. A child can teach you . . .

Why don't you finish that last sentence? What are your children teaching you?

February 8

I bow my knees before the Father of our Lord Jesus Christ, for Whom every family in heaven and on earth is named (Ephesians 3:14,15, AMP).

*W*hat is a family? Can you answer that question with one word, a phrase, or a paragraph?

Everyone has their own thoughts about what a family is, and sometimes the response varies depending upon the day, the time of day, or the current behavior level of the children. As you read Edith Schaeffer's answer to that question, perhaps you'll identify with the feelings she has described in her words. Or, maybe she will encourage you to venture in a new direction with your family.

> What is a family? A family is a mobile. A family is an art form. A family is an exciting art career, because an art form needs work.
> God's mobile—a human being—two human beings—a family of human beings. Mobiles that can reproduce. Constantly changing patterns, affected by each other, inspired by each other, helped by each other. A family which is real in space and time and history, with roots in the past and stretching out into the future.[7]

> What is a family? A family is a blending of people for whom a career of making a shelter in the time of storm is worth a lifetime! A Christian family is meant to be different because of its knowledge that human beings are significant in this life and through eternity. A Christian family has been given enough in God's verbalized Word to know that when one part of the body hurts, the rest of the body is affected and does something to help. The rest of the body doesn't just "give up," but goes on. Because we have a handicap or broken ribs, a foot in a cast, dizziness or headache, we don't come to a DEAD STOP with the rest of our bodies—we go on in the best way we can.[8]

That's quite a bit to digest, isn't it? But what a difference it makes when our own family reflects this.

February 9

Only be careful, and watch yourselves closely so that you do not forget the things your eyes have seen or let them slip from your heart as long as you live. Teach them to your children and to their children after them (Deuteronomy 4:9).

*P*atrick Morley shares an interesting approach he and his wife used to encourage their children to develop a personal devotional life. What do you think about it?

Patsy and I offered our children a deal. "If you will do a daily devotion for at least twenty-five days each month, we'll buy you a tape or compact disc."

"That's nice, Dad."

"That's not all. In addition, if you do your devotions at least twenty-five days each month for ten out of twelve months we'll pay you $250. You can miss any two months and still get paid." Their eyes popped open.

"Wow, Dad! Are you kidding?"

"No, we're not kidding. But that's not all. If you will do your devotions all twelve months in a row, we'll double the amount and pay you $500. And you still only have to do twenty-five days a month."

By this time the children had become quite interested! They asked questions, and a great discussion ensued. We agreed they could use any youth devotional materials they wanted; our goal was to form the habit more than anything. We suggested they spend about five minutes a day; we didn't want them to think of time spent with the Lord as a burden. If they missed a day they could make it up; we wanted to communicate grace, not law. We suggested they keep track by marking off on a calendar; we proposed an honor system to demonstrate we trusted them.

At the end of the first year both children not only received the full bonus, but both had a perfect record of 365 days. They are well on their way to establishing a spiritual discipline which can keep them close to their Lord all their days. Some might call it bribery. I like to think of it as giving our children what they *need* in the context of what they *want*.

The greatest gift we can give our children is a heart that thirsts for God. We cannot force our children to love God, but we can create the most probable environment in which they will.[9]

February 10

But God demonstrates his own love for us in this: While we were still sinners, Christ died for us (Romans 5:8).

*F*athers. They come in all sizes, strengths, temperaments, and abilities. And many of us, when we were children, began to fashion our understanding of God based upon our own father. For some of us, that was good. But for others, that wasn't so good.

Rather than base our beliefs upon a human father, it's better to look to Scripture to understand who God is. You may want to look up each Scripture reference cited along with the following statements:

- He is the loving, concerned Father who is interested in the intimate details of our lives (Matthew 6:25-34).
- He is the Father who never gives up on us (Luke 15:3-32).
- He is the God who sent His Son to die for us though we were undeserving (Romans 5:8).
- He stands with us in good and bad circumstances (Hebrews 13:5).
- He is the ever-active Creator of our universe. He died to heal our sickness, pain, and grief (Isaiah 53:3-6).
- He has broken the power of death (Luke 24:6,7).
- He gives all races and both sexes equal status (Galatians 3:28).
- He is available to us through prayer (John 14:13,14).
- He is aware of our needs (Isaiah 65:24).
- He created us for an eternal relationship with Him (John 3:16).
- He values us (Matthew 10:29-31).
- He doesn't condemn us (Romans 8:1).
- God values and causes our growth (1 Corinthians 3:7).
- He comforts us (2 Corinthians 1:3-5).
- He strengthens us through His Spirit (Ephesians 3:16).
- He cleanses us from sin (Hebrews 10:17-22).
- He is for us (Romans 8:31).
- He is always available to us (Romans 8:38,39).
- He is a God of hope (Romans 15:13).
- He helps us in temptation (Hebrews 2:17,18).
- He provides a way to escape temptation (1 Corinthians 10:13).
- He is at work in us (Philippians 2:13).
- He wants us to be free (Galatians 5:1).
- He is the Lord of time and eternity (Revelation 1:8).

February 11

Each of us has one body with many members, and these members do not all have the same function (Romans 12:4).

A few days ago in this devotional we asked the question, What is a family? Then we considered some thoughts from others about what a family is. I'd like to share more insights and begin by saying that it's important for your child to have a positive regard for your family. Why? This is the first place where a child learns to love. It's your child's launching pad into the big outdoors. As your child participates in your family, he or she can experience the diversity of life without having to bear full responsibility for what happens. Family is a place of joy and sadness, a place to learn to take and share responsibility, a place to express feelings and discover a positive identity.

That's a lot, isn't it? But it's not all. A family provides even more. Consider what Edith Schaeffer says in her book, *What Is a Family?*:

> Unity and diversity. Form and freedom. Togetherness and individuality. A family.
>
> Age, youth, childhood, infancy—strung together on tiny threads. Blowing in delicate movement, independently, yet together. A family—belonging to each other, affected by each other, compassionate for each other, concerned about each other, interested in each other—a living mobile, never static. A family. . . .
>
> What is a family? A family is a well-regulated hospital, a nursing home, a shelter in time of physical need, a place where a sick person is greeted as a sick human being and not as a machine that has a loose bolt, or a mechanical doll that no longer works—to be shoved aside because it is no more fun, nor is it useful! A family should be a training place for growing human beings to know how to care for a great variety of sicknesses, and for people who have just had accidents or operations, because each one has received both knowledgeable and loving care, and has watched it being given to others.[10]

Share with another family member what you learned about a family today.

February 12

He who covers and forgives an offense seeks love, but he who repeats or harps on a matter separates even close friends (Proverbs 17:9, AMP).

A Letter to a Child about to Be Married

After you've married, a day will come when you will need to practice one of the elements of God's grace to all of us—forgiveness. I'd like to be honest with you: Some days you won't feel that your partner deserves your forgiveness. That's all right. It's nothing new. None of us deserve the forgiveness we receive.

Sometimes you may find it hard to forgive your husband or wife. You may be concerned that by forgiving your partner you're letting him or her off the hook and that what happened may reoccur. That's a risk you have to take. After all, the only other option is resentment and revenge.

Forgiveness hurts. There is pain involved. But eventually it will diminish. Forgiveness is also costly because when you forgive, you're saying to your partner, "You don't have to make up to me for what you did." You're actually releasing your partner and reaching out in love instead of relishing resentments.

When you have truly forgiven your partner, you never have a need to dwell upon the problem, believe it is going to happen again, or bring it up again!

A mature marriage is a forgiving marriage. Be sure to verbalize the phrases, "Will you forgive me?" as well as, "I forgive you." You know you have what it takes to forgive one another—anyone who knows Jesus as their Savior has been given that power. You have been loved, accepted, and forgiven by God. So the gift given to you is yours to use with other people.

If you wonder whether you've truly forgiven your spouse, just keep this in mind: You've forgiven your partner when in your heart you wish him or her well and are able to ask God's blessing upon his or her life.

February 13

... living ... with complete lowliness of mind (humility) and meekness (unselfishness, gentleness, mildness), with patience, bearing with one another and making allowances because you love one another (Ephesians 4:2, AMP).

A family is comprised of several unique creations of God. All sizes, shapes, personalities, preferences, and metabolisms will be found under the same roof. Everyone has received gifts that need nourishment in order to bloom. A spouse becomes a gardener toward his or her partner as does a parent toward a child. As in any garden, the soil must be prepared and cultivated and each plant must be tended, protected, fed, watered, and given the ultimate in care.

Family members shouldn't merely be left to just develop their interests and talents, they need to be challenged, and above all encouraged to do so. When you do this to others, they tend to respond back to you in like manner. As a family you don't grow separately and independently of one another, nor do you dream independently of each other.

A home is not a place where one person dominates or fashions the uniqueness of the others. When God's Word talks about "making allowances because you love one another," it means we are to learn to be flexible and adapt to the differentness of each person. We are to learn to understand how each is different and then accept this differentness as part of God's creation.

We *need* the differentness of one another. That becomes an opportunity to rejoice in each other's uniqueness. Perhaps one of the greatest favors we can do is to permit family members to be who they are and what they will become and help them develop into the kind of people God has ordained them to be. With this attitude, family members of all ages and sizes have room to sprout and grow.

Here are some questions to think about: How is each family member the same? In what ways are they different? Have you thanked God for those differences? That's the first step in accepting and enjoying them.

February 14

Now if we are children, then we are heirs—heirs of God and co-heirs with Christ, if indeed we share in his sufferings in order that we may also share in his glory (Romans 8:17).

Your children could turn out to look just like you! That's right. They may have the same height, weight, build, eyes, hair (or lack of), nose, mouth—you name it, they may have or get it. They can become a mirror reflection, made in your image for better or for worse.

But both you and your children were created in another image—the image of God. That's what gives you and your child so much value! It's true the image was distorted by sin, but when you accept Christ as your Savior there is a restoration.

Have you ever looked at your child and said, "That boy or girl has been created in the image of God!" It puts them and their lives in a brand-new perspective, doesn't it?

There's another exciting truth about your children: They're adopted. "No", you say, "they're mine. My spouse and I gave birth to them. They carry our genes."

That's true, but your children are also adopted if they have accepted Jesus as Savior. If they haven't yet, you could tell them that when they do accept Him they will become adopted, chosen by God to be part of his family. That's something special!

There's yet another exciting truth. Do you have a will or a living trust? If so, you've arranged for your children's inheritance. So has God. He has provided a rich inheritance for all of His children. When you know Jesus, you're well provided for, according to the book of Ephesians:

> God raised us up with Christ and seated us with him in the heavenly realms in Christ Jesus in order that in the coming ages he might show the incomparable riches of his grace, expressed in his kindness to us in Christ Jesus (2:6,7).

So . . . if you were created in God's likeness, and if you know Jesus, you're adopted and you have an inheritance. What does that say about how much you and your children are worth? You're very, very rich!

February 15

All have sinned and fall short of the glory of God (Romans 3:23).

*A*s our children grow up, what do they need to know about themselves so they have a balanced perspective on who they really are? We don't want them to turn out conceited or proud or have an inflated view of who they are. Nor do we want them to end up with a poor perspective of their worth. What is the message we need to get across to them?

That's a good question. Here are three messages a child (or an adult, for that matter), needs to understand:

First, children, just like their parents, are sinful. Sin is sin and needs to be labeled for what it is, and each person is responsible for the sin in his or her life. Sin also has consequences. But when you share this, you aren't demeaning your children's character or worth. Rather you are looking at who they are through God's perspective. See Romans 6:23 (as well as 3:23): "The wages of sin is death, but the gift of God is eternal life in Christ Jesus our Lord."

Second, children need to know they are wonderful. They were made in God's image, and are a unique, wondrous creation. A child is a person with the potential to glorify God in a way no one else has ever done before. That's an amazing thought. A wonderful creation like this needs to be the recipient of praise—plenty of praise from his or her parents.

Third, children need to experience acceptance—unconditional acceptance based upon who they are, not what they do. Equal praise, equal recognition, equal affection for each child must be the pattern. God accepts and loves the gossiper, the murderer, the thief, and the good Samaritan equally. He is love with open arms. Our children need to see God's love and acceptance through us.

So . . . you, me, our children—we're a strange blend, aren't we? Sinful, yes. Wonderful, yes. Accepted by God, yes. That's a balanced view. Maybe it's not the world's view, but that's okay. This view is much better.[11]

February 16

Thy will be done (Matthew 6:10).

*P*arents want their children to obey them. It's good for the child and the parent. When a child doesn't obey, parents usually get upset.

But it's not only children who disobey. Adults disobey as well. One area of disobedience is our resistance to the prayer, "Thy will be done."

Oftentimes we're afraid of God's will. Why? Perhaps it's because we're not sure what His will is and we wonder whether it's really best for us or not. Some of us are afraid that God will allow us to experience all the bad circumstances in life in order to discipline us. But a major reason has to do with control. We want to be in control of our lives rather than surrender our will to God, so it's a struggle to be obedient. But God already knows that, doesn't He? Adam and Eve showed Him that.

"Thy will be done" is a prayer that says, "God, You know what's best for me and I know You want the best for me. I will learn to trust You."

And there are benefits in doing this:

When we pray "Thy will be done," we accomplish a number of things, all of which contribute to our basic feeling of well-being and happiness:

+ *We demonstrate that we can trust the God we claim to be our Savior.* Those who see our faith will be drawn to Him through this trust.

+ *We reveal our understanding that all of life is finally under the control of God.*

+ *We place all our troubles under God's protection*, claiming that the blood of Christ has redeemed all that is sinful and restored all that is not whole.

+ *We demonstrate our understanding of the role suffering plays in God's redemptive plan.* We cannot grow without suffering.

+ *We free ourselves of unnecessary worry and anxiety.* If God's will is being done, then why should we fret and rage?

+ *We avoid wasting energy on trivial problems.* We can see the "whole" much better and understand how God works in *all* of our life.

+ *We confront our own desires and face the truth about ourselves,* even though this may be painful, even humiliating, in the final analysis.[12]

February 17

The memory of the righteous will be a blessing (Proverbs 10:7).

*T*here used to be a syrupy, popular song out years ago in which the singer drew out the words, "Memories . . . memories. . . ." It was almost too much. Yet memories, especially family memories, are very important. Some are instantaneous or spontaneous. Others are built on traditions. But some of the most meaningful family memories have nothing to do with traditions. They're built on relationships, experiences, and the investment of time. Bart Compolo wrote this letter to his father, Tony, about his favorite family snapshots:

> . . . The times that I remember best, though, are the times I spent with you. I love those memories best of all, Dad, and they're a big part of who I am. That's the whole point of these letters for me. My childhood is gone, and I will never be able to be with you the way I was with you as a little boy. I will never be that small, and you will never seem that big again. But I have my stories, and they comfort me when I am overwhelmed by the world, when I am too old all of a sudden, when I lose my sense of wonder. They are all I have of my boyhood, and the reason I wish we had spent more time together is that I wish I had more of them now. It isn't that you didn't do enough, you see, for I would always want more. You were the king of the world back then, the imp of fun, the man with all the answers, the one who could always fix what was broken. You made life seem magical to me.
>
> When you die, Dad, I will surely go to pieces for a while, because I still count on you more than anyone knows, but in the end I will be all right. I will have my stories, and in them I will always have part of you, the part that tells me who I am and where I came from. I only wish there was more because what there is means all the world to me.
>
> Love,
> Bart[13]

This is a good time to build stories, to invest time, and to help develop a new life for the next generation.

February 18

The prayer of a righteous man is powerful and effective (James 5:16).

*I*n the following excerpt from a book entitled *Two-Part Harmony*, Patrick Morley tells us about one family's approach to prayer and then shares his own prayer list for his children.

Rick and his wife have four beautiful children. Everyone in the family is walking with the Lord. Rick has been a genuine spiritual leader in his home. Recently he explained how it all started.

When Rick was a youngster, his mother and three other ladies would meet once each month to pray for the salvation of their children. Between them they had nine kids. Today all nine children know Christ and live for Him.

In *The Man in the Mirror,* I included my own daily prayer list for my children. Since then I've added some additional items. Here is the revised list. You may find that by adding and subtracting a few subjects you can tailor-make your own list:

+ That there will never be a time they don't walk with You
+ A saving faith (thanksgiving if already Christian)
+ A growing faith
+ An independent faith (as they grow up)
+ Persevering faith
+ To be strong and healthy in mind, body, and spirit
+ A sense of destiny (purpose)
+ A desire for integrity
+ A call to excellence
+ To understand their spiritual gifts
+ To understand the ministry God has for them
+ Values and beliefs, a Christian worldview
+ To tithe and save 10 percent of all earnings
+ To set and work toward realistic goals as revealed by the Lord
+ That I will set aside time to spend with them
+ To acquire wisdom
+ Protection from drugs, alcohol, tobacco, premarital sex, rape, violence, and AIDS
+ The mate God has for them (alive somewhere, needing prayer)
+ To do daily devotions
+ Forgiveness and be filled with the Holy Spirit
+ Glorify the Lord in everything

The prayers of righteous parents are both powerful and effective.[14]

February 19

...and gave him [Jesus] the name that is above every name (Philippians 2:9).

S hakespeare penned the question, "What's in a name?" There's a lot in any name. It's a means of identification, but names can also reflect special meanings.

Most prospective parents hear the question, "What will you name your baby?" Responses vary from, "If it's a boy..." or, "If it's a girl..." to, "Well, we have it narrowed down to...." Sometimes people say, "Why in the world would anyone give a child a name like that!"

Did you struggle over the names of your children? Why did you select what you did? What do the names signify? What do they mean?

In previous centuries, people's occupations were often reflected in names such as Smith, Miller, Carpenter, and so on. In the Scriptures, names were sometimes changed to reflect or to signify a new direction or even a new nature for the person involved. *Abram* was changed to *Abraham* and *Jacob* to *Israel*. *Jacob* meant "supplanter," but *Israel* meant that as a spiritual prince, he had power with God. Jesus changed Simon's name to *Peter*, which meant "rock." And you probably remember the changing of Saul's name to *Paul*.

Have you ever wanted to change your child's name? Probably. Most parents have. There are all kinds of names we use when we're frustrated with our children! And your children probably have some choice labels for you, too, when you're not around.

The person who probably has more names than anyone else is our Lord. Not only did God give Him "the name that is above every name," He gave Him more than 100 names and titles throughout the Old and New Testaments. Why would He do that? Keep in mind that a name is not only descriptive but also restrictive. No one name could be used to describe or define Jesus. Each name and title reveals some unique aspect of who He is and His purpose.

In each of the months that follow, we will learn and explore one of the names or titles of Jesus. As we do, you'll discover that the more you know about Jesus, the more there is to learn and the more you'll want to learn.

What's in a name? Everything.[15]

February 20

Be on your guard; stand firm in the faith; be men of courage; be strong (1 Corinthians 16:13).

*I*t's time. Perhaps you've experienced it or it's yet to come. Your child is no longer a child but an adult. It's time for your child to launch and for you to let go. How will you do it? Consider what Stu and Linda Weber did for their son. They gave him this letter, which was written on parchment and framed:

"As arrows in the hand of a warrior, so are the children of one's youth. How blessed is the man whose quiver is full of them."

To a world very much needing his character, his gifts, his skill, and his love for Christ, we, Stu and Linda Weber, do proudly and humbly announce in the manner of our heavenly Father, this is our beloved son, Kent Byron Weber, in whom we are well pleased. Like an arrow fashioned not to remain in the quiver, but to be released into the heart of its target, we release Kent to adulthood. We know him to be thoughtful, capable, and mature. He is the message we release to a world we will never see. He is a man. We release him to his manhood and all of its responsibilities. To the finding and cherishing of a godly and supportive wife, to the begetting and raising by God's grace and design of believing children. And to the commission of the Lord Jesus Christ Himself to go into all the world, making followers of all people, teaching them to observe the rich and life-giving truths of His holy scriptures. Kent, we love you, we're extremely proud of you, and we release you to the target of being all you can be in Christ. You will always be our son. You will never again be our little boy. Thank you, Kent, for having graced our lives with your remarkable sonship. You have blessed us richly.

"Be strong, therefore, and show yourself a man" (1 Kings 2:2).

"Be on the alert, stand firm in the faith, act like men, be strong. Let all that you do be done in love" (1 Corinthians 16:13).

Your very fulfilled parents,
Stu and Linda Weber
Mom and Dad, Spring 1992[16]

February 21

O LORD, you have searched me and you know me. You know when I sit and when I rise; you perceive my thoughts from afar. You discern my going out and my lying down; you are familiar with all my ways. Before a word is on my tongue you know it completely, O LORD (Psalm 139:1-4).

Child: I've got a question. Does God ever learn anything? Did anyone ever teach Him? Is He ever surprised by anything? Does . . .

Parent: Stop! Enough. Boy, the questions you ask.

Child: Haven't you ever thought about this stuff?

Parent: Well . . . I guess I have.

Child: So, what's the answer?

Parent: Hmmm. There's a big word that's used for this. It's called God's *omniscience.* It means He is all-knowing. He doesn't learn, doesn't have any need to learn, and has never learned. He can't.

Child: He can't?

Parent: No, He couldn't be God if He had to learn, could He? God just knows everything. You and I wonder about things. God doesn't. He doesn't need to. In Jeremiah He says, " 'Am I only a God nearby,' declares the LORD, 'and not a God far away? Can anyone hide in secret places so that I cannot see him?' declares the LORD" (23:23,24). He is never surprised by anything we ask Him in prayer, either.

Child: If He knows everything, why ask?

Parent: In Matthew 6 Jesus says our Father already knows what we need before we ask Him. There is nothing you can tell God that will shock Him or change His feelings about you. Yet He wants us to talk and fellowship with Him so we can learn to be dependent upon Him and receive all that He is waiting to give us. I guess that's the best answer I can give now.

Child: I'm trying to understand, but it's hard.

Parent: I'm still trying to understand too. But your questions help. Just keep asking. It makes me ask God more. I guess that's the whole point, isn't it?[17]

February 22

How long, O LORD? Will you forget me forever? How long will you hide your face from me? (Psalm 13:1).

*H*ave you ever fallen flat on your face? Perhaps you know what it's like to be walking somewhere and suddenly trip and have your entire body hit the ground. You lie there with your nose either burrowed an inch deep or flattened against your face. That's one way to be flat on your face. But there is also another way.

David, the writer of the above psalm, was flat on his face because he was despondent. He was down. He felt abandoned by God. Sound familiar? David had experienced so many trials for so long. In The Living Bible, Psalm 13:1 says, "How long will you look the other way when I am in need?" David had come to the place where he was focusing on his misery. It's easy to do that, just like it's easy to focus on what the kids do wrong rather than on what they do right.

Perhaps part of the problem is seen in verse 2: "How long shall I take counsel in my soul?" (NASB). David was trying to work out the problem himself, in his own mind, but we see the result of that. He ends up with "having sorrow in my heart all the day" (NASB). Carrying our burdens by ourselves keeps us flat on our face.

But, David came to his senses. Instead of complaining and berating God, he then said, "Consider and answer me, O LORD, my God; enlighten my eyes" (verse 3, NASB). He doesn't see God as distant; he is asking God for the answer. "Enlighten" means "to cause to shine." David wanted God's brightness to reflect what came from his eyes. David had moved from being flat on his face to being on his knees. Have you been there lately? It's not that uncomfortable; praying places problems in perspective.

Later in verse 5, we read, "I have trusted in Thy lovingkindness; my heart shall rejoice . . ." (NASB). In contrast to being on his face, David is now on his feet moving, rejoicing, delighting in God. Did his circumstances change? No. His position changed. From face to knees to feet.

Read this psalm. Follow it. After all, a change of position may be all you need.

February 23

The LORD said to Moses, "I will do the very thing you have asked, because I am pleased with you and I know you by name" (Exodus 33:17).

*W*hy were you born? Is that a strange question? Perhaps—but who of us hasn't wondered? Obviously you are the product of your parents' involvement. But what else? Isn't there more to your existence than that?

Yes, there is. You were born to know God. That's why you're here. "What is the chief end of man?" the Westminster Catechism asks, and then answers, "To glorify God and to enjoy Him forever." Many people acknowledge God, but few have learned to truly know and enjoy Him because they have a distorted image of who He is and who He created them to be.

The Scriptures tell us, "This is eternal life: that they may know you, the only true God, and Jesus Christ, whom you have sent" (John 17:3). Our growing knowledge of God leads to a greater realization of the goodness and grace He wants to lavish on us.

As we journey through life learning to know God, we discover a wonderful truth: God knows us completely and loves us just as we are. God knows us through and through. He said to Jeremiah, "Before I formed you in the womb I knew you, before you were born I set you apart" (Jeremiah 1:5). And Jesus said to His followers, "I am the good shepherd; I know my sheep and my sheep know me" (John 10:14).

Perhaps the importance of being known by God is best expressed by J.I. Packer in one of the all-time classics, *Knowing God:*

> What matters supremely, therefore, is not, in the last analysis, the fact that I know God, but the larger fact which underlies it—the fact that *He knows me.* I am graven on the palms of His hands. I am never out of His mind. All my knowledge of Him depends on His sustained initiative in knowing me. . . .[18]

Do these concepts generate hope within you? Do they give you a sense of security, relief, comfort? That is their purpose. You have so much more value and significance than you can possibly grasp. God has much in store for you.[19]

And for your children.

February 24

Bless the Lord, O my soul (Psalm 103:1, NASB).

*L*et's bow our heads and ask God to bless this meal." Have you ever said that? What would you say if one of the children asked, "Why? Why do we do this?" That's a good question; do you have a good answer? Asking God to bless the meal is a way of acknowledging that He is the giver of life and the giver of gifts both large and small. We're letting Him know that we realize we are dependent upon Him for everything.

Sometimes this asking of the blessing strays from its original intent. It may be tempting to use it as a means to get a message across to a family member and coerce him or her back into line. It could also become a routine using the same repetitious phrases, uttering them with little meaning and with such speed that what was said was unintelligible. Then there is verbosity, which not only puts people to sleep, but lets the food get cold as well!

In some families, the person who asks the blessing uses it as an opportunity to display his or her gift (or lack) of humor. The intent of such a person is not to thank the Lord but to elicit laughter by being a clown. Statements like, "Rub-a-dub-dub, pass the grub, amen and amen" or, "Through the teeth and around the gums, watch out stomach, here it comes, amen" may be good for a laugh, but they lack appropriate reverence.

Let's consider some creative steps you can take when you ask the blessing.

First, think before you pray. Create your prayer out of the reality of life itself. Thank God for specific circumstances or items. Call them by name. Thank Him not only for providing the food, but for the hands that prepared it.

Second, why not involve everyone in prayer by asking for one- or two-sentence prayers? You might even prefer to pray after the meal sometimes.

Third, you could sing a brief hymn or the doxology. Or you could learn some sign language for a prayer or hymn and have everyone sign it.

And . . . after the meal, why not ask everyone if they remembered what was prayed for before the meal.

February 25

The fruit of the Spirit is love, joy, peace, patience, kindness, goodness, faithfulness, gentleness and self-control. Against such things there is no law (Galatians 5:22,23).

A Message from a Parent
to a Child Embarking upon Adolescence

Dear Inbetweener,

Well, guess what? You've got one foot on the launching pad and one hovering over. You're an inbetweener. Part of you has some roots remaining in childhood and part is flailing around for a place to settle in adolescence. It's an exciting time. It can also be a frightening time as well.

You're going to struggle at this crossroads in your life. You're faced with two roads to choose from. And you will have to decide which one to travel. One road will be very enticing—it offers you happiness and satisfaction based on circumstances. The other road offers you joy regardless of what happens.

One road will be very attractive with relationships that are not friendships. They carry hidden agendas and a price tag you won't know about in advance. The other road offers a simple uncomplicated love and acceptance.

One road will entice you with immediate thrills and pleasure, but the price tag may be addictions. The other road offers you peace and self-respect. You'll be able to hold your head up high.

One road is going to look attractive to you with its promises and vows, but they can be broken. Most likely, they will be. The other road offers you something that will never change and can always be trusted. The promises are true.

Finally, to help you in your choice, memorize these words. Feed upon them. They're your road map. Your direction finder. Let them speak to you:

> Do not love the world or anything in the world. If anyone loves the world, the love of the Father is not in him. For everything in the world—the cravings of sinful man, the lust of his eyes and the boasting of what he has and does—comes not from the Father but from the world. The world and its desires pass away, but the man who does the will of God lives forever (1 John 2:15-17).

Your Loving Parents[20]

February 26

God created man in his own image, in the image of God he created him; male and female he created them (Genesis 1:27).

*I*n his fascinating book *The Pleasures of God*, John Piper talks about God singing and asks, "What would it be like if God sang?":

What do you hear when you imagine the voice of God singing?

I hear the booming of Niagara Falls mingled with the trickle of a mossy mountain stream. I hear the blast of Mt. St. Helens mingled with a kitten's purr. I hear the power of an East Coast hurricane and the barely audible puff of a night snow in the woods. And I hear the unimaginable roar of the sun, 865,000 miles thick, 1,300,000 times bigger than the earth, and nothing but fire, 1,000,000 degrees centigrade on the cooler surface of the corona. But I hear this unimaginable roar mingled with the tender, warm crackling of logs in the living room on a cozy winter's night.

I stand dumbfounded, staggered, speechless that he is singing over me—one who has dishonored him so many times and in so many ways. It is almost too good to be true. He is rejoicing over my good with all his heart and all his soul. He virtually breaks forth into song when he hits upon a new way to do me good.[21]

Dr. Piper compares our relationship with God to a marriage. He goes on to talk about how the honeymoon ends for all married couples. Reality sets in and the level of intensity and affection experienced during the honeymoon diminishes. But it's different with God:

God says his joy over his people is like a bridegroom over a bride. He is talking about honeymoon intensity.

And to add to this, with God the honeymoon never ends. He is infinite in power and wisdom and creativity and love. And so he has no trouble sustaining a honeymoon level of intensity; he can foresee all the future quirks of our personality and has decided he will keep what's good for us and change what isn't.[22]

What does that say to you about your worth? Does that fling open the doors of possibility for you to make choices in your life that will lead to hope and eventually to change and blessing? It can.[23]

February 27

Jesus was in the stern, sleeping on a cushion. The disciples woke him and said to him, "Teacher, don't you care if we drown?" (Mark 4:38).

S uch an honest cry, a doggedly painful cry. I've asked that one before, haven't you? It's been screamed countless times. . . .

A mother weeps over a stillborn child. A husband is torn from his wife by a tragic accident. The tears of an eight-year-old fall on a daddy's casket. And the question wails.

"God, don't you care?" "Why *me?*" "Why *my* friend?" "Why *my* business?"

It's the timeless question. The question asked by literally every person that has walked this globe. There has never been a president, worker, or businessman who hasn't asked it. There has never been a soul who hasn't wrestled with this aching lament. Does my God care? Or is my pain God's great goof?

As the winds howled and the sea raged, the impatient and frightened disciples screamed their fear at the sleeping Jesus. "Teacher, don't you care that we are about to die?" He could have kept on sleeping. He could have told them to shut up. He could have impatiently jumped up and angrily dismissed the storm. He could have pointed out their immaturity. . . . But he didn't.

With all the patience that only one who cares can have, he answered the question. He hushed the storm so the shivering disciples wouldn't miss his response. Jesus answered once and for all the aching dilemma of man, Where is God when I hurt?

Listening and healing. That's where he is. He cares.[24]

February 28

Discipline your son while there is hope . . . (Proverbs 19:18, NASB).

For some parents, discipline means exasperation, hair pulling, and sleep-losing frustration. But it doesn't have to be that way, nor is it supposed to be.

The word *discipline* means "to take action; to restrain or rectify the behavior of someone under you." Discipline is given to help someone improve or learn a lesson that will make him or her a better person. Sometimes the way we discipline our own children is identical to the way we ourselves experienced the process. Let's consider, though, what may be a different idea about discipline.

It's this: discipline positively. That's right, positively. There's a new "Certificate of Award" now available for use by parents. It says, "You were caught being good." It's much more effective in child training (and dog training) to encourage and reinforce good behavior than to correct misbehavior. When you *expect* positive and healthy behavior, you're more likely to see it.

It has been suggested that the 10-to-1 ratio in discipline is best. It's better to give 10 responses praising good behavior for every 1 that corrects wrong behavior.

You may find it helpful to keep track of the words you use when you respond to your child. Sometimes parents find they're using an abundance of the negatives such as "no," "stop that," "quit doing that,""don't," and so on when they could be using positive responses.

Expect the best and look for it. If on a given day 25 percent of the time your child behaved, talk more about that than the 75 percent of the time they misbehaved. You may find the percentages changing based on how you respond.[25]

February 29

To the Jews who had believed him, Jesus said, "If you hold to my teaching, you are really my disciples. Then you will know the truth, and the truth will set you free" (John 8:31,32).

From time to time it's best just to stop, pray, and ask God for His strength in our life. William Barclay's words voice what all of us need.

O God, our Father, direct and control us in every part of our life.
Control our tongues,
that we may speak no false, no angry, no impure word.
Control our actions,
that we may do nothing to shame ourselves or to injure anyone else.
Control our minds,
that we may think no evil, no bitter, nor irreverent thought.
Control our hearts,
that they may never be set on any wrong thing, and that they may ever love only the highest and the best.
O God, our Father, to whom the issues of life and death belong, preserve us from all ills.
Preserve us in health of body,
that we may be able to earn a living for ourselves and for those whom we love.
Preserve us in soundness of mind,
that all our judgments and decisions may be sane and wise.
Preserve us in purity of life,
that we may conquer all temptation and ever do the right, that we may walk through the world and yet keep our garments unspotted from the world.
And if illness, misfortune, sorrow come to us, preserve us in courage, in endurance, and in serenity of faith, that, in all the changes and the chances of life, we may still face life with steady eyes, because we face life with you.

This we ask for your love's sake. Amen.[26]

March 1

Commit your way to the LORD; trust in him and he will do this . . . (Psalm 37:5).

Sometimes parents are frustrated when they ask their child to do a task. They hear, "Oh, sure, I will," but nothing ever happens.

By the same token, sometimes children are frustrated when they make a request to their parents and get the same kind of response. It works both ways: Promises requested. Promises given. Promises broken. And the result? Lowered trust.

All of us want certainty. We want something and someone to depend on. We need security in the midst of an insecure world. You can't always depend on people. After all, we're marred because of the fall and sometimes our actions don't match our words. There is One, however, who will always deliver on what He says. Read these passages over every morning and evening for a month (out loud!). Not only will your sense of security rise, the Scriptures will also become your own.

"Never will I leave you; never will I forsake you" (Hebrews 13:5).

"Surely I am with you always, to the very end of the age" (Matthew 28:20).

"Trust in the LORD with all your heart and lean not on your own understanding; in all your ways acknowledge him, and he will make your paths straight" (Proverbs 3:5,6). If God says He will, then He will!

"You may ask me for anything" (John 14:14).

"All that the Father gives me will come to me, and whoever comes to me I will never drive away" (John 6:37). "I will" means just that.

"Then you will know the truth, and the truth will set you free" (John 8:32).

I will . . . I will . . . I will. These are absolute promises that we can depend on. They are especially encouraging when we've been let down by others.

By the way, children will need time to learn to follow through on their promises. After all, aren't we still learning, too?

March 2

Now the Lord God said, "It is not good [sufficient, satisfactory] that the man should be alone; I will make him a helper meet (suitable, adapted, completing) for him" (Genesis 2:18, AMP).

A Letter to a Child about to Be Married

Dear Child,

As you're about to embark upon your wedding, let me share some thoughts about this journey—that I have gleaned from the pen of Richard Exley and his wisdom.

Getting married is wonderful and also scary. A marriage may be made in heaven, but the maintenance must be done on earth. May you always consider each other first, before others.

Don't destroy each other with words, especially in public. Words are very powerful, they can kill love faster than roses can mend it. Always work toward the best for each other. Never leave each other without a kiss or an "I love you." Three little words, but they mean so much. Respect each other or the stars won't come out at night. Even in a crowd always let each other know you are aware of them.

Romance is a fragile flower, and it cannot long survive where it is ignored or taken for granted. Without commitment and imagination, it will slowly wither and die. But for those who are committed to keeping romance in their marriage, the best is yet to come.

Marriage is what you make it. Under God, it must be the most important relationship in all your life. If your marriage is good, you can overcome anything—financial adversity, illness, rejection, anything. If it is not good, there is not enough success in the world to fill the awful void. Remember, nothing, absolutely nothing, is more important than your marriage, so work at it with love and thoughtfulness all the days of your life.

Guard it against all intruders. Remember your vows. You have promised, before God and your families, to forsake all others and cleave only to each other. Never allow friends, or family, or work or anything else to come between you and your beloved.

Marriage is made of time, so schedule time together. Spend it wisely in deep sharing. Listen carefully and with understanding when he in turn shares his heart with you. Spend it wisely in fun—laugh and play together. Go places and do things together. Spend it wisely in worship—pray together. Spend it wisely in touching—hold each other—be affectionate.[1]

March 3

. . . put on a heart of compassion (Colossians 3:12, NASB).

*T*hat's an interesting verse, but how does a person put on a heart of compassion? Is it a matter of developing "new feelings"? If so, how do you do that?

True compassion is not just a feeling for another person. Nowhere in Scripture does it say to be compassionate or loving or kind "if you feel like it." The Bible just says to *do* it. Compassion, as taught in the Scripture, is not expressed by feeling, but by action. Let's look at some examples of Jesus' compassion as recorded in the Gospel of Matthew.

> Jesus went through all the towns and villages, teaching in their synagogues, preaching the good news of the kingdom and healing every disease and sickness. When he saw the crowds, he had compassion on them, because they were harassed and helpless, like sheep without a shepherd (Matthew 9:35,36).

Jesus knew what the people needed. He ministered to them for their physical, spiritual, and emotional needs. When He saw a problem, He acted. "When Jesus landed and saw a large crowd, he had compassion on them and healed their sick" (Matthew 14:14).

When two blind men confronted Him, He wasn't taken aback. They said to Him, "Lord we want our sight" (Matthew 20:33). Moved with compassion, Jesus touched their eyes; and immediately they regained their sight and followed Him.

Who in your life needs a touch of compassion today? Perhaps someone needs a literal touch, such as a hug or a shoulder rub. A touch could be a note in a lunch sack, a phone call of encouragement, or the statement, "I want you to know that I will be praying for you today for that test" (or sporting event, or whatever).

But keep in mind, true compassion can be costly. It involves a sacrifice without even calling attention to it. It means giving to give, not to eventually receive. And it means seeing life and the needs of others through their eyes, not yours. It's learning to care about what they care about.

March 4

Children are a gift of the LORD (Psalm 127:3, NASB).

*T*here are times when even the best of parents have mixed feelings about one of the gifts God has entrusted to them—their children. Sometimes they don't seem like much of a gift. But they are. The Israelites of the Old Testament had such a high regard for children that you will find passages that praise birth and discuss the anxiety and concern for those who were barren. Scripture celebrates children, and the more the better.

> Behold, children are a gift of the LORD;
> The fruit of the womb is a reward.
> Like arrows in the hand of a warrior,
> So are the children of one's youth.
> How blessed is the man whose quiver is
> full of them (Psalm 127:3-5, NASB).

Your family can bring glory to God because of your children. How? God's Word indicates that children are a blessing just because they are a gift from God. They can glorify God as you lead them to a saving knowledge of Jesus Christ and see His character developed in them.

Not only can children be a glory to God, they also can help in your own spiritual development. Married couples learn to bend, become flexible, and give up pockets of selfishness. The process begun in marriage is continued and deepened by the coming of children.

Yes, you will be inconvenienced, challenged, and made uncomfortable by your children. But rejoice. Their presence stretches you and causes you to learn in a way unknown to you before their coming. Family love was described by C.S. Lewis in this way: "Dogs and cats should be brought up together.... It broadens their minds so."[2]

Your children will be a source of satisfaction that cannot come from anywhere else. Even when your children are imperfect, that sense of satisfaction will remain unmatched. This is some gift God has given to you![3]

March 5

*If we confess our sins, he is faithful and just and will forgive us
our sins and purify us from all unrighteousness* (1 John 1:9).

A story is told of a time when Sir Arthur Conan Doyle decided to play a practical joke on 12 of his friends. He sent
each of them a telegram that read, "Flee at once . . . all is discovered." Within 24 hours, all 12 had left the country.

Most of us don't feel quite that guilty, yet many people go
through their entire lives struggling with the emotion of guilt.
Webster's Dictionary defines guilt as "the fact of having committed
a breach of conduct, especially violating law and involving a
penalty."[4] A person who is guilty is justly chargeable with or responsible for a grave breach of conduct.

Guilt is a powerful emotion that, like other emotions, can have
a positive or negative effect on our lives. It can warn us of danger
and motivate us to take corrective action. It can rob us of our joy
or open the door to greater joy. It can distort our views or help us
see things from God's perspective. We can allow guilt to keep us
imprisoned in our past or let it serve as a motivator to learn and
grow beyond our past.

Healthy guilt is constructive. It is an appropriate emotional response to the clear violation of a civil, spiritual, or relational standard. Healthy guilt is from God. Guilt is to our spirit what pain is
to our body. It warns us when something is wrong and needs attention or correction.

As Christians, it's important to remember that God has given
us a way to remove the painful feelings of guilt. In Leviticus chapters 4–6 God gave the Israelites three specific steps they could
take to resolve healthy guilt. First, confession (5:5); then restitu-
tion (6:1-5); and finally, sacrifice (6:6,7). In Psalm 51:17 we read,
"The sacrifices of God are a broken spirit; a broken and contrite
heart, O God, you will not despise."

Healthy guilt leads to a contrite heart that produces a positive
change in behavior. This, in turn, results in a closer walk with our
Lord.

How could 1 John 1:9 help you and your child resolve your
guilt?[5]

March 6

Cease striving and know that I am God; I will be exalted among the nations, I will be exalted in the earth (Psalm 46:10).

*Y*ou've probably had it happen to you. Your kids have been on an outing all day long. They chugged down Cokes, candy, and lots of chocolate. They played hard all day and now it's evening. They're exhausted. You're exhausted. And . . . you're hoping they're going to crash, fall asleep, and give you a chance to recover. Right? Wrong. They're so exhausted they're running around shrieking, bouncing from wall to wall, totally out of control. It's panic time. They're like frantic animals running themselves to death trying to outrace a fire. And you've reached your limit.

At the top of your voice you scream, "That's enough! Quiet!"

Suddenly there's a deathly calm. Everything comes to a halt. The only sound is that of silence. You spoke to your children and they got the message.

As a parent, our Father God speaks to each of us. Have we gotten the message?

He says to us in the midst of our own chaos and panic, "Cease striving and know that I am God." The Hebrew word for "cease" means "relax, do nothing, be quiet." But you say, "I can't! There's too much to do, too many places to go, too many people to tend to." God says, "It's okay. Take a break. Don't sweat it. Let me handle your situation."

Can you refuse such an offer? It's for your good. God didn't design us to live a life at a frantic pace. He has designed and reserved a spirit of rest for you, as it says in Hebrews 4:9: "There remains, then, a Sabbath-rest for the people of God."

This doesn't mean you cop out, throw up your hands, and walk away. Not at all. Instead, just set aside a few minutes, sit down, turn off the television, the phone, the answering machine, take a deep breath, and say, "God, here I am. Calm me, relax me, empower me, cause me to move and work more slowly and in Your strength." Once you've done that, go back to your battle and face it with Him. It may help to read Psalm 46 out loud—to the entire family—slowly.

March 7

As for me and my household, we will serve the LORD (Joshua 24:15).

*H*ow do you pray for your children? What do you pray for? One of the best steps a parent can take is to pray frequently and specifically for their child or children. All children need prayer whether or not they know Jesus or are walking with the Lord. Quin Sherrer and Ruthanne Garlock have given us some helpful suggestions in this regard.

One especially effective tactic involves personalizing verses of Scripture as you pray, such as replacing the pronouns with the names of the children or people for whom you're interceding. For example, Psalm 23:3 could be personalized in this way: "Thank you, Lord, that you guide my son Keith in the paths of righteousness for your name's sake." The verse takes on added potency as both an expression of praise to the Lord and a declaration of truth to the enemy.

We pray differently for children during various phases of their lives. For instance, the following prayer for a child who is either a student or an employee combines several verses:

Lord, may my child, like Daniel, show "... aptitude for every kind of learning, [be] well informed, quick to understand and qualified to serve in the king's palace" (Daniel 1:4). May he/she "speak with wisdom and tact," and may he/she be "found to have a keen mind and knowledge and understanding and also the ability... to solve difficult problems" (Daniel 2:14; 5:12). Lord, endow my child with "wisdom and very great insight, and a breadth of understanding as measureless as the sand on the seashore" (1 Kings 4:29).

Another way to personalize these same Scripture verses would be to speak them aloud about your child: "My child will be found to have a keen mind and knowledge and understanding and ability to solve difficult problems. He/she does have wisdom and insight and breadth of understanding as measureless as the sand on the seashore." By hearing the Word of God—even from our own lips—we stand firm on his truth as applied in our very own family. And in doing this we have strengthened our own faith.[6]

Try to discern your child's needs, and search the Scriptures to find verses that apply. Your prayers will take on an entirely new meaning.

March 8

Do not worry about tomorrow, for tomorrow will worry about itself. Each day has enough trouble of its own (Matthew 6:34).

*Y*ou've been invited to the governor's mansion for a special reception and dinner a month from now. But the surprise and excitement of the invitation is soon overshadowed by a very common question: "What shall I wear?" The anticipatory delight is soon disappointed by the concern over what rags to throw on for the evening.

Or, let's say you've invited guests over for dinner. It's the new pastor and his wife, as well as several other church staff members. Is your concentration and energy directed toward the enjoyment and fellowship of the upcoming event? Or does a sense of panic rise as you ask, "What are we going to serve?" and, "How can we get the house cleaned up in time?"

Those are legitimate questions to be asked and answered. But too often, we let our concerns about the future drain our joy in the present. Some people live in a constant state of preimagining the future and thus fail to derive the most from the present. Jesus had something to say about this:

> Do not worry, saying, "What shall we eat?" or "What shall we drink?" or "What shall we wear?" For the pagans run after all these things, and your heavenly Father knows that you need them. But seek first his kingdom and his righteousness, and all these things will be given to you as well. Therefore do not worry about tomorrow, for tomorrow will worry about itself. Each day has enough trouble of its own (Matthew 6:31-34).

If you worry about the future, then who is trying to be in control? And consider what we worry about so much of the time. Even when Matthew 6 was written, people had worries about food and clothes. Back then, such concern was legitimate. Many people were barely surviving. They worried out of scarcity and survival. Most of us today, however, worry out of abundance.

In either case, let God into your decision-making, your concerns, and your difficulties. Let Him have an opportunity to dispel your concerns, fill you with peace, and give you the ability to handle what you'll face today. Let go of tomorrow. It will be here soon enough.

March 9

I will do whatever you ask in my name, so that the Son may bring glory to the Father. You may ask me for anything in my name, and I will do it (John 14:13,14).

*W*hy do you pray? Go ahead—take a moment to answer that question.

Now, how would you answer the question if it were put to you by a three-year-old? A seven-year-old? A 15-year-old?

There are many reasons for praying. One is that praying for other people not only brings us closer to them, but it also can change our attitudes toward them. Another reason is that when we pray we become much closer to God. It's our way of communicating with Him. We didn't just learn to do this; He created us for that purpose.

Yet another reason to pray is that God has resources and blessings for us that we won't receive until we go to Him in prayer. And Dr. Lloyd John Ogilvie shared still another reason for prayer which may surprise you. It's a thought that you will want to think about the rest of today:

> We pray not so much to *change* but to *receive* the mind of God. As we pray our prayers and listen to God, He is able and willing to impress His mind upon us. Too often we think of prayer as changing God's mind on a subject. This is not the purpose of prayer.[7]

Perhaps that's a new thought for you—prayer is not to change but to receive the mind and will of God. Talking to God is not our idea, but His. We don't have to get His attention. He is there waiting . . . for our attention. Ask the Holy Spirit right now to stir your spirit and create a greater hunger and thirst for your heavenly Father.

March 10

Rejoice with those who rejoice; mourn with those who mourn (Romans 12:15).

Carry each other's burdens, and in this way you will fulfill the law of Christ (Galatians 6:2).

Some homes have an atmosphere that is pleasant, comfortable, and friendly. You know what it's like to enjoy such a home. Yet some families experience that all too infrequently. For others, that's the way it is most of the time. Have you ever wondered what makes the difference?

Some homes have an atmosphere that is tense, on edge, uncomfortable, and strained. You probably know what that's like, too. Every family experiences that once in a while. But for some families, that's the way it is most of the time. Have you ever wondered what makes the difference?

Think about this:

Part of a family's function is to shoulder one end of our burdens and to share the delight of our blessings.

Robert Frost said, "Home is the place where, when you have to go there, they have to take you in." . . . It is that, and a whole lot more. It is a center of fellowship, where families can be friends, where power and blessing abound.

Helping us to celebrate God's love is the chief blessing our families can give us. The unity that our psalmist calls "good and pleasant" is as much dependent on God as the anointing oil that made Aaron a priest or the dew that watered Zion when there was no rain. Only as we know how much God loves each of us can we begin to know how to love each other.

Friendly families are not those where there are no differences or disagreements, but those where God's love provides the strong glue that binds them together whatever the differences may be. Families can be friends but only when true love takes charge. The Bible says this love comes from God. Have you found any better source?[8]

God's love not only gives us eternal life with Him, but it also makes life much better here when we allow it to permeate our thoughts, feelings, and the way we respond to one another.

How could God's love be implemented to impact your family life today?

March 11

Before the mountains were born or you brought forth the earth and the world, from everlasting to everlasting you are God (Psalm 90:2).

Child: Does God ever change? Does He ever get better or worse? Does He change His moods? Does He . . .

Parent: All right, already! Wow—these are questions to ask the pastor!

Child: Pastor isn't here right now. You are. And I want to know.

Parent: Well, let's see if I can explain this so it makes sense to you (and to me!). God doesn't change. In the Psalms it says He is always the same (102:26). God Himself said, "I am the first and I am the last" (Isaiah 48:12). God has always been there. He wasn't made. He exists forever and He is always the same. He can't become better because He is already perfect. Does that make sense?

Child: I guess so . . . but go on.

Parent: Well, God's character doesn't change either. In James 1 we read about God's goodness, holiness, generosity, and His reaction to sin. James speaks of God as one "with whom there is no variation or shadow due to change" (James 1:17, RSVB). You see one minute I might be loving and kind, but the next I might get upset or angry. Right?

Child: Right!

Parent: Well, not God. He can't become less truthful or merciful or loving than He used to be. When you go to Him in prayer, you never have to wonder if He's in a good mood or not. He doesn't keep office hours or put up an "Out to lunch" sign. A thousand years ago, 500 years ago, and today God feels exactly the same toward people as He did when He sent His Son into the world to die for mankind. God Himself said in Malachi 3:6, "I the LORD do not change." That's something we can depend on, okay?

Child: Yeah, I'm beginning to understand. You sure gave me something to think about.

Parent: Well . . . you gave me something to think about, too![9]

March 12

Blessed are those who mourn, for they shall be comforted (Matthew 5:4, NASB).

*L*oss. It's a simple four-letter word that is one of our constant companions throughout life. But we don't talk about it often. Like a silent conspiracy, we seem to have an unspoken agreement with other people not to talk about our losses. Yet with each and every loss comes the potential for change, growth, new insights, understanding, and refinement—all positive descriptions and words of hope. But these benefits are often experienced in the future, and we fail to see that far ahead when we are in the midst of our struggles.

You may have faced many losses in your life already. You may not even be aware of some of them, or you may not have realized that what you experienced were actually losses. Some losses are overcome in 24 hours. Others last for years.

How you respond to your losses or what you let them do to you can affect the rest of your life. You can't avoid loss or shrug it off. Loss is not the enemy; not facing its presence in our lives is.

Are there any benefits to loss? God's Word tells us that loss produces maturity. The character qualities of patience, endurance, humility, long-suffering, gratitude, and self-control can all develop through our losses:

> Not only so, but we also rejoice in our sufferings, because we know that suffering produces perseverance; perseverance, character; and character, hope (Romans 5:3,4).

When you experience loss, you will discover the extent of God's comfort:

> Praise be to the God and Father of our Lord Jesus Christ, the Father of compassion and the God of all comfort (2 Corinthians 1:3).

Remember these thoughts when you encounter your next loss.[10]

March 13

*My son, give attention to my words . . . for they are life to those
who find them* (Proverbs 4:20,22, NASB).

*W*hat makes a dad successful? What are the ingredients?
For some answers, let's look at a young father who reflected on his own dad. He believed that his father was an excellent example of what God requires and desires in fathers. Here is
what he says:

> As I searched my childhood, I tried to recall the keys that made
> my father a successful family man. And so, from my father's ex-
> ample, I have observed several keys that I believe can help all fa-
> thers raise a family that is successful in God's eyes.

1. *Dad was always available.* I cannot remember a time when Dad
   did not immediately drop whatever he was doing to answer
   my questions or help me solve a problem.

2. *My father made a sacrifice for me.* Recently I have learned that
   every day since I have been born, my father and mother have
   knelt beside their bed and prayed individually for me, as well
   as my brother and sisters.

3. *Dad was a man of consistency, who set a strong example.*

4. *My father's affection built lasting bonds of friendship.* Dad never hes-
   itated to reach out and hug me or pat me on the shoulder.

5. *My father had a wife who loved and encouraged him.*

6. *Dad always expected the best of me.* When Dad gave me a job or
   responsibility, he always assumed that I would carry it out to
   the best of my ability.

7. *Dad loved me for who I was.* From the time I was just young
   enough to understand, my parents always made it clear to me
   that they loved me unconditionally.

8. *Dad was always proud of me.* Dad took every opportunity to introduce me to his friends and colleagues. "I'd like you to meet
   my son, Ron," he would say. "We're proud of him because . . ."

9. *Dad built memories for me.*

10. *My father learned early where his real priorities were.* Talk to my
    Dad about his business, and he'll be glad to discuss it with you.
    But ask him about his family, and his eyes light up and a fire
    flickers within. I only pray that my children, and yours, may
    one day be able to say the same things about their father.[11]

March 14

Then his father Isaac said to him, "Come here, my son, and kiss me" (Genesis 27:26).

*P*erhaps your children have asked you to come into their room and rub their backs. They enjoy the relaxing and soothing quality of your touch. Have you ever had the opportunity to experience a full-hour body massage? If so, you know the effect of touch on your muscles.

In the Old Testament, touch was important. In Genesis 27:26 we see Isaac asking his 40-year-old son to come and hug him as he blessed him. In another instance of blessing, touch was also important: " 'They are the sons God has given me here,' Joseph said to his father. Then Israel said, 'Bring them to me so I may bless them.' Now Israel's eyes were failing because of old age, and he could hardly see. So Joseph brought his sons close to him, and his father kissed them and embraced them" (Genesis 48:9,10).

We can never know how important it is to be touched by someone we love. Just for our physical well-being we need to be touched at least a dozen times a day. In rest homes where dogs have been brought in for several hours a day to be petted, held, loved, and talked to, the residents who spent time with the dogs lived longer than those who didn't. They also developed a much more positive attitude toward life.

Why is it that when people are apart for a long time and they meet again they touch or shake hands or embrace? It's because the message conveyed by the touch says much more than words could. There are times when your arms around another person at a time of loss speaks volumes whereas any words would not have been heard. Have you noticed the difference in your child's response when you say, "I love you," compared to saying, "I love you," and touching him or her at the same time? Perhaps touching makes our words more believable.[12]

March 15

The Lord gives skillful and godly Wisdom (Proverbs 2:6, AMP).

A Personal Note from the Author

Joyce and I raised two children—a daughter, Sheryl, and a son, Matthew. Matthew was a profoundly mentally retarded boy who went into the presence of Jesus in 1990 at the age of 22. When he died, his mental development equalled that of an eighteen-month-old child.

Recently I asked our daughter, who is in her thirties, how Matthew affected her and what problems she experienced in having a disabled brother.

"When I was young, his condition didn't bother me," she said. "It was like riding in an airplane or going through an earthquake when I was a child. I didn't fully understand the significance and all the ramifications of those situations, nor of retardation. When I became an adult I understood, and then it was difficult to deal with. I couldn't handle going to Matthew's home and seeing all the other disabled children. It just tore me to pieces. I have a difficult time seeing retarded children now."

After Sheryl said that, we talked a bit more. I told her that I understood and have a similar response and sensitivity to seeing anyone who has a disability. It took me years to discover that what I was feeling was the wish that I could reach out and heal that person—make him or her whole—followed by the frustration of knowing I couldn't.

Sheryl floored me with her response: "I don't think Matthew's retardation was something for us to try to heal. I think his purpose was to bring healing to all of us. We're all different because of him. I know I'm a different person because of Matthew."

I just stood there silently, letting the truth of her profound statement sink in. Her words left me with nothing to say. My tears were the only response. When she came across the room to hug me, I told her that was one of the most special things she had ever said.

There will come a time when your children's wisdom will make your life different, too.

March 16

He is like a father to us, tender and sympathetic to those who reverence him. For he knows we are but dust . . . (Psalm 103:13,14, TLB).

*W*hat is the role of a Christian father? God's Word gives us some clear pictures regarding the father-child relationship. In the above Scripture passage, God is compared to a father who knows that his children are not angels. He knows they're not perfect, and he accepts it. He can handle it. Fathers are not called to be perfectionists toward themselves nor their children.

> See, I will send you another prophet like Elijah before the coming of the great and dreadful judgment day of God. His preaching will bring fathers and children together again, to be of one mind and heart, for they will know that if they do not repent, I will come and utterly destroy their land (Malachi 4:5,6, TLB).

These verses are full of hope. They show that it's possible for fathers and their children to be drawn back together and united if there has been estrangement. Wouldn't it be wonderful for a parent and child to be in accord—no hassles, no disagreements, no divisions between them?

> You know that Timothy has proved himself, because as a son with his father he has served with me in the work of the gospel (Philippians 2:22).

Timothy is mentioned quite a bit in Paul's writing. The close relationship that they enjoyed is possible between a father and son when there is respect and admiration. When a son respects and admires his father, that's one thing, but when it's reciprocated by the father, the son feels loved and accepted. For this to occur takes time and a willingness to accept the giftedness and uniqueness of each other.

It's important for a father to be involved with his son and talk about everything with him. It may be easier to talk about grades, sports, and activities, but the time spent communicating about spiritual matters is what counts for eternity.[13]

He will be the sure foundation for your times, a rich store of salvation and wisdom and knowledge; the fear of the LORD is the key to this treasure (Isaiah 33:6).

*C*ontrol! I want to be in control of my life!" All of us have said that. But some people have taken this desire to the extreme and have become controllers. You've probably met them before.

People with rigid personalities, who are highly dominating or perfectionists, have difficulty handling life because they aren't flexible. Instead of being resilient, they are brittle. The more unexpected the problem, the more trouble they have. Setbacks cause them to make adjustments and changes, and this causes them difficulty. In addition to their rigidity, they lack a wide range of coping skills, and this exacerbates the problem. Consider the fallacy and futility of being in rigid control through the words of Dr. Lloyd John Ogilvie:[14]

> I wonder how controllers like these get along with God. I wonder how they learn to trust Jesus Christ as Savior. I wonder how they try to determine God's will for their lives (or maybe that question never enters their minds). I wonder how controllers handle the unexpected and uncontrollable losses of life and learn to view these upsets with a spiritual perspective. A controller cannot trust God because he fears the control of his life resting in anyone's hands but his own.[15]

What we all need to remember is this: We never *were* in total control! We are not in total control now. We never will be in total control. *God*, not us, is in control. Why stay in bondage to the myth that we must be in control? There is a better way to live.

March 18

The word of the LORD came to me, saying, "Before I formed you in the womb I knew you, before you were born I set you apart; I appointed you as a prophet to the nations" (Jeremiah 1:4,5).

*D*oes God create mistakes? That's a tough question! But think about it for a minute. Some of us do wonder about that. For example, have you ever wished that your child's physical characteristics were different? What about the sound of his or her voice? Have you ever said, "How could our child be so small with two tall parents?" What about your child's personality? Perhaps you're organized, structured, punctual, and bright and cheerful in the morning. But your child doesn't seem to have one drop of blood from your genes in him or her. Why did your child have to be that way? Some days you wonder about that more than others.

Jeremiah brings us back to an important fact. God said, "I made you," and the psalmist reiterates that truth with even greater clarity: "You created my inmost being; you knit me together in my mother's womb. I praise you because I am fearfully and wonderfully made; your works are wonderful, I know that full well" (Psalm 139:13,14).

God created you and your child for a specific purpose. You may not be all that you wanted to be. Your child may not be what you expected. But you and your child are very important to God. Both of you have high value in His sight.

Some days you may not feel significant. We all have days like that—some of us more than others. But every day, every minute, you and your child have great significance to God. Think about that! Bask in it. Delight in it. God is an architect. He designed you and every child you have. Mistakes? No. Not at all. There's a purpose. You may not always know what it is, but it's there. So when you look in a mirror or at your child, you're looking at a design fashioned by God.

Treat yourself and your child with the regard God has for you. After all, you both belong to Him.

March 19

For as the Father has life in himself, so he has granted the Son to have life in himself (John 5:26).

I can do it myself. I don't need anyone's advice or help." You've heard that before and perhaps have even said it yourself. You're self-sufficient . . . or at least you think so. Children say this much of the time in their eagerness to try new adventures or to let you know that they're growing up. This is the battle cry of the independent, strong-willed child.

Fortunately, as we go through life we realize that we aren't self-sufficient. We don't know it all or have all the capabilities we need—especially as parents. Something new always seems to come up just when we think we've got it all together. You have needs. We all have needs. And part of our calling is to help meet each other's needs.

God doesn't have any needs. He's different. You may have heard a speaker at some time say, "God needs you to do this or that . . ." but it's not true. God does not need us. He is not lacking in any area. He is not incomplete and waiting for us to help out. If He were, He would be an incomplete God. Where would that put us?

God is so complete He can't be elevated. No one can promote Him or degrade Him. If every person on earth became an atheist, it wouldn't affect God. He is what He is regardless of anyone else.

But if He is all-sufficient, where do we come in? That's simple: Our holy God doesn't need us, but He desires us. He doesn't need you, but He loves you more than you can fathom. Our fulfillment comes by living a life of faithful obedience to Him. That's what He desires. Just thinking about that should make you grateful and thankful. After all, He didn't need to create us, did He?[16]

March 20

Do not seek revenge or bear a grudge against one of your people,
but love your neighbor as yourself (Leviticus 19:18).

This is a message from one of America's favorite pastors about relationships:

Relationships. America's most precious resource. Take our oil, take our weapons, but don't take what holds us together—relationships. A nation's strength is measured by the premium it puts on its own people. When people value people, an impenetrable web is drawn, a web of vitality and security.

A relationship. The delicate fusion of two human beings. The intricate weaving of two lives; two sets of moods, mentalities, and temperaments. Two intermingling hearts, both seeking solace and security.

A relationship. It has more power than any nuclear bomb and more potential than any promising seed. Nothing will drive a man to a greater courage than a relationship. Nothing will fire the heart of a patriot or purge the cynicism of a rebel like a relationship.

What matters most in life is not what ladders we climb or what ownings we accumulate. What matters most is a relationship.

What steps are you taking to protect your "possessions"? What measure are you using to ensure that your relationships are strong and healthy? What are you doing to solidify the bridges between you and those in your world?

Do you resolve conflict as soon as possible, or do you "let the sun go down when you are still angry"? Do you verbalize your love every day to your mate and children? Do you look for chances to forgive? Do you pray daily for those in your life? Do you count the lives of your family members and friends more important than your own?

Our Master knew the value of a relationship. It was through relationships that he changed the world. His movement thrived not on personality or power but on championing the value of a person. He built bridges and crossed them. Touching the leper... uniting the estranged ... exalting the prostitute. And what was that he said about loving your neighbor as yourself?

It's a wise man who values people above possessions. Many wealthy men have died paupers because they gave their lives to things and not to people. And many paupers have left this earth in contentment because they loved their neighbors.[17]

March 21

He will be called . . . Everlasting Father (Isaiah 9:6).

*R*emember the day you were born? Hardly. Remember the day your chid was born? Absolutely. How could you forget it? That was the beginning. You and your child had a beginning, and you will have an ending. Right now people refer to you and your child as "who you are." But one day that will change and people will refer to you as "who you were" or say, "Do you remember . . . ?" Not so with Jesus Christ. One of His titles is "Everlasting Father," or as the Amplified Bible states, "The Father [of Eternity]." In this verse the word "Father" actually means "author."

You see, *Jesus always was.* There wasn't a moment in time when He wasn't. He has always been with the Father and was there when this and all the other planets were created. Paul said, "He is before all things" (Colossians 1:17). Our minds cannot compute that fact.

When you and I talk about time, we use the terms B.C. and A.D. But when Paul talks about Jesus, he is talking about another kind of time—preworld! You and I have a here and now and hereafter. Jesus has a before, a here and hereafter. He is forever. In John 17:5 He asked God to "glorify me in your presence with the glory I had with you before the world began" (John 17:5).

Many parents struggle over the future. They wish they could gaze ahead into the upcoming years and know either what's going to happen or how to control and determine future events. But that's impossible. And remember, Jesus is in charge of time. He's the one who holds the future in His hands.

Every year as we get older, a bell goes off somewhere in the recesses of our mind to remind us there are fewer days remaining in our schedules. Someday the quota will run out. Your time here will be exhausted. As a believer, life on earth is just a time of preparation. At death, your journey with the Father of Eternity begins. Jesus has made you a joint heir with Him (*see* Romans 8:17), and you get to share eternity with Him. That makes you special.[18]

March 22

There is . . . a time to be silent and a time to speak (Ecclesiastes 3:1,7).

Communication—a family cannot exist without it. No relationship can continue without interaction. That's true not only between us and other people, but also between us and God!

Of all the books written on communication, the best and most practical resource is the Word of God. Read the following verses and endeavor to practice these biblical principles of communication even more than you have been doing up to this point. It can make a significant difference in the life of your family.

"Speaking the truth in love, we are to grow up in all aspects into Him, who is the head, even Christ" (Ephesians 4:15, NASB).

"A man who refuses to admit his mistakes can never be successful. But if he confesses and forsakes them, he gets another chance" (Proverbs 28:13, TLB).

"Let him who means to love life and see good days refrain his tongue from evil and his lips from speaking guile" (1 Peter 3:10, NASB).

"Some people like to make cutting remarks, but the words of the wise soothe and heal" (Proverbs 12:18, TLB).

"A wise man controls his temper. He knows that anger causes mistakes" (Proverbs 14:29, TLB).

"Gentle words cause life and health; griping brings discouragement. . . . Everyone enjoys giving good advice, and how wonderful it is to be able to say the right thing at the right time! (Proverbs 15:4,23, TLB).

"Timely advice is as lovely as golden apples in a silver basket" (Proverbs 25:11, TLB).

"Pride leads to arguments; be humble, take advice and become wise" (Proverbs 13:10, TLB).

"Love forgets mistakes; nagging about them parts the best of friends" (Proverbs 17:9, TLB).

"Let all bitterness and wrath and anger and clamor and slander be put away from you, along with all malice. And be kind to one another, tender-hearted, forgiving each other, just as God in Christ also has forgiven you" (Ephesians 4:31,32, NASB).

March 23

Set your minds on things above, not on earthly things (Colossians 3:2).

*C*hoices—life is full of them. You make choices all day long. For most of us some choices are good and others are not so good. And as a parent, you try to give your children the opportunity to make choices. Years ago there was a television program in which contestants had to choose one of three doors. Behind two of the doors were comparatively worthless items, but behind the other was a new car or a similar prize. It was interesting to see how many contestants were immobilized by the fear of making the wrong choice.

There is a choice, though, that doesn't have a wrong door. It's the decision to choose to be happy, content, and fulfilled. How is that possible with a house full of demanding children? Choose your attitude. You'll find it helpful to read the following out loud each morning for a week and note the difference.

Just for today I will set my affection on things above, not on things on the earth.

Just for today I will not worry about what will happen tomorrow, but will trust that God will go before me into the unknown.

Just for today I will endure anything that hurts or depresses me because I believe God controls what happens to me.

Just for today I will not dwell on my misfortunes. I will replace my negative thoughts with happy and hopeful thoughts.

Just for today I will choose to do some things I do not like doing, and I will do them cheerfully and with a happy spirit.

Just for today I will make a conscious effort to love those who don't show love to me and be kind to those who do not appreciate me.

Just for today I will be patient with those who irritate me and longsuffering toward those who are selfish and inconsiderate.

Just for today I will be courageous. I will take responsibility for all my actions and not blame others for the way I behave.

Just for today I will choose to BE HAPPY![19]

March 24

Judah is a lion's [cub] . . . and as a lion, who dares rouse him up? Naphtali is a doe let loose, he gives beautiful words. Joseph is a fruitful bough, a fruitful bough by a spring (Genesis 49:9, 21,22, NASB).

*W*hat a strange passage of Scripture. Jacob was talking about his children as though they were animals. Isn't that an unusual way of describing your children? Not really. In the process of giving each child a blessing, he used word pictures to describe them. He was sharing how much he valued and accepted them by picturing their qualities in a way that isn't always tied to their performance. In Genesis we read, "All these are the twelve tribes of Israel, and this is what their father said to them when he blessed them, giving each the blessing appropriate to him" (49:28).

Why was Judah depicted as a lion's cub? In the Word of God, a lion portrayed strength. It was also considered to be a symbol of royalty in the Near East. A lion, then, signified the strength of character and leadership qualities that Judah possessed.

Naphtali was described as a doe. Portraying a son in this way may seem strange, but Naphtali was a man who possessed artistic qualities. What better way to illustrate this than with the grace and beauty of a gentle animal? This son spoke and wrote words of beauty.

Then there was Joseph. Why was he described as a fruitful bough by a spring? This picture shows how his trust in the Lord resulted in providing a place of refuge for his family. A similar picture was used of Jesus in Psalm 1:3: "He is like a tree planted by streams of water, which yields its fruit in season and whose leaf does not wither. Whatever he does prospers."

Have you ever been described in a positive way by some type of word picture? Have you described anyone else in your family like that? Most recipients not only understand what is said but appreciate the description. List the qualities and characteristics of your family members. Then create your own pictures. That will help give you a greater appreciation for each person's uniqueness.[20]

March 25

Do not withhold good from those who deserve it, when it is in your power to act (Proverbs 3:27,28).

*A*t funerals and memorial services, oftentimes one or more family members or friends will deliver a eulogy. They share the positive qualities, characteristics, and accomplishments of the deceased. They extol the person's virtues and go into detail as to why the person will be missed. Everyone present hears the kind and affirming words except one—the person who is being talked about. Sometimes you wonder if they knew, while they were alive, that this was how other people felt about them. You wonder how much of what was shared in the eulogy was ever told to them directly when they were alive. Perhaps some of it was, or none of it.

Proverbs 3:27,28 certainly gives us clear directions about this. There are some families who have taken this to heart in a dramatic way. They have conducted living eulogy services with a family member who is terminally ill. The family members and friends come together in the hospital room or home and each one shares face to face with the individual what they would say if they were giving the eulogy at a memorial service. One large family of 16 members spent three hours one afternoon sharing in this way and videotaped the proceedings. What a rich experience! It may seem sad, but what would really be sad is if a family member died without having heard the good others had to say about him. What a difference it might have made in the life of a deceased person if he had known what other people had to say.

So many parents and children end up saying, "If only I had told them how much I loved them, what I appreciated, how much they meant to me . . .". "If only" are words of regret and sadness over missed opportunities. The presence of positive words can motivate, encourage, and lift up someone. The absence of such . . . well, perhaps the deceased would never know what they missed. Or they could have been living with the longing for a few well-chosen words.

We can't change the times we've missed, but we can fill the lives of our family members in the future. Who needs words of love and encouragement from you? And who do you need to hear from? Sharing what you have to say may help other people do likewise.

March 26

Confess your sins to each other and pray for each other so that you may be healed. The prayer of a righteous man is powerful and effective (James 5:16).

*I*n order to love, accept, and respond to our children in the way God has called us to do so, we need to be refreshed by God Himself with His grace. Only then can we be faithful to our calling. Some parents have found it beneficial to pray this prayer out loud each day for several weeks to allow the truths to penetrate into their hearts and minds.

Prayer for Trust in the Spirit of God

I will not worry, fret or be unhappy over you.
I will not be anxious concerning you.
I will not be afraid for you.
I will not blame you, criticize you or condemn you.

I will remember first, last and always
that you are God's child,
that you have his Spirit in you.
I will trust this Spirit to take care of you,
to be a light to your path,
to provide for your needs.
I will think of you always,
as surrounded by God's loving presence,
as being enfolded in his protecting care,
as being kept safe and secure in him.

I will be patient with you,
I will have confidence in you,
I will stand by in faith
and bless you in my prayers,
knowing that you are growing,
knowing that you are finding the help you need.
—Anonymous[21]

March 27

You are the light of the world. A city on a hill cannot be hidden. Neither do people light a lamp and put it under a bowl. Instead they put it on its stand, and it gives light to everyone in the house. In the same way, let your light shine before men, that they may see your good deeds and praise your Father in heaven (Matthew 5:14-16).

There's a light shining from your house. You may not see it, but it's there. That light is you. Jesus said we are the light of the world. But what does that mean? A light has got to shine. A person who knows Jesus as Lord and Savior can't keep it to himself. You can't be a private Christian. We aren't to live as solitary hidden believers, but obvious visible ones.

It's as though Jesus was saying, "I've started something—a ministry to people. But I'm going back to the Father. So each of you needs to continue My ministry."

When Jesus spoke again to the people, he said, "I am the light of the world. Whoever follows me will never walk in darkness, but will have the light of life" (John 8:12).

While I am in the world, I am the light of the world (John 9:5).

The first place that we need to be a light is in our homes. And our light needs to shine in such a way that when others see it they will say, "If that's Christianity, then I want it," not, "If that's Christianity, you can have it."

Listen to what children who have seen their parents' light say about it:

"My mom didn't only talk about her faith. I saw it in action. She was willing to be different. Sometimes she made decisions that weren't popular, but I respected her."

"Dad showed us what it meant to be a Christian by what he said, how he said it, and by what he didn't say. He was different from other men at home and at the factory."

Perhaps the best way to be a light is summed up in James: "In the same way, faith by itself, if it is not accompanied by action, is dead" (2:17).

March 28

Blessed are those who hunger and thirst for righteousness, for they will be filled (Matthew 5:6).

*M*ost parents would like their children to be ambitious. After all, isn't that the opposite of being lazy? You want them to be industrious—to do the best they can and achieve.

There is nothing wrong with ambition. To get anywhere in this life it's a must. That's what this beatitude is talking about. But the ambition described here is to be a person whose life is based upon what is right.

It's so easy for our ambition to be misdirected. Many young couples just starting out today are not content to take a step down economically from their parents' standard of living. They want to have everything right now. Their ambition is a bit misdirected.

Scripture abounds with stories of misguided ambition. In Isaiah 14 we read the story of one of God's magnificent creations, Lucifer. He had an intense driving ambition—to be like God! He wanted power. We read what happened to him in Isaiah 14:15: "You are brought down."

In Luke 12 we read about a rich man who had done well with his crop. He wanted more abundance so he tore down his barns and built larger ones. He was a pleasure seeker. He died before he could enjoy it all.

In the book of Daniel, King Nebuchadnezzar's ambition was to make himself as famous as possible. He ended up going mad and eating grass from the fields like the wild animals.

What form should a parent's ambition take? Toward what goal should we direct our children? Righteousness. We're called to possess righteousness. The righteousness of Christ was given to us when we accepted Him. We're called to practice righteousness. Which means that what we say, where we go, what we do, and who we spend time with will be different. That, of course, will set a positive example for our children.

We're also called to ambitiously promote righteousness—to do the right thing and work against the wrong thing. That's a big task. But we don't have to do it in our own strength.[22]

March 29

Forgive us what we owe to you (O God our Father) as we have also forgiven those who owe anything to us!" (Matthew 6:12, Phillips).

Forgive us our debts, as we also have forgiven our debtors (Matthew 6:12).

*Y*ears ago there was an old song with the words, "I owe my soul to the company store." Many people go through life owing everyone, or so it seems. Sometimes we'll do a favor for someone and he or she will say, "You owe me." And with our children we sometimes feel like they owe us for all we've done for them.

Being in debt to someone is not a comfortable feeling. We feel pressure hanging over our heads until we can repay. What's especially sad is that today we see many families that have experienced financial bankruptcy.

We were never called to be people in debt. "Let no debt remain outstanding, except the continuing debt to love one another, for he who loves his fellowman has fulfilled the law" (Romans 13:8). Of course, it's difficult to purchase a house or other large items without incurring debt. But there *are* many other items that we could choose to wait on so we don't have to go into debt.

Who do you owe? And what do you owe? There are many things we can owe other than money. Is there anyone to whom you owe a letter? Is there anyone to whom you owe an apology? What about owing someone a visit or a call or a bit of your time? And, what do you owe yourself? A bit of solitude, time to sit and read, or a lunch with a friend? Sometimes we're in debt to ourselves as much as to others. There are more debts to be aware of, as Phillip Keller points out:[23]

> The debt of common courtesy for each other.
> The debt of promises made but never fulfilled.
> The debt of cheerful encouragement in adversity, withheld.
> The debt of insensitivity for those who suffer.
> The debt of neglect for one another in loneliness.
> The debt of just not caring about others.
> The debt of silence, when praise is needed.[24]

Wouldn't it be wonderful to begin to live debt-free!

March 30

We have different gifts, according to the grace given us. . . . if it is teaching, let him teach. . . ." (Romans 12:6,7).

Some parents instill within their children a quest for knowledge and a thirst for learning. It's as though they are able to turn every situation into a classroom. These parents have been given the gift of teaching. It's true that all parents are to teach and will teach, but for some it's natural and it happens constantly. The word *teach* means "to train . . . to give lessons to (a student or a pupil); to guide the study of; to instruct . . . to give lessons in . . . to provide with knowledge, insight."[25]

If you as a parent have this gift (or your spouse), you are usually sharing information or knowledge with a joyful attitude. It's easy. It's natural. The opportunities are unlimited. Children raised in this type of home will have an abundance of stimuli such as books, cassette tapes, and other research materials. These parents usually surround their children with whatever will assist them in learning.

Learning occurs not only in a formal setting but at any time. Deuteronomy 6:6,7 tells us, "These commandments that I give you today are to be upon your hearts. Impress them on your children. Talk about them when you sit at home and when you walk along the road, when you lie down and when you get up."

Wise parents know the value or strength of their gift as well as the weakness of its overuse. For example, a wise parent-teacher does not overburden a child with too many details and thus douse enthusiasm. When your child asks the time, you don't tell him or her how the watch or clock was made!

A wise parent-teacher also allows for individual differences within children and looks for teachable moments. And they work with their children to help them discover their own uniqueness or giftedness.

All parents can and will teach. For some it's a natural ability with a joyful attitude. Don't be down on yourself if you don't see this gift in your home. God can bring other people who will supply it. The gift you have will be a blessing for your family. Discover your gift, rejoice in it, and use it.[26]

March 31

Jesus answered, "Do you think that these Galileans were worse sinners than all the other Galileans because they suffered this way? I tell you, no! But unless you repent, you too will all perish. Or those eighteen who died when the tower in Siloam fell on them—do you think they were more guilty than all the others living in Jerusalem? I tell you, no! But unless you repent, you too will all perish" (Luke 13:2-5).

*J*esus had some strange words for the crowd He was talking with, but they're applicable for today as well. Sometimes we think that the reason bad things happen to people is because those individuals deserved what they got. They brought it on themselves. Sometimes that's true and sometimes it's not.

When something bad happens to someone you don't like, don't get along with, or compete against, how do you respond inside? All of us have probably struggled with this at one time or another. We have a tendency to gloat silently. We may even feel gratified and justified over another person's misfortunes. That's easy to do if it's obvious that person is wrong or has violated some law. We think he deserves it. Sometimes we have that attitude when we watch trials or investigative reports or talk shows on television. We see a person confronted and squirming under the heat of the investigation. We make comments about him, and our children hear, listen, and . . . learn. We're teaching our attitude to our children without knowing it.

Sometimes we think our brother's adversity makes us look better. Or we think we must be doing something right because we're not having the same problems he is.

But there's a better way to respond. It's found in 1 Corinthians 13:6: "Love does not delight in evil." When someone else is having a hard time, don't ask, "What did you do to deserve that?" Rather, ask, "How can I pray for you?" It will make a difference for you, for the other person, and for your children![27]

April 1

"Honor your father and mother" . . . is the first commandment with a promise (Ephesians 6:2).

*T*here's a fascinating book parents ought to read that's titled *The Tribute: What Every Parent Longs to Hear*. The author, Dennis Rainey, talks about how to make it as easy as possible for your children to honor you. As he read through the multitude of tributes that were mailed to him while he was writing this book, he found that again and again children felt that the following three factors were important:

1. Their parents' involvement

2. Their parents' emotional support

3. Their parents' character[1]

This is what he says about parents' involvement:

Your children want more than anything else for you to be involved in their lives. They need more than your time—they need your attention. They flourish when you focus on them.

That means more than just showing up at soccer games with a cellular phone in your pocket. Your children need your heart knitted to theirs as they make their choices and hammer out their character. They need you to know what's going on in their lives. They need you to help them think about the clothing they wear, the type of person they date, and the peer pressure they face.

In order to be a parent worthy of honor you can't just "be there." As much as possible, you have to "be *all* there."

That may sound simple, but it's easy for all your hours away from work to be filled with television shows, projects, finances, books, shopping, and housework. If you were able to add up how much time you actually spend focusing on your children each week, you might be shocked to discover your total measured in minutes, not hours. Occasionally I am so exhausted that, when I do arrive home or at one of our children's activities, I am really oblivious to what is going on.

Being all there does not mean you have to do it perfectly every time. It does mean that you are keeping the lines of communication firmly open and intact.[2]

April 2

. . . making the most of your time (Ephesians 5:16, NASB).

*T*he clock reminds us. Our stomach reminds us. Others remind us of this precious commodity called time. For some people it's a treasure. When you're young, you think it's endless. Time moves so slowly. When you're in your seventies you wonder how much is left, for you know it's limited.

As a parent, you look at your child and think, *Where has the time gone? It seems like just yesterday they were starting school, and now they're graduating.* Sometimes we feel as if a thief came through the door and stole some of our time.

We all have a different value on time and its usage. Some people actually wonder what they can do to fill their time each day. They must not be parents! Sometimes you ask your children, "What have you been doing?" You hear the reply, "Just hanging around. You know, spending time bumming around." But time is more than something to be spent. When a portion of time in our life is gone, it can never be retrieved. It's gone forever.

One of the greatest gifts we can ever give another person is he gift of our time, whether it be to a family member, friend, or stranger.[3] Consider what Phillip Keller says:

> That really is what the Master meant when He said:
>
> "I was hungry—hungry for human companionship—human warmth—good cheer—and you gave me meat."
>
> "I was thirsty—thirsty for loving care, for a bit of your time—and you gave me to drink."
>
> "I was a stranger—a stranger to the winsome warmth of a genial family—and you took me into your life!"
>
> "I was naked—naked and exposed and vulnerable in a society that strips a man of feeling 'he belongs,' but you clothed me in compassion and tender concern."
>
> "I was sick—sick in soul, sick in spirit, yes, sometimes sick in body—but you cared enough to visit me."
>
> "I was in prison—the prison of my own loneliness, my own fears, my awful sense of being forgotten—*then you came.*" Came to set me free from bondage to my own loneliness.[4]

Moreover [let us also be full of joy now!] let us exalt and triumph in our troubles and rejoice in our sufferings, knowing that pressure and affliction and hardship produce patient and unswerving endurance (Romans 5:3, AMP).

*L*osses. Your children will experience many of them. Some daily. Part of your calling will be to assist them to handle and learn from them. But before this can occur we have to make sure we've handled the childhood losses in our own life and recovered from them. Some adults haven't.

Think about your life as a child. Have you identified the losses? Do they loom out of proportion to all of your experiences and affect the way you perceive all of your life? Frequently this happens. We all perceive life from our backlog of experiences.

The way we perceive is similar to a camera. Photographers can alter the image of reality through the use of various lenses or filters. Thus what the camera records may not be an accurate view of the world. A wide-angle lens gives a much wider panorama, but the objects in the picture appear more distant and smaller. A telephoto lens has a much narrower and more selective view of life. It can focus on a beautiful flower, but at the same time it shuts out the rest of the garden. A normal lens will capture happy and smiling people, but those same people seen through a fish-eye lens will become distorted and unreal. Filters can blur reality, break images into pieces, bring darkness into a lighted scene, and even create a mist.

Like the lenses and filters on a camera, our perception of the world can distort reality. A photographer, however, is aware of the distortion in his perception of reality, and sometimes we are not aware of what our perception is doing. When we are depressed, we are practically blind without knowing it. Depression focuses upon the darker portions of life and takes away the warmth and joy from a scene. The greater the intensity of our depression, the greater the distortion. All this can happen because of overwhelming losses as children.[5]

In spite of this, there can be joy in the midst of difficulty. As you learn this, teach your children about life, loss, and joy. It will prepare them for the future.

April 4

I urge you, brothers, by our Lord Jesus Christ and by the love of the Spirit, to join me in my struggle by praying to God for me (Romans 15:30).

This is a blunt question: Do you pray regularly with your partner? If you're a single parent, do you pray regularly with a prayer partner or a close friend? Praying together with another person engaged in the parenting vocation can keep you going when times are tough. But why is it so important for a married couple, especially parents?

A Christian marriage is not a relationship between two people, but a partnership between three—God, husband, and wife. And partnerships really do work better when there is daily or frequent communication between the partners.

One husband and father suggested that praying together as a couple at bedtime does several things. It's difficult to stay angry and distant from your spouse when you pray with him or her. When you pray at the end of the day it forces you to deal with those unresolved issues that you've been putting off. When the Scripture says, "Don't let the sun go down upon your wrath," there's a good reason for it.

Second, when you pray together, it seems that the Holy Spirit bonds your marriage together in a stronger way. It builds the depth of intimacy because praying openly takes vulnerability. It helps you to be more open in other areas as well. Many couples have said prayer even improves sexual intimacy!

Third, when you pray together it reminds you of what is important not only to you but to your partner. In a way you are forced to become more a part of the other person's concerns.

Fourth, parenting is teamwork, not just between a couple but with God. Throughout the journey of parenting you will have a multitude of issues and concerns to pray about. And among the worst moments are the times when you feel that you're carrying the load alone as a parent. When you pray together, the burden is shared and lessened.

Perhaps prayer is already a major part of your life together. If not, why not begin now? It can only help and may become a life-changing experience.[6]

April 5

. . . give thanks in all circumstances, for this is God's will for you in Christ Jesus (1 Thessalonians 5:18).

*P*raise the Lord!"
      You've heard other people say that. Perhaps you have said that, too. It's easy to praise God for what He has already done because we can reflect back and measure the results. But what about praising Him for what He is *going* to do? When you do that, you not only become more of a risk taker, but you also become aware of what He wants for you.

You will have circumstances in which there appears to be no answer or solution. You may feel blocked. Have you ever stopped at such times and taken a moment to praise God?

Lloyd John Ogilvie has an interesting thought along this line: "Consistent praise over a period of time conditions us to receive what the Lord has been waiting patiently to reveal to us or release for us."[7]

We are to recognize and rejoice in God. We are to praise Him for who He is in response to His love, goodness, faithfulness, and unbelievable concern for each one of us. When we praise God, we are recognizing His sovereignty and capability. In praising God we are making a transfer—giving trust and dependence to Him rather than trusting and depending upon our own efforts and abilities.

What would you do if someone sent you a letter admonishing you 20 times to rejoice—and four of those times he said to rejoice *always?* Paul wrote such a letter to the church at Thessalonica—a letter that applies to us today. When you and I rejoice in the Lord, we do so not because we feel like it. Rather, it is an act of our will, a commitment. When we rejoice in the Lord, we begin to see life from another point of view. Praise is our means of gaining a new perspective and new guidance for our bogged-down lives.

You may be thinking that you are too busy during the day to stop and praise God. That, however, is just the time to praise Him—when you are too busy, fretful, and overwhelmed. Stop, clear your mind, and praise God. You will feel refreshed.

April 6

For God so loved the world that he gave his one and only Son,
that whoever believes in him shall not perish but have eternal
life (John 3:16).

*F*amily—what does it mean to you? What images unfold in your mind as you focus upon that word? For many of us, family means the people you can count on no matter what. Those special people who are there when you need them. Those with whom you share your joys and sorrows. Those who show up at your graduation, your wedding, and when you're in the hospital.

Family usually includes the people who you look to immediately for help, support, love, and acceptance. The ones you want to be among the first to see your newborn baby. Those with whom you may experience your deepest emotions, your greatest joys, and your most painful hurts.

Family means times of reunion, traditional holiday gatherings, brief airport encounters when one passes through on business, and partings that are sad and painful. And family also means times of stress, tension, disagreements, and sometimes painful distancing.

Family can mean welcoming a new member by marriage ... and in time seeing someone leave when divorce invades your family structure. Family means learning to grieve, not in isolation, but together as strength is shared in times of deepest need. A family is a grouping that expands through births and marriages and shrinks a bit when a member leaves for whatever reason.

What does your family mean to you? Who has come and gone? What marks have different people made on your life? What imprints have you made and are you making on others? Who are the people in your life that you consider family?

We are part of an even larger family than our immediate relatives. As believers, we are all related, all joint heirs in Christ. Our call within this family of God is to relate to one another, serve one another, love one another. But this family is not to be an exclusive one that keeps others on the outside. Our mission as a family is to expand God's family by inviting other people to join through a personal relationship with Jesus Christ.

Therefore, I urge you, brothers, in view of God's mercy, to offer your bodies as living sacrifices, holy and pleasing to God—this is your spiritual act of worship. Do not conform any longer to the pattern of this world, but be transformed by the renewing of your mind (Romans 12:1,2).

*H*ow is your body today? Take a look at it in the mirror. How are the bodies of your other family members? You've probably got all shapes and sizes in your household.

It's interesting to note and understand what Scripture says about your body. First, you don't own your body. It's not yours. It never was, never will be. Your children's bodies are not their own either. Our bodies belong to God. We are to present them to God as a sacrifice. When sacrifices were presented to God in the Old Testament, the animals offered had to be the best, without blemish. But ours is a *living* sacrifice. We're a walking-around, breathing sacrifice. People should be able to look at us and say, "That's a sacrifice to God." But will they end the statement with an exclamation point or a question mark? An exclamation point says, "You're in great shape! Wow!" A question mark says, "You're a living sacrifice? You've got to be kidding!"

Which are you? How are you treating your body? What shape are you in? We live in a health-conscious age. And what we do to ourselves is observed by our children. What we eat or don't eat, whether we exercise regularly (four times of aerobic activity a week—sorry, golf doesn't qualify), and whether we get sufficient sleep all contributes to the shape we're in. And it does matter to God.

Our body is a temple of the Holy Spirit (*see* 1 Corinthians 6:19). It belongs to God. He is saying, "Treat well what I've given to you, for in doing so, you honor Me and you become a testimony to others about your relationship with Me."

Is that a thought you've considered in your life?

April 8

Dear children, let us not love with words or tongue but with actions and in truth (1 John 3:18).

I love you." Three of the most commonly expressed words. Three of the most desired words to hear from loved ones. Parents and children exchange them, sometimes with deep feeling and thought. At other times, we say them automatically as if we were giving a conditioned response. The words are easy to say, but difficult to do. If there are no actions to back them up, they have a hollow ring to them.

Parents want their children to be loving in all their relationships. But more than anything, children need to see practical expressions of love not just in the home but in the world around us. Consider these words from the prophet Isaiah:

> Is not this the kind of fasting I have chosen: to loose the chains of injustice and untie the cords of the yoke, to set the oppressed free and break every yoke? Is it not to share your food with the hungry and to provide the poor wanderer with shelter—when you see the naked, to clothe him, and not to turn away from your own flesh and blood? Then your light will break forth like the dawn, and your healing will quickly appear; then your righteousness will go before you, and the glory of the LORD will be your rear guard. Then you will call, and the LORD will answer; you will cry for help, and he will say: Here am I (58:6-9).

Those words were spoken many years ago, but conditions haven't changed much. The needs are still with us. Have you and other family members ever read this passage aloud? Try it. Have you ever discussed what it would mean to put these admonitions into action daily? Do it. God is saying, "If you say you love Me and other people, don't tell Me. Show Me. Be a person or a family of action. Do something about the needs of other people. Then experience all the blessings I have for you.

That's quite an offer. In addition, God wouldn't ask us to do something we're incapable of doing. Are you ready to apply what you've learned . . . today? This could be an interesting day for you.

Where can I go from your Spirit? Where can I flee from your presence? If I go up to the heavens, you are there; if I make my bed in the depths, you are there (Psalms 139:7,8).

Child: I've got another question.

Parent: I figured as much. What is it?

Child: At church I heard someone say, "Let's go into God's presence and worship Him." Does that mean when we leave church we are walking out of God's presence? Does that mean God isn't here in our home? When we're not allowed to pray at school, does that mean we've taken God out of the classroom?

Parent: You sure ask good questions. I just wish I could answer them better.

Child: Oh, you do all right. What about it, though? Where is God?

Parent: God is everywhere. God isn't limited, and there's no limit to His presence. The Bible teaches that there is no place in heaven or hell where anyone can hide from Him. When we're here at home or in the car or at the grocery store, God is with us just as much as He is at church. When Paul was preaching, he found that people believed that God was only in the sanctuary or the temple. Paul said, "The God who made the world and everything in it is the Lord of heaven and earth and does not live in temples built by hands" (Acts 17:24). God is always here and He is always everywhere. He is here right now with us, He is with the native in the jungle in Africa, and He is with the Japanese family in Tokyo. I know it is hard to understand how He can be everywhere.

Child: Yes, it is. But He doesn't have a body like us. It's impossible for us to be everywhere, but it's possible for Him, right?

Parent: Yes. He is everywhere. He's at school, at home, at your soccer games. And no matter what we face, we can be hopeful because God is always there. You don't have to feel His presence. He's there anyway.

Child: That's awesome. Someday, maybe I'll understand it all better.[8]

April 10

He who loves Me will be loved by My Father, and I will love him and manifest myself to him (John 14:21, NKJV).

*F*ive of the most wonderful words that you can ever hear are, "I will always love you." They are said by teenagers to their first love when nothing else in the world seems to matter. They are said by couples standing in the front of a church as they recite their wedding vows.

They are said by little children as they look up into the faces of their parents as they're being tucked into bed at the end of an exciting day. They are said by parents to their child as they close the door of their child's overloaded car before he or she departs for college.

They are said with a look, a touch, a whisper, a note, or a shout. They are cherished by the person who receives them, for they bring inner peace and joy when all else has fallen apart. They are also noted by their absence, for there is an empty place in every person's heart that can only be filled by these five simple words. Without these words, we may come to question our worth.

There is, however, one person who never stops saying, "I will always love you." Even when you don't hear it, it's being said. Even when you think you don't deserve it, it's being said. Remember the words. Remember who is saying it over and over again.

Perhaps the summation of the extent of this love is reflected in this Bible passage: "Keep yourselves in God's love as you wait for the mercy of our Lord Jesus Christ to bring you to eternal life.... To him who is able to keep you from falling and to present you before his glorious presence without fault and with great joy" (Jude 21,24).

You can't ask for more than that, can you?

April 11

Since we are surrounded by such a great cloud of witnesses, let us throw off everything that hinders and the sin that so easily entangles, and let us run with perseverance the race marked out for us (Hebrews 12:1).

*W*e live in a world of gadgetry: airplanes, ships, and missiles, all of which have guidance-control systems. That system is there for an important reason—to keep the object on course so it will arrive at its prescribed destination. A plane leaving Los Angeles for New York can end up hundreds of miles off course with just the slightest variance in directional readings.

For us as parents to be successful we need to stay on course, know what we want to accomplish, let nothing distract us, and persist in doing it.

What do you want to accomplish as a parent? What is your goal for your children? And is it really yours? I mean *really*? Or is it what is wanted by your spouse, parents, in-laws, church, or school? Sometimes, in a desire to appear successful, parents cave in to the pressures around them. But does every child have to be in soccer, ballet, Little League, home school, and so on? Think about what you want. Think about the pressure to do what other people want. And then, think about this:

> Most of us are familiar with the story of Helen Keller, the blind and deaf woman who broke through the prison of her limitations and lived her life to the fullest. But not many of us know much about Anne Sullivan, the gifted teacher who empowered Helen Kellers' transformation.
>
> As a child raised in a mental institution, Anne was one of the least likely to succeed. But a nurse saw a spark of hope for this little girl, and she took a compassionate interest in her. When the apparently hopeless child was released, Anne had a heart full of compassion to help others. Because someone had seen potential in her, Anne was able to detect potential in Helen Keller and draw it out. Each life that was touched in this remarkable chain of caring went on to touch other lives.
>
> Who was successful—the institutional nurse, Anne Sullivan, or Helen Keller? Each was successful, because *each woman knew what she wanted to do with her life and did it.*[9]

April 12

In these last days he has spoken to us by his Son, whom he appointed heir of all things, and through whom he made the universe (Hebrews 1:2).

*W*hen families come together in an attorney's office to go over someone's will, there is usually an air of expectation along with the feelings of loss. Sometimes what you get is not what you expected, or what you didn't get is what you did expect. There will be limitations to what you can receive, just as there will be limitations to what you can pass on to your children. You may feel as though you have a right to receive certain family heirlooms. But so might some other people, especially if you were one of several children.

Jesus Christ is also an heir. This is one of the 100 or more titles given to Him in Scripture. But with Him there is absolutely no restriction or limitation. "Heir of all things" is what God's Word says (Hebrews 1:2). And in the book of Revelation the thought is expanded: "The kingdom of the world has become the kingdom of our Lord and of His Christ, and he will reign for ever and ever" (Revelation 11:15).

Sometimes people challenge the right of an heir or the recipient of a will. Why should the other person receive all that he or she has been given?

Have you ever wondered that about Jesus? There are good reasons why He should receive everything.

First, He has the right because He is the Son of God. *Heir* is a legal term used to denote a person who receives an inheritance by natural right rather than through a will. It's determined by the bloodline, usually the nearest of kin. But second, Jesus is also an heir by divine appointment. There is no way anyone can contest His right to the inheritance from the Father.

There is a third reason. Jesus has a right to His inheritance because He was involved in the act of creation. He was there to bring the world into being. And He had a part in creating you and your child.

No matter what your inheritance here on earth, you have an inheritance waiting for you in heaven—one that can't be measured. That's a gift to look forward to, isn't it?[10]

April 13

Can you pull in the leviathan with a fishhook or tie down his tongue with a rope? . . . He looks down on all that are haughty; he is king over all that are proud (Job 41:1,34).

*H*ave you run into any crocodiles lately? The word "leviathan" actually means "crocodile." Crocodiles are strange, savage, brutal creatures. Job 41 gives a thorough description that shows they would never qualify as household pets. Crocodiles are not easily intimidated by anything or anyone. No one wants to run into one.

Job 41:34 states that the crocodile "is king over all that are proud." It is arrogant and forceful. So is a proud person. In fact, a proud person is a pain in the neck. So is a proud child. Some people become so enamored with themselves they become a legend in their own minds! Satan loves it when people create an inflated view of themselves.

Remember when Satan told Jesus He could have all the kingdoms of the world? He was trying to appeal to Jesus' pride. Satan knows that when we elevate ourselves, we are going counter to the calling God has for us—to serve others.

It's easy for us to fall into the trap of pride by calling attention to what we have, what we've done, who we married, or where we live. Pride creeps in as we talk about our children's abilities, awards, and accomplishments. Sometimes our children become filled with pride because we filled them with it! Another problem is that when we're proud, we don't listen to others, we're defensive, and we harden our heart.

Give thanks and glory to God for what you have and who you are. When you become impressed with yourself, you take away from God the credit that is due Him.

I'd like to close with this thought from Proverbs: "Pride goes before destruction" (16:18, NASB). A better way to live is summed up in the word *humility*. "A humble spirit will obtain honor" (Proverbs 29:23, NASB).

April 14

Do not conform any longer to the pattern of this world, but be transformed by the renewing of your mind. Then you will be able to test and approve what God's will is—his good, pleasing and perfect will (Romans 12:2).

*H*ow much have you changed recently?

Perhaps change isn't uppermost in your mind because you feel that you are doing all you can just to keep up with life as it is. And yet we are changing, even though we may not realize it. Or, at least we hope we are changing. For the opposite of change (which means grow) is stagnation. We either change for the worse or the better. Your children are constantly changing. So is your spouse (although you may not see it!).

Do you resist change or encourage it? Do you allow other people to encourage you to change?

According to God's perspective, change is a crucial part of life. As one author expressed it:

> You are a caterpillar, and so am I. Just as caterpillars are in metamorphosis, we are "in-process" people. That is what we are intended to be. That is what we will always be.
>
> Throughout our personal metamorphoses, God sees us as complete and perfect if we are Christians. And God is neither surprised nor disappointed that we are not completely perfected in our current lives on earth. God loves us so much that he *accepts* us right where we are. But he loves us too much to *leave* us right where we are.
>
> God has a plan for us caterpillar Christians, and he calls it transformation. According to Romans 12:2, this transformation is the result of a lifelong process of mind renewal.[11]

How would you like your partner to change? How would you like your children to change? How will you be changing today? How would other people in your family like you to change? You'll want to talk about these questions as a family.

April 15

You turned my wailing into dancing; you removed my sack-cloth and clothed me with joy, that my heart may sing to you and not be silent. O LORD my God, I will give you thanks forever (Psalm 30:11,12).

*W*hat do you believe about life? How does your theology affect what you believe? When you encounter the difficulties and rough times in life, how do you reconcile everything? What explanations do you have? Did you know that sometimes it's our beliefs that create some of our tensions?

Some Christians live by assumptions that are not biblically based. For example:

+ Life is fair.

+ I can control what happens to me.

+ If I follow Christ and His teachings, nothing tragic will happen to me.

+ If I am suffering, it is because I sinned or am sinning.

+ My body was meant to live forever...at least until age 90.

+ If I tithe, God will bless me financially.

It's important to face your beliefs and make sure they're founded on the Word of God—especially before you hit the rough times in life.

In her excellent book *Helping People Through Grief*, Delores Kuenning writes that we cannot:

> suddenly draw from deep reservoirs of faith within ourselves if nothing has been done to nurture our spiritual lives in the past....[12]

Daniel Simundson, in *Where Is God in My Suffering?* reminds us of the following:

> [W]hen we cry out to God in our times of suffering, we know that we will be heard by one who truly knows what we have gone through. It is a great comfort for a sufferer to know the presence of an understanding and compassionate God, who not only invites our very human prayers but also knows what it is like to be in so much pain. God hears. God understands. God suffers with us. The lament is heard by One who has been there.[13]

April 16

He answered: "Love the Lord your God with all your heart and with all your soul and with all your strength and with all your mind"; and "Love your neighbor as yourself" (Luke 10:27).

*M*ost parents want their children to be loving individuals. They tell them this in many ways—sometimes in a soft, loving voice and other times in a loud, harsh manner. We all laugh at the frustrated parent who yells at her son, "You're going to love your brother or I'll give you a spanking so you will remember!"

Well, we've been commanded to love, too—by God. He wants us first of all to love Him with all our being, and we're also to love our neighbors as ourself.

But talking about love isn't enough. Talk is cheap. Love must be experienced, especially by our children. What's the best way to teach them? By the three *E's:*

The first *E* is *example.* Why is it that in track meets today it's commonplace for runners to run a mile under four minutes whereas years ago people believed that was impossible? Roger Bannister of England broke that milestone, showing that it was possible. He changed the world's belief by his *example.*

Our children will learn to be loving by the *expectation* that we have for them. People generally rise to whatever level of *expectation* someone has for them. It's a way of saying, "I believe you have the capability to do this." God expects us to live in a certain way and believes in our capability. Positive expectations can be realized. But so can negative expectations!

Your child will also learn to be loving by *experiencing* God's love. The love of God is the only power that can change people whom we have given up on. When we experience God's love, we're enabled to follow through and love the way He wants us to.

If your child ever says, "I can't love; it's too hard," don't buy into that excuse. Your child (and perhaps even you at times) needs to know that. When God asks us to do something, He will equip us so we can do it! That's a great promise![14]

April 17

At that time the son born in the ordinary way persecuted the son born by the power of the Spirit. It is the same now (Galatians 4:29).

*R*eflect back to a time when you were a bit younger (perhaps a *lot* younger), when you were in grade school and had to play on teams. Next to being the captain of the team, what was the best thing that could happen? Wasn't it being the first person chosen? The captain locked eyes with you, pointed his finger, and said, "I choose you." At that moment in time you knew how wonderful it was to be a chosen person.

Of course, it's possible that you were never the first one chosen. Maybe you were always the last. Whatever your situation, the good news is that those days are over. Like Abraham, you are the object of God's attention.

Abraham was born during a time when, as far as we can tell, there wasn't much interaction going on between God and man. But one day, out of the clear blue sky, God spoke to Abraham. You can imagine what a shock it must have been, but there was no doubt: Abraham knew it was God. The Lord said, "Leave your country, your people and your father's household and go to the land I will show you" (Genesis 12:1).

For Abraham to have God speak to him was a miracle. But there was more. God told Abraham that he was special. Abraham was a chosen one, the patriarch of blessing. And Galatians 4:28,29 affirms that we who are in Christ are "Abraham's seed" and heirs to the promise of blessing.

Paul wrote, "*He chose us* in him before the creation of the world to be holy and blameless in his sight" (Ephesians 1:4, emphasis added). You have been chosen by God. His selection of you has nothing to do with any of your characteristics or qualities. God chose to declare you holy and blameless apart from your merits and despite your shortcomings. You weren't chosen to be perfect. God simply chose you to be with Him. Why did He do this? Because He loves you. Doesn't being a chosen person make your feel better?

April 18

Do not store up for yourselves treasures on earth, where moth and rust destroy, and where thieves break in and steal. But store up for yourselves treasures in heaven, where moth and rust do not destroy, and where thieves do not break in and steal. For where your treasure is, there your heart will be also. . . . But seek first his kingdom and his righteousness, and all these things will be given to you as well (Matthew 6:19-21,33).

*O*ne of the lessons of life that children (and parents) have to learn is how to put "first things first." Kids usually like to play before doing homework or practicing their music lessons. There are days when all of us look at the tasks to be done and feel like thumbing our noses at them. We'd rather kick back and put off until tomorrow the unpleasant or even the necessary. And sometimes we struggle with trying to decide what is most important. We make lists and lose them. We have good intentions of what we're going to accomplish on Saturday, and then the distracting phone call and invitation comes in.

Today's passage from Matthew 6 helps us refocus our priorities. What we do and where we commit our time may need to be evaluated frequently. Two questions we need to ask ourselves are, "Why am I doing what I'm doing?" and, "For whose benefit or glory is this being done?" (That's a thought provoker!) A third question you may find helpful is, "What would your life be like if you weren't doing some of what you're doing now?" Give that some thought; you may be able to free up some time by changing or eliminating some of your activities.

Jesus said in Matthew 6 that our worries rob us of our attention, energy, and effort. It's good to have concerns because they motivate and direct us, but do our concerns fit into the priorities that make a difference in our life spiritually? Also, someone once said that when we express worry, we are teaching our children a certain set of values.

Why not read Matthew 6:19-21,33 to your family and discuss the following:

1. What does it mean?
2. How can we apply it?
3. What changes would it make in our family life if it were applied?[15]

April 19

Give thanks in all circumstances, for this is God's will for you in Christ Jesus (1 Thessalonians 5:18).

*T*hank you. *Thanks. Thanks a lot.* All these are phrases that we begin teaching our children at an early age. We want them to be polite, appreciative, and thankful. But did you know there is another important reason for them and us to be thankful? Thankfulness is actually a prerequisite for worship. Scripture says, "Enter his gates with thanksgiving and his courts with praise; give thanks to him and praise his name" (Psalm 100:4).

Thankfulness is an attitude that needs to be developed. How? By becoming more aware of every good thing that you have and experience in your life. It's a refashioning of our attitude not to demand or expect something, but to experience it as a gift. It means stopping, looking back over the last few hours, and saying, "I didn't deserve what I just experienced. There are many people alive today who will never experience this. I don't understand why, but I have been blessed by God."

If you need some help with thankfulness, here are some suggestions:

Thanking God

+ *Thank God* for the gift of life. Live it triumphantly.
+ *Thank God* for your special gifts and abilities. Dedicate them to His service.
+ *Thank God* for opportunities and challenges that make work possible and dreams fulfilling.
+ *Thank God* for each new day by living it to the fullest.

Thanking Others

+ *Thank someone special* today for their love and consideration.
+ *Thank your friends* for their faithfulness and willingness to tolerate you.
+ *Thank your spouse,* children, or other relatives for the happiness they share with you.[16]

April 20

Rejoice in the Lord always (Philippians 4:4).

*D*o you ever want to resign from life? Especially on the days that Murphy's Law is in effect? Do you remember those laws? Here are some of them:

+ Nothing is as easy as it looks.
+ Everything takes longer than you think it will.
+ If anything can go wrong, it will.

Have you ever had a day when...

...you walked into the bathroom and stepped on a fur ball the cat left on the floor?

...during the night you changed the baby's diaper and took it into the bathroom to drop it in the diaper pail only to have it land on your bare foot?

...your child ate into a huge ripe delicious strawberry and found an earwig in the remaining half?

...you walked into the kitchen to discover the dog was eating your toddler's breakfast and the toddler was eating the dog food?

...you left work at the end of the day and discovered why everyone snickered whenever you walked by—you had buttoned your sweater one button off?

The list goes on (by the way, all these have happened to me!).

At times like these, you pray for patience—immediately. And speaking of patience, J.I. Packer once wrote,

> Patience means living out the belief that God orders everything for the spiritual good of his children. Patience does not just grin and bear things, stoic-like, but accepts them cheerfully as therapeutic workouts planned by a heavenly trainer who is resolved to get you up to full fitness.
>
> Patience, therefore, treats each situation as a new opportunity to honor God in a way that would otherwise not be possible, and acts accordingly. Patience breasts each wave of pressure as it rolls in, rejoicing to prove that God can keep one from losing his or her footing.[17]

April 21

We, who with unveiled faces all reflect the Lord's glory, are being transformed into his likeness with ever-increasing glory, which comes from the Lord, who is the Spirit (2 Corinthians 3:18).

You're holding a camera in front of you. You snap the shutter and then . . . a strange winding noise and a piece of coated paper slides out of a slot on the camera. At first it is blank. But the seconds tick by and soon some vague shapes begin to emerge. Gradually, the process continues. Thirty seconds more and the picture takes on a unique recognizable form . . . it's your child. His or her picture developed right before your eyes. Isn't that amazing? But it's nothing new. It's the same process a gifted artist uses, only it's much more rapid and mechanized.

An artist begins with a blank canvas. A brush or pallet knife is dipped into a glob of paint, lifted to the canvas, and the application begins. For a while, that's all that seems to happen . . . dip, lift, and apply; dip, lift, and apply. Colors are laid over colors, and outlines that at first are vague become distinct. The artist glances every now and then to the model, who is motionless (unless it's your child!) to make sure what is captured on the stretched cloth is an accurate representation of the person. Slowly and gradually the face begins to resemble more and more who it is supposed to reflect.

Some portraits take hours, and others take days or even weeks. All portraits take time. They progress slowly . . . like you. Like your child, you are a portrait in progress, never completed. The artist is constantly at work refashioning, remaking, changing you. He doesn't make mistakes. He knows what needs to be added or deleted. A still-life model or a person who has commissioned an artist doesn't peek over the artist's shoulder to give advice. He trusts, sits patiently, relaxes, and allows the expert to create.

God is the Artist who is shaping us. And the finished product is more than a portrait. You're being made into the image of Jesus Christ. So is your child. Let your Artist work. You will praise Him for the result!

April 22

Encourage one another and build each other up, just as in fact you are doing (1 Thessalonians 5:11).

*W*hen a son or daughter marries it can be a major adjustment for everyone in your family. How do you share your thoughts and feelings with your child at such a time? A letter—yes, a simple letter of belief, affirmation, and release is a great way to communicate your thoughts. When our own daughter married we gave her such a letter:

Dear Sheryl,

You probably didn't expect to receive a letter from us at this time, but we have always wanted to write a letter to our about-to-be-married daughter. And that time is here—finally!

For years we have prayed for your choice of the man with whom you will spend the rest of your life. Patience does have its rewards, doesn't it?

Sheryl, our desire for you is that you have a marriage which is fulfilling, satisfying, and glorifying to God. You, as a woman, have so much to offer. You have God-given talents and abilities which, with each year of your life, emerge more and more. You have a sensitivity and love to give Bill that will enhance your marriage.

We know there are times when you get down on yourself and feel discouraged. Never give up on yourself. God never has, nor will, and we never have, nor will. Treat yourself with the respect that God has for you. Allow Him to enable you to continue to develop now as a married woman. Jesus Christ has started a new work in you, and He will bring it to completion.

Sheryl, you have brought so much delight and joy into our lives, and we thank God that you have been our daughter for all these years. We have all grown together through learning to accept one another and through some difficult times of hurt and pain. That's life! But because of Jesus Christ, we all learn through those hard times.

We look forward to becoming parents of a married daughter. Mrs. Bill Macauley: doesn't that have a great sound!

Sheryl, thank you for how you have enriched our lives. Thank you for who you are.

We love you,

Mom and Dad

What will you say in your letters to your children? No matter their ages, now is the time to think of what you'll say when they marry.

April 23

He chose us . . . to the praise of the glory of His grace, which He freely bestowed on us in the Beloved (Ephesians 1:4,6, NASB).

*T*here may be a thief living in your home—one that steals joy and satisfaction. It could be residing in the lives of one or more people in your family. It's called perfectionism. Sure we all want to be successful, but perfectionism can become a mental monster.

Have you ever met perfectionists? They strive to do the impossible and expect it from their children. The standards they set for themselves and their children . . . forget it. No one could consistently attain them.

Perfectionists have a pet statement: "It could always be better." Things are never good enough even when they are outstanding. It's as if there's a tape that plays inside their head which says, "It isn't good enough. If you do better, you'll get some approval. Try harder. But don't make a mistake." And this same message is often conveyed to their children as well.

Did you know that perfectionists are also procrastinators? They are. They don't want to try something unless they know they'll be successful at it. So the job is put off again and again. Does anyone in your home reflect this pattern?

Keep in mind that perfectionism is not attainable nor is it a spiritual calling. We are who we are because of what God has done for us, as Ephesians 1:4,6 tells us. He calls us to live a life of *excellence.* Kevin Lehman describes the difference:

> The perfectionist reaches for impossible goals, whereas the pursuer of excellence enjoys meeting high standards that are within his reach.
>
> The perfectionist bases his value of himself upon his accomplishments, while the person who pursues excellence values himself simply for who he is.
>
> The perfectionist tends to remember his past mistakes and dwell on them. He is convinced that everyone else remembers them, too. The pursuer of excellence, on the other hand, will correct his mistakes, learn the lessons they have to offer, and then forget about them.[18]

April 24

*We have different gifts, according to the grace given us. . . . if
it is showing mercy, let him do it cheerfully* (Romans 12:6,8).

*D*o you know someone who especially enjoys informal social gatherings or who is sensitive to the atmosphere of a
get-together? Or perhaps this person likes to listen to a speaker
who is emotional rather than someone who is logical. Have you
run into the highly sympathetic person, who tends to cry easily?
What about a person who is very tactile, always touching others?
This person reflects empathy, compassion, sympathy, and is
highly attentive while listening sincerely. The people I've just described have the gift of mercy.

A parent or anyone else who has this gift seems to have an an-
tenna that picks up the emotional responses of other people. They
long for harmony in their home. They go out of their way to
soothe people who have faced disaster. Physical contact is highly
valued in all of their relationships. They seem to be able to read
the body language of other people very well. There are some limitations, though, as with the other gifts. Being so caring sometimes makes it difficult to discipline or correct others. Sometimes
these people are too tolerant of situations that could hurt others.
And they are often swayed and influenced easily.

But a child with such a parent knows he or she is loved, understood, and accepted because his or her feelings are validated and
accepted. *Mercy* means "to console or to succor one afflicted." The
Amplified Bible says, "He who does acts of mercy, [does so] with
genuine cheerfulness and joyful eagerness" (insert added). That's
the true manifestation of this gift. It leaps from the heart. There's
no resistance to showing mercy; they don't begrudge.

Sometimes people with a different gift wonder, "How can you
as a parent keep doing what you do?" They can't do it by themselves. Like the other items listed in Romans 12:6-8, mercy is a gift
from God. And what do we do when we receive a gift? Rejoice.
Be thankful. And use it![19]

April 25

Though the L*ORD* *is on high, he looks upon the lowly, but the proud he knows from afar* (Psalms 138:6).

*G*od is holy. There's an unapproachable holiness to God. But sometimes we have a wrong picture of God because of the way we perceive His holiness.

Our Father is not a stern or harsh God. Consider what A.W. Tozer says about Him:

> How good it would be if we could learn that God is easy to live with. He remembers our frame and knows that we are dust. He may sometimes chasten us, it is true, but even this he does with a smile, the proud tender smile of a Father who is bursting with pleasure over an imperfect but promising son who is coming every day to look more and more like the One whose child he is.
>
> Some of us are religiously jumpy and self-conscious because we know that God sees our every thought. We need not be. God is the sum of all patience and the essence of kindly good will. We please Him most, not by frantically trying to make ourselves good, but by throwing ourselves into His arms with all our imperfections, and believing that He understands everything and loves us still."[20]

What a pattern and model for us in our response to our family. Think about it:

Do we burst with pleasure when we see our partner, son or daughter? If so, do they know it?

What does it take for other family members to please us? How do they know they've pleased us?

When we show our appreciation to our family members we are demonstrating God's love in us. The only way we can do this is by allowing His love to flow through us.

April 26

*His delight is in the law of the LORD, and on his law he medi-
tates day and night* (Psalm 1:2).

*A*re you as a parent looking for surefire ways to help your
children learn to live godly lives? There is a way that will
develop character and help your children resist the pressures of
life. The procedure is found in Psalm 1:2. In The Living Bible it's
paraphrased, "They delight in doing everything God wants them
to, and day and night are always meditating on his laws and
thinking about ways to follow him more closely." The law is the
Scripture, so if children want a clear, unwatered-down standard
of right and wrong, they'll find it in the Scripture.

Do you know what the word "delight" means? Psalm 1:2 is
saying that a godly person enjoys and wants the Word of God in
his or her life. And meditation is not a nebulous, vague procedure.
It means to place your mind on the Word, ponder it, think about
it.

In Psalm 119 two more verses tell us how to live a pure life:
"How can a young man keep his way pure? By living according
to your word....I have hidden your word in my heart that I
might not sin against you" (verses 9, 11).

Commit your verses to memory and they will come to mind
when you need them.

The first three verses of Psalm 1 share a message. Verse 1 gives
us a promise of happiness. Verse 2 tells us how to experience it,
and verse 3 tells us the final result.

Take a moment and read these verses. How can you apply
these truths to you and your children's lives?

Remember:

+ If you're planted—you have roots—you're stable.

+ If you're fruitful—you are productive.

+ If you don't wither—you're undaunted.

+ If you're prosperous—you fulfill the goals God has
for your life.

Who could ask for anything more?

April 27

The Lord is always good. He is always loving and kind, and his faithfulness goes on and on to each succeeding generation (Psalms 100:5, TLB).

A couple stood at the doorway of their home watching their last child drive away to take a job across the country. As they closed the door, they turned and walked silently through the house. It was still filled with furniture, but there was an emptiness about it. They held hands without saying a word. They didn't need to, for each knew the others' thoughts and heart at this moment. They each thought to themselves, *It seems so empty. So many years devoted to the children. Alone once again as a couple. Thirty-one years devoted to nurturing, training, providing, and teaching. We hope we did the best we could.*

They knew they would be sad for a while. They had talked about this day, planned for it, and knew there would be some sadness. They had traveled the road that all parents will. You sink your very life into your children just to have them leave your nest. That's the way it is. It's hard, but it's good. If you haven't experienced it yet, you will. You're helping to build the future generation. Here are some words to help you when your children leave home:

> To relinquish our children is to set them free. The earlier we relinquish them the better. If we unthinkingly view them as objects designed for our pleasure, we may destroy their capacity for freedom. We may also cripple ourselves. Having made our children necessary to our happiness, we can so depend on them that we grow incapable of managing without them.[21]

> Having children is a little like building ships. There comes a day when you have completed everything, and the ship needs to be launched. You christen it and send it sliding down to the sea of life. You trust it will not only float but sail. With your children, it's now up to God, and you trust Him even though you know all about the storms that may overtake them.[22]

April 28

Before they call I will answer; while they are still speaking I will hear (Isaiah 65:24).

*H*ave you ever tried to call someone repeatedly only to get a busy signal? Perhaps you use the redial button, and the results are still the same . . . busy! Ever have one of those days? You spend more time trying to get through to a person than actually talking to him or her. It's frustrating, isn't it?

Have you ever felt that way when it comes to praying . . . the line is busy? Some people have. But God is not too busy. He always hears. He knows what you're going to say before you say it.

But there's another problem we sometimes encounter on the phone that can be even more frustrating. Have you ever received a phone call during which the other person talked on and on and on? The person would ask you a question, but before you could get your mouth open, he or she would answer it! You had something to say, but then that person hung up before you had a chance to do so. That's frustrating!

Our prayers are like that at times. We cut short some of our conversations with God or we don't listen. Consider what Dr. Lloyd John Ogilvie says about that:

> God has more prepared for us than we are prepared to ask. We need to spend as much time seeking what God wants us to ask for as we do asking. Then our asking will be in keeping with His will. The desire to pray is God's gift. Praying is not to get God's attention but focusing our attention on Him and what He has to say to us. Don't make prayer a one-way telephone conversation in which we hang up before we listen to what He has to say!
>
> Prayer is seeking God with all our hearts. God can use our imaginations to give us a picture of His future for us, but with one qualification: that we seek Him with all our hearts. Many of us aim at nothing and hit it because we have not taken God at His Word. We all become what we envision. Prayer is the time to let God paint the mind picture of what we are to be and do.[23]

Think about that today!

April 29

For that very reason I was shown mercy so that in me, the worst of sinners, Christ Jesus might display his unlimited patience as an example for those who would believe on him and receive eternal life (1 Timothy 1:16).

*U*nlimited patience. Wouldn't you like to have that? It would be especially helpful with the children, on the freeways, in the lines at the supermarket, and when we're using the new phone menus when we call a business number.

Patience shows compassion for the frailties of others. Jesus gives us an example of when we need to be patient with other people. He was patient toward forgetfulness. The disciples were with Him when He fed 5,000 and had 12 baskets left over. But a little later when their boat got caught in a storm, they forgot His power. And when another 4,000 needed dinner, they forgot what He did with the 5,000.

We forget. We want others to accept our forgetfulness, but how do we respond when *they* forget what we said? Sometimes we think, *If I've said it once, that's sufficient. It's enough. If they didn't catch it, they weren't listening.* We tell ourselves it couldn't possibly be that we weren't clear, or that we shouted to them from the other room, or . . . well, you know how it goes.

Jesus was also patient toward ingratitude. Are there times when you feel taken advantage of—as if nobody cares or recognizes your efforts? No thank-yous, no praises, and they can't even take their dishes from the table. You're disappointed. But look what happened to Jesus. Ten lepers came to Him, ten were healed, and ten left. Only one turned back and said, "Thank you." Jesus was disappointed, too. "Were there not ten cleansed?" He asked. "But the nine—where are they?" He asked, but He didn't demand. Galatians 6:9 says, "Let us not become weary in doing good, for at the proper time we will reap a harvest if we do not give up."

One last thought: Could there be times when we've forgotten the power of Jesus? Could there be times when we've forgotten to say thanks? Sure, we've all done that. But we have a Lord who has unlimited patience. He knows we'll do better next time.[24]

April 30

I can do everything through him who gives me strength (Philippians 4:13).

*H*ave you heard your child making statements such as these? Are these phrases a regular part of your vocabulary?

+ "I can't..."
+ "That's a problem."
+ "I'll never..."
+ "Why is life this way?"
+ "If only..."
+ "Life is a big struggle."
+ "What will I do?"

For today and tomorrow let's consider some of these phrases. Did you know that by using phrases like these, you reinforce the control these problems or hurts have over your life?

Let's consider what happens when you exchange these phrases for words that better express your position in Christ.

"I can't." Do you realize that these words are prompted by some kind of unbelief, fear, or lack of hope? When you say "I can't," you are saying that you have no control over your life. It's no harder to say, "It's worth a try," and you'll like the results of this positive approach much better.

"That's a problem." People who see life's complications as problems or burdens are immersed in fear and hopelessness. But with every obstacle comes an opportunity to learn and grow—if you hold the right attitude. Using phrases such as, "That's a challenge" or "That's an opportunity to learn something new" leaves the door open for moving ahead.

"I'll never..." This victim phrase is the anchor of personal stagnation. It doesn't give yourself or God an opportunity. Instead, say, "I've never considered that before" or, "I haven't tried it, but I'm willing to try" and open the door to personal growth.

That's enough to think about today. It may help to notice who in your family uses these phrases. Encourage them to learn the alternatives.

May 1

I can do everything through him who gives me strength (Philippians 4:13).

*Y*ou may want to begin by reviewing what you read yesterday. Now let's consider the remaining problem phrases and what can be done about them.

"Why is life this way?" This is a normal response to the deep pains and sudden shocks of life. Some people experience one hurt and disappointment after another. Others experience a major setback and choose to linger in its crippling aftermath without recovering. They inappropriately ask this question over and over again for months and years.

"Why is life this way?" and its companion statement, "Life isn't fair," are often overused for the normal, minor upsets of everyday life. Life *is* unpredictable and unfair. But our response to life is our choice, and the healthiest response is reflected in James 1:2,3: "Consider it wholly joyful, my brethren, whenever you are enveloped in or encounter trials of any sort, or fall into various temptations. Be assured and understand that the trial and proving of your faith bring out endurance and steadfastness and patience" (AMP).

These verses encourage us to welcome or be glad about adversity. Joy in life is a choice. And change in life can be a choice.

"If only . . ." This phrase makes us yesterday people and imprisons us in lost dreams.

But there is another phrase that can release us from yesterday and usher us into the future. When instead we say, "Next time," we show that we have given up our regrets, learned from the past, and are getting on with our lives.

"Life is a big struggle." This victim phrase reinforces the difficulties of life. Struggles can and should be turned into adventures. Yes, changing your perspective will take work. You may be stretched. You may feel uncomfortable for a time. But that's all right.

"What will I do?" This question is a cry of despair coupled with the fear of the future and the unknown. Instead, say, "I don't know what I can do at this moment, but I know I can handle this. Thank God I don't have to face this issue by myself. I can learn and become a different person."

May 2

The LORD God said, "It is not good for the man to be alone. I will make a helper suitable for him" (Genesis 2:18).

A Letter to a Child About to Be Married

Of all the strengths you bring into a marriage, none is more valuable than your character. That may not sound as exotic as romance, wit, or charm, but character is the beam that holds the structure together. Without it marriage is little more than cotton candy or shifting winds.

Good character is never fickle. People who have it stand like rocks when the going gets tough. They aren't dependable one day and flaky tomorrow. They don't run like scared rabbits when the relationship starts to rattle. Character means we stay. . . .

Character takes its vows seriously. Very seriously. It still believes that a promise is a promise, a commitment a commitment, and that two people in love dedicate themselves to each other for life.

"In sickness and in health, for richer and for poorer" means what it suggests. Character doesn't believe marriage is a turnstile, a stop on the road, or a phase in life. Marriage isn't an experiment to dabble at to see if it works out.

Love isn't for irresponsible people. It isn't for the immature. Marriage wasn't created for those who can't tell time, keep appointments, call home, leave notes, or keep in touch. Love is too good to be wasted on independent souls. Only the truly interdependent know how to share meaningful affection. Only those who learn to blend reach true intimacy.

I can't say your mother and I never thought about leaving.

Why did we stay? Only God can answer that. But I'm glad we did. I'd like to think it's because most of the time we liked each other. We loved each other, too, but sometimes "like" is the determining factor. We enjoy each other's company.

On days we didn't appreciate each other God gave us the grace to reach back and pull up all the character we could muster. We determined to find a way to happiness again even if we had to break our necks.

Character means you give everything double effort when you need to. Character means if need be you will stand tall in the wind and the rain and the darkness, determined that you will see the light again.[1]

My son, pay attention to my wisdom, listen well to my words of insight . . . (Proverbs 5:1).

*H*ow will you prepare your child for dating? Consider what Dennis Rainey did as described in his book *The Tribute.*

Barbara and I allowed our oldest daughter, Ashley, to begin double-dating at age sixteen. And for some time beforehand we made it clear that any boy who wanted to date Ashley needed to come and meet me to have a "little chat" before they went out.

So when the first young man asked her out, Ashley told him he needed to set up an appointment with me. One day after school he rode his motorcycle (?!) to my office. After several minutes of small talk, I looked him in the eye. I began to tell him how valuable a woman is, how she is God's finest creation. He nodded dutifully.

Then I said, "You know, Kevin, I was a teenage boy once. And I want you to know that I remember what the sex drive is like for an eighteen-year-old man." His eyes were getting bigger—he was really listening.

"And I want you to know that I expect you to treat my daughter just like God would have you treat His finest creation—with all respect and dignity. Whether you go out with her one time or one hundred times, I want to be able to look you in the eyes and ask you if you are treating my daughter with respect and dignity—especially in the physical area.

"And you know, Kevin, God may want her to be another man's wife. So you'd better be very careful to keep this relationship pure."

I paused.

"Are we communicating, Kevin?"

His eyes were fully dilated. He nodded. We shook hands and I commended him on his courage to be willing to meet with me.

Later, as I arrived home, I couldn't help but wonder if I was an "old fuddy-duddy dad." I wondered if I was being too intrusive into the lives of my kids. Then over dinner my doubts evaporated as I shared what had happened with our family.

It wasn't just that Ashley's response was one of appreciation for me. It was that Benjamin, fourteen at the time, put it in context. He said, "Dad, I hope that the father of a girl I ask out wants to meet with me. I'll know I'm at the right house if that happens!"[2]

May 4

You are the salt of the earth. But if the salt loses its saltiness, how can it be made salty again? It is no longer good for anything, except to be thrown out and trampled by men (Matthew 5:13).

*H*ave you ever eaten food that needed salt but didn't have it? Or have you picked up food that you thought hadn't been salted and dumped more on it? Either way, I'm sure you had a negative reaction. Job even asked the question, "Is tasteless food eaten without salt?" (Job 6:6).

Notice that in Matthew 5:13 Jesus didn't ask, "Do you want to be salt?" It wasn't a request. You are salt—clear and simple. But what does it mean to live as salt.

Salt is distinctive. It has its own task. It stands out. And if we're salt, we're to do the same. In Jesus' time, salt was associated with purity. Probably its glistening whiteness brought it that distinction. Similarly, we as believers are called to be pure in our lifestyle, the standards we hold, and in what we teach our children.

One of the major qualities of salt in Jesus' day was its ability to preserve quality. It was used to hold off decay and keep things from rotting. It kept things fresh. Can you imagine what would have happened if fishermen had not packed their fish in salt when they sent it to the market?

Every believer has been called to have a purifying influence—like an antiseptic—on the world around them. We're to be people who, by our presence, impact corruption and make it easier for others to have a higher value system. How? By what we stand for in the home, the schools our children attend, and the entertainment that's presented in our community and television.

Become a little salt. Speak up with an attitude of love. And the best way to be salt is to bring others to a saving knowledge of Jesus Christ.

So . . . how's the salt content of your life? You are the kind of salt that's all right to have in abundance.[3]

May 5

Why spend money on what is not bread, and your labor on what does not satisfy? Listen, listen to me, and eat what is good, and your soul will delight in the richest of fare (Isaiah 55:2).

*Y*ou're at the doctor's office for your annual physical. You've reached the age where it's necessary to take a treadmill stress test for your heart. You go into the room, get wired up, and once the treadmill is running, you step on and keep walking. Three minutes go by, then six minutes. The pace picks up, your legs move faster, and the oxygen is slowly seeping out of the room. You pass the ten-minute mark and your heart is pounding. Finally, it's over. You walked rapidly for 12 minutes and got . . . nowhere. You got on and off in the same location.

One parent who heard that description said, "That's a lot like my life. I do and do and do and get nowhere. I get up each day, go to the same places, see the same people, do the same things, go home, and go to sleep. Every day is a replica of the day before. It seems like I'm pursuing a lot of things but either they don't satisfy or I'm not getting anywhere. Life is one big treadmill. Always going, never getting there."

Do you feel that way? If so, it could be because often we just respond to what happens around us rather than creatively orchestrating our future. Or, it could be because our priorities are not God's priorities. That's why some of the dreams we chase don't offer fulfillment when they're captured. They leave us feeling empty. We end up asking, "Why did I want this? It's a waste. I'm no better off now."

Before you make a decision about what to do, you'll find it helpful to ask God His opinion. For example, when you want something for your children that many other families have, first ask God what He has to say about it. Or, if you're working three jobs not just to survive but to get the extras of life, ask yourself: Do they really satisfy? If no one else in the world knew you had those extras, would you still want them?

It's all right to want to have abundance. But if it doesn't satisfy, it just takes up space. Fortunately, God's abundance does satisfy.

May 6

Since we are surrounded by such a great cloud of witnesses, let us throw off everything that hinders and the sin that so easily entangles, and let us run with perseverance the race marked out for us (Hebrews 12:1).

*R*unners are a different kind of men and women. Have you ever watched them in a marathon mile after mile after mile? It's exhausting to watch them.

As a parent, perhaps you've had times when you felt like you were running a marathon race as well. You keep on going and going no matter how tired you get. Jeanne Zorner reminds us of four things as we run this race.

1. Remember you're watched—we're actually on display in our Christian life. Our friends, co-workers and children are watching to see if the faith we claim is all that we say it is. Does it really work? As others have been our example, we become the example to others.

2. When you run, run light—when runners prepare for a race they leave nothing to chance. They run at a high altitude to strengthen their lungs and they strap weights on their legs. But the day of the race, watch out. They get the lightest material for their running outfit. They strip off every possible ounce. Likewise we're to strip off everything that keeps us from doing our best such as anger, lack of control, procrastination, eating habits that aren't healthy, overloaded schedules, addictions....

3. Never give up. Don't quit. Persevere and continue to trust God to bring that finish line into view. Time spent talking with Him makes it possible. Did you know there's a difference between endurance and perseverance? The first asks you to hold up, bear up, and to withstand difficulties without giving up. Perseverance is the same, but it adds to it a goal. It asks that we focus on God's purpose and don't give up....

4. Keep your focus—you're not running for you but for God. Fix your eyes on Jesus—when you do, you draw strength from Him to finish the race and to cope with the children when you put them to bed at 9:00 P.M., get them to sleep at 10:00 P.M. and comfort them from a bad dream at 2:17 A.M.![4]

When I call to remembrance the unfeigned faith that is in you, which dwelt first in your grandmother Lois and your mother Eunice, and I am persuaded is in you also (2 Timothy 1:5, NKJV).

*D*r. Lloyd John Ogilvie tells this moving story about his own mother.

Some years ago I had an experience I will never forget. It was a gala occasion. I had just finished preaching in the church where I began my ministry. It was a time for memories and reflection.

Suddenly I was face to face with a gracious, radiant woman in her early seventies. She had tears of joy in her eyes, and somehow a handshake was not enough for us. She embraced me and drew me close. Then she kissed me and whispered in my ear, "Pay no attention to me. You belong to these people tonight." I kept an eye on her throughout the evening, catching a glimpse every so often through the crowd. She sat alone, greeted every so often by some of the people. She waited until most of the people had left. We looked long and hard at each other... and then laughed with joy. "Mother, how are you?" I said.

She had come to attend the service from a nearby community which had been my hometown, and to have a few hours together before I returned home. The memory of the visit has lingered pleasantly, but her words to me in the crowd have persisted for deep thought and reflection. She did not know all that she had said, but the true meaning of Christian motherhood was affirmed: "Pay no attention to me; tonight you belong to these people. ..."

In so speaking, she proclaimed the true essence of Jesus' message about the family and the special calling of mothers to prepare their children for service and then give them away to follow Him.[5]

May 8

O LORD, you have searched me and you know me. You know when I sit and when I rise; you perceive my thoughts from afar (Psalm 139:1,2).

*P*atience. A commodity most of us want . . . right now. We need it as we deal with our children, our spouse, and even ourselves. Some of us are impatient with our own progress or lack of it as we struggle to be different in some way. One area in particular that is a source of turmoil for many of us is our thought life. What goes on in our minds is often a battleground that we wouldn't want anyone to view if it were on a video! We have negative thoughts about ourselves, friends, employers, or employees and our children. We know we want to change for the better, yet we don't seem to change very much or as fast as we want.

But you will change. You can change. And so can your children. In fact, you're in for a radical change. The Scripture says that because the Holy Spirit dwells in your heart, you are going to be transformed: "We, who with unveiled faces all reflect the Lord's glory, are being transformed into his likeness with ever-increasing glory, which comes from the Lord, who is the Spirit" (2 Corinthians 3:18).

Yet transformation takes time. It's slow. Sometimes you focus so much on what you want to become you fail to see the progress. If you've ever grown fruit trees or berries you know what I mean. At first there's some new growth on the plant, then a blossom which turns into the fruit. Then the colors change. But even when the fruit has the right color, if you pick it too soon, it's bitter. It hasn't become mature. You have to wait on it. Likewise, you have to wait on yourself.

Scripture promises that even something as difficult as our thought life (from which comes our feelings, action, and words) can change. Second Corinthians 10:5 says to "take captive every thought to make it obedient to Christ." Romans 12:2 says, "Do not conform any longer to the pattern of this world, but be transformed by the renewing of your mind."

If you struggle with your thoughts, turn back to the Scriptures and ask God's intervention to help your mind become new. He wouldn't have made these promises if they couldn't happen.

May 9

I have fought the good fight, I have finished the race, I have kept the faith. Now there is in store for me the crown of righteousness, which the Lord, the righteous Judge, will award to me on that day—not only to me, but also to all who have longed for his appearing (2 Timothy 4:7,8).

*A*s believers, we will someday receive four different and wonderful crowns.

One is the Crown of Righteousness, which is mentioned in the verses above. This crown is for believers who look forward to the return of Jesus.

Then there is the Crown of Life, which is for those who allow the love of God to permeate and sustain them. "Blessed is the man who perseveres under trial, because when he has stood the test, he will receive the crown of life that God has promised to those who love him" (James 1:12).

Third, there is a Crown of Rejoicing. For Paul it was comprised of the people he had brought to Jesus. There is no greater joy than leading another person to the Lord. "Surely you remember, brothers, our toil and hardship; we worked night and day in order not to be a burden to anyone while we preached the gospel of God to you" (1 Thessalonians 2:9).

Finally, there is the Crown of Glory. "When the Chief Shepherd appears, you will receive the crown of glory that will never fade away" (1 Peter 5:4).

Keep in mind, though, that you need to guard your crown. Jesus said, "I am coming soon. Hold on to what you have, so that no one will take your crown" (Revelation 3:11). You need to guard your crown against teaching that is contrary to the Word of God. This could include legalism or claims about the date of Christ's return.

There is one other crown we need to remember. It was Jesus' crown. It wasn't made of gold or silver. Rather it was made of woven branches with two-inch spikes. It was a crown of thorns that He wore for you, for the entire world. His crown enables us to someday wear a crown also.[6]

May 10

In my Father's house are many rooms; if it were not so, I would have told you. I am going there to prepare a place for you (John 14:2).

*Y*ou may have heard people who are elderly or terminally ill say, "I'm just waiting around for heaven." Sometimes Christian rest homes are called "heaven's waiting room."

Have you given much thought to heaven? How many of us in the prime of life have a longing for heaven? Not many, perhaps, because we don't know or understand what it will be like.

We may think we're waiting for heaven. *But heaven is waiting for us.* God is not, as many say, getting our mansions ready. *He's getting us ready for our mansions.*

Heaven will be fulfilling. As Charles Wesley wrote, we'll be "lost in wonder, love, and praise." We'll serve God (Revelation 22:3) in glad, tireless, fulfilling service. Above all, in heaven we'll see Jesus.

"And I—in righteousness I will see your face; when I awake, I will be satisfied with seeing your likeness" (Psalm 17:15).

"What will be has not yet been made known. But we know that when he appears, we shall be like him, for we shall see him as he is" (1 John 3:2).

Sometimes I think I couldn't bear to see Jesus. I'd be overwhelmed by my own unholiness in the blinding glare of his perfect holiness. Moses took off his sandals before the Lord's manifestation in a burning bush. Isaiah was so desperate in his holy vision that he cried out, "Woe to me, I am ruined!" (Isaiah 6:5).[7]

Will you feel comfortable in the presence of Jesus? When you're standing in front of Jesus looking Him in the face, what will He be like? That's difficult to comprehend, but John says we'll be like Him (1 John 3:2), so in our new and changed state, we ought to feel comfortable in His presence.

Perhaps by now you can't wait to get to heaven. Yet what we need most is to be faithful and patient as we prepare and wait for heaven and wonder what it will be like to see Jesus. After all, once we become a Christian, every moment of our lives goes toward getting ready for heaven.[8]

. . . so that you, your children and their children after them may fear the LORD your God as long as you live by keeping all his decrees and commands that I give to you, and so that you may enjoy long life (Deuteronomy 6:2).

A family is made up of more than you and your children. You have a heritage. You have your parents and they had theirs. Each generation has something to pass on. A former seminary president once wrote,

> Family relationships are not just sentimental ideas; they are indispensable ties that keep us steady and secure amid the loneliness and uncertainty of life. Grandparents, aunts and uncles, parents, brothers and sisters play a very special part in our maturing. They show us something of where we have come from and what we will be. They are instruments of heredity and environment used by God to shape us for his purposes.[9]

What can you pass on to your children from the lives of those who came before you? How much do your parents know of their grandparents, great-grandparents, and so on? Each family member, past and present, is part of the collage—the body that makes up your larger family. And there's a purpose in the life of each member. As Edith Schaeffer says,

> A family—parents and grandparents and children, the larger combination of three or four generations, or one little two-generation family—is meant to be a picture of what God is to His Family. "Hear my cry, O God; attend unto my prayer. From the end of the earth will I cry unto thee, when my heart is overwhelmed: lead me to the rock that is higher than I. For thou hast been a shelter for me, and a strong tower from the enemy" (Psalm 61:1-3). Our earthly family is meant to be a shelter, a solid, dependable "ear" that will hear and understand, as well as a place to which to run. Then this family, these parents, this father and mother, are to make clear to their children the understanding of the faithfulness of God. We should be able to say, "You know something of the way we love you. You can always come to us in any kind of trouble. You will always find forgiveness and understanding and help. Yet we are nothing in comparison to God, our heavenly Father, whose faithfulness is perfect compared to our imperfection."[10]

May 12

Those who know your name will trust in you, for you, Lord, have never forsaken those who seek you (Psalm 9:10).

Special Thoughts for Mothers

Ruth Bell Graham once said, "As a mother, my job is to take care of the possible and trust God with the impossible."

A famous preacher from many years ago, Henry Ward Beecher, said, "A mother has, perhaps, the hardest earthly lot; and yet no mother worthy of the name ever gave herself thoroughly for her child who did not feel that, after all, she reaped what she had sown."

Glen Wheeler adds, "Through the ages no nation has had a better friend than the mother who taught her child to pray."

Helen Steiner Rice, in her eloquent way, wrote, "A mother's love is patient and forgiving when all others are forsaking, and it never fails or falters, even though the heart is breaking."

James Keller put it this way: "Every mother has the breathtaking privilege of sharing with God in the creation of new life. She helps bring into existence a soul that will endure for all eternity."

Lisa Alther summed up the work of a mother quite well when she said, "Any mother could perform the jobs of several air traffic controllers with ease!"

An anonymous writer illuminated the loyalty of a mother when he said, "A mother is the one who is still there when everyone else has deserted you."

A wise woman, Judith Clabes, observed, "A woman who can cope with the terrible twos can cope with anything!"

First Corinthians 3:9 reminds mothers and fathers that we are laborers together with God. Commenting upon this verse, Ruth Vaughn says, "Parenthood is a partnership with God. . . . You are working with the creator of the universe in shaping human character and determining destiny."

And finally, because Ecclesiastes states there is a time to laugh, consider these last two thoughts. Imogene Fey said, "A mother finds out what is meant by spitting image when she tries to feed cereal to her baby." And Lionel M. Kaufman quipped, "Children are a great comfort in your old age—and they help you reach it faster, too."

Thomas said to him, "My Lord and my God!" (John 20:28).

*J*esus Christ was a man, right? And Jesus Christ was also God, right? But suppose your preschool or elementary-age child came to you and asked those questions? If you affirmed that Jesus was God, your child might think for a minute, the silence hanging heavily as he gets ready to ask the next question. Then it comes: "How can Jesus be God? I thought He was the *Son* of God."

That's a good question. Do you have an answer ready?

Let's look at how Jesus can be God. Paul wrote this about Jesus: "Who, being in very nature God" (Philippians 2:6). You've probably used the word *nature* at times in reference to your child. Maybe you've said, "That's just his nature" or, "He's got his father's/mother's nature." In Philippians 2:6, "nature" means Jesus is permanently identified with the nature and character of God. His divinity has always been there and comes from within Him.

But what about Jesus' humanity? Jesus was a man, too. Jesus was "found in appearance as a man" (Philippians 2:8). "Appearance" doesn't just refer to how He looked, but rather the human side of Him. In contrast to His divinity, which came from within, His humanity is assumed from the outside. He was both. If you don't completely understand how this could be, you're not alone. Just keep in mind that the Jesus you follow was not only a man, He is also God. Scripture speaks of this again and again: "In Christ all the fullness of the Deity lives in bodily form" (Colossians 2:9). "We wait for the blessed hope—the glorious appearing of our great God and Savior, Jesus Christ" (Titus 2:13). Too often what we believe about Jesus is a bit limited.

Do you ever stop to consider that the person you call Jesus is God? Maybe that explains the miracles that still happen today. Or the radical transformation of a wasted life into a productive one. Or the comfort you experience when you share your struggles and griefs with Him.

Jesus is different. He is unique. He is special. He is risen and alive. After all, He is God.[11]

May 14

Confess your sins to each other and pray for each other so that you may be healed. The prayer of a righteous man is powerful and effective (James 5:16).

Some parents read books about parenting. That's good. Some parents make sure their children go to church, read their Bible, and attend Christian schools. That's good, too. Some parents are intercessors for their children through faithful prayer. That's even better!

If you want to see an example of a parent who prayed for his children, look at Job. In the first chapter you discover that after Job's children feasted, Job would have them purified. "Early in the morning he would sacrifice a burnt offering for each of them, thinking, "Perhaps my children have sinned and cursed God in their hearts" (verse 5). He was concerned and faithful in bringing them before the Lord.

John Bunyan made an interesting comment about prayer many years ago. He said,

> You can do more than pray
> after you have prayed
> But you cannot do more than pray
> until you have prayed.

There are many ways to pray. Bible teacher Kent Hughes and his wife Barbara share the concept of taking prayers from the Scripture and modifying them for your own family. Read Ephesians 3:16-18 out loud now. Then come back and read this family's adaptation of the same passage. This is an activity you may want to do with your own family.

> *Ephesians 3:16-18* for the family: Father, we pray that out of your glorious riches you will strengthen our children with power through your Spirit in their inner beings, so that Christ may dwell in their hearts through faith. And we pray that our children, being rooted and established in love, may have power, together with all the saints, to grasp how wide and high and deep is the love of Christ, and to know this love that surpasses knowledge—that they may be filled to the measure of all the fullness of God.[12]

Preface your own prayers with the Word of God. There's nothing better.

May 15

...and have put on the new self, which is being renewed in knowledge in the image of its Creator (Colossians 3:10).

*H*ave you ever thought about yourself as a work of art? You are. So is each child. A Sculptor has been chipping away at you for some time and will continue to do so. Consider this:

> When a fanatic dealt several damaging blows to Michelangelo's Pieta, the world was horrified. It surprised no one when the world's best artists assembled to refashion the disfigured masterpiece.
>
> When the sculptors arrived in Italy, they didn't begin repairing the marred face immediately. Rather they spent months looking at the Pieta, touching the flowing lines, appreciating the way each part expressed suffering yet ecstasy. Some spent months studying a single part such as the hand until finally the sculptors began to see more and more with the eyes of Michelangelo and to touch and feel as the master artist would have done. When the sculptors finally began repairing the face, the strokes belonged almost as much to Michelangelo as to themselves.
>
> Not Michelangelo's but rather God's sculpturing hand fashioned us from soil-dust into a masterpiece which surpassed even the Pieta (Genesis 2:7). It would not surprise us that God constantly refashions us—that as soon as we disfigure ourselves, He's already sculpturing the pieces back together.[13]

Sometimes we disfigure ourselves by what we think about ourselves rather than what we do to ourselves. Some people have been disfigured emotionally because of what others did to them when they were children. Sometimes our memory banks become a warehouse of beliefs and feelings that cripple our progress.

In a sense, you are also a sculptor fashioning your children. The words and looks you use are the tools that leave imprints. The younger the child, the more he or she is like moldable clay rather than hard granite. As you allow the Holy Spirit to rework and refashion your beliefs about yourself and draw you closer to Christ's image, your skills as a potter or sculptor will be refined.

Yes, you're a work of art. You're a masterpiece. God's art created in Jesus Christ. And you're more valuable to Him than any museum piece. What do you think about that?!

May 16

One who was there had been an invalid for thirty-eight years. When Jesus saw him lying there and learned that he had been in this condition for a long time, he asked him, "Do you want to get well?" "Sir," the invalid replied, "I have no one to help me into the pool when the water is stirred. While I am trying to get in, someone else goes down ahead of me" (John 5:5-7).

*W*hen you go to your doctor seeking treatment for some malady, does he or she ever ask if you want to get well? Probably not, because we consider the desire to get well a forgone conclusion.

When Jesus discovered the paralyzed man, He asked him one of the strangest questions in all of Scripture: "Do you want to be healed?" Or, to put it another way, "Do you want to change?"

The man was probably taken aback by Jesus' seemingly unsympathetic question. That's not what a doctor would ask. Didn't Jesus understand that he had been brought to this pool day after day, week after week, year after year, for healing? Didn't Jesus understand that he had asked person after person to help him get into the pool?

Or could it be that Jesus knew what was really going on inside this man, and that is why He asked the question? It is possible that after so many years of frustration in the same state of paralysis the man's helplessness had turned into hopelessness.

It may even be possible that the lame man had actually achieved a degree of contentment in being an invalid for the rest of his life. He knew that if he were cured, he would have to assume some new responsibilities, such as finding a job. Other people would expect much more of him than they did now.

Whatever the man's inner condition, Jesus tells him exactly what to do. He told the man to do the impossible—to get up and walk and carry his bed with him. The man trusted Jesus and he got up! The atrophy in his legs disappeared, and he immediately began to walk.

Consider Jesus' question for your own life: Do you want to change? If so, in what way? Are you willing to pay the price?

Come to me, all you who are weary and burdened, and I will give you rest (Matthew 11:28).

*E*veryone wants something from me. My spouse, my children, the church, my boss. There's not enough of me to go around! When do I get something for me?"

There will be those days when all you see and feel are people grasping and grabbing for you. Eventually you come to feel like a waiter or waitress taking everyone's order and when you turn around to give the order to the cook, you find out that you're the cook, too!

Many parents have certain times of the day that they dread. Max Lucado describes one such time in his own family's experience:

> In our house we call 5:00 P.M. the piranha hour. That's the time of day when everyone wants a piece of Mom. Sara, the baby, is hungry. Andrea wants Mom to read her a book. Jenna wants help with her homework. And I—the ever-loving, ever-sensitive husband— want Denalyn to drop everything and talk to me about my day.
>
> When is your piranha hour? When do people in your world demand much and offer little?
>
> Every boss has had a day in which the requests outnumber the results. There's not a businessperson alive who hasn't groaned as an armada of assignments docks at his or her desk. For the teacher, the piranha hour often begins when the first student enters and ends when the last student leaves.
>
> Piranha hours: parents have them, bosses endure them, secretaries dread them, teachers are besieged by them, and Jesus taught us how to live through them successfully.[14]

Isn't that descriptive—piranha hours? Piranha are small vicious fish with teeth that can tear you apart as they consume you with their voracious appetite.

There is a good side, however, to being burdened. It teaches you that you can't do everything alone. You won't make it by yourself. Jesus told us how to make it: Whether you're running or walking, frantic or lethargic, fresh or worn out, lift up your hand and reach out to the hand that's always extended to you. It's the hand of Jesus waiting to gently encompass your own. When you come to Him, He will drain away your weariness, remind you that you're special to Him, and give you strength.

May 18

Don't be misled; remember that you can't ignore God and get away with it: a man will always reap just the kind of crop he sows! . . . And let us not get tired of doing what is right, for after a while we will reap a harvest of blessing if we don't get discouraged and give up. That's why whenever we can we should always be kind to everyone, and especially to our Christian brothers (Galatians 6:7,9,10, TLB).

*D*ean Merrill, in his helpful book *Devotions for Busy Parents,* has some insightful advice that relates to the above Scripture verses.

When you're switching Laundry Load No. 6 into the dryer and there are two loads yet to wash . . . when you write the check for your child's music lessons and *again* there's nothing left for an adult night out . . . when you play an after-supper game with your kids, then read them a bedtime story, pray with them, and finally tuck them in, only to realize you're too tired to tackle that job you'd saved for this evening . . . you need the apostle's exhortation in verse 9: "Let us not get tired of doing what is right, for after a while we will reap a harvest of blessing if we don't get discouraged and give up."

Parenting is like farming: a lot of hard work, day in and day out, month in and month out, and the "harvest of blessing" doesn't come quickly. It takes a special kind of perspective to raise kids.

Having kids is the easy part: a nine-month incubation that climaxes in the thrill of a new arrival. *Raising* kids, by comparison, takes twenty-five times as long and probably a hundred times as much endurance and fortitude. Lots of parents bail out early—not officially, of course, but practically. Somewhere along about junior high, they quit trying, quit pouring their energy and creativity into the process, start coasting, just hoping their offspring don't do anything *really bad* in the remaining months or years of their liability.

This Scripture, by contrast, says that "if we don't get discouraged and give up," the Holy Spirit will smile on us, and we will be able to finish our task with pride.[15]

Come to me, all you who are weary and burdened, and I will give you rest. Take my yoke upon you and learn from me, for I am gentle and humble in heart, and you will find rest for your souls. For my yoke is easy and my burden is light (Matthew 11:28-30).

*D*o you understand the significance of the phrase, "My yoke is easy and my burden is light"? Many of us don't because we've never seen a yoke. Jesus was describing a yoke that was used to train young oxen, which was called a training yoke. Since Jesus was a carpenter, He probably made a number of these during His lifetime. These yokes had two openings on them. One was a large opening for the older, experienced, already-trained ox. The smaller opening on the other side was for the younger ox.

When the yoke was put on the oxen, it rested on the shoulders of both but the weight of the plow was carried by the experienced ox. As the farmer directed the oxen to plow his field, the young ox learned how to respond to the reins and do the job it was supposed to do. He didn't dare try to do his own thing, or the yoke would rub his neck raw.

Which yoke do you think you're wearing? Some of us try to put ourselves in the larger opening and soon we're worn out. God calls us to get into the training side of the yoke and stay there. That side is easier for us to handle, but let's clarify the word *easy*. It means "for use" or "able to be used" or "gracious." Thus, effort is still required on your part. But the good news is that we're in the yoke with Jesus. He is always carrying more of the burden than we are. So why do we fight Him for a larger share of the load? That's the real question. Jesus pulls the majority of the load. Our part is to trust Him.

Imagine for a moment that everything you do during the day is done side by side with Jesus. You're in a yoke together. Remember who is carrying most of the load. He's there to make your burden lighter. Let Him lead.[16]

May 20

Honor your father and your mother (Exodus 20:12).

*H*ow old are you today? How many more years will it be until you're 65? 75? 80? Kind of scary, isn't it? Have you ever tried to imagine what you will be like at 80 years of age? With computers it's possible to take your picture and "age" you so you can get an idea of what you'll look like. You will also change in ways that can't be seen in the picture—your bones will be more brittle, your vision and hearing won't be as sharp, you'll have less energy. In fact, you could be quite dependent on other people by then.

It's ironic—we start out in life dependent on others, and in some ways end up like that. We start out being parented. Later we get married, become parents, and then ... we may end up being parented again. Only this time by our own children.

How will your children respond to you when you're old? How will they treat and parent you? There are two possibilities: Either they will treat you the way they were parented, or the way they observed you parenting your parents. That makes you stop and think, doesn't it? You're not only raising your children to be functional, responsible, independent adults, you're also raising them to take care of you when you're elderly.

What do your children hear and observe from you about the way you relate to your parents? They're learning every day by overhearing your conversations, watching your attitudes, noticing the amount of time and money you spend on them, and ... well, you know what I'm talking about.

It's a privilege to honor our parents regardless of their frailties and faults. Honoring them is a way of showing that Jesus Christ has made a difference in our life. Many families have discovered a book titled *The Tribute* by Dennis Rainey, which talks about the tools necessary for building cross-generational relationships.

Your children will provide for you if they see a loving example. Isn't it interesting that one of the last things Jesus did on the cross, in the midst of His agony and dying, was to provide for the care of His mother? (*see* John 19:26,27).

May 21

"Come, follow me," Jesus said, "and I will make you fishers of men" (Matthew 4:19).

I have absolute confidence in you. I believe you have the ability and the wisdom to do what I'm asking you to do. Go for it!" Great words of encouragement, aren't they? That's what Jesus is saying to every believer in Mark 4:19. He is saying, "Tell other people about Me. You can do it!"

Many Christians hesitate, however. It's a bit scary to tell other people about Him.

But notice in Mark 4:19 that Jesus says, *"I will* make you. . . ."* In Luke 5:10 Jesus says, "Do not be afraid. From now on you will catch men" (NKJV). The Aramaic word for "catch" in that verse means "to take alive." This passage defines our call to become fishermen—of people. But let's go back to the question most of us have. "What will I say?"

Luke 21 has a second "I will" statement that tells how you will be effective: "It will turn out for you as an occasion for testimony. Therefore settle it in your hearts not to meditate beforehand on what you will answer; for I will give you a mouth and wisdom which all your adversaries will not be able to contradict or resist" (verses 13-15). Isn't that some promise! God will give us the words when we need them. You don't have to struggle to assemble a collection of pat phrases ahead of time. Ask Him for both opportunities as well as the words, and believe that He will give them.

There's one other "I will." It's both a word of encouragement and alarm: "Whoever acknowledges me before men, I will also acknowledge him before my Father in heaven. But whoever disowns me before men, I will disown him before my Father in heaven" (Matthew 10:32,33).

Jesus doesn't want us to be silent about Him. Being silent is a form of denial—just like Peter's denial. But the more we confess Him, the more He attests to the fact that we belong to Him.

Jesus empowers us to share and then proclaims that we are His. He has confidence in us. Doesn't that make it a lot easier for you to share your faith?[17]

May 22

You then, my son, be strong in the grace that is in Christ Jesus. And the things you have heard me say in the presence of many witnesses entrust to reliable men who will also be qualified to teach others (2 Timothy 2:1,2).

*T*he Scripture gives us a model for parenting that is based upon our relationship with God Himself. If you read through the Psalms you can discover some of the roles a father has in relation to his children—roles that are based upon how God responds to us. These poems portray a father as a person whom a son can run to for protection. Indeed, God is our source of security:

You are a shield around me, O LORD, you bestow glory on me and lift up my head (Psalm 3:3).

The LORD is my light and my salvation—whom shall I fear? The LORD is the stronghold of my life—of whom shall I be afraid? (Psalm 27:1).

A father who is a refuge is both available and a haven. A father is also a person of graciousness and compassion:

The LORD is gracious and compassionate, slow to anger and rich in love (Psalm 145:8).

A father is approachable.

In the morning, O LORD, you hear my voice; in the morning I lay my requests before you and wait in expectation (Psalm 5:3).

A father supports his children during the difficult times in life:

The righteous cry out, and the LORD hears them; he delivers them from all their troubles. The LORD is close to the brokenhearted and saves those who are crushed in spirit (Psalm 34:17,18).

As parents, we will be called upon many times to be our children's source of security and a refuge who is approachable and supportive. But to be able to do this consistently we will need to rely upon our heavenly Father in the same way to have our own needs filled. Yes, our children will depend upon us, but it's so much easier when, at the same time, we're dependent upon God.

Woe to you, teachers of the law and Pharisees, you hypocrites! You clean the outside of the cup and dish, but inside they are full of greed and self-indulgence. Blind Pharisee! First clean the inside of the cup and dish, and then the outside also will be clean (Matthew 23:25,26).

The Pharisees were image-conscious. They worked at looking a certain way to make an impression on others. They really weren't all that different from us today. Instead of working on developing inner character qualities, we concern ourselves with polishing our image. In the world of politics, presidential and gubernatorial candidates hire "personality polishers." Most of the energy and effort put into television debates focuses on image. To some degree, aren't we all politicians?

We want our children to behave perfectly when we're with company and at certain functions. Why? We want our home to look impeccable when guests come over. Why?

In many ways we are like that little lizard that children like to have as a pet—the chameleon. We change colors frequently. Put us on a green background, and we turn green. Put us on a brown background, and we turn brown. We do that to blend in so we can avoid predators.

We don't change colors to avoid danger (as the lizard does), but to gain approval. But in doing this we may give up some freedoms, lose who we really are, and become captive to the approval of others.

So, how do we stop being hypocritical? First, remind yourself that you don't need the approval of others. After all, no matter what you do, some people will never give you their approval anyway. Then pay heed to Galatians 1:10: "Am I now trying to win the approval of men, or of God? Or am I trying to please men? If I were still trying to please men, I would not be a servant of Christ."

Let God work on changing you on the inside. When that's done, you'll feel more secure and the necessary outward changes will begin to take place. Your true colors will show. After all, who wants to be a lizard?[18]

May 24

We preach Christ crucified, to the Jews a stumbling block and to the Greeks foolishness, but to those that are called, both Jews and Greeks, Christ the power of God and the wisdom of God. Because the foolishness of God is wiser than men and the weakness of God is stronger than men (1 Corinthians 1:23-25, NKJV).

*P*ower failure. The lights dim, then go out. The sounds of machinery—the refrigerator, or air conditioners—come to a halt. An eerie silence hangs in the air. Usually it happens when the people who are tapping into the power source overload it. Or, it could be that there is a short in the system or a transformer that wore out. Sometimes it's as simple as a person tripping over a cord and unplugging it from the wall socket. But no matter what the cause, a power outage is no fun. If it goes on for an extended period of time, the food rots in the refrigerator, work cannot be done, and the heat can rise along with the tempers. Your life is totally thrown off course.

In relation to our personal lives, there are two important questions to consider. First, who's your power source? Is it you? Your spouse? Your friends? The Lord? Some of us go through life connected to a real power source, and others run their lives on a portable battery pack powered by their own energy. And naturally they run out of juice after a while. But when your source is the Lord, there's never any lack of potential power.

In Acts 2:32,33 we read, "God has raised this Jesus to life, and we are all witnesses of the fact. Exalted to the right hand of God, he has received from the Father the promised Holy Spirit and has poured out what you now see and hear."

He gives us the gift of power—the Holy Spirit.

But the second question is this: Are you plugged in? An electric saw won't work when you run the blade back and forth by hand. It's got to be connected.

We're connected when we pray, listen, and read the Word. Busy? Yes, we all are. But we can pray lying down, sitting, standing, walking, or driving. We can read at any time just for a minute at a time. Those who begin their day with Jesus realize they are connected to a power source that won't overload or run out. That's a pretty good source.[19]

. . . you shall teach them diligently to your sons and shall talk of them when you sit in your house and when you walk by the way and when you lie down and when you rise up (Deuteronomy 6:7, NASB).

A young man was asked where he had learned most of his values. "Well, it really wasn't in school," he said. "It wasn't in books that I read or from sermons I managed to stay awake through. It was my mom and dad. They were people of truth. They never lied to me or anyone else even when it would have been easy to do so and escape some negative consequences. I could depend on them to be truthful. They didn't hammer away at me not to be a certain way. They didn't have to. Their example was enough for me." Not a bad commentary on the impact of parents' lives rather than their lectures!

In her bestseller *What Is a Family?* Edith Schaeffer devotes her longest chapter to the idea that a family is a *perpetual relay of truth.*[20]

Dr. Charles Swindoll says that the family is . . .

a place where principles are hammered and honed on the anvil of everyday living. Where character traits are sculptured under the watchful eyes of moms and dads. Where steel-strong fibers are woven into the fabric of inner constitution.

The relay place. A race with a hundred batons.

+ *Determination.* "Stick with it, regardless."
+ *Honesty.* "Speak and live the truth—always."
+ *Responsibility.* "Be dependable, be trustworthy."
+ *Thoughtfulness.* "Think of others before yourself."
+ *Confidentiality.* "Don't tell secrets. Seal your lips."
+ *Punctuality.* "Be on time."
+ *Self-control.* "When under stress, stay calm."
+ *Patience.* "Fight irritability. Be willing to wait."
+ *Purity.* "Reject anything that lowers your standards."
+ *Compassion.* "When another hurts, feel it with him."
+ *Diligence.* "Work hard. Tough it out."

And how is this done? Over the long haul, believe me. This race is not a sprint, it's a marathon. There are no 50-yard dash courses on character building. Relays require right timing and smooth handoffs—practiced around the track hour after hour when nobody is looking. And where is this practice track? Where is this place where rough edges cannot remain hidden, must not be left untouched? Inside your own front door. *The home* is God's built-in training facility.[21]

May 26

. . . mount up with wings like eagles (Isaiah 40:31, NKJV).

*D*r. Lloyd John Ogilvie tells the story of an old trapper who ran out of provisions during the middle of winter. There was nothing he could do but make the long trek through the snow to town. Since he hadn't yet sold his pelts he was low on money, but he managed to scrape together $50. He arrived at the store and very carefully selected each item while checking the price.

After a while he had all the supplies his money would buy. He then noticed a number of stuffed animals and birds on a shelf along with an eagle in a cage. It wasn't stuffed. It was alive. There was a price tag on the cage—$50. The trapper looked at his supplies and then back at the confined bird. He looked at the storekeeper and in an upset voice said, "An eagle wasn't meant to be in a cage." The merchant replied, "So, buy it and you can do what you want with it."

The trapper was torn. He needed the supplies, but his heart went out to the caged eagle. Sweeping aside the supplies, he put down the money and said, "I'll take that bird."

Once he was outside, the trapper opened the cage door, pushed the eagle out, and watched it begin to fly. It circled around and around and then caught the updrafts with its wings and began to soar higher and higher. The trapper laughed and said, "Go on, eagle—soar, soar away on your wings. Eagles have to soar. You were never meant for a cage."

We too weren't created to be in a cage that we or other people have built. But sometimes we find ourselves there. Do you feel like you're in some kind of a cage? Who put you there? Jesus came to set us free from everything—the effects of the past, the struggles of the present, and the fears of the future. Trust Him. God wants you to soar. Take Jesus' hand as He helps you step out of the cage.[22]

May 27

Cast all your anxiety on him because he cares for you (1 Peter 5:7).

*W*hat does a "good enough" parent look like? The best model can be found in Scripture's description of the way God parents. Myron Chartier describes seven attributes of God's love that show us what "good enough" parenting involves.

1. *God cares for people.* Although this is preeminently demonstrated in the incarnation, death, and resurrection of Christ, numerous biblical passages stress the caring nature of God (see Luke 15:11-32; 1 Peter 5:7).

2. *God is responsive to human needs.* We see this in the covenant God established after the flood (see Genesis 9:8-17), in God's rescuing of Israel from Egypt (see Deuteronomy 32), and in God's freely giving grace, mercy, and restoration (see John 3:16; Titus 3:3-7).

3. *God reveals love by giving.* God gave his only Son (John 3:16) and the power to become his children (John 3:1,2). He also gave us the Holy Spirit as our Comforter (John 14:16,17).

4. *God shows respect.* This is an attitude of considering the importance of the other person as someone valued and cherished who is free to be rather than being dominated or possessed.

5. *God knows us.* His Son was made in human likeness (see John 1:14; Philippians 2:5-8; Hebrews 2:17,18; 4:15), and his knowledge of us penetrates to the core of our existence (see Psalm 44:21; John 2:25).

6. *God forgives us* (see Ephesians 1:7; John 3:17; Hebrews 4:15,16).

7. *God disciplines us as an expression of love* (see Proverbs 3:11,12; Hebrews 12:5-8; Revelation 3:19). The discipline God exercised over Israel can be seen as an attempt to create a faithful and obedient people.[23]

Look up the verses listed above and study them carefully for a biblical model of good parenting.

May 28

I have been crucified with Christ and I no longer live, but Christ lives in me. The life I live in the body, I live by faith in the Son of God, who loved me and gave himself for me (Galatians 2:20).

There's no doubt about it. Paul was a committed apostle. He was committed to Jesus, and he committed his difficulties to Him as well. He told Timothy, "I know whom I have believed and am persuaded that He is able to keep what I have committed to Him until that Day" (2 Timothy 1:12, NKJV).

In that verse, the Greek word for "committed" refers to a deposit committed to another person's trust for safekeeping. Keep in mind that banks did not exist in Paul's day. So it was a sign of trust to ask someone else to guard your money. The word "keep" means to guard against any kind of loss. Paul was telling Timothy that Jesus was totally reliable and that he could depend on Him.

Commitment is a big word, and it's an important part of marriage. Someone has said that marriage is an unconditional commitment to an imperfect person. There's a commitment between parents and children, too. Life is made up of commitments.

What's involved in a person's commitment to the Lord? Dr. Lloyd John Ogilvie suggests three elements:

The first is *repentance*. This means returning to the Lord and changing our belief that we're on our own and that we have to face life in our own strength. It's changing direction and deliberately turning our lives and circumstances over to God.

The second is *relinquishment* of our struggles and facing what is driving us up the wall. It's letting God help us see clearly what's going on in our lives and establish priorities.

The third part of commitment is *responsiveness*—it's asking this question several times a day: "I wonder what the Lord has in store for me with this?" and then doing what He asks. When you commit to Him, He will never let you down.[24]

The tongue of the wise commends knowledge, but the mouth of the fool gushes folly (Proverbs 15:2).

The patron was browsing through the public library looking for new books. Her eye was drawn toward what looked like a new mystery called *The Case of the Flapping Tongue*. The author's name was one word: Solomon. She opened the book and, much to her surprise, discovered that it was a selection of verses from the book of Proverbs. As she glanced through the book she was amazed to learn that the words "tongue," "mouth," "lips," and "words" were used in Proverbs almost 50 times.

Intrigued by this little book, the parent read on. There were times when she had problems controlling not only what her children said, but what she said as well.

The book of Proverbs is a wonderful and practical book for families to live by—especially in what they say to one another. Our mouths can be used in healthy or unhealthy ways. Let's consider what Proverbs says about an uncontrolled tongue. Do you ever hear these kinds of words from anyone in your family?

Deceitful flattery. "Food gained by fraud tastes sweet to a man, but he ends up with a mouth full of gravel" (Proverbs 20:17). We want to stay clear of flattery because it reflects insincerity and will backfire.

Gossip and slander. "He who conceals his hatred has lying lips, and whoever spreads slander is a fool" (Proverbs 10:18). God has some very strong words to say about gossip.

Angry, strifeful words. "An angry man stirs up dissension, and a hot-tempered one commits many sins" (Proverbs 29:22). Anger and strife usually reflect stubbornness and rigidity.

Boasting. "Like clouds and wind without rain is a man who boasts of gifts he does not give" (Proverbs 25:14). Calling attention to ourselves usually pushes others away from us.

Talking too much. "When words are many, sin is not absent, but he who holds his tongue is wise" (Proverbs 10:19). When we talk, we aren't listening. It's only when we listen that we learn.

Are any of these familiar? Tomorrow you'll learn about a better way.

May 30

We all stumble in many ways. If anyone is never at fault in what he says, he is a perfect man, able to keep his whole body in check (James 3:2).

*C*ontrol. It's highly desired, frequently absent, and sometimes overused. But when it comes to controlling our mouths, it is essential. A mouth out of control is like a runaway train ready to jump the track and create havoc all around it.

If you want some guidance on positive ways of speaking to your children (and each other!), look to the book of Proverbs.

First, parents (and all of us) are to give wise counsel and sound advice: "The lips of the righteous know what is fitting, but the mouth of the wicked only what is perverse" (Proverbs 10:32). "The lips of the wise spread knowledge; not so the hearts of fools" (Proverbs 15:7).

Parents are called upon to give reproof, rebuke, and especially spiritual exhortation: "A fool spurns his father's discipline, but whoever heeds correction shows prudence. . . . He who listens to a life-giving rebuke will be at home among the wise. He who ignores discipline despises himself, but whoever heeds correction gains understanding" (Proverbs 15:5,31,32).

Parents are also asked to witness, teach, and comfort as well: "A word fitly spoken and in due season is like apples of gold in settings of silver" (Proverbs 25:11, AMP).

Did you know that the word of God also asks you to have a sense of humor? "A happy heart makes the face cheerful, but heartache crushes the spirit. . . . All the days of the oppressed are wretched, but the cheerful heart has a continual feast" (Proverbs 15:13,15). Humor is healthy. It's a lifesaver. You need to laugh not a little, but a lot. As one man prayed, "Lord, loosen us up and activate our funny bones." Humor will help you survive. And be sure to laugh at yourself as well.

Remember, Scripture committed to memory is reflected in changed lives. Which of these verses can you ask God to help you apply?

For this reason he had to be made like his brothers in every way, in order that he might become a merciful and faithful high priest in service to God, and that he might make atonement for the sins of the people. Because he himself suffered when he was tempted, he is able to help those who are being tempted (Hebrews 2:17,18).

Satan is subtle. Or at least he tries to be. He attacks us in numerous ways, laying out temptations in front of us like stones on a path, hoping we'll trip over them.

He tried to tempt Jesus. Satan tempted Jesus with food when He was hungry, and he tried to get Jesus to jump off the pinnacle of the temple. Such a spectacular act would have gotten the attention of the people; Jesus could have reversed gravity. Instead, Jesus countered Satan, saying "You shall not tempt the LORD your God" (Matthew 4:7, NKJV; see also Deuteronomy 6:16).

Finally, Satan offered Jesus the kingdoms of the world if He would worship him. Again Jesus confronted Satan with Scripture.

Notice that Jesus gave us an interesting strategy that we can use when we are tempted: We can cite Scripture to kick Satan out of our lives.

How does Satan try to get through to you? Have you been pressured by other people to give in to what they want or believe? They say, "Times have changed; loosen up. You're not going to deprive your child of that movie or video game, are you? What will their friends say? You want your child to be well-rounded, don't you?" Or perhaps we feel pressure from other people to home-school our children, or send them to a Christian or a secular school. It's easy to fold against the pressure of other people just to get them to keep quiet!

But is that best for us? We conform because we don't want to be different. Yet it's okay to be different—to take an unpopular stand. To follow Jesus' leading. Think about that the next time you feel pressured.[25]

June 1

Bless the LORD, O my soul (Psalm 103:1, NASB).

*W*hat does it mean to bless someone?
To bless generally means to speak good or to do good for another person. There are many types of blessing in Scripture. One is the blessing *God communicates to people.* When God blessed Abraham by saying, "I will make you into a great nation and I will bless you; I will make your name great, and you will be a blessing" (Genesis 12:2), He was pronouncing a benediction promising His favor.

A second type of blessing is *spoken by people to God.* In Psalm 103:1,2, King David blesses God by saying, "Bless the LORD, O my soul; and all that is within me, bless His holy name. Bless the LORD, O my soul, and forget none of His benefits" (NASB). Speaking well of or expressing praise to God is blessing Him. When we bless Him we acknowledge Him as the source of all we have.

Yet another type is a blessing *spoken by God or people over things.* We see this in Deuteronomy 28:4,5: "The fruit of your womb will be blessed, and the crops of your land and the young of your livestock—the calves of your herds and the lambs of your flocks. Your basket and your kneading trough will be blessed." Even in our secular age it's common in many coastal communities to have an annual "blessing of the fleet" ceremony at the beginning of each fishing season.

The fourth type of blessing is *spoken by one person to another,* often invoking the name of God. When we bless someone superior to us, as when Jacob blessed Pharaoh in Genesis 47:7, we are showing honor or respect.[1]

The Old Testament Hebrew word for *blessing* refers to the transmission or endowment of the power of God's goodness or favor. And Scripture affirms that God is the source of the favor and well-being we receive. Blessing must be important; it's mentioned 415 times in the Old Testament alone.

Do you feel blessed? What about your children? Sometimes it's easier to give a verbal blessing than to be a blessing to someone. Think about that.[2]

June 2

Love is patient, love is kind. It does not envy, it does not boast, it is not proud. It is not rude, it is not self-seeking, it is not easily angered, it keeps no record of wrongs (1 Corinthians 13:4,5).

A Letter to a Child About to Be Married

In a healthy marriage, the support, affirmation, and encouragement of your courtship does not dissipate over time but grows. Each of you feels loved and valued by the other. You are willing to learn to express love in a way that registers with your loved one.

One of the best descriptions I've read of the healthy expression of marital love was written by Mel Krantzler in his book *Creative Marriage*.

> Marital love requires the ability to put yourself in your partner's place, to understand that the differences that divide you are the differences of two unique personalities, rather than betrayals of your hopes and dreams. The unconditional willingness of each of you to understand and resolve these differences through the sharing of your deepest feelings, concerns, attitudes and ideas is a fundamental component of marital love.
>
> Postponement of your need for instant gratification when your partner feels no such need; sharing the struggle to triumph over adversities as well as sharing the joys and delights of being together; nurturing each other in defeat caused by forces beyond our control and renewing each other's courage to prevail in the face of despair; carrying necessary obligations and responsibilities as a flower rather than as a hundred-pound knapsack; acknowledging the everyday value of your partner in a look, a smile, a touch of the hand, a voiced appreciation of a meal or a new hair style, a spontaneous trip to a movie or a restaurant; trusting your partner always to be there when needed; knowing that he or she always has your best interests at heart even when criticism is given; loyalty and dedication to each other in the face of sacrifices that may have to be made—all of these are additional components of marital love that courtship knows little about.[3]

June 3

I became greater by far than anyone in Jerusalem before me. . . .
I hated life, because the work that is done under the sun was
grievous to me. All of it is meaningless, a chasing after the wind
(Ecclesiastes 3:9,17).

*T*alk about extremes! One minute the writer of Ecclesiastes
seems to be applauding himself, and the next he's in despair
and regretting all that he had done. He is looking back after a life of
effort and achievement and saying that he feels empty. "It wasn't
worth it," he says. What a feeling of futility! He says,

> I hated all the things I had toiled for under the sun, because I
> must leave them to the one who comes after me. And who knows
> whether he will be a wise man or a fool? Yet he will have control
> over all the work into which I have poured my effort and skill un-
> der the sun (Ecclesiastes 2:18,19).

Lest we too experience such feelings of futility, perhaps we
should take a moment to look at our priorities and our use of
time. It's never too late to correct our ways. Dr. Jim Dobson says,

> I have concluded that the accumulation of wealth, even if I
> could achieve it, is an insufficient reason for living. When I reach
> the end of my days, a moment or two from now, I must look back-
> ward on something more meaningful than the pursuit of houses
> and land and machines and stocks and bonds. Nor is fame of any
> lasting benefit. I will consider my earthly existence to have been
> wasted unless I can recall a loving family, a consistent investment
> in the lives of people, and an earnest attempt to serve the God who
> made me. Nothing else makes much sense.[4]

Project yourself down the road a bit—to the end of your life.
What do you want to be able to say about your life? How do you
want to feel about your life? You can determine that by what you
do now.

June 4

Love bears up under anything and everything that comes, is ever ready to believe the best of every person, its hopes are fadeless under all circumstances, and it endures everything [without weakening] (1 Corinthians 13:7, AMP).

*W*hat can parents do to help their children accept who they are? How can parents help their children avoid feelings of unworthiness? Here are some steps you can take.

1. Ask God to help you be aware of how you feel about yourself. Many parents are hard on their children because of their own identified and unresolved issues. Because they were never accepted for who they are, they may have a difficult time accepting their children for who they are. They may want them to be bigger, stronger, quicker, smarter, prettier, bouncier, more aggressive, more compliant, and more or less of any number of characteristics.

2. Ask God to help you appreciate the uniqueness of each one of your children and to be aware of their real needs.

3. On a daily basis, tell your children that you love them. Nothing defends against the attacks of shame or unworthiness like the security a child receives from the love and acceptance of his or her parents. When your children know that you love and appreciate them for who they are, they are free to grow into the unique people God intended them to become.

4. Affirm your children several times a day. Let them know that they are of infinite worth and value and are precious to you. The Bible commands us to love one another, build up one another, nourish one another, cherish one another, and encourage one another. Each week pick one of the *one anothers* and ask God for creative ways to model it for each of your kids.

5. Give them quality time. This can be especially powerful after they have made a mistake or done something wrong. This tells them that even when they make mistakes, they are significant, they are of infinite value and worth.

6. Listen for your kids' statements of guilt and shame.[5]

By the way, do you treat yourself in this way? It's a good place to begin.

In all your ways acknowledge Him, and He will make your paths straight (Proverbs 3:6).

*D*o you ever catch yourself looking at the clock and wondering, *Will I make it? Is there enough time to get everything done? I need to hurry up!*

Rush, rush, rush—that's the story of our lives. We're on the go all the time at a rapid pace. Who piles on the work? God? No. We do. We often plan more than is humanly possible to accomplish.

We need to pace ourselves. In races—whether horse, auto, or human—there is often one who sets the pace. What we need is a pacesetter. This rendition of Psalm 23 by Toki Miyashina can help put your life into a better perspective:

> The Lord is my Pacesetter, I shall not rush;
> He makes me stop and rest for quiet intervals.
> He provides me with images of stillness,
>   which restore my serenity;
> He leads me in the ways of efficiency through
>   calmness of mind,
> And His guidance is peace.
> Even though I have a great many things
>   to accomplish each day,
> I will not fret, for His presence is here.
> His timelessness, His all-importance,
>   will keep me in balance.
> He prepares refreshment and renewal in
>   the midst of my activity,
> By anointing my mind with His oils of tranquility.
> My cup of joyous energy overflows.
> Surely harmony and effectiveness shall be the
>   fruits of my hours,
> For I shall walk in the pace of my Lord, and
>   dwell in His house forever.[6]

June 6

This is the secret: that Christ in your hearts is your only hope of glory (Colossians 1:27, TLB).

*H*ave you ever felt like a ball of yarn with the threads starting to come unraveled . . . and there's no way to stop it? Perhaps you've had the experience of using a ball of twine and unexpectedly discovering a second end of twine becoming tangled with the end you're working with. That's the way life is sometimes—it's slowly unraveling. We have a phrase for that—"I feel like I'm at loose ends!" We say that when we feel out of control on a downhill slide.

We all want to have complete control over our lives, but we can't. God never intended for us to be in control of our lives. Does that thought stress you or relax you?

What happens when we try to take control of our lives? Does it work? No. Do we tend to mess up? Yes. God knows that. Adam and Eve got into a power play with God and we're all experiencing the result. They sure didn't do us a favor by trying to take control. God knows we can't handle controlling our lives, so He gave that task to someone else—His Son Jesus.

There's just one catch. (Isn't there usually?) We need to surrender our will to Him and admit we can't control our lives. We also need to surrender to Him our desire to be in control.

Can you handle all the loose ends . . . the undone, the unresolved, the unexpected, or the unfulfilled dreams?

We can make a choice about who has control of our will—us or Him. We can make a choice about who should run our lives—us or Him. Why not let Jesus have it all? Putting Jesus in control brings rest, relief, and resolution to your lives.[7]

Encourage (admonish, exhort) one another and edify (strengthen and build up) one another, just as you are doing (1 Thessalonians 5:11, AMP).

*Y*ou can't change another person, so forget it."
Have you ever heard that statement? It's not necessarily true. All of us have a part in helping to change the lives of other people. If you're a parent, you're called to be a change agent with your children.

Another word for *change* is *grow*. You certainly would like your children to grow. And if you're truthful, you probably would like to see your partner grow or change in some way.

Some people object to the idea of trying to change others. Yet the Bible calls us to help other people grow or change:

> When [Apollos] wished to cross to Achaia (most of Greece), the brethren wrote to the disciples there, urging and encouraging them to accept and welcome him heartily (Acts 18:27, AMP).

> We beseech and earnestly exhort you, brethren, that you excel [in this matter] more and more (1 Thessalonians 4:10, AMP).

What are we to exhort, teach, or encourage one another to do? In 1 Thessalonians 4:10, the word "exhort" means "to urge one to pursue some course of conduct." It looks to the future. Exhorting one another is a threefold ministry in which a believer 1) urges another person to action in terms of applying scriptural truth, 2) encourages another person with scriptural truth, and 3) comforts another person through the application of Scripture.

In Acts 18:27, the word "encourage" means "to urge forward or persuade." In 1 Thessalonians 5:11 it means "to stimulate another person to the ordinary duties of life."

Perhaps the idea of exhorting and encouraging is new for you. Read the Scriptures and their meaning again. Consider how you might follow these verses as you raise your children and interact with your partner. But remember: Any change you request in other people needs to be for their benefit! Present your requests thoughtfully and prayerfully.

June 8

*After Paul had seen the vision, we got ready at once to leave for
Macedonia, concluding that God had called us to preach the
gospel to them (Acts 16:10).*

*A*s parents, we want to know the will of God for our lives as
well as for our family. How can we know? Dr. Lloyd John
Ogilvie points the way:

> F.B. Meyer, a biblical expositor of another generation, illustrates
> how to know God's will by describing an incident when he was
> crossing the Irish Channel on a dark, starless night.
> "I stood on the deck by the captain and asked him, 'How do
> you know Holyhead Harbor on so dark a night as this?' He said,
> 'You see those three lights? Those three lights must line up behind
> each other as one, and when we see them so united, we know the
> exact position of the harbor's mouth.'"
> Meyer spells out the implication. "When we want to know
> God's will, there are three things which always concur—the in-
> ward impulse, the Word of God, and the trend of circumstances.
> God in the heart, impelling you forward; God in the Book, collab-
> orating whatever He says in the heart; and God in circumstances.
> Never start until all three things agree."[8]

If we have the inclination to know His will, if we have looked
into His Word, then

> we need the third light of seeing what the Lord is doing in our cir-
> cumstances and what He wants us to do to cooperate with Him in
> the accomplishment of His will. The infilling of the Spirit creates
> the impulse, the inspiration, and the insight we need. The in-
> dwelling Lord creates the desire to do His will, convinces us of our
> new life in Him, and clarifies what we are to do in specific circum-
> stances.
> There are also three precious keys to the secret of guidance:
> commitment of our will, freedom from dependence on contempo-
> rary values which are not rooted in Christ, and bringing our out-
> ward life into conformity with the indwelling Christ through
> moment-by-moment renewal of our relationship with Him.[9]

Do not worry about tomorrow, for tomorrow will worry about itself. Each day has enough trouble of its own (Matthew 6:34).

*W*hen young men and women interview for a prospective job, they usually ask, "What are the retirement benefits? What kind of pension do you have?" Sometimes they will refuse a job offer because of what isn't offered 40 or 50 years down the line. Many people today are concerned (and rightly so) about the future of social security payments or whether there will be any medical payments available for them when they reach retirement.

In other areas of life, we often fall into the pattern of worrying about the future and fail to enjoy today. We allow what may or may not happen years from now to rob us of our joy at the present time. But 90 percent of our worries about the future never come to pass—except in our minds. W. Phillip Keller describes in graphic terms what we tend to do:

> We fret and fume and fuss about the unknown future.
> We drag tomorrow's imagined difficulties into this day.
> So we desecrate each day with stress and strain.
>   Our Father never intended us to live that way.
> He gives us life one day at a time.
>   Yesterday is gone.
>   Only today is mine to relish at a gentle pace.
> It is too precious to overload.
>   So it is to be enjoyed in serenity and strength.
>   Put first things first.
>   The petty distractions can wait.
>   Time erases most of them.[10]

What can you do with the gift of today? A gentle pace is not a hurried pace. Does God hurry? No, He doesn't, but we do. We want to get things done and move onto the next activity. But in doing so we miss the joy of the present because we're so focused on the end result. Is that what we want? Not really.

Perhaps we can learn to move slower through life, to enjoy each moment. When we stop worrying about tomorrow, we can take our eyes off of the unknown future and experience the here and now.

June 10

I know your deeds. See, I have placed before you an open door that no one can shut. I know that you have little strength, yet you have kept my word and have not denied my name (Revelation 3:8).

*M*ost of us have been told to look for the "open doors of opportunity." Open doors are much easier to get through than closed doors. But not everyone sees an open door in a positive light. Hans Sachs wrote a book with a chapter that he titled, "Locked in a Room with Open Doors." In this chapter he describes a little boy who has an intense fear of open doors. This boy's brother had told him, "One day I will tie you up in a room with all the doors open." How terrifying that must have been for the boy! You can imagine how the parents reacted when they discovered this attempt at terror.

In real life, sometimes people become tied up by others. Yet some people have not been tied up by others. Rather, they've done it to themselves. Nathaniel Hawthorne said, "What dungeon is so dark as one's own heart! What jailer is so inexorable as oneself."

We do that at times—lock ourselves up and stay imprisoned. But Jesus said to the church at Philadelphia, "I have placed before you an open door" (Revelation 3:8). He wants us to walk through the open doors of life, to try the untried, to be willing to be different, and to confront challenges that will push us to grow.

Perhaps there are new opportunities to serve other people in your neighborhood and introduce them to Jesus. Paul talked about these opportunities when He said, "As we have opportunity, let us do good to all" (Galatians 6:10, NKJV).

The open doorway that is beckoning to you is providing you with a unique opportunity to love others, to care in a new way, to do something that will make a difference. No one is going to shut the door from the outside. It stays open. Don't be immobilized. Walk through that doorway and discover what God has for you.

The love of money is a root of all kinds of evil. Some people, eager for money, have wandered from the faith and pierced themselves with many griefs (1 Timothy 6:10).

*W*e all need money. Prices climb and the paycheck shrinks. The battle gets especially rough as our children grow up. How do you save for a college education when tuition at many schools can cost as much as $12,000 to $16,000 a year? Then there is the cost of room and board and books! How do you continue to pay the bills with such expenses? It's a struggle for all of us.

Some people have a different problem with money—they love it. It becomes the reason for their existence, the source of their ambition, their goal in life. It's their god.

What part does money play in your life? Think about these questions:

What percentage of the day do you spend worrying about money?

Do you spend more time thinking or worrying about money than you spend praying each day?

When you're feeling down, discouraged, or hurt, do you jump in the car and go on a shopping spree to help make you feel better?

Does the value you attach to yourself as a person fluctuate in accord with the fluctuation of your net worth?

To what extent is money the source of arguments between you and other family members?

If you listed all of your cancelled checks, what message would they tell about the place money has in your life?

To what extent do you operate on a well-defined budget that the entire family is aware of and has some voice in creating?

To what extent do you have a plan to handle extra money that comes in unexpectedly? (That does happen, you know.)

To what extent do you and your family members pray about money and the direction God wants you to take in using it for His kingdom and glory?

Think over these questions and come up with some answers with your spouse or family.[11]

June 12

*Do not be anxious about anything, but in everything, by prayer
and petition, with thanksgiving, present your requests to God.
And the peace of God, which transcends all understanding, will
guard your hearts and your minds in Christ Jesus* (Philippians 4:6,7).

*A*s parents, one of the struggles you face is ministering to
your children when they are sick. There are many illnesses
they might get—colds, the flu, mumps, chicken pox, ear infections,
and ailments you've never even heard of! Fortunately, there are
gifted doctors and nurses available to help. In addition to these,
bringing your children to the Lord in prayer will be a source of
comfort and strength to each of you. This prayer, though you may
not need it today, may be useful in the future.

> O God, our Father,
> bless and help (name)
> in the illness which has come upon him (her).
>
> Give him (her) courage and patience,
> endurance and cheerfulness
> to bear all weakness and all pain;
> and give him (her) recovery all the quicker.
>
> Give to all doctors, surgeons and nurses
> who attend him (her)
> skill in their hands,
> wisdom in their minds,
> and gentleness and sympathy in their hearts.
>
> Help us not to worry too much,
> but to leave our loved one
> in the hands of wise and skillful men (and women)
> who have the gift of healing,
> and in your hands.
>
> Lord Jesus,
> come to us and to our loved one
> this day and at this time,
> and show us that your healing touch
> has never lost its ancient power.
> This we ask for thy love's sake. Amen.

—William Barclay
A Book of Everyday Prayer

June 13

Now when he saw the crowds, he went up on a mountainside and sat down. His disciples came to him, and he began to teach them, saying . . . (Matthew 5:1,2).

*W*hat would it have been like to sit on a mountainside and listen to Jesus teach? Probably uncomfortable. Why? Not only because the ground was hard and the rocks rough, jagged, and unmoving. In addition, Jesus' teaching probably made the listeners uncomfortable. Jesus was calling the people of His time—as well as ours—to a new way of living.

The Sermon on the Mount is profound, practical, and lifechanging. It is a call to live differently. If you follow it you will be seen as different, distinct, unique, even odd. It's a call to be different in every area of your life, including the way you parent.

There are four ways in which this difference is expressed. First, your *morality* will be different. Scripture is clear, cut and dried about that. You don't have to wonder or speculate. Jesus said there is a system of morality that works. But it means what you do and what you teach your children to do will be different from the world's ways.

Your *mentality* will be different. Jesus' teachings are different because they didn't originate here on earth. They came from heaven. What you teach your children will be contrary to what the world teaches.

Mastery is third. You are not in charge of your life. We're all called to surrender our lives, to lose our lives in Him. This is letting someone else run your life.[12]

And last, you are going to be a *minority*. That's all right. Jesus chose 12 men, empowered them, and set them loose. Your morality, mentality, and mastery will set you apart as a minority. In today's world, there's more benefit to being in the minority than in the majority.

Think about that . . . today. Then act.

June 14

Wait for the LORD*; be strong and take heart and wait for the* LORD (Psalm 27:14).

*M*uch of our life is spent in waiting. There are waiting rooms in hospitals, airports, and train stations. People often say to us, "Why don't you sit down and wait over there?"

Do you ever get the feeling that much of life is one big waiting room? We spend so much time waiting for our children to finish playing, get ready for school, get out of the bathroom, or come to dinner. It's aggravating to spend hours preparing a meal wait for the rest of the family while it gets lukewarm.

But we can more or less handle such episodes. We're used to them. What's more difficult is waiting on God for answers to the turbulent episodes that threaten to disrupt our life. This kind of waiting is expressed best by Sarah Doudney.

> There are days of silent sorrow
> In the seasons of our life;
> There are wild despairing moments,
> There are hours of mental strife;
> There are times of stony anguish,
> When the tears refuse to fall;
> But the waiting time, my brothers,
> Is the hardest time of all....
>
> We can bear the heat of conflict,
> Though the sudden, crushing blow,
> Beating back our gathered forces,
> For a moment lay us low;
> We may rise again beneath it
> None the weaker for the fall;
> But the waiting time, my brothers,
> Is the hardest time of all.[13]

Is there a purpose or benefit in waiting? Yes. It makes us realize how much we need God. It makes us more willing to receive Him. And it makes us able to handle what life throws our way. "Those who hope in the LORD will renew their strength. They will soar on wings like eagles; they will run and not grow weary, they will walk and not be faint" (Isaiah 40:31).

Waiting brings with it great rewards.

June 15

Praise be to the God and Father of our Lord Jesus Christ, the Father of compassion and the God of all comfort, who comforts us in all our troubles, so that we can comfort those in any trouble with the comfort we ourselves have received from God" (2 Corinthians 1:3,4).

*W*hen we travel through a time of loss, we are eager for our grief to end. But grief doesn't have to be a thief in the night that comes to steal away your joy. It can be just the opposite: It can help us experience joy once again. Grief is normal, necessary, and inevitable. You, your spouse, and your children will experience losses together and separately.

When a loved one enters into the valley of grief, they need someone—namely you. But perhaps you have found it difficult to offer comfort. You don't know what to do or say.

Comfort is not fixing the other people so they're no longer sad or crying. It is not telling them to pull themselves together and get on with their lives. It is not just giving them time and space so they can get their act together. It is not quoting Romans 8:28 to them so they will change their perspective.

Comfort is sitting in silence while your child or spouse cries until it seems his or her heart will break. It is sitting with your arms around him or her and listening—no matter whether what is said makes sense or not. It's helping to draw out the soreness of his or her wound with a few well-placed questions that are open-ended. It is being willing to pray with and for him or her consistently (if that's what the person wants). It is clarifying to other well-meaning individuals what is needed most at this time because so many people say and do the wrong thing. It is doing something for the person that he or she usually does but can't do right now. It is . . . well, how would *you* like to be comforted when you're feeling down? Perhaps thinking about that will help you know what to do.

June 16

A record of the genealogy of Jesus Christ the Son of David (Matthew 1:1).

A family tree is the history of how you came to be. The further back you trace your roots, the more complex your research can get. Some families can trace their heritage back generation after generation for centuries and to other countries.

For many people, keeping track of all the relatives and researching family roots has become quite a pastime. And it is a worthwhile venture to pass on to your children. One day you too will be an ancestor on that family tree!

Jesus was from the house of David. That may not mean much to you today, but had you lived in Jesus' day, that information was vital. Every Jewish person knew the Messiah had to come from the house or lineage of David. In Matthew chapter 1 you will find Jesus' genealogy described in three divisions of 14 generations each. You'll find it interesting to go through each name listed and look back into the Old Testament to read about each person. You'll both find men and women—including a woman who was a harlot (Rahab), and Ruth, who wasn't even Jewish. Some of the people who are named didn't achieve greatness, but they are still important because they are part of the Messiah's lineage.

Jesus' title as the Son of David brings in His connection with humanity. On the one hand He was God. But He was also man. He had two parents like everyone else. He was born with afterbirth on Him and probably yelling like every other newborn. He has always existed, yet one day He was born like the rest of us. One minute He wasn't here as man, and the next minute He was. He created this world, then came to live here with an ordinary family. The Son of God and the Son of David. Have you introduced other living members of your past and present family tree to Jesus' family tree? How much do they know about Him?[14]

June 17

Let us stop passing judgment on one another. Instead, make up your mind not to put any stumbling block or obstacle in your brother's way (Romans 14:13).

*I*f you have ever grown any plants, you know they often require as much care as children. One of the problems plants can have is to be hit by some sort of blight. *Webster's New World Dictionary* says a blight is any kind of an atmospheric or soil condition, parasite, or insect that kills, withers, or retards the growth of plants. It could be a plant disease like rust or mildew. The word *blight* is also used to describe anything that either destroys, prevents growth, or causes devastation—such as a problem in a community or city. The word can also be used to speak of a person or thing that withers someone's hopes or ambitions.[15] Now it's getting personal.

One of the blights that will destroy a relationship or friendship quicker than anything else is gossip. You know, the sharing of speculative information about someone to see if it's true or not. Usually gossip doesn't present the best about a person. Gossip more often than not is a rumor.

Family members gossip about one another. Families gossip about other families. People at church often gossip under the guise of "sharing a prayer request."

Some people use gossip as a cover for criticism. The person who does the gossiping makes other people feel defensive, uneasy, and guarded because, after all, they could be the object of gossip next time. Gossipers say what they do to make themselves look better. But the big danger of gossip is that it's usually not accurate.

How can you overcome this? It's quite simple: Pray for the person, check out a rumor to see if it's true, and don't say anything about another person you haven't said or aren't willing to say to that person within 24 hours. This could make a major difference in the way you talk![16]

June 18

These commandments that I give you today are to be upon your hearts. Impress them on your children. Talk about them when you sit at home and when you walk along the road, when you lie down and when you get up (Deuteronomy 6:6,7).

*M*any fathers do a wonderful job of raising their children. Too often we focus more on what they haven't done rather than what they have done right. We can learn the most from those examples which are positive because they act as a guide for our life.

Below are some statements from sons who talk about their dads. You may want to think about your own father and what he did for you. And if he's still living, he may want to know what you feel.

My father showed his feelings in actions, but most important, he verbalized them. When he was angry, he was honest with his anger but he would admit responsibility for feeling that way. He didn't blame us for the way he felt. I've also seen him grieve. He wept when our dog died. He even cried at my wedding. But most important of all, he told me why he was crying. One of my favorite statements he would make was, "I really feel the joy of the Lord today." And all this came from a quiet, introverted man. I feel privileged to have him as my dad.

Dad expressed delight by the expression on his face, sorrow by withdrawing, frustrations by being busy and involved, but love by telling me, "You're special, son. I love you. God blessed me when you came along."

When I was 12, I hated church and refused to go. My dad said he would go with me to a new church for several Sundays if I wanted to. And if I liked it he would go through the new members class with me and we would join the church together. We did. That started my involvement and I practically lived there during junior high and high school. I was eventually led into ministry by the people at the church and have had a wonderful life serving the Lord for thirty years. Thanks, Dad, for what you did.

What would you like your children to say about you when they reach adulthood? What happens now in your relationship with your sons or daughters will affect what they say about you in the future.

June 19

That they all may be one, as You, Father, are in Me, and I in You; that they also may be one in Us, that the world may believe that You sent Me. And the glory which You gave Me I have given them, that they may be one just as We are one (John 17:21,22 NKJV).

I was in a world of my own as I flew home. I had just finished a very emotional talk with my sisters and brother. We had prepared the old family home in Kenosha, Wisconsin, for sale. All the furnishings had to be cleared out and keepsakes divided among us. My sister, Elaine, had put in a box all the personal things left to me by my father: pictures, his diary of the First World War, some Ogilvie tartans, and his pocket watch. I had rushed to meet my flight, and then, in the anonymity of 3½ hours to myself, I opened the box and sorted through the precious gifts of memory. The pictures of my father, taken through the years, made me laugh and cry—the family portraits, the pictures of fishing trips and never-to-be-forgotten times together. I relived a portion of my life and was thankful for a father who had loved me and believed in me.

About this time in June each year, we set aside a day to honor our father. It's a time for memories and gratitude, a time to say to our fathers still with us, or those with the Lord, "Dad, I love you!" But it's also a special day to claim one of Jesus' most awesome promises. We can be like our heavenly Father. He came in Jesus Christ so that we could reclaim our family likeness. In a way, He gave us a photograph of Himself so that we could never forget our divine destiny to be children of the Father, and a part of His forever family.[17]

What is the significance of Father's Day for you?

June 20

From the ends of the earth I call to you, I call as my heart grows faint; lead me to the rock that is higher than I. . . . I long to dwell in your tent forever and take refuge in the shelter of your wings (Psalm 61:2,4).

*D*on't cling to me. I can't stand it. You're old enough to stand on your own." Those words are spoken in frustration by many parents at one time or another. Children will cling especially when they're learning to walk or they're frightened. Then there are some children who we call clingers. They just won't let go!

There are times, though, when we encourage clinging. We tell children to "hang on" and sometimes punctuate it by saying, "No matter what, don't you dare let go!"

Adults cling sometimes. Several years ago Hurricane Diane was taking apart the Carolina coastline. As usual, the television networks were there in spite of the 100-mile-per-hour winds. They graphically captured cars upended, boats thrown on shore, and damaged homes. Trees were torn apart as the winds toyed with them. One scene showed a man in a raincoat clinging for dear life to a telephone pole as the rain and wind tried to pluck him away and devour him.

There are times when we all hang onto something in an effort to survive. A mother said, "I hang on every day to the fact that my husband walks in the door at six o'clock sharp, takes over the feeding of the twins, and allows me the luxury of a bubble bath."

Sometimes it's not just physical stress that we battle. Mental or emotional stress can upset us as well. That's when we need something solid and secure to hang onto so we can make it through. There are times when we feel overwhelmed like David did in Psalm 61. David found a place of safety and trust in the arms of God.

All through life we will face many different blowing winds—from a slight breeze to a hurricane. Hang on tight to God and His Word. Hang on as He wraps His arms around you. He won't be uprooted.

June 21

The LORD God said, "It is not good for the man to be alone. I will make a helper suitable for him" (Genesis 2:18).

O ne of the concerns of all parents is not only who their son or daughter dates, but who they will marry. Many parents become anxious about this—especially when their child's choice of a partner appears to lack wisdom. Some parents begin praying for their son or daughter's future partner when their child is just an infant. This is a wise decision and can bear fruit later on when the time arrives for the choice of a mate. You may want to begin praying about this now. You may find that the following prayer serves as a good initial step for you.

Prayer for the Future Spouse of a Daughter or Son

Dear Father God,
please send your Holy Spirit
in search of a good spouse
for my daughter (son).

I pray that this chosen one
may be full of love for you, God,
and one who accepts your Son, Jesus,
as his (her) Savior.

May the spouse of my adult child
be strong, good, loving and prudent.

Please give my child
the patience to wait
for the spouse you have chosen.

If she (he) has impatiently
gotten close in hurtful or sinful ways
to another man or woman
please heal and cleanse her (him)
of the wounds and stain
of those relationships.

Please give (name of adult child)
the gifts and virtues he (she) needs
to be a good spouse
for the one you have chosen.[18]

June 22

. . . for the Lord will be your confidence and will keep your foot from being snared (Proverbs 3:26).

*N*o. It's a simple two-letter word which, interestingly enough, is one of the first words our children learn to say. And we probably tire of hearing it. Yet it's a powerful little word and a very necessary one. It's become the slogan of the war on drugs: "Just say no." E. Stanley Jones says that "your ability to say no determines your capacity to say yes to greater things."

In the musical play *Oklahoma* there's a song titled, "I'm Just a Girl Who Can't Say No." Is it difficult for you to say no? Sometimes we're either afraid of the reaction we'll get if we say no, or we fear offending the person who made the request.

Some people are noted for saying, "No" immediately. They say no in a firm voice, then eventually get around to considering the request. It's kind of frustrating for the person asking the question, who knows the first response will be no.[19]

God wants us to say no—not to Him, but to many other situations in life. Temptations swirl around us every day just looking for a place to land. How can we be consistent in saying no when we need to?

Dr. Lloyd John Ogilvie has a ready answer for that question:

> There's no other way than through consistent communion with God. We get ready for crises before they hit—not in them. A constant surrender of our minds to think God's thoughts and our will to do His will will give us the moment-by-moment discernment about what we should do.
>
> People with silent strength are not pushovers for the pressures of people or the subtle strategies of Satan. They know the Lord will guide and will provide the course. A good test is [asking the following]: "Will saying yes bring me closer to the Lord?" If not, we can be sure it's time to say "no." This involves not only the more obvious sins, but also getting so busy that we have little time left for the secret place and prayer where we receive silent strength.[20]

June 23

Do not fear, for I am with you (Isaiah 41:10, NASB).

*F*ear is a part of life. There are many things to fear when you're a parent. There are times when you need to be afraid. But why does Scripture tell us 365 times to "fear not"? Because fear can immobilize us.

Fear blocks our relationship with God. It keeps us from experiencing the blessings of God. Why? Because it short-circuits our choices and keeps us from changing. We have freedom in Christ, yet we often choose to walk through life in the prison of fear.

There are many ways that fear keeps us from getting the most out of life. Fear can talk you into limiting your vision, and as a result you do less than you are capable of doing. You say, "What if I attempt too much and don't make it or it takes away from my time with other activities?" Fear can cause us to imagine the worst possible outcome of our efforts. It can also cause us to limit the experiences to be had by our children. We focus on what could happen to them and imagine the worst.

Fear has a warping effect. It warps our perceptions of life and what we could do to move ahead in a positive way. You can get to the point where unchecked fears soon begin to destroy the reality of what might have been.[21]

Fear keeps us from saying, "I can . . .", "I will . . .", "I'm able . . ." as well as "God is able . . ."!

Fear turns people into yesterday people. Their resistance keeps them from experiencing the blessings that God has for them. They are unable to focus their thinking and beliefs and move ahead.

If you're afraid of making choices, try this. Write down your fear, then ask three other people if they believe it's realistic. If it is, spend five minutes a day committing it to God. List everything that could go wrong with your vision because of this fear. For every possible thing that could go wrong, list two things you could do to correct it. Finally, for every reason you have created to keep yourself from moving ahead, list two reasons why it actually *is* possible to move ahead.[22]

Conquer your own fears, and when your children ask you how to handle fear in their own lives, you'll have suggestions and encouragement you can give to them.

June 24

Train up a child in the way he should go [and in keeping with his individual gift or bent], and when he is old he will not depart from it (Proverbs 22:6, AMP).

*T*here are so many books about parenting. We hear about permissive, restrictive, neglectful, and authoritarian styles. Which is best? What are parents to do? Here are some answers from Jack and Judith Balswick:

> While some parenting styles encourage growth and are empowering, others hinder or block growth either by fostering dependency or by expecting self-reliance prematurely.
>
> Early attempts to understand parenting styles made a distinction between *permissive* versus *restrictive* parenting. Proponents of the permissive style, while not rejecting the need for discipline, stressed that a child's greatest need is for warmth and security. Those holding to the restrictive style, while not rejecting parental affection, emphasized that a child's greatest need is for discipline, responsibility, and self-control.
>
> In hundreds of studies done on parenting styles over the last thirty years, two factors—parental control and parental support—have emerged as the most important elements in good parenting. The term *parental control* means that you, as a parent, actively provide guidelines, set limits, direct and redirect your child's behavior in some desired direction. The term *parental support* refers to the affirmation, encouragement, and general support that you give to assure your children that they are accepted and cared for.
>
> Some parents are great at teaching right behavior but not so good at following through in their own lives. In effect they tell their children, "Do as I say, not as I do." Children will understandably feel resentful when parents fail to live by the standards they preach. Children recognize the incongruence and may be disrespectful or rebellious when parents make demands.
>
> On the other hand, parents who model right behavior but never provide explanations and good reasons for the values and beliefs they hold are also lacking appropriate skills. It is important that parents guide, equip, and empower their children by taking time to give the *whys* of the behavior they expect from them. It's balance we're looking for, perhaps best described as a disciplining role.[23]

What type of parent are you?

June 25

Be still, and know that I am God; I will be exalted among the nations, I will be exalted in the earth (Psalm 46:10).

A little boy snuck into the kitchen while his parents were busy in another room. He headed straight for the cookie jar, took off the lid, and slid his hand down to the bottom, where two of his favorite cookies were waiting for him. He clutched them in his fist and tried to lift them back out of the jar, but his hand got stuck. He pulled and pulled, but all that he succeeded in doing was to crush the cookies. Chocolate oozed out between his fingers. But he just wouldn't let go. He then heard his parents coming to the kitchen and he panicked. As he headed for the back door he swung his hand around and the jar exploded into pieces as it hit the refrigerator. Oh, he got the cookies all right, but he also got something else!

Many parents go through life with a clenched fist and are holding on for dear life. It's easy to hang on to something—especially when there is an insurmountable problem to deal with. We hold on to the way we've handled circumstances in the past. We hold on to patterns of thinking that are nonproductive. Some of us even hold on to addictive patterns of behavior that affect every family member in a negative way.

There's a far better way to face each day. It's found in the words, "Be still, and know that I am God." But it's hard to be still when we're faced with a problem. We want to be active—to do something. God's Word tells us to be still. Did you know that when we're being still we are doing something? The word "still" in the Hebrew text implies that we "let loose, leave off, let go."

Instead of worrying or fretting, Psalm 37 tells us to *commit* our situation to the Lord and *trust* in Him. We are to open our hand and let go—with no string or rubber band attached to make the situation come back. Letting go is the way we trust, commit, and be still. Then perhaps we will realize who God really is and how eager He is to help us. No one can help us more than God.

What can you be still about today?

June 26

Do not be anxious about anything, but in everything, by prayer and petition, with thanksgiving, present your requests to God (Philippians 4:6).

Once again it's time to face the inevitable. One day they'll be gone. No, not your hair or your teeth. Your kids. They'll walk out your front door and become the next generation. It's normal to wonder what that experience will be like, how your kids will do, and how you'll cope. Perhaps this mother's prayer voices what many parents struggle with. What do you think?

Lord, as I face an empty nest, I am afraid. I'm afraid for Jason's safety. I'm afraid he doesn't really understand what's involved in his choices. I'm afraid he'll be introduced to habits and language that are foreign to his protected life. I fear an unworthy woman may steal his affection.

God, I'm afraid the house will be so empty without the noise of a teenager's laughter and the reverberation of his karate practice. I'm afraid to pass his unslept-in bed and fearful of facing the next stage of my own life. I'm not used to less laundry, greater freedom. I may feel worthless with no lunch bags to fill or carpooling to provide. God, I worry that he may not need me anymore, and my anxious heart feels unable to put this in Your hands.

Father, teach me that "letting go" involves a total surrender of my will and a faith-filled decision to practice what Mary said: "Be it unto me according to Thy will." Help me to affirm my son's manhood and trust his choices. Teach me to "be anxious for nothing" and to quit worrying about tomorrow.

Lord, with Your help, I will quit making my son feel guilty for growing up. Help me to stop depending on him to make me happy and to realize that only You can fill the empty places in my heart. I dedicated him to you when he was in my womb, and I affirm today that he belongs to You and is only "on loan" to me. Help me to look around and use my gifts to help others now that my "hands on" parenting is almost over. Amen.[24]

June 27

I, the Teacher, was king over Israel in Jerusalem. I devoted my-self to study and to explore by wisdom all that is done under heaven (Ecclesiastes 1:12,13).

Think back a few years to when you were a child. (Perhaps that is more than a few years!) What do children think about constantly? What do they have on their minds while they're awake? What do they want to do most? Play!

What were your favorite toys, games, and activities? Do you remember? Do your children know what you did? Do they realize that you grew up at a time in history called BVG—Before Video Games?!

Playing was one of the ways we prepared for the adult world. We emulated what we saw and put our daydreams into action. Our play may even have influenced what we ended up doing the rest of our life. When you play, you transport yourself into another world. You enjoy what you're experiencing at the moment.

Hopefully, you play often with your children. And what about your own play? What do you do that you thoroughly enjoy, that rejuvenates you, that brings a sense of joy and changes your outlook and approach to the tasks of life? Do you feel free to play? Or when you do play, do you feel a twinge of guilt that carries the message, "You're too busy for this. You're wasting time. You're too old for this"?

Everyone needs a break. We need to play...like a child...to love ourselves, enjoy life, laugh, be silly, and cut loose. If we don't do that, we not only become too serious, we also stagnate and then wear out.

Is there a new sport you would like to take up? Or a hobby? Experiment with something new. You don't have to explain why you're doing it. You don't have to defend it. Just say, "I'm becoming more healthy, more balanced, and more what God wants me to be." And then do it.

June 28

There is a time for everything, and a season for every activity under heaven (Ecclesiastes 3:1).

*W*e've talked about rhythm and balance earlier in this devotional, and I'd like to talk about that again. Why? Because we all need reminders—some of us more than others.

We learned earlier that the four ingredients needed for balance are work, worship, rest, and play. It's easy to get them mixed up, as Gordon Dahl points out:

> Most middle-class Americans tend to worship their work, to work at their play, and to play at their worship. As a result, their meanings and values are distorted. Their relationships disintegrate faster than they can keep them in repair, and their lifestyles resemble a cast of characters in search of a plot.[25]

That's an unnerving thought. Consider what Scripture has to say about the importance of rhythm and balance in life:

> As long as the earth endures, seedtime and harvest, cold and heat, summer and winter, day and night will never cease (Genesis 8:22).

> I have seen something else under the sun: The race is not to the swift or the battle to the strong, nor does food come to the wise or wealth to the brilliant or favor to the learned; but time and chance happen to them all (Ecclesiastes 9:11).

> The LORD said to Moses on Mount Sinai, "Speak to the Israelites and say to them: 'When you enter the land I am going to give you, the land itself must observe a sabbath to the LORD. For six years sow your fields, and for six years prune your vineyards and gather their crops. But in the seventh year the land is to have a sabbath of rest, a sabbath to the LORD. Do not sow your fields or prune your vineyards. Do not reap what grows of itself or harvest the grapes of your untended vines. The land is to have a year of rest (Leviticus 25:1-5).

Is there balance in your family's work, worship, rest, and play? Talk about this with another family member.

June 29

Consider it all joy . . . (James 1:2 NASB).

*I*f you had to define joy, what would you say? And why is joy so important? Are those heavy questions? Yes. Are they answerable? Yes.

One parent said, "I think joy is a good feeling. You know, when everything is right." Another parent said, "Joy is when you're adjusted. It's when you understand yourself and everything going on around you." Yet another said, "Joy is the good life."

All of these answers focus on what is temporary. They're built on what we are doing or can do. What if there is no good feeling? On some days things just don't seem right. You may not feel adjusted. And the good life? What is that? It's here today and gone tomorrow.

Is it possible to have joy when there's not enough money to pay the bills or you've been out of work for seven months or your child has been ill for a year?

According to the word of God, yes. Think about these words written on joy:

> Joy at its highest meaning calls for the vertical, or spiritual, dimension that translates superficial happiness, productive adjustment, and self-help techniques into an encounter with God. Joy becomes the power of God's grace, the process of God's spirit, and the presence of God's nature in our lives.
>
> In the biblical sense, joy then becomes a spiritual balance between expectations and achievements—the ability to approach problems objectively by accepting things as they are and working toward solution and adjustment. Assuming this stance, joy is a sense of imperturbable gladness that sings when rejected, praises when persecuted, and stands when attacked. (See Acts 16:25; Acts 5:41; 2 Chronicles 20:14-30.)
>
> In this sense, joy is taking our crises in stride and utilizing our circumstances to bring glory to God. It is seeking first the kingdom of God and His righteousness.[26]

Perhaps we could say joy is our response of faith as we look to God as our source of security—no matter what our circumstances. It's adopting God's perspective on what is going on in our life. Is it worth a try? Definitely.

June 30

There is a time for everything . . . (Ecclesiastes 3:11).

"When I've finished this, accomplished this, perfected this, then I'll be able to . . ." We've all said that when we're pre-occupied with a major task. During such times we shut all other people and things out of our life. But why? Sometimes there are good reasons. But sometimes there are not. And in some cases, that "perfect" end result we are waiting for never happens.

There's another option, as this poem suggests:

> Go barefoot in the wet grass.
> Don't wait
> Until all the problems are solved,
> Or all the bills are paid.
> You will wait forever.
> Eternity will come and go
> And you
> Will still be waiting.
> Live in the now,
> With all its problems and its agonies,
> With its joy,
> And its pain.
> Celebrate your pain,
> Your despair,
> Your anger.
> It means you're alive.
> Look closer,
> Breathe deeper.
> Stand taller.
> Stop grieving the past.
> There is joy and beauty
> Today.
> It is temporary,
> Here now and gone.
> So celebrate it
> While you can.
> Celebrate the temporary.[27]

What would you like to celebrate today? What would your family like to celebrate? Talk about it, then do it.

July 1

Jesus continued: "There was a man who had two sons. The younger one said to his father, 'Father, give me my share of the estate.' So he divided his property between them. . . . The older brother became angry and refused to go in" (Luke 15:11,12,28).

We call the story in Luke 15 the story of the Prodigal Son, but is that accurate? Couldn't it just as well be called "The Forgiving Father" or "The Older Critical Brother"? It's an old portrayal of family relationships that applies to the present day. Perhaps you know of a child who decided to leave not only home but what he was taught. Maybe you're familiar with the shedding of tears and sleepless nights experienced by the parents of such a child.

Jesus carefully portrays both what a father is called to be and a glimpse of our heavenly Father. Do you remember the story? If not, read it . . . and then read this prayer by Ken Gire, who brings the story home to each of us.

Dear Beloved Son of the Father, how it must crush you when I turn my back on you and walk away. How you must weep when you see me disappear over a far horizon to squander my life in a distant country.

Thank you that although I have sometimes left home, I have never left your heart. Though I have forgotten about you, you have never forgotten about me.

Thank you for the financial crisis or the famine or the pigsty or whatever it took to bring me to my senses. And thank you that even though what brought me home were pangs of hunger instead of pangs of conscience, yet still, even on those terms you welcomed me back.

Thank you for the forgiveness and the restoration you have lavished upon me, the one who needed them most but deserved them least.

I confess that there is inside me not only a prodigal son but also a critical older bother.

How dutiful I have sometimes been, and yet so proud of the duties I have done. How generous I have been in my opinion of myself, and yet so judgmental in my opinion of others. How often I have entered into criticism, and yet how seldom I have entered into your joy.

Gather both the prodigal part of myself and the critical part of myself in your loving arms, O Lord. And bring them home. . . .[1]

July 2

Love bears up under anything and everything that comes (1 Corinthians 13:7, AMP).

A Letter to a Child About to Be Married

Here are some thoughts to help you walk the pathway of marriage:

Love is what love does. To define love at rest is impossible because love never rests. If love rests it is no longer love, but indifference.

Love is always doing. Love is always in motion.

Love is the glue that holds our marriages together and the oil that keeps us from rubbing each other the wrong way.

Share the extremes of life with one another—the embarrassing moments, the great victories, the dark temptations, the tragic failings, the ecstatic joys. Laugh, cry, sing, and dance. Make beautiful music together. Smell the flowers. Joke around. Lighten up. Be real. You are stuck with each other! Enjoy it.

The strongest expression of love we can make is to sacrifice ourselves for one another. When we deny ourselves for our mates we prove by our actions that we "get it" about the true meaning of love.

The deepest expression of our love comes through our willingness to share in the tedium of each other's daily routines and frustrations.

When husband and wife are more focused on pleasing each other than getting their own way, God will free them to mutually love and respect each other.

God has given couples no greater gift than the ability to laugh at life together. The joy of sharing humorous secrets and private jokes breathes energy into a marriage.

Nothing our spouse can do for us can touch us so deeply as faithfully praying for us day after day—long after another person would have moved on to something new.

It is easier to pray *for* each other than it is to pray *with* each other. To pray with each other is a brave step toward intimacy.[2]

A patient man has great understanding, but a quick-tempered man displays folly (Proverbs 14:29).

I'm so frustrated! That makes me mad!" We all have moments when our tempers flare.

Three major culprits feed our frustration. One is our *expectations*. We all have them—for ourselves, our mate, our children, and even for our friends. Unfortunately, too many of these expectations remain unspoken, and when they are not fulfilled they often turn into demands. Then they lead to frustration, and ultimately, anger. Expectations keep us focused upon what we are not getting and limit our options in life.

Another major cause of frustration is the attitude of *entitlement*— the simple belief that if I want something, I ought to have it. "I'm entitled to it," people say.

Entitlement confuses desire with obligation. If I want something, people say, then others have no right to say no. Unfortunately, this mindset is saying that another person must give up his or her limits and boundaries for you. Such an attitude can overshadow care and concern for another person. And frustration is inevitable because entitlement is doomed to failure.

The third culprit is the belief that *life should be fair*. We believe that relationships should be fair. We believe that if we do certain things, there will be prescribed results. However, fairness is subjective. It can be defined so that we can call anything either fair or unfair. We must recognize that life is not fair; that is a fact.

So, what can you do?

One way to deal with frustration is to *internalize the guidelines from God's Word*. God has preserved those Scriptures through the centuries for a major reason: His guidelines for life are the best because they work.

Here are two fundamental truths from Proverbs. Memorize them, practice them, and watch your frustration shrink:

A wise man controls his temper. He knows that anger causes mistakes (14:29, TLB).

It is better to be slow-tempered than famous; it is better to have self-control than to control an army (16:32, TLB).

July 4

Now faith is being sure of what we hope for and certain of what we do not see (Hebrews 11:1).

*I*t's hard to trust my child now that he's into his teen years." Some parents say that, and even more think it. But let's consider this issue of trust for a moment.

The starting point in trusting your teenager is trust in God. Why? There are three reasons. First, you've come to know God's reliability in your own life, and you can trust God to be working in the life of your teenager as well. God hears the prayers of His children, so when you pray for your teen, you can trust Him to work in his life, even if he is resisting God.

Second, as parents learn to trust God in greater and more intimate areas of their lives, they learn how to trust people, including their teenager. Even though their teenager is unreliable, God is still reliable.

Third, the parents' trust in God can be a model for their teenager to follow. The clearest picture of *active* faith in God that a teenager will be able to see is his parents trusting God in regards to him. We parents are called to trust God in front of our teenagers so they can come to understand God better through our lives.

Not only is God trustworthy, reliable, and faithful, He also invests in us, His children. His greatest investment was to send His only Son, Jesus, to die on a cross for us so that we might have life through Him. And God continues to invest His riches, His reputation, His love in us even when we mismanage His trust repeatedly. Consider this: What businessman would continue to invest in a venture that yielded such low returns as God's investments in us?

As parents of teenagers, we experience times when the returns on our investments of trust are low. It's at these times that we are most tempted not to trust anymore. It's at these times that we most need to trust God, then invest more trust in our teenagers. By doing so, we demonstrate living trust.

July 5

We do not have a high priest who is unable to sympathize with our weaknesses, but we have one who has been tempted in every way, just as we are—yet was without sin. Let us then approach the throne of grace with confidence, so that we may receive mercy and find grace to help us in our time of need (Hebrews 4:15,16).

*Y*ou worked from sunup to sundown making sure every task was done. You tried to meet the needs of every person. You went out of your way, did more than your share, and worked your fingers to the bone. Not only did you make extra stops on the way home from work, you even missed lunch. Your muscles ached, your head was pounding, your feet were sore and then . . . you received a phone call and were asked to do three more tasks.

It wasn't so much the requests that bothered you. It was the comment, "You're not that busy, are you? You can work it in." You were ready to scream! Nobody understood. You felt taken for granted, used, unappreciated, and just plain exhausted.

That's the life of a parent. The problem is, there's no relief in sight. And it's the expectations other people have of you that disturb you the most.

When no one understands you, it hurts. Sometimes you may feel like saying, "Why bother?!" You do and do and do, and there's no appreciation.

But wait! Perhaps there *is* something you can do—like informing other people (in a calm voice) what you're capable of handling, what you can and can't do, and what you expect from others. If you don't say anything, how will people ever know?

Whether you take any action or not, take heart in this: Yes, it's unfair to be misunderstood, but life isn't fair. No one knows that better than Jesus. He was misunderstood and He was tempted "in every way" (Hebrews 4:15). He knew fatigue and lack of appreciation from friends.

But here's some good news: Guess who does understand? Guess who does care? Guess who has love and strength and grace to give you when you feel isolated and used? Jesus does. Tell Him, ask Him, and then praise Him.

July 6

We have different gifts, according to the grace given us. If a man's gift is . . . leadership, let him govern diligently (Romans 12:6,8).

*R*uling is not limited to kings and presidents. We all have to rule to some degree. And the person who has this spiritual gift is usually obvious. He or she is organized, structured, and likes to get things done. Sometimes children may say that a parent who has this gift is "the boss" or perhaps "bossy." But it is a biblical gift that is necessary. In the Amplified Bible, Romans 12:8 says, "He who gives aid and superintends, [let him do it] with zeal and singleness of mind." The King James version says that those who lead should do so "with diligence."

In the above passage, "leadership" can mean "take the lead, to superintend, preside over." Sometimes there's conflict in a marriage if both the husband and the wife have this gift. Hopefully such couples not only delegate but also give and take. A parent with this gift orchestrates the household and organizes the life of each child and sometimes even each pet! This person is a good juggler and can balance many things at once. Parents who don't have this gift often wish they did. If this is your situation, find someone who does, and follow his or her example as much as possible.

A parent with the gift of administration can usually determine his or her children's abilities and channel them in the proper direction. But keep in mind that the way this gift is manifested is crucial. Some parents become unbending and rigid controllers. A loving tone of voice giving suggestions rather than directives is a must.

Parents with this gift value reliability and responsibility. The word *tenacious* describes them well because they remain firm and steadfast even when problems arise. Keeping commitments is highly valued for themselves and their children.

If you have this gift, remember this: You need the gifts of other people to bring a balance into the tight ship you run. You want your gift to be seen as a plus, a benefit, an asset, not a liability. At this point in time, is your gift of leadership helping or hindering your family?[3]

July 7

A friend loves at all times, and a brother is born for adversity (Proverbs 17:17).

*H*ow do you respond to your children's friends? They're an investment, you know.

By taking time, energy, and interest in your children's friends, you are saying, "I love you" to your children or teens. Your offspring expect you to invest in them because they are yours. But investing in their friends is an unexpected bonus they'll appreciate. By taking an interest in their friends . . .

You affirm your trust. In effect you say, "Any friend of yours is a friend of mine. I trust you to choose wisely." Your trust is likely to be reciprocated.

You enhance your child's self-image. By believing in your child and making that belief obvious to his friends, you enhance his belief in himself. He can then exert a stronger influence on his friends.

You build a climate of inclusion. By investing in your children's friends, even those whom you find unattractive, you make it easy for them to include you rather than exclude you from their decisions. They will feel that you haven't pitted yourself against their friends making them choose between you and their friends.

You have a positive influence. You make it easier for your children to lead their friends to Christ. Their friends can see the kind of relationship you have with your children. If the friends are drawn in, they will be affected by your values. They will at least become aware of the alternatives you represent.

The Bible has much to say about friendships—especially the book of Proverbs, which talks about our choice of friends.

1. Determining what kind of friends your friends are—Proverbs 9:7-9; 10:8-11; 17:4,5,17; 19:22; 20:11.

2. Choosing friends carefully—Proverbs 13:20; 20:6,7; 27:17; 28:7; 29:24.

3. Avoiding some "friends"—Proverbs 14:7; 18:24; 20:19; 22:24,25; 23:20,21; 29:3.

You may want to read these passages with your children and consider how they can help you as an adult and them as children.

July 8

*They replied, "Believe in the Lord Jesus, and you will be saved—
you and your household"* (Acts 16:31).

*T*he verse for today expresses the desire most parents have for
their children. There are numerous examples of this in Scripture. Consider these passages and comments by a parent:

"What must I do to be saved?" the Philippian jailer asked Paul
and Silas after the Lord had supernaturally freed them from their
prison stocks. *"Believe in the Lord Jesus, and you will be saved—you
and your household,"* they replied (Acts 16:31). That very night the
jailer and all his household believed.

A parent can speak for the household as illustrated by Joshua's
statement: *"But as for me and my household, we will serve the Lord"*
(Joshua 24:15).

Salvation for a whole household had its beginnings in the Old
Testament. In Exodus chapter 12, God gave Passover-night instructions when He told the Israelites He was going to bring them
out of Egypt, *"Each man is to take a lamb for his family, one for each
household"* (verse 3). The lamb's blood on the doorposts prevented
the destroyer from coming into the houses of His chosen people.
Today we know that the Lamb of the Passover is Jesus Christ and
that we are the spiritual Israelites. When we are in right relationship with Him, our household is included in His promises.

Even as the early Jews, we must keep His words before our families, *"Teach and impress them diligently upon the [minds and] hearts of
your children"* (Deuteronomy 6:7, AMP). When we do this, we can expect God to do His part and draw our children to Himself.

Another Old Testament scripture offers assurance for our families: *"I will pour out my Spirit on all people."* When Joel speaks of sons
and daughters, young and old men, and servants, he is talking
about whole households (Joel 2:28,29).

When we read, *"The promise is for you and your children"* (Acts
2:39), we need to keep in mind that this refers to both our present
households and to future generations.[4]

Reading these verses can give you not only hope, but also can
encourage your own Bible study and prayer life. Let's begin now
to praise God for His faithfulness.

July 9

You are to give him the name Jesus, because he will save his people from their sins (Matthew 1:21).

*T*he Promise Keepers host meetings nationwide and many men come—as many as 50,000 to 75,000. Every so often during the meetings, a chant will break out that is quickly taken up by every man there. The chant, "Jesus, Jesus, Jesus" is shouted over and over again.

Hymn books abound with Jesus' name. How many hymns can you recall with the name Jesus in the title? You've probably sung, "Take the Name of Jesus with You" or, "All Hail the Power of Jesus' Name" or "Jesus, the Very Thought of Thee." Next Sunday, glance through your church hymnal and count how many times the name Jesus appears in the song titles.

Not only do Christians say the name of Jesus; people who don't believe in Him or know Him use His name frequently.

Even though there are more than 100 different names and titles given to Him, Jesus is His main name. It appears over 500 times in the Gospels and over 900 times in the New Testament. In this devotional, you've read about Him being called the Everlasting Father, an heir, God, Son of David, and now Jesus.

Who named Him? Did Jesus select His name? No. God said, "Name Him Jesus." Then God defined His purpose: "He shall save His people from their sins." That's the purpose of Jesus' life. Some people know, talk, teach, and preach about Him, yet still miss out on knowing Him as Savior.

The Hebrew equivalent for the name Jesus is Joshua. The two names are the same. There's an interesting parallel here, too. Joshua led the children of Israel from their days of wandering in the wilderness and took them to the Promised Land. What a change of life that must have been for them! But there is an even greater change of life available: It's when Jesus leads a person from the wandering lifestyle of sin into the promised land of a new life and eternity with Him. That's good news. Who can you share this good news with this week?[5]

July 10

Be kind and compassionate to one another, forgiving each other, just as in Christ God forgave you (Ephesians 4:32).

*W*hat a verse to help a family! How can we apply it in the daily interaction between a parent and child or teenager? Here are some possibilities:

Cancel debts. Forgiving other people, just as God in Christ has forgiven us, means cancelling the debts. It means resisting the impulse to bring up the past. It may mean asking our children to forgive us if we bring up old problems on impulse in the heat of an argument.

Be kind. Webster's dictionary defines kindness as being sympathetic, gentle, benevolent. Forgiveness springs much easier from an attitude of kindness than from an attitude of defensiveness.

When we feel threatened, we tend to become defensive. Replacing defensiveness with kindness means we become vulnerable to being taken advantage of again. That's why being kind is sometimes difficult. It takes a strong person to be gentle, and sometimes we don't feel strong. But we are called by Scripture to be kind, so we are promised strength as well. Psalm 28:7 says, "The LORD is my strength and my shield; my heart trusts in Him, and I am helped; therefore my heart exults, and with my song I shall thank Him" (NASB).

Be tenderhearted. Being kind implies some vulnerability. But being tenderhearted implies even more vulnerability. It means absorbing some hurt so our children can grow. It means letting our walls down and inviting our family to feel our emotions with us. It also means feeling their emotions with them. When we are tenderhearted, it becomes much easier to forgive.

The opposite of tenderheartedness is hardness of heart. In Mark 10:5, Jesus says hardness of heart was the reason Moses wrote the law on divorce. In other words, tenderhearted couples don't need divorce. Tenderhearted people can forgive. This also applies to parent-child relationships. It takes tenderhearted, forgiving parents to develop tenderhearted, forgiving children and teenagers.

. . . that we love one another (2 John 1:5, NASB).

*P*aul Lewis, the founder of Dad's University, a ministry to fathers, has made many practical suggestions for fathers. Some of these could be applied to mothers as well.

1. If you're going away on a business trip, you may want to record on audiotape some bedtime stories for your children to listen to while you're gone. If the stories you read are from books, leave the books so your children can follow along. Be creative. Put in as many sound effects as you can. You may also want to encourage your children to tape a story you can take with you on your trip.

2. Some evening, have all the family members switch places at the dinner table. During the meal, they need to talk and behave just like the family member whose chair they're sitting in. Get ready for an educational experience!

3. Some parents take photos of their children doing things right and post the pictures somewhere in the house during the week. This follows the principle of focusing on what your children do right and ignoring what they do wrong.

4. Some fathers make an effort to plan out how they will greet each family member when they arrive home from work. They try to vary the greetings so they don't become predictable. They've learned the principle that what happens during the first four minutes you set foot in the house sets the tone for the rest of the evening.

5. This is the age of the business cards. Some fathers and mothers also put on their card, "Father of _____" or "Mother of _____" followed by the names of their children. This not only generates conversation, but makes your children feel special as well.

Take a moment now to put your creative talents to work and develop some additional creative ideas. That will do wonders towards building the family connection.[6] And it puts the words "I love you" into action.

July 12

The LORD reigns, He is robed in Majesty (Psalm 93:1).

They will speak of the glorious splendor of your majesty, and I will meditate on your wonderful works (Psalm 145:5).

Child: I've been thinking . . .

Parent: That's nothing new.

Child: Sunday we sang a hymn in church. It was called, "Majesty, Majesty" or something like that. I don't really understand. What does *majesty* mean?

Parent: Majesty means greatness. When we use the word *majesty* to describe someone like the queen of England or God, we are acknowledging the fact that he or she is great. And God is very great.

Child: But He's much greater than the queen of England, isn't He?

Parent: Of course He is. You know, some people just don't realize what His greatness means. There are two things we can do to understand His greatness. First, we need to get rid of anything in our thoughts about God that would make Him small in any way. Psalm 139 tells us that God is not limited in His knowledge of us nor in His power.

Second, we can compare God with powers or forces that we think of as great. Let's look at Isaiah 40:12-26 [read this passage together]. God says, "Look at the tasks I have done. Could you or anyone else ever do these?" And because God's people were afraid of other nations, God said, "Look at them! I am greater than any of them. They're a drop in the bucket." God also said that He is so big that we are like grasshoppers. He is greater than this world and everything in it. God is also greater than any ruler who has lived here on earth. Isaiah 40:23 says, "He reduces the rulers of this world to nothing" (NASB). In verse 24 God says, "You may be overwhelmed by the stars, but that's okay. Just remember who made them." Verses like these help us understand how great God is.

Child: Now I understand what *majesty* means. God really is a great God. I'll remember that.[7]

July 13

Practice what you have learned and received and heard and seen in me, and model your way of living on it (Philippians 4:9, AMP).

*W*hen your child becomes a teenager, your role as a parent changes. That's the only way to survive, but it's also beneficial.

When we parents change and grow we show our teenagers that it is all right for them to change and grow. In fact, one of the best ways we can restructure our relationships with our teenagers is to begin building two-way accountability. What is that? Let's look at its opposite to help define it.

The world structures relationships by setting up a series of one-way accountability systems that comprise a line of authority. At the bottom is the guy who is accountable to his boss, who is in turn accountable to *his* boss, and so on all the way up the ladder to the top. The president or manager may be accountable to a board, and in some companies there is a profit-sharing program that makes the president indirectly accountable to lower-level employees.

One-way accountability is the system most families are familiar with. Kids are accountable to adults, especially parents, but not vice-versa.

In two-way accountability, a dad would be willing to go to his teenage son and say, "Son, I'm working on not being anxious and committing everything to God in prayer. I'd like to report my progress to you each evening, and I'd like you to ask me how I'm doing. I'd like you to suggest ways I can learn quicker. And when you notice me getting anxious about something, I'd like you to remind me to commit it to the Lord right away. Okay?"

When a parent initiates two-way accountability, he or she sets the stage for several things to happen: 1) Teenagers will have a model for change that will make change and growth easier to accomplish; 2) teenagers will have a model for voluntary accountability, which, if they develop, will increase their self-discipline and responsibility greatly; 3) parent-teen communication can become more adult-to-adult rather than adult-to-child.

So . . . are you there yet? Or is the best yet to come?

July 14

He said to me, "My grace is sufficient for you, for my power is made perfect in weakness." Therefore I will boast all the more gladly about my weaknesses, so that Christ's power may rest on me. That is why, for Christ's sake, I delight in weaknesses, in insults, in hardships, in persecutions, in difficulties. For when I am weak, then I am strong (2 Corinthians 12:9,10).

*D*o you ever feel as if you're living your life in a courtroom? You're not in the jury box, though, nor the judge's bench nor at the table where the attorneys sit. You're on the stand, but not as a witness for the prosecution. You're standing trial!

Some people seem to go from one trial to another. As one parent cried out, "Trials! Who needs them?" You do. I do. We all do. Trials are an educational experience, though there may be times when we wish we didn't have to face them. Chuck Swindoll offers an excellent perspective on the purpose of trials.

Trials are designed for us, not for our surroundings. God wishes to train us, to mold us. He uses the distressing circumstances of life as His tools. He allows the icy feelings of despondency to linger within us. In doing so, He deals bountifully with us . . . deep within where no one else can see or touch.[8]

It may be difficult to fathom, but trials are actually good for us. The psalmist, David, said so: "It was good for me to be afflicted so that I might learn your decrees. . . . I know, O LORD, that your laws are righteous, and in faithfulness you have afflicted me" (Psalm 119:71,75).

The apostle Paul talked repeatedly about his weakness. We're all weak in some way. It's just evidence of the fact that we're human. Any trial that you and I experience—whether in a marriage, job, or with the children—carries the potential for God to do some of His mightiest work in our lives. We may not like it at the time; that's normal. But asking, "What can I learn from this about myself and God?" can put trials in a whole new light.

July 15

The teaching of the wise is a fountain of life, that one may avoid the snares of death (Proverbs 13:14, AMP).

*H*ave you ever flown in a helicopter? What's amazing about this machine is that it can climb straight up, hover in one spot, and dart around in different directions like a giant fly. A helicopter can even take people into the depths of a volcano crater to see the sights.

Helicopters make a lot of wind and noise. They're not noted for going fast. But they have a job to do. They hover, rescue, and protect.

Some parents are like helicopters. They hover overhead to provide constant protection. Perhaps you've seen them. They pick up all the slack for their children. They're the ones who show up at school frequently to bring the lunches, coats, and equipment their children forgot. They hover overhead just waiting for an opportunity to dart in and get their children off the hook. They're a self-appointed search-and-rescue team.

Why do they do this? They say it's because they love their children. They can't stand to see them hurt. Perhaps that's because when their children hurt, they hurt as well. Yet these parents may be confused. They think that love, protection, and caring are all the same, but they aren't.

These parents won't allow their children to fail. That's sad. Failure is one of the greatest learning experiences of life. When you do something wrong, it provides you with the opportunity to do it right the next time. But helicopter parents see their children's failures as their own. They rescue because of their own needs. It's interesting to note in the Bible that God used failures for some of the greatest lessons of life. All through the Scripture He used people who failed.

Just keep this thought in mind: If we rescue our children from failure now, someday they will really fail and we won't be there. And they won't know how to handle it. Let them learn now so they can be prepared later.[9]

July 16

Brothers, if someone is caught in a sin, you who are spiritual should restore him gently. But watch yourself, or you also may be tempted. Carry each other's burdens, and in this way you will fulfill the law of Christ (Galatians 6:1,2).

A group of prospective parents came together to hear an older couple share with them some guidelines on raising children. This is what the couple said:

Discipline is a must. If you want to enjoy either children or dogs, they need to be disciplined early in life. Now, I mentioned dogs just to get your attention. As we look at the children you're going to have, you want three things. You need to expect and train your children to respect you in both their actions and even non-verbal responses. Sarcasm and insolence must be confronted at the first infraction so the behavior does not give a foothold. Proverbs says, "The eye that mocks a father, that scorns obedience to a mother, will be pecked out by the ravens of the valley, will be eaten by the vultures" (30:17).

But remember it's easier for your child to respect you if you behave in a way that calls for respect. Provide an example.

Teach your child to speak the truth. This is difficult. You're asking something of them that isn't prevalent in our world today. You will need to teach your children to behave in a counter culture manner. "Instead, speaking the truth in love, we will in all things grow up into him who is the Head, that is, Christ . . ." (Ephesians 4:15, NIV). They will learn this easier if they see it consistently in your life as parents.

Finally, expect your child to obey immediately. Don't let your discipline become negotiable. It's your time schedule they learn to adhere to and not the other way around. The word "later" must be agreed upon but never instituted by just your child.

Why are these three things necessary? Simple. You're working yourself out of a job. One day you relinquish your control so two other forms of control can occur. Self-control and God's control. That's your goal. Enjoy your parenting![10]

July 17

The prayer of a righteous man is powerful and effective (James 5:16).

Sometimes the obstacles to the spiritual and emotional well-being of our children are present not just in us as parents, but also in other members of the family.

Prayer for Healing of the Family Tree

God, the Father, almighty
Creator of all beings. . . .

We know that since the fall
of our original parents
our family ancestry includes
not only talents and virtues
but also much tragedy and sin.

Today . . . I ask that You would
    heal our family tree.

I call to mind each member of the family
I have heard of
or known personally
and I ask for Your healing
graces to bless him (her).

We know that in You, eternal God,
all of time is one,
and so we ask You
to bring the light
of Your Son's redemption
into the darkness of the past.

Especially, I beg You,
loving God,
to cleanse me
of any bad patterns
coming from my family background. . . .

Come, O Holy Spirit,
to teach us how to mingle necessary sacrifice
with proper self-love,
that we may be able to respond
to the needs of our babies
in ways that are prudent and sound.[11]

July 18

Do your best to present yourself to God as one approved, a workman who does not need to be ashamed and who correctly handles the word of truth (2 Timothy 2:15).

You're in the doctor's office waiting with your child. Soon you're called into the examining room, where the doctor takes out a needle and carefully injects the contents into the arm of your wide-eyed child. While the shot may have hurt momentarily, it is of important and lasting consequence. Your child was just inoculated against a life-threatening disease.

How did that happen? In the shot, your child was given a small dose of the disease. This weakened form triggered the body's immune system in a way that activated its forces and built some antibodies to fight off the disease.

This preventative action serves as a good example of helping children learn how to handle the everyday problems and stresses of life. The best way to help them develop the character they need is to inoculate them against what they will encounter. But how?

Don't keep your children in a protected hothouse environment. This will weaken their resistance. Expose them gradually, bit by bit, to problems and stresses. While you're doing it, talk with them and show them how to handle what they are going to encounter. That way, they're better prepared and not thrown off course.

Gradual exposure means giving your children responsibilities, not shielding them from the unpleasant situations of life. It also requires being truthful even when your children are hurt. It means holding back the urge to rescue your children from problems and letting them learn how to solve them. If your children experience a hurt or a loss, let them experience it fully. Teach them how to grieve and how to say good-bye to what they lose. If children don't grieve their losses, they accumulate them, which will compound the losses they experience in the future.

Yes—sometimes this is hard to do. But the motto that has existed for generations in the Boy Scouts of America program is applicable here for both you and your child: Be prepared.

For this reason, since the day we heard about you, we have not stopped praying for you and asking God to fill you with the knowledge of his will through all spiritual wisdom and understanding (Colossians 1:9).

One of the most frequent questions parents ask is, "How should I pray for my children when they're in trouble?" But the other side of the coin is, "What's the best way to pray for my children when they're doing well and living for the Lord?"

In Colossians 1:2, Paul called the Colossians "faithful brothers in Christ." They were living for the Lord, but Paul saw they still had a need for prayer. If your children are committed to the Lord, keep in mind that Satan, the great deceiver, is not too happy about this. Godly children are still going to face temptations. They can get discouraged and will face greater peer pressure and ridicule than other people. That's because they're nonconformists living in a society that has totally different values.

In Jesus' great prayer in which He committed His followers to God's keeping, He prays:

> I have revealed you to those whom you gave me out of the world. They were yours; you gave them to me and they have obeyed your word.... For I gave them the words you gave me and they accepted them.... I pray for them. I am not praying for the world, but for those you have given me, for they are yours.... Protect them by the power of your name—the name you gave me—so that they may be one as we are one (John 17:6,8,9,11).

If Jesus prayed this way for His spiritual children, then we as parents should pray even more for our believing children that they will be protected by the power of Jesus' name. We can pray, "Dear Lord, I bring my children to you. They have heard the Word of God which I have taught them, and they have believed. Now keep them, protect them by the power of Your name, Lord Jesus Christ. Don't let the Evil One steal away the teaching they have received, but rather let it grow in them. Make them mighty men and women of God to Your honor and glory."[12]

How will you pray for your family today?

July 20

We love because he first loved us (1 John 4:19).

*I*s there love in your family? Is there affection in your family? But why ask about love and affection in two different questions? Aren't they the same? No, not really. We're supposed to love one another. This love comes as a sense of family duty and loyalty. But liking one another . . . that's something else. That's family affection. It's best expressed in this way:

> Happy families . . . own a surface similarity of good cheer. For one thing, they like each other, which is quite a different thing from loving. For another, they have, almost always, one entirely personal treasure—a sort of purseful of domestic humor which they have accumulated against rainy days. This humor is not necessarily witty. The jokes may be incomprehensible to outsiders, and the laughter springs from the most trivial of sources. But the jokes and the laughter belong entirely to the family.[13]

Kent and Barbara Hughes suggest that there are three elements to growing in affection. The first is loving God, because it connects you with the source of love (1 John 4:8) and gives you an example of ideal love (1 John 4:10,11). It also empowers you to love (1 John 4:19). When you love God, your love for other people will endure.

The second element is loving each other. Children need the assurance of their parents' love for one another. Elton Trueblood said:

> It is the father's responsibility to *make* the child know that he is deeply in love with the child's mother. There is no good reason why all evidence of affection should be hidden or carried on in secret. A child who grows up with the realization that his parents are lovers has a wonderful basis of stability.[14]

The third element for family affection comes through clear communication. Healthy communication reflects truth expressed delicately, as mentioned in Proverbs: "An honest answer is like a kiss on the lips" (24:26). It involves adapting what you say so the other person can accept and understand it. And both ears and eyes must be involved in listening.

Building family affection . . . it's not a chore, it's a pleasure.[15]

*The father of a righteous man has great joy; he who has a wise
son delights in him. May your father and mother be glad; may
she who gave you birth rejoice!* (Proverbs 23:24,25).

*A*s they go through life, your children are going to be faced
with a multitude of decisions. And they're not the decisions of a few generations ago! Will they say yes or no to drugs?
Will they say yes or no to premarital sex? Will they say yes or no
to an attractive cult leader? Will they say yes or no to the wrong
person to marry? There will be times when they, like you, will
need insight, wisdom, and help.

It's frightening to think about all the present and future decisions your children will have to make. What if they end up just
drifting through school or into some "job" with little or no meaning? What if they never tap into and activate the potential that
God has given to them? What if . . . ?

Now isn't the time to ask, "What if . . . ?" Right decisions come
from wisdom and discernment. James 1:15 tells us these qualities
come from God: "If any of you lacks wisdom, he should ask God,
who gives generously to all without finding fault, and it will be
given to him."

Read, study, and memorize God's Word. Pray for wisdom for
you and your child. And consider these words:

> Trust in the LORD with all your heart and lean not on your own
> understanding; in all your ways acknowledge him, and he will
> make your paths straight (Proverbs 3:5,6).

> Wisdom is supreme; therefore get wisdom. Though it cost all
> you have, get understanding. Esteem her, and she will exalt you;
> embrace her, and she will honor you (Proverbs 4:7,8).

> For wisdom will enter your heart, and knowledge will be pleas-
> ant to your soul. Discretion will protect you, and understanding
> will guard you. Wisdom will save you from the ways of wicked
> men, from men whose words are perverse (Proverbs 2:10-12).

Your hope is that your children will learn to make wise decisions. They can and they will . . . when they walk hand in hand
with God.

July 22

It is for freedom that Christ has set us free. Stand firm, then, and do not let yourselves be burdened again by a yoke of slavery (Galatians 5:1).

*W*hat did you inherit from your parents? What have your children inherited from you?

We all know we can inherit our mother's eyes, our father's nose, or the color of our grandmother's hair. But did you know that we can also inherit a bad temper, a propensity for lying, depression, self-pity, envy, unforgiveness, perfectionism, and pride? These and other entrenched characteristics that have a spiritual base can also be passed along from our parents to us and from us to our children. In a particular family there may be a tendency toward such things as divorce, constant sickness, infidelity, alcoholism, addiction, suicide, depression, rejection, or being accident prone—all mistakenly accepted as "fate" or "the way I am."

"These things just happen to my family," we hear people say.

Some of what we accept about ourselves and our lives are actually family bondages, for children inherit the consequences of their ancestors' sins. The Bible says God will visit "the iniquities of the fathers upon the children to the third and fourth generations of those who hate Me" (Exodus 20:5). This Scripture is referring to people who don't walk in a loving relationship with God, but how many of our ancestors didn't walk with God and how many times have we been less than lovingly obedient to Him? The point is, we all qualify for the judgment in this verse, but by the grace of God, through Jesus Christ, we don't have to endure it. The very next verse continues by saying that God shows mercy "to those who love Me and keep My commandments" (Exodus 20:6).[16]

To break a destructive family pattern, pray specifically for yourself and your child that Jesus Christ will break the bondage of the past. Above all, read, claim, and believe the truth of what Paul said in 2 Corinthians 5:17: "If anyone is in Christ, he is a new creation; the old has gone, the new has come!"

July 23

Fathers, do not exasperate your children; instead, bring them up in the training and instruction of the Lord (Ephesians 6:4).

*F*athering is tough. It's on-the-job learning with insufficient time for just trying to keep up with the kids, the payments, and life itself. Many of us can identify with the feeling of this dad:

> "...I love my three kids more than life itself," a father told me. "I have sacrificed some very important dreams so that I can have a career that allows me to provide for my children. I have overcome substantial personal problems because I am determined to keep my marriage and family together. I am doing the best I know to do, but I am often frustrated. It takes so much work to stay competitive in my field, to provide financially, to coordinate schedules, to maintain a healthy relationship with my wife—that I never seem to have enough time with my kids. It's not a matter of wasting time on personal interests. I just don't have enough time with them, and it's not a matter of choice."

In a national survey, dads were asked to describe their feelings about fathering by using word pictures. Their answers included the following:

"I feel like a lone lion roaring in the jungle."

"I feel like a duck out of water."

"I feel like a loved teddy bear with all the fuzz rubbed off."

"I feel like the sun on a partly cloudy day, warm and nice when it's there, but not there quite as much as my children would like."

"I feel like I'm swimming against a river of things that are demanding my time, struggling to get to the island where my children are waiting."

"I feel like water in the shower, which runs hot and cold depending on who is using water in other parts of the house."[17]

Wow! What about you? If you're a father or mother, how would you describe, in word pictures, what you're doing?

July 24

Confess your sins to each other and pray for each other so that you may be healed. The prayer of a righteous man is powerful and effective (James 5:16).

Sometimes songs convey our thoughts better than anything else, as does this song for a child: "Above All Else" by Stormie Omartian.

> So much to say and just a lifetime to say it.
> How quickly time passes.
> If I had my way, I'd keep you safe within
>   my arms
> While the storm of life crashes.
>
> I won't always be with you, my child,
>   but words I can give.
> When the winds of hope are dying down,
>   these words will live.
> Above all else, know God's the One who'll
>   never leave you.
> Look to Him above all else.
> He is love you can depend upon,
>   a heart set to care.
> If in the darkest night you should be lost,
>   He will be there.
> He's the everlasting Father,
> In His hands you'll never fall.
> He's the One who holds it all,
> Above all else.
> He's the Author of your laughter,
> He's the Keeper of your tears,
> He's the One who you must fear
> Above all else.
>
> He's the Giver of the kingdom
> Bought for you right from the start,
> And He'll ask you for your heart
> Above all else.
> So much to say
> And not enough time left to say it.
> Just love the Lord
> Above all else.[18]

July 25

Even to your old age and gray hairs I am he, I am he who will sustain you (Isaiah 46:4).

*Y*ou're growing older, aren't you? We don't really like to admit it. We live in a society that celebrates the vitality of youth. But we all hit our thirties, forties, fifties, sixties, and beyond. If we don't hit them, it's because . . . well, we know the alternative.

We have a condition in this country described as "the graying of America." More and more people are in their sixties. And the people in this age bracket face many new stresses, problems, and challenges. You know what some of them are if you are approaching this time yourself or if you have aged parents. Health issues, retirement, and memory loss seem foremost in our minds. These are the concerns of aging.

How we face and handle aging is an education for our children. We can take the pessimistic approach or the biblical approach. Old age can be a time of strength, as reflected in Isaiah 46:4, the theme verse of today's devotion.

E. Stanley Jones, in his book *Christian Maturity*, shares how this promise of God from Isaiah was fulfilled in his advanced years. He writes that God said to him when he passed seventy, "I'm giving you the best ten years of your life—the next ten ahead." Jones adds, "Two of them have passed and they have literally been the best two years of my life. Eight to go! . . . Practically all my question marks have now been straightened out into dancing exclamation points."[19]

We can live in the past and dread our future or look toward the future and live with faith and hope. Have you ever considered that there just might be joy in aging? When your children are on their own and you're moving through the decades, remember the promise of God: "They will still bear fruit in old age, they will stay fresh and green" (Psalm 92:14).[20]

July 26

Instead, it should be that of your inner self, the unfading beauty of a gentle and quiet spirit, which is of great worth in God's sight (1 Peter 3:4).

*H*ave you ever had one of those days where you've got a case of the blahs? You're not feeling up, you're not down—you're just feeling *blah*. Your spouse says a positive, uplifting, and affirming word to you. Your reaction? "Blah."

Years ago there was a movie called *Ordinary People*. We don't like to feel ordinary. Do you like being known as an ordinary parent with an ordinary spouse and ordinary children? Ordinary never seems to end.

We all want to be unique, special, unusual, or even spectacular. But why? What will that do for us? Where will it get us? And more importantly, who sets the standard for what or who is special? You? The world? God?

We need to remember that God is the one who sets standards in life, not the world. God sees you in two ways: He sees you as ordinary, and He delights in the ordinary. Is He impressed by your accomplishments, status symbols, and positions of prominence? I don't think so. He doesn't need to be, and neither do you. He already sees you as special because you are His creation. He looks inside and delights in your inner beauty and calm spirit.

Paul told us where we're to look for our significance when he wrote to the Colossians, "Whatever you do, work at it with all your heart, as working for the Lord, not for men, since you know that you will receive an inheritance from the Lord as a reward. It is the Lord Christ you are serving" (Colossians 3:23,24).

You aren't called to be a people pleaser. Rather, you are called to please Him. Each little unassuming ordinary faithful step you take and task you fulfill is pleasing to your heavenly Father. And when you please Him, do you know what happens? The ordinary turns into the extraordinary!

July 27

Arise, cry out in the night, as the watches of the night begin;
pour out your heart like water in the presence of the Lord. Lift
up your hands to him for the lives of your children, who faint
from hunger at the head of every street (Lamentations 2:19).

*W*henever you apply for a job, you usually ask if you can look at the job description. You want to know what to expect and what you'll be doing with your time. That's a wise step to take because you want to make sure the job is right for you. As a parent, you might find it helpful to draw up a job description of the task of parenting because it entails so much of your life. There's a fascinating description in the book *The Power of a Praying Parent* by Stormie Omartian. You'll probably identify with this!

It's the best of jobs. It's the most difficult of jobs. It can bring you the greatest joy. It can cause the greatest pain. There is nothing as fulfilling and exhilarating. There's nothing so depleting and exhausting. No area of your life can make you feel more like a success when everything is going well. No area of your life can make you feel more like a failure when things go wrong.

PARENTING!

The word itself can bring contradictory emotions to the surface. We try to do the best we can raising our children. Then, just when we think we've got the parenting terrain all figured out, we suddenly find ourselves in new territory again as each new age and stage presents another set of challenges. Sometimes we sail through smoothly. Sometimes we encounter tempests and tidal waves. Sometimes we get so tired that we just want to give up—let the storm take us where it will.

But I have good news. We don't have to be tossed and turned by these winds of change. *Our children's lives don't ever have to be left to chance.*[21]

What makes the difference? Prayer. Praying specifically for each child. When Jesus Christ is your resource and your source of strength as a parent, let the problems come. You're not alone. Knowing that can be a real source of calm.

July 28

Why is life given to a man whose way is hidden, whom God has hedged in? (Job 3:23).

*C*hildren are constantly asking, "Why?" But so are adults. Especially when circumstances go wrong. We ask that question of ourselves, other people, and even God.

You won't be the last person to ask God, "Why?" And you're definitely not the first. Many years ago, one of His prophets asked the same question, and he wasn't indirect or timid, either. He was appalled by all the suffering he saw, just as some of us are pained by what we see today. This is what he said to God:

> How long, O LORD, will I call for help, and Thou wilt not hear? I cry out to Thee, "Violence!" Yet Thou dost not save. Why dost Thou make me see iniquity, and cause me to look on wickedness? Yes, destruction and violence are before me; strife exists and contention arises. Therefore, the law is ignored and justice is never upheld. For the wicked surround the righteous; Therefore, justice comes out perverted (Habakkuk 1:2-4, NASB)

When we encounter the deep valleys in our lives, they soon reflect our theology and philosophy of life. Unfortunately, our expectations and beliefs sometimes don't correspond to Scripture. Now that doesn't mean we're heretics, but we can look at the trying times in life as an opportunity to bring our thinking and perspectives more into line with God's Word.

Many Christians believe, for example, that life is (or ought to be) fair. They think, *If I'm a Christian, I should be immune to tragedy.* God does not insulate us from misfortunes, however, and He never promised He would. Sometimes God does intervene in negative circumstances in a strange and marvelous way, but He does so at His sovereign choosing and not through our demanding.

So, hard times are an opportunity to become more dependent upon God and discover that even when things don't go our way, we will still survive. It is these times that are learning experiences for us.

By the way, if you want to know what happened to Habakkuk, take a look at chapter 3, verses 17-19.

July 29

Even a child is known by his actions, by whether his conduct is pure and right (Proverbs 20:11).

*W*hat do you want your children to be known for? What kind of reputation do you want them to have? A label or series of descriptive adjectives, once applied, seems to stick to us like super glue. Most parents want their children to be known for doing what is right. But the question is, by whose standards? There are many sets of values in operation in our world today.

The Bible is the standard that Christian parents want their children to follow. That standard can be summed up in one word: purity. Not only does Proverbs talk about that, but so did Paul. He said, "Keep yourself pure" (1 Timothy 5:22, NKJV). That's hard because it means you have to go counterculture. And if you think it's difficult for an adult to do that, imagine what it must be like for a child. You see, being pure means being free from anything that taints, impairs, or infects—free from defects and sin. That's asking a lot!

But . . . do we want our children to be known for their purity or impurity? Can they have a pure life in the world that we live in? Yes, they can. But they must be in submission to God and His Holy Spirit. What can you do as a parent to help your children? The author of *The Power of a Praying Parent* suggests this:

> Let's pray for our children to be attracted to holiness and purity like a magnet, so that when anything entices them that isn't holy or pure, they detect the pull immediately and are made uncomfortable enough to thoroughly reject it. "For God did not call us to uncleanness, but to holiness" (1 Thessalonians 4:7). To live purely within the boundaries of God's law is to find wholeness in the total person. That wholeness is what holiness is all about. Children who have a desire for holiness and seek God's enabling power to help them achieve it can never be anything but blessed and fulfilled.[22]

July 30

They are the Israelites who are to be given wholly to me. I have taken them as my own in place of the firstborn, the first male offspring from every Israelite woman (Deuteronomy 8:16).

*W*hy me?" Many parents ask this question when everything they've tried with their child has gone wrong. "Why me?" is a way of asking, "What did I do to deserve this? Where did I go wrong?" It's a normal question. Part of the time, though, it's a question, and part of the time it's our cry of protest. Either way, it's all right to express it. Just keep in mind that you won't always get an answer. Why not? Because getting an answer probably wouldn't make much difference nor would it suffice.

If you get stuck with "Why me?" as your posture in life, you'll come to have a narrow perspective that focuses on the apparent unfairness of your predicament and end up nurturing a case of self-pity. Self-pity can warp and absorb you. And it can generate the acid of cynicism.

A better question is this: "What now?" Asking "What now?" instead of "Why me?" turns your eyes away from yourself and onto someone else—God. You start looking to see what He has in store for you. God won't give you an answer to every "Why me?" But He *will* give an answer to "What now?" This question gives you hope because it's future-oriented. Life can move forward again. Isn't that a great perspective to pass on to your children to help them live life to the fullest?

We have a choice: We can think that the best of life is behind us or in front of us. Which perspective would encourage you the most?

A cheerful heart is good medicine, but a crushed spirit dries up the bones (Proverbs 17:22).

Humor is one of the most powerful influences in a family. It can be used very effectively in discipline. We're called to discipline our kids, not punish them. The word *discipline* actually means "to learn." It doesn't mean to put chains on our kids.

One day I asked a friend how hard it was to discipline his kids. He said, "Well, one day my kid really goofed up. He was being stubborn and disobedient. So I just grabbed him and said, "I'm going to tickle you until you wet your pants unless you promise never to do that again." And he looked up at me and said, 'What?' So I started tickling him and tickling him, and he was laughing and laughing. And I got him to promise never to repeat what he had just done."

My friend used humor and tickling to bring about behavior change. Of course, he did it lightheartedly; we have to be careful not to abuse our kids under the guise of kidding them. I've started using humor for discipline too, and it works well with my sons.

Laughter is a powerful medicine for a family. Proverbs 17:22 says, "A cheerful heart is good medicine, but a crushed spirit dries up the bones." Humor, laughter, and joy release endorphins—chemicals that create positive emotions—into the bloodstream. Humor is a miracle substance for families. It's easy to overreact when our kids make mistakes, but if we learn not to take ourselves *too* seriously, they will find it easier to correct their errors....

Laughter is so important that I've made it a high priority. John Powell once said, "He who learns to laugh at himself shall never cease to be entertained." We need to learn to laugh at ourselves, because the human predicament is so notoriously difficult. Life can be so preposterously hard that if we didn't learn to laugh at ourselves, we wouldn't survive. Families today are going through more stress than ever before, but a well-developed sense of humor can keep them from breaking.[23]

August 1

In the same way, the Spirit helps us in our weakness. We do not know what we ought to pray for, but the Spirit himself intercedes for us with groans that words cannot express (Romans 8:26).

*H*ave you ever been at a loss for words? That happens to all of us at one time or another. Someone gives you an unexpected outrageous compliment in front of other people and your mind goes into space. What do you say?

Or your children have misbehaved all day long and now you've hit the last straw with them. They look up innocently and lovingly at you in the midst of the seventeenth chaotic episode of the day. Your brain freezes, your mouth sputters, and the choice words that you want to spit out to correct, control, and corral those kids just don't come out. You're so upset and frazzled that you're at a loss for words. Yes, you've arrived; welcome to the world of parenting.

But these aren't the only places where we've been at a loss. It happens when we pray, too. We have needs, burdens, requests, and even praise, but somehow we seem so blocked and bottled up in our thoughts and words. So we try harder, and even though some words come, we wonder, *Is this what I should be praying?*

If you were sharing your heart with one of your closest and most trusted friends, what would the conversation be like? It would probably just flow. Think of talking with God in the same way... it's a conversation. And most conversations are dialogues (not monologues) between two hearts and two minds. Two friends can also sit in silence and converse. They hear one another in the still sounds of silence.

However, there is one difference when you talk with God. Someone else is helping and speaking for you when you're at a loss for words. The Holy Spirit knows how to express what is bottled up within you that can't be translated into words. So, don't fret. Don't get down on yourself. Just praise God for His Holy Spirit and pray to the Holy Spirit to speak for you and free you up to speak.

August 2

*Be strong and very courageous. Be careful to obey all the law
my servant Moses gave you; do not turn from it to the right or
to the left, that you may be successful wherever you go. Do not
let this Book of the Law depart from your mouth; meditate on
it day and night, so that you may be careful to do everything
written in it. Then you will be prosperous and successful.
Have I not commanded you? Be strong and courageous. Do
not be terrified; do not be discouraged, for the LORD your God
will be with you wherever you go* (Joshua 1:7-9).

*T*he words the Lord gave to Joshua on how to be a successful
leader are applicable for you as parents because you are the
leaders of your family.

First, there is the promise of the *presence of God* in your life. If a
person is strong and courageous as a leader, fear and discouragement have difficulty gaining a foothold.

Second, the Lord said Joshua didn't need to be afraid nor dismayed. God wouldn't fail him. We, too, are promised the same
protection of God. How does that make you feel?

The third promise is the *provision of God*. Joshua and the children of Israel experienced God's provision as they entered the
Promised Land. Philippians 4:19 states, "My God will meet all
your needs according to his glorious riches in Christ Jesus." What
are your needs at this time? God wants us to be specific in our requests, seek His will, and depend upon Him to provide.

Joshua was also promised the *power of God*. God said Joshua
would receive the power he needed to lead as long as he obeyed
the Word of God. Families that look to the Word of God as their
source of guidance and insight will find stability. Can you imagine what it would be like if everyone in your community lived
their lives according to what the Scripture teaches? Or your own
family, for that matter? All types of power have to come from a
source. Our source is the Holy Spirit. His presence in our lives,
too, is a promise from Scripture.

So, Joshua was promised the presence, the protection, the provision, and the power of God. The same promises have been
given to you. Remind yourself of this each morning; it will make
your day go better.

August 3

Better a patient man than a warrior, a man who controls his temper than one who takes a city (Proverbs 16:32).

I get angry as a parent—is that wrong? Is that a sin?"

Does Scripture label anger as a sin? No, it doesn't. If anger is a sin then God is capable of sin, because there are numerous references in Scripture to God's anger. Indeed, anger is a God-given emotion. He is glorified when we express this emotion in constructive ways.

But, unfortunately, we sometimes respond to the emotion of anger in ways that lead to sin. That is one reason why both the Old and New Testaments teach us to be slow to anger (see Proverbs 16:32 and James 1:19).

The starting point for the positive use of anger is to understand that it is a God-given emotion. Anger is not an evil or destructive emotion in itself. Anger isn't necessarily dangerous. Unfortunately, many people confuse anger with the ways some individuals choose to express or act out that emotion. They confuse anger and aggression. Anger is an emotion, aggression is an action.

When we don't understand our anger and allow it to get out of control it can lead to aggressive behaviors that are sinful, dangerous, destructive, and even deadly. But the emotion of anger isn't the problem. The real problem is the mismanagement and misunderstanding of it—the emotional immaturity of the individual who allows himself or herself to be controlled by the anger-energy.

We can't always control when or how we experience anger. However, with God's help, we can learn to control how we choose to interpret and express that emotion. Because God has made us rational creatures, we are free to choose how we will respond to external events. In fact, we have more control than we give ourselves credit for. Often, however, our past experiences, memories, and patterns of response tend to hinder us from exercising this control. With understanding, time, and practice we can overcome these influences and develop constructive and healthy responses to our anger.[1]

August 4

Jesus answered her, "If you knew the gift of God and who it is that asks you for a drink, you would have asked him and he would have given you living water" (John 4:10).

*Y*ou've been walking for hours in the desert. It's hot, dry, and dusty. The land is parched and so is your mouth. All you can think about is water—cool, wet, thirst-quenching water poured into your mouth. You may have had such an experience. Most of the time, however, we have sufficient water for our needs. You may live in an area with an abundance of lakes or near a large river. The Mississippi River starts as a very small stream in the woods of Minnesota and then takes off for 2,562 miles on its way to the Gulf of Mexico. As it goes along gaining depth and width, the size and volume it reaches becomes enormous. When it stays within its banks it's extremely useful and productive for crops and travel. But sometimes it rages out of control and causes tremendous destruction.

We all need water. We can live without food for 10 to 15 days. But three days without water can be a disaster.

We who are Christians have been given another type of water: Jesus, the fountain of life. Scripture describes us as being conveyers of water, too. Jesus said, "Whoever believes in me, as the Scripture has said, streams of living water will flow from within him" (John 7:38). Now, what does that mean?

We've received God's grace through Jesus Christ. We then are called to become rivers of blessing. Where? In our homes, at work, in the world. How? By living according to His Word. By reflecting His teaching—especially at home, where we tend to let down. Remember that the Mississippi River flows and grows as it makes its journey. Are we doing the same?[2]

August 5

You will seek me and find me when you seek me with all your heart (Jeremiah 29:13).

*A*s parents, there's a game we all end up playing with our children. It's called hide-and-seek. Kids love it. They enjoy hiding from us and fooling us so much that they win. You probably played this game when you were a child, too. It's a game for kids . . . not for adults.

Sometimes adults continue to play hide-and-seek, but the results aren't so much fun. Parents hide themselves from their children—they hide their time, love, feelings, or personal involvement. There are problems when adults engage in this activity.

Husbands and wives can engage in a marital game of hide-and-seek, too. Often the person hiding or distancing themselves from their partner never stops in one place long enough to allow themselves to be caught. They live in fear of being known or getting too close to another person. Could it also be they're afraid of themselves in some way?

Some adults play a perpetual game of hide-and-seek with God. They look for God halfheartedly and say, "He's not around. I can't find Him." Or they look in the wrong places and always seem to miss Him. Or the God they are looking for exists only in their own mind. Some people have been known to create God in their own image instead of looking to Scripture to discover who He really is. Jesus gave us some guidance about this: "Ask and it will be given to you; seek and you will find; knock and the door will be opened to you. For everyone who asks receives; he who seeks finds; and to him who knocks, the door will be opened" (Matthew 7:7,8).

There's one other thought to consider. With God being who He is, how could we ever really hide from Him? It's odd . . . why would anyone want to hide from someone who loves us so much and wants the best for us? I wonder. . . .

August 6

Now that I, your Lord and Teacher, have washed your feet, you also should wash one another's feet (John 13:14).

*L*ife involves a constant change of roles. Who knows—someday you may have a position in a company where your former supervisor becomes your supervisee! That's a role switch. Perhaps it's happened in your family. The person who was the main wage earner is now the one taking care of the home and the former homemaker is the wage earner.

When you were younger, your parents took care of you. If it hasn't happened yet, there may come a time when you will become a parent to your parents and care for them. And your children, whom you cared for, may end up reversing roles with you in a number of years! Scary thought, isn't it? But that's life. We all experience role changes. Fortunately, Jesus experienced a role change, too.

> As Paul declares, "You know the grace of our Lord Jesus Christ, that though He was rich, yet for your sakes He became poor" (2 Corinthians 8:9). In Philippians 2:7, Paul says that Christ, who was equal with God, who in fact *was* God, "made Himself nothing, taking the very nature of a servant." More than that, "He humbled Himself and became obedient to death—even death on a cross!"[3]

Before Jesus came to earth, angels worshiped Him in heaven. He made a choice to be poor so we could be rich. How are we rich? We are rich because God has forgiven our sin. We are rich because we have the promise of eternal life. We can't purchase these riches for any amount because they are free gifts from God. That's quite a role reversal! He didn't have to do that. He wasn't forced to do it. He chose to. He wanted to. Why? Simply because He loves you. Think about that the rest of today. You are so loved that someone gave up riches and became poor so that you, who lived in spiritual poverty, could become rich. That's real love![4]

August 7

He who covers and forgives an offense seeks love, but he who repeats or harps on a matter separates even close friends (Proverbs 17:9, AMP).

*A*re your parents still living? If so, how is your relationship with them? And even if they are deceased, how is your relationship? That's not such a strange question; many deceased parents still exert a tremendous amount of control over their living children. Often you still hear their voices, experience their training, reflect on their values, or even feel inhibited in your life because of something they did or said. If there are any problems or residual effects that still affect you because of your parents, the solution just may be to forgive them.

"But," you say, "they haven't asked for forgiveness." Or, "They don't deserve it." That may be true, but that's what forgiveness is all about, isn't it?

The reason this is important is because it will not only help you, but also your children. They will know if there is a problem between you and your parents. And they will learn from your example.

There are some steps you can take to help you come to the place of wanting to forgive your parents. And remember that forgiveness is a process.

First, read portions of Scripture that talk about forgiveness.

Next, thank God for your Mom and Dad. Thank God for what your parents did right . . . and what they did wrong. That demonstrates faith in God, doesn't it? Hebrews 11:6 tells us that faith pleases God. Keep in mind I'm not saying you have to *feel* thankful, but that as an act of faith in God's wisdom and provision you can say, "Thank you for my parents."[5]

Then identify what it is that still bothers you about them. In some cases it may be specific offenses from years ago or even recently. Write them out, and then say, "I forgive you for . . ." Then hand your list to God and thank Him for helping you learn to forgive. You'll be surprised at the result.

If there is no residue of bad feelings from your parents, praise the Lord. If there is, forgive them, and you'll become free to praise the Lord in a new way.

August 8

. . . train yourself to be godly (1 Timothy 4:7).

*N*ow I'm going to meddle a bit in another area of life. Do you have a regular aerobic exercise program that you follow, say, at least 3 to 4 times per week? Are your muscles toned up or are there a few bulges that are becoming more and more evident? When you walk up two flights of stairs, does your heart rate stay the same or is it racing?

We live in a world that is health-conscious, an age of physical fitness. Look at the joggers. They're everywhere. People watch their diet, their cholesterol, the water they drink, and the vitamins they take. Most people want to be physically fit. That's great.

There's another kind of fitness that's even better. It's called spiritual fitness. It's easy to become so busy that it, like physical fitness, can be neglected. Physical fitness helps us in this life. Spiritual fitness helps us even more so in this life, but also for eternity. Paul encouraged Timothy to watch his physical health, but then said, "Have nothing to do with godless myths and old wives' tales; rather, train yourself to be godly. For physical training is of some value, but godliness has value for all things, holding promise for both the present life and the life to come" (1 Timothy 4:7,8).

If your child were to ask you, "How can I stay spiritually fit?" what would you say? Spiritual fitness will happen when we:

+ Spend time each day in prayer—praising, adoring, asking, interceding.

+ Spend time each day in worship—this can occur in your home as well as at church.

+ Spend time in your local church serving and ministering to others.

But remember, many people do the above yet are not spiritually fit. Routines won't work here. It must come from the heart— a heart that has been changed because of the love of Jesus. He makes it possible for us to be spiritually fit.

August 9

Children's children are a crown to the aged, and parents are the pride of their children (Proverbs 17:6).

*W*hat did you call your father? Everyone has different names for their dad, some formal and some informal. Sometimes when a child reaches adulthood he or she calls father by his first name. Others continue to call him Daddy. Chuck Swindoll shares some memories about his own father:

My dad has not always been "Pop" to us. We, my brothers and sister, as well as mom, called him "Daddy" when we were young. He was able to make even folding clothes on Saturday fun with tickle fights amidst freshly washed garments strewn all over the living room floor. He would roll and pretend at vulnerability on the carpet and grab each tiny, groping hand that attempted to tweak his ribs. We seldom won, of course. Daddy could mercilessly tickle the toes off a dead giant, not to mention take on four lively kids.

And, yes, there were serious times as well. We knew of them, too. He could spank the tears out of any of us, not because the physical pain was so incredible, but because it hurt us to think that we had brought him pain by having earned that spanking.

Looking back, I can see that my parents, by joint effort, have done an exceptionally good job raising us. High moral values, spiritual priorities, academic excellence—all these have been held out to us as important. My pop has instilled in us kids a sense of trust. He's been available, especially in emergencies. He has done what he thinks best for us, even when we might not agree—as an example, in the business world, our family, our church. My dad has a corner on the upper echelons of fatherhood.[6]

August 10

So I tell you this, and insist on it in the Lord, that you must no longer live as the Gentiles do, in the futility of their thinking (Ephesians 4:17).

*A*sk your children, "How are you?" and often you get an automatic, nonthinking response of, "Fine." But if you want a puzzled look and rapt attention, ask them, "How's your mind today?" They may look at you like you've lost yours!

The condition of our mind may be more important than how our body feels. What happens in your mind, and your children's, can make or break an entire day. Your thoughts can determine your feelings and even the health of your body.

As Christians, we have a calling to use our mind in a right way. Jesus said, "Love the Lord your God with all your heart and with all your soul and with all your mind" (Matthew 22:37). Your heart may be responding to God, and your soul may be responding, but if your mind isn't then there's a problem. The mind needs to be involved. Paul said, "I *know* whom I have believed" (2 Timothy 1:12). Peter said, "Grow in the grace and *knowledge* of our Lord and Savior Jesus Christ" (2 Peter 3:18).

How are you using your mind in relationship to God? What do you think about? What goes on inside your head when you read the Scripture and it tells you to do something that is different from what you've been doing? You see, for your children to make a decision to obey you, they have to use their mind and decide to do it. The same is true for us. We're called to obedience. God wants us to think about what He is saying in His Word and to discover the benefits of following it.

Obedience to God's Word is not distasteful, restrictive, or limiting. It's the greatest way to experience the best life and freedom ever devised!

August 11

The Son of Man did not come to be served, but to serve, and to give his life as a ransom for many (Matthew 20:28).

A parent sitting in church one day heard the pastor read the passage above. Because she had a particularly draining week, her first response was, "I don't think I'm being sacrilegious, but there *are* days when I feel that way—serve, serve, serve. That's all I do!" Perhaps you have also felt that way at times.

It's important to note how Jesus was using the term "Son of Man" in Matthew 20:28. He was the only one to use this title. "Son of Man" reflects His humanity, as does serving. He wanted to identify with us and our experiences. Think for a moment what you experience each day:

Do you laugh? Jesus laughed.

Do you cry? Oh, He wept.

Do you get tired? So did He.

How about hunger? He knew the contractions of an empty stomach.

What about thirst? Yes, of course. Especially when He was hanging on the cross.

Have you ever suffered? He did in many ways.

You haven't died . . . yet. He did in a very painful manner.

Some people ask, "How can Jesus be both the Son of God and the Son of Man?" Consider these thoughts:

This title is associated not only with the humanity of Jesus Christ but with His divinity as well. We cannot neatly compartmentalize His humanity. He was a mysterious and majestic composite of man and God. This title is linked with some of the sublime declarations of Christ. Among them:

"When the Son of Man comes in His glory, and all the angels with Him, He will sit on His throne in heavenly glory. All the nations will be gathered before Him, and He will separate the people one from another" (Matthew 25:31-32). "In the future you will see the Son of Man sitting at the right hand of the Mighty One and coming on the clouds of heaven" (Matthew 26:64; Mark 14:62; see Luke 22:69).

Our text at the beginning reminds us of Christ's mission as the Son of Man. It was a role assumed to serve (to minister), to suffer (give His life), and to save (ransom for many). The Son of God became the Son of Man that we might become sons of God.[7]

August 12

You have forgotten that word of encouragement that addresses you as sons: "My son, do not make light of the Lord's discipline, and do not lose heart when he rebukes you, because the Lord disciplines those he loves, and he punishes everyone he accepts as a son" (Hebrews 12:5,6).

*W*hen I become an adult, get married, and have children, I'm going to discipline my children different than my parents disciplined me. Just wait and see." Thus spoke a 15-year-old. And if we waited around for another 15 years and observed this adolescent-turned-parent, he or she would probably be following the pattern of his or her parents regardless of the earlier self-proclaimed intentions. But at least there was a desire to discipline.

Some parents violate God's pattern by failing to discipline. You don't show love nor do your children a favor when you neglect to discipline them. Hebrews 12:11 says, "No discipline seems pleasant at the time, but painful. Later on, however, it produces a harvest of righteousness and peace for those who have been trained by it." There is a purpose for discipline.

The Old Testament gives a dramatic portrayal of what happens when a parent fails to apply discipline (1 Samuel 2:12-36). Eli did not restrain his sons, and the Scripture states they were wicked. They were spiritually bankrupt.

As a parent you really don't have the option *not* to discipline. It's a duty, but it's also a privilege. A time of correction is an opportunity to train, educate, and demonstrate love. Make it a learning experience. Don't take all the responsibility upon yourself to explain. Ask your child what happened, what the consequences ought to be, and what he or she will do differently the next time. In addition, both mother and father need to agree on every aspect of the disciplining process—the infraction, the mode of discipline, and so on. Make every discipline encounter a growth experience for each person involved, not just the child. Ask yourself the same question you ask your child: "How might I respond differently the next time I need to discipline?" It may make a difference in all of your lives.

Give thanks in all circumstances, for this is God's will for you in Christ Jesus (1 Thessalonians 5:18).

*A*ttitude. What is it? It's a choice we make to look at life in a certain way. It determines the atmosphere of our home and the way we interact with other people.

Some people claim they were born with a gloomy disposition. Perhaps some of your children seem to have been born with an abundance of gratitude genes whereas other children seem to be shortchanged. Some have a sore disposition whereas others can be ridiculously cheerful and grateful.

Yet we don't inherit gratitude genes from our parents. We choose to display gratitude. We can choose to be thankful and look for the best and the blessings rather than the defects. We can make a choice to search, discover, and not take for granted what we have or experience.

Gratitude unexpressed is wasted. If kept private, its benefit is never fully experienced by you or others. A sense of gratitude can be infectious; it can impact the attitude of others.

We teach our children to say, "Thank you." It's even more important to teach them to thank God for all that we are, all that we have, and all that we delight in. Again and again the psalms say, "Oh, give thanks to the Lord" or, "I will give thanks to the Lord."

What are you thankful for? Take a few moments and write your answer. Could it be there is some gratitude that needs expression in a phone call or a note? What are your children thankful for? I wonder what will happen when you look at your child and say, "I'm so thankful for you"?

Ask each family member today what he or she is thankful for. Never take one another for granted, but let everyone know your heartfelt thanks. If it's difficult to see what you can be thankful for, begin to look with new eyes—with God's perspective. Ask Him to illumine the eyes of your heart.

August 14

Be very careful, then, how you live—not as unwise but as wise, making the most of every opportunity, because the days are evil. Therefore do not be foolish, but understand what the Lord's will is (Ephesians 5:15-17).

*Y*ou're wasting time." Perhaps you grew up hearing that phrase again and again. For some of us it stuck in our minds and became a guilt-prodding stimulus that still exerts its control today. But for others of us, it had no impact whatsoever. Somewhere there's got to be a balance.

Sometimes the generations clash over how people use their time. Those who were raised in the depression of the thirties and the war years of the forties lived in a survival mode that is much different from the way we live today. Values and long hours for the sake of survival have been replaced by new values and long hours for the sake of obtaining more material items. How we use our time, though, is still an issue no matter what generation we're from.

Perhaps you make good use of your time and are diligent and hard-working. How do you feel and respond when you see another family member just lounging around and accomplishing nothing? Or maybe your marriage partner is a compulsive workaholic who can't stand to see you rest when you're exhausted.

The real issue, however, is not *how* you make use of your time. You can be busy and still not do much. It's *what* you do that has value. Paul said to "make the *most* of your time."

Have you ever asked the other members of your family, "What did you do of value today?" Try it. You'll also want to look back over the last seven days and ask yourself that same question for each day.

Start each day by asking, "What will I do of value today?" Some families gather at the end of the day and ask, "What did each of us do of value today, and what would the Lord like us to do tomorrow?" This discussion time has changed many a family. It's worth a try.

August 15

Moses built an altar and called it The Lord is my Banner. He said, "For hands were lifted up to the throne of the Lord. The Lord will be at war against the Amalekites from generation to generation" (Exodus 17:15,16).

*H*ow long are you able to hold your hands up over your head? Try that sometime with your children. Aside from the laughter you'll all experience, you'll discover some new muscles. Your arms get tired when you try to hold them up by yourself.

Moses knew all about that. The children of Israel were engaged in a battle against the Amalekites. While this was going on, Moses was on a hill praying to the Lord. As long as his arms were lifted up in prayer, Israel was winning. But just like us, his arms got tired, and when he dropped them the Amalekites began to win. So Aaron and Hur came over and held up his arms as he prayed. The result? Israel won.

Figuratively speaking, wouldn't you like someone to hold up your arms like that? Sometimes we say, "We're holding up another person in prayer."

There are different ways we can support and help one another. When our spouse or child is feeling down or exhausted, we can give him or her a back rub. We can ask other family members how they would like us to pray for them during the day. We can let them know that we're holding them up in prayer even when they don't request it.

As a family, who could you hold up in prayer? Is it your pastor, your child's teacher, your employer? If your children see you ministering to other people in this way, this practice may become a part of their lives.

There's one last question to consider. In what way do *you* need to be held up by others? Family members sometimes need to be reminded that you, too, have needs. It's all right to mention your needs. In fact, it's all right to discuss them together as a family.

August 16

Do not conform any longer to the pattern of this world, but be transformed by the renewing of your mind. Then you will be able to test and approve what God's will is—his good, pleasing and perfect will (Romans 12:2).

*P*ut off until tomorrow..."

Wait a minute—we're told not to put things off until tomorrow. But there are exceptions, as Lloyd Ogilvie has suggested.

When a difficult problem must be solved or a hard choice must be made, tell the Lord about it, praise Him for it, and then put off the resolution until He has full access to your mind and imagination. After the initial praise, thank Him constantly that the answer is on the way and that, in time and on time, you will know what He wants you to do.

A woman came to see me about her "unsolvable problems." When we got into the specific problems, she confessed that she did not know how to pray. We talked through the potential of praise for each of the needs. In a time of prayer with her, I asked for the anointing of the Holy Spirit on her will and imagination. She started experimenting with a kind of "release through rejoicing" prayer therapy. She is a competent executive with a large company. Her thoroughness and attention to detail were utilized in keeping a log which has become a kind of spiritual autobiography. She kept track of problems surrendered with praise. The amazing thing to her was the new freedom to imagine solutions to the very problems that had brought her to see me.

Henry Drummond once said, "There is a will of God for me which is willed for no one else besides. It is a particular will for me, different from the will He has for anyone else—a private will—a will which no one else knows about."

By the use of the word "private," he did not mean that the will of God for each of us is separatistic, freeing us from responsibility for others. Rather, God has a personal will for each of us, as a part of the eternal purpose of God.[8]

August 17

Even to your old age and gray hairs I am he, I am he who will sustain you (Isaiah 46:4).

*W*eary? Frazzled? Worn out? Children get this way and need the arms of their mother or father. Parents get this way and also need another person's arms. Consider these words:

Yesterday, I observed a young child in the mall, laughing and running without a concern in the world. When she suddenly drooped, as small children will, her father picked her up, positioned her head so it rested on his shoulder and carried her. She went instantly and soundly to sleep.

I really wouldn't want to be two years old again. But sometimes I think it would be grand to experience that pressure-free existence when Mom and Dad took care of *everything*.

On one of my draggy, dreary days God showed me that He does exactly that! Even though my gray hairs now outnumber the brown, God still cares for me as His *child*.

I read the following passage slowly, then inwardly shouted, *Hallelujah!* Isaiah 47:3-4 says, "Listen to me . . . you whom I have upheld since you were conceived, and have carried since your birth. Even to your old age and gray hairs I am he, I am he who will sustain you. I have made you and I will carry you; I will sustain you and I will rescue you."

I grabbed a pen and paper and scribbled:

> God *upholds* me when I am about to fall.
> When I am despondent and discouraged,
>   He's the "lifter of my head."
> He *carries* me when I have no strength of my own,
>   when I am helpless,
>   and for all of my life—from birth to death.
> He *sustains* me when I am weary, worn out,
>   when those I love can't,
>   when friends turn away,
>   when support systems collapse.
> He *rescues* me when fear overtakes me,
>   when enemies surround me.
> What a fantastic Father![9]

August 18

A patient man has great understanding, but a quick-tempered man displays folly (Proverbs 14:29).

*H*ave you ever...

✦ waited in line at the bank for ten minutes only to discover that the person immediately in front of you has a stack of business deposits and receipts to reconcile with the bank teller?

✦ waited in the grocery line while the person in front of you pulls out 200 coupons to wade through?

✦ put gas in your car only to have the pump break down and the nozzle stick in your gas tank?

✦ had the key you're using to open your car door (which also fits the ignition) break off in the door?

Yes! Welcome to life in the fast lane! We fuss, fume, fret, and flip out over "minor" daily occurrences like these. And then someone tells us to be patient.

These are the times when it's so easy to light the fuse that soon leads to a blowup. And usually the eruption is more intense than the circumstances warranted.

How can a parent or anyone handle these unexpected delays? The answer is in the question—the unexpected. Always expect the unexpected. That's not being pessimistic, but realistic. Life will not always go the way you think it should. Begin each day by saying, "Something is not going to go the way I want it to go today, and that's all right. I can handle it." Then when the unexpected happens, you're ready for it.

Part of our problem with unexpected delays is that we may be trying to put two quarts of time into a one-quart container. Some people look at the amount of time they have available and determine they can accomplish seven tasks during that time. It doesn't always work. Cut the number of tasks in half, and your day is likely to go smoother.

Life with its twists and turns can take charge of you, or you can exercise patience and take charge of it in a new way. It's your choice.

August 19

And I will do whatever you ask in my name, so that the Son may bring glory to the Father. You may ask me for anything in my name, and I will do it (John 14:13,14).

*W*hen you pray for your children, do you also pray for yourself? Sometimes the changes we pray for in our children don't materialize because we're not seeking some needed changes in our own lives.

What change needs to be made in your life? What do you need to pray about? Sometimes the insight of other parents can help us develop sensitivity to changes we need to make. Consider this prayer from *The Power of a Praying Parent.*

Lord,

I submit myself to You. I realize that parenting a child in the way You would have me to is beyond my human abilities. I know I need You to help me. I want to partner with You and partake of Your gifts of wisdom, discernment, revelation, and guidance. I also need Your strength and patience, along with a generous portion of Your love flowing through me. Teach me how to love the way You love. Where I need to be healed, delivered, changed, matured, or made whole, I invite You to do that in me. Help me to walk in righteousness and integrity before You. Teach me Your ways, enable me to obey Your commandments and do only what is pleasing in Your sight. May the beauty of Your Spirit be so evident in me that I will be a godly role model. Give me the communication, teaching, and nurturing skills that I must have. Make me the parent You want me to be and teach me how to pray and truly intercede for the life of this child. Lord, You said in Your Word, "Whatever things you ask in prayer, believing, you will receive" (Matthew 21:22). In Jesus' name I ask that You will increase my faith to believe for all the things You've put on my heart to pray for concerning this child.[10]

August 20

...all night I soak my pillow with tears...for the Lord has heard the voice of my weeping (Psalm 6:6,8, AMP).

*D*o you cry? Oh, everyone cries at some time or another. But some people cry only on the inside. Do you allow yourself the expression of tears? After all, they are one of God's gifts. Consider this from the pen of Max Lucado:

Before we bid goodbye to those present at the cross, I have one more introduction to make. This introduction is very special.

There was one group in attendance that day whose role was critical. They didn't speak much, but they were there. Few noticed them, but that's not surprising. Their very nature is so silent they are often overlooked. In fact, the gospel writers scarcely gave them a reference. But we know they were there. They had to be. They had a job to do.

Yes, this representation did much more than witness the divine drama; they expressed it. They captured it. They displayed the despair of Peter; they betrayed the guilt of Pilate and unveiled the anguish of Judas. They transmitted John's confusion and translated Mary's compassion.

Their prime role, however, was with that of the Messiah. With utter delicacy and tenderness, they offered relief to his pain and expression to his yearning.

Who am I describing? You may be surprised.

Tears.

Those tiny drops of humanity. Those round, wet balls of fluid that tumble from our eyes, creep down our cheeks, and splash on the floor of our hearts. They were there that day. They are always present at such times. They should be; that's their job. They are miniature messengers; on call twenty-four hours a day to substitute for crippled words. They drip, drop, and pour from the corner of our souls, carrying with them the deepest emotions we possess. They tumble down our faces with announcements that range from the most blissful joy to darkest despair.

The principle is simple; when words are most empty, tears are most apt.[11]

When you cry, and you will as a parent, be thankful for your tears. And never apologize for them. After all, you don't have to apologize for something that's a gift from God.

August 21

*Forgetting what is behind and straining toward what is ahead,
I press on . . .* (Philippians 3:13,14).

*T*he past. What do you do with it? Or, what do you let it do to you? We think about what happened yesterday with the children, or less recently during our adolescent years, or even back to our own dealings with our parents. And sometimes we feel regret. We say, "If only I had . . ." or "Oh, how I regret . . ." or, "If only I could have done it differently I wouldn't be in this plight today." Have you ever made a list of your "if onlys"?

Whether we *regret* what was done to us by others or what we have done to others, looking back at the past only cripples the blessings of the present and deters us from entering the future. It's not that we should never regret the past. There is a place for regret—once! And then we must begin moving in a new direction.

Another dangerous tactic we use in handling the past is *recrimination*. We attempt to make others atone for what they did to us in the painful past. Blame and recrimination bring us to resentment, which leads to a lack of forgiveness, and we end up with memories that fester within us.

Another common response to the past is *renunciation*: We promise to change and do things differently. Past behaviors and attitudes are simply renounced, but they are not confronted and cleansed.[12]

Instead of dragging along the unnecessary baggage of regret, blame, and renunciation, have you ever tried *rejoicing* over the past? That may sound strange, but rejoicing eventually brings release. Rejoicing over the past doesn't mean that you deny the hurtful incidents or the pain they brought you. Rather, it helps you come to the point where you no longer ask *why* but *how:* How can I learn from what happened to me and be a different person because of it?

Eventually, your children will need to learn how to deal with their past. How they see you handling your past will be a model for them. What a wonderful opportunity you have to teach them how rather than *why!*

August 22

Love . . . is not easily angered, it keeps no record of wrongs. . . .
It always protects, always trusts, always hopes, always perse-
veres. Love never fails. . . . And now these three remain: faith,
hope and love. But the greatest of these is love (1 Corinthians
13:4,5,7,8,13).

A Prayer to Give to a Child About to Be Married

Lord, we believe that You ordained marriage
and that You also sustain it.

Help us to exercise faith.
Faith that You answer prayer
and heal wounded hearts.
Faith that You forgive and restore.
Faith that Your hand of love
will clasp our hands together.
Faith that You build bridges of reconciliation.
Faith that all things will work for good
to those who love You.

Help us to hold on to hope.
Hope that enables us to endure
times of trial and testing.
Hope that fixes our gaze on possibilities
rather than problems.
Hope that focuses on the road ahead
instead of detours already passed.
Hope that instills trust, even in the midst
of failure.
Hope that harbors happiness.

Help us to lift up love.
Love that doesn't falter or faint
in the winds of adversity.
Love that is determined to grow and bear fruit.
Love that is slow to anger and quick to praise.
Love that looks for ways of saying,
"I care for you."
Love that remains steady during shaky days.

Lord, may Your gifts of faith, hope and love find plenty of living room in our hearts. Thank You that these three abide—and the
greatest is love. Make our home an outpost for Your kingdom and
an oasis for wandering pilgrims. In the name of Jesus who blessed
the marriage at Cana with a miracle. Amen.[13]

The law was given through Moses; grace and truth came through Jesus Christ (John 1:17).

*R*ules, rules, rules. We all have to live by them to a certain extent. Our society wouldn't be able to function without rules. As a parent, you're the creator and enforcer of certain rules in your own household. Unfortunately, in some families people go to the extreme with rules. They make life restrictive and burdensome, and live in a self-imposed bondage. And they expect others to do likewise. This becomes legalism.

Fortunately, the Christian life is one lived by grace. If you were asked to define *grace*, what would you say? To understand grace, you need to know about an old Hebrew term that means "to bend or to stoop." Eventually it came to encompass the idea of "condescending favor."[14]

The best description comes from Charles Swindoll, who says,

> If you have traveled to London, you have perhaps seen royalty. If so, you may have noticed sophistication, aloofness, distance. On occasion, royalty in England will make the news because someone in the ranks of nobility will stop, kneel down, and touch or bless a commoner. That is grace. There is nothing in the commoner that deserves being noticed or touched or blessed by the royal family. But because of grace in the heart of the queen, there is the desire at that moment to pause, to stoop, to touch, even to bless.
>
> To show grace is to extend favor or kindness to one who doesn't deserve it and can never earn it. Receiving God's acceptance by grace always stands in sharp contrast to earning it on the basis of works. Every time the thought of grace appears, there is the idea of its being undeserved. In no way is the recipient getting the idea of its being undeserved. In no way is the recipient getting what he or she deserves. Favor is being extended simply out of the goodness of the heart of the giver.[15]

How is grace manifested in your home? In what way would an expression of grace on your part cheer up another family member? In what way would an expression of grace cheer you up?

Jesus was the manifestation of grace to each of us. Time and time again Jesus smiled with favor on others. That's grace. Our world could use a lot more of it. Wouldn't you agree?

August 24

He did right in the sight of the Lord and walked in all the ways of David his [forefather], and turned not aside to the right hand or to the left (2 Kings 22:2, AMP).

*T*his verse is talking about a man by the name of Josiah, who came from a dysfunctional family. In fact, he came from a family that was dysfunctional for generations. His parents, grandparents, and more were idolators, sorcerers, and murderers. That is the legacy Josiah brought with him to the throne when he became king. But he didn't let that influence him. He chose to turn that around. He left a positive legacy as evidenced by 2 Kings 22:2.

All of us will leave a legacy. Some of that legacy will be etched on our tombstones, and some of it on other people's hearts. Tim Kimmel's family has a burial plot that includes five generations. Sometimes he goes there to visit the site. These are his thoughts from one of his visits.

Below the names on these tombstones are epitaphs, marble and granite phrases that try to say in a handful of words what a person's life said over many years.

But true epitaphs are not carved in stone. They are carved in the souls and memories of men and women, boys and girls. Regardless of what my ancestors' tombstones say, the words can never overwrite what those individuals *were*. That's why God leaves the last word on our life to those we leave behind.

Maybe this helps you understand why I like to come out here. It's not some morbid preoccupation with the past. It's perspective. It's a reminder to me that I, too, am going to get my turn at being a memory...that I am writing my epitaph now, on the hearts of my children.

They will sum up my life some day. And that sum total will have a deep and abiding effect on the lives that they end up leading.

By the way, how are you doing on writing your epitaph?

We all have to remember that we are not curators of the dead, we are stewards of the living. We are surrounded by the children we must move into tomorrow. Someday we will stand before the God who bought our eternal souls on the cross.

Now we are leaving a legacy. Then we will give an account. Between now and then is all the time that we have left.[16]

Come, all you who are thirsty, come to the waters; and you who have no money, come, buy and eat! Come, buy wine and milk without money and without cost (Isaiah 55:1).

*M*om . . . Mom . . . Mother! I'm thirsty!"
      "Daddy! Daddy! I need you . . . now!"
You've heard it before. You'll hear it again. The cry of a child who has a basic need that requires fulfillment.

You have some of the same needs, the same longings. You were born with these God-given longings, and Scripture describes them as hunger and thirst:

> Everyone who thirsts (Isaiah 55:1, NKJV).
> My soul thirsts . . . my flesh longs (Psalm 63:1, NKJV).
> My soul longs (Psalm 84:2, NKJV).
> The longing soul . . . the hungry soul (Psalm 107:9, NKJV).

All of us, including our children, desire to be wanted by another person. We want to be valued by another. We want to be accepted for who we are rather than what we do. We want some significant person to reach out and say, "I choose you. I want you in my life." We want to be loved with no conditions and no reservations. We want to belong and to have someone who never fails to know our needs be there to meet our needs and never fail. That's a tall order!

Where are the people who can do all that? Where are the spouses, the parents, the children who can fit this description? They're non-existent except in our fantasies. It would be nice to have other people be this consistent, but we'd feel uncomfortable with them. Why? Because we're not that consistent. We couldn't meet their needs in the same way. The only one who can do all this is God.

> O God, you are my God, earnestly I seek you; my soul thirsts for you, my body longs for you, in a dry and weary land where there is no water (Psalm 63:1).

> He satisfies the thirsty and fills the hungry with good things (Psalm 107:9).

It's reassuring to know there is someone who *can* truly quench our thirst.[17]

August 26

After the Feast was over, while his parents were returning home, the boy Jesus stayed behind in Jerusalem, but they were unaware of it (Luke 2:43).

*H*ave you ever left your child somewhere, thinking all the time that he or she was with your spouse? It happened to Jesus' parents.

Imagine not being able to find your child for three or four days. What would go through your mind? Would you feel panic, anxiety, worry, blame, or guilt? You wouldn't be able to sleep and eventually soon you would imagine the worst.

Jesus' parents were just like you. You see, Jesus was a child like other children. And the scene described above is a common one for parents.

Then they found Him. He was sitting in the temple teaching the teachers. When Jesus was confronted by His parents, He simply said, "Didn't you know I had to be in my Father's house?" (verse 49).

Jesus our Savior started out as a baby much like all other babies. But He was different as a boy. When He sat and talked with some of the brightest minds of the day in the temple, they were amazed. And His parents were astonished. It seems as if a new side of their son was revealed that day.

That's the way it is when you're a parent. Your baby becomes a child, then a teenager, and finally an adult. Each stage brings you the opportunity to be astonished.

How have your children astonished you? Have you written that down? Have you shared that with anyone? Be sure you save your memories because someday they will be very important to you.

There's a beautiful response from Mary about what she learned that day when she found Jesus: "His mother treasured all these things in her heart" (verse 51). Children provide us with experiences to treasure. What do you treasure right now? If you've noticed something to be treasured, why not let your child know?[18]

August 27

*But God will redeem my life from the grave; he will surely take
me to himself* (Psalm 49:15).

*H*ave you ever done anything wrong? Of course. Have your
children? Definitely! Will they continue to do wrong
things? Yes, they will. What is one way we respond when we say
or do something we know we shouldn't have done? We try to
make up for it.

Perhaps you've had times when your children's behavior is exceptionally good to the point that you get a bit suspicious. It's as
though you sense they've done something wrong and you don't
know what it is, but they're trying to make up for it. Such behavior is typical and normal. We all do it. Pastor Rudolph Norden
shares an interesting example of a man who did this:

> On the fateful night that President Abraham Lincoln was shot,
> the assassin, John Wilkes Booth, having suffered a broken leg in
> jumping from the presidential box onto the stage of Ford's Theater,
> rode off into Maryland. There a country doctor, Dr. Samuel A.
> Mudd, set the leg, apparently without asking any questions. For
> aiding and abetting a criminal, Dr. Mudd was sentenced to prison.
> A few years later, when an epidemic broke out at Fort Jefferson in
> the Florida Keys, Dr. Mudd rendered heroic services and was in
> 1869 pardoned by President Andrew Johnson. In a way, the doctor
> made up for his misdeed, if such it was.[19]

The Word of God sometimes calls sin "error" or "errors":

> Who can discern his errors? Forgive my hidden faults (Psalm
> 19:12).

> Remember this: Whoever turns a sinner from the error of his
> way will save him from death and cover over a multitude of sins
> (James 5:20).

Some people don't like the word *sin*, so they call their misdeeds
mistakes, mishaps, or even errors. But it's all the same. The problem is that when it comes to sin, we can't make up for it. That's
the bad news. The good news, however, is that Jesus can make up
for it. He has covered us with His blood. Our redemption is complete, and we can rest in that thought the rest of our lives![20]

August 28

For God so loved the world that he gave his one and only Son, that whoever believes in him shall not perish but have eternal life (John 3:16).

Several kinds of love are mentioned in Scripture. There is *eros*, the romantic kind of love that gives you funny feelings in your stomach. And there's *storge*, the love that we experience for our family members. And of course there's *phileo*, which is known as friendship love.

But the sacrificial love that Jesus modeled for us is called *agape*. It's an unselfish love that gives of itself and doesn't expect anything back. Of course, that's easy to say and hard to do.

Agape is the love that grows and expands as you give it. It's the unconditional love God gives us regardless of who we are or what we've done. It is undeserved love. It's what God wants us to practice toward other people, especially fellow family members.

It's not natural to love this way. We want others to deserve our love. But does anyone ever really deserve love? No, because we're all inconsistent.

How do you make *agape* love a part of your life? Like the ads say, just do it. When you took music lessons, what one word did the teacher constantly stress? *Practice.* If you went out for sports, the coach stressed practice. "Show up for practice. Don't miss practice." The more you practice *agape* love, the *more* you will have to give other people, the more you will *feel* like giving, and the more you *will* give. Can you imagine a world where everyone practices *agape* love?

Some people think it's impossible to love this way. That's true; it is. It's only as you experience and receive the love of Christ that *agape* love is possible.[21]

August 29

Blessed are the peacemakers, for they will be called sons of God
(Matthew 5:9).

*D*o you want a peaceful home? So many parents cry out, "If only we could get along and have peace between the kids!" or, "All I want is some peace and quiet!" Many homes are characterized more by warfare than by peace and mutual love.

Peace, in the Bible, doesn't just mean freedom from all trouble. Rather, it means focusing on and promoting everything that is beneficial and good. Peace means overcoming hostility.

Most people say they love peace. But Scripture says, "Blessed are the peace*makers*," not just the peace lovers. It's possible to love peace so much that we won't take action to correct something that is wrong.

Consider your family members. Who are the peacemakers? On the other hand, who creates the storms that trouble and upset other people? Who are the quarrelers? These family members need to be shown a better and more productive way to live.

How can you bring peace into a family? Consider these words from Paul: "Do not repay anyone evil for evil. Be careful to do what is right in the eyes of everybody. If it is possible, as far as it depends on you, live at peace with everyone" (Romans 12:17,18).

Paul is realistic. He said, "If it is possible. . . ." You work at peace regardless of what the other person does. Sometimes we allow ourselves to be drawn into the same behavior that's shown by the other person. Don't retaliate. There's a better way. If another person gets defensive, don't bring out the artillery for an onslaught. Tear down your own defenses. Become vulnerable. Don't assume a person is out to attack you. He or she may change when you change your responses first. When you do the unexpected, it throws the other person off balance. Peter says, "Whoever would love life and see good days must keep his tongue from evil and his lips from deceitful speech. He must turn from evil and do good; he must seek peace and pursue it" (1 Peter 3:10,11).

August 30

To this you were called, because Christ suffered for you, leaving you an example, that you should follow in his steps (1 Peter 2:21).

*A*s a parent you've probably told your child, "Now watch me. Do this the way I do it. Just follow me." But what does it really mean to follow another person—especially the way today's verse states?

Perhaps (years ago) in school you heard about or read Walt Whitman. He's best known for his work *Leaves of Grass*. What most people don't know about Walt was the deep love and concern he had for people. During the Civil War he volunteered to help some 80,000 wounded soldiers. That experience had a great impact upon him, and his feelings of sympathy and empathy grew to such an extent that he would feel what the hurting soldiers felt. One time he said, "I don't ask the wounded person how he feels; I myself become the wounded person."

Have you as a parent done that when your children are hurting? The Good Samaritan did that for the wounded man on the road. He put himself in the man's place.

You know, we're all spiritually wounded. Left to ourselves we would all expire quickly. But someone has rushed to our rescue just as you rush to help your children: Jesus Christ. He doesn't ever pass us by. He becomes what we are—wounded.

> He was pierced for our transgressions, he was crushed for our iniquities; the punishment that brought us peace was upon him, and by his wounds we are healed (Isaiah 53:5).

> He himself bore our sins in his body on the tree, so that we might die to sins and live for righteousness; by his wounds you have been healed (1 Peter 2:24).

Not only does Jesus save us, He also sets the example for the way we're to reach into the lives of other people who need help. Who do you know that is wounded and needs you to feel what he or she is experiencing? What can you do to rescue him or her?[22]

August 31

*You, my brothers, were called to be free. But do not use your
freedom to indulge the sinful nature; rather, serve one another
in love* (Galatians 5:13).

Sometimes getting information from the horse's mouth will
give us the best advice and guidance. Read what three grown
children said about how their parents helped them grow.

A daughter shared,

> My parents have made a lot of decisions for me and yet have
> made me make a lot of decisions. They have given me freedom
> when I've shown I can handle it responsibly—and even when I
> haven't been responsible, just to let me know I'm an individual
> who has worth and importance. Later on I will become responsible
> in certain areas that I might not be doing well in right now.

A son shared,

> As I look back, I know my parents have really cared about our
> lives and what we've been interested in. They haven't said, "Kids,
> we're going to do this because your father and I want you to do
> this," or anything like that.
>
> They consulted us about activities we wanted. We spend at least
> an hour or two doing something with our parents each weekend—
> different kinds of activities that kids usually do. My dad and I got
> a little airplane that we put fuel into, and we held it by a string as
> it flew around in the air. We also got interested in train sets and
> spent some of our activity time on them. That was really fun! I know
> most of my friends' parents never took time for special activities
> with them; so I feel that really shows my parents' interest in my life.[23]

In a letter to his father Tony, Bart Campolo reflected on how his
parents helped him grow:

> . . . That's what real freedom is, I think: the understanding that
> in a world filled with choices and decisions, under tremendous
> pressure from other people and our own desires, amid the para-
> lyzing fear of mistakes or failure, loving God and loving His
> people are the only things that really matter, and doing those
> things is a decision that we genuinely have the ability to make in
> every situation.
>
> You and Mom didn't let me do whatever I wanted to, Dad, but
> you gave me my freedom nonetheless. I think I finally appreciate it.
>
> Love, Bart[24]

September 1

Children's children are a crown to the aged, and parents are the pride of their children (Proverbs 17:6).

*T*hat's my dad." "That's my mom. She's the second one from the left, with the funny hat on." "My dad is the greatest fisherman in our family." These are statements of pride coming from the mouths of children.

What qualities or abilities do your parents have that you're proud about? To be proud of another person means you have delight or satisfaction in who that person is or what he or she has achieved. When have you told your parents (or an aunt or uncle) that you're proud of them and why you're proud? Doing that could really make their day.

It's all right to be proud of other people. It begins early in life with our children. We take pride in our children's expressions, first steps, ability to read, and so on. It's common to hear parents say, "Her reading ability is three years above where she should be!" or, "We took our daughter deep-sea fishing when she was six years old and she hooked and landed three big barracudas all by herself!"

Children can also be proud of their parents. In fact, if children are proud of certain character qualities they see in their parents, they may want to incorporate those qualities into their own lives.

What qualities in your life can your child be proud about? It could be an achievement, your position at church or in the community, or an ability. But what about pride over what you believe, what you stand for, your values, and the way you are consistent and fair in your love and response to your children? These actually have more value for your children's lives.

Give your children something to be proud of. It's all right if they brag about you. It's all right for them to look out into the audience and, with a smile on their face, say, "That's my mom. That's my dad. They're special." What a gift to you!

September 2

Commit your way to the Lord, trust also in Him (Psalm 37:5, NASB).

A Message to a Child on the Eve
of His or Her Marriage

Marriage—A Lifetime of Memories

As you begin your marriage, you will begin to accumulate memories. What will make the difference in the quality of your memories? There is just one word—commitment.

One word? Yes, but a costly word that can bring tension and questions at the same time it brings peace, maturity, and stability.

As you walk through life, which brings rapid, unexpected changes, unfairness, tragedy, and unanswered questions, commitment to living by faith will guide you through the journey.

Commit your life to the person of Jesus Christ, who is the Son of God. Make this a daily decision together.

Commit your life to the Word of God, which brings stability and peace. Read this daily together.

Commit yourself to seeing your spouse as having such worth, value, and dignity that God sent His Son to die for him or her.

Commit yourselves as a couple to prayer. There is no greater intimacy than when a couple opens their hearts to God together. This enhances the completeness and oneness of a couple and helps put their differences and adjustments in a better perspective. Lines open to God are invariably open to one another, for you cannot be genuinely open to God and closed to your partner.

Commit your life to giving your marriage top priority in terms of time, energy, thought, and planning for growth.

Commit yourself to a life of fidelity and faithfulness regardless of your feelings or the lure of life around you.

Commit and open yourself to the working of the Holy Spirit in your life. "When the Holy Spirit controls our lives he will produce this kind of fruit in us: love, joy, peace, patience, kindness, goodness, faithfulness, gentleness and self-control" (Galatians 5:22,23, TLB).

Faith, hope, and love will grow out of your commitment to one another and to God and His Word.

September 3

The character of even a child can be known by the way he acts—whether what he does is pure and right (Proverbs 20:11, TLB)

If you must choose, take a good name rather than great riches; for to be held in loving esteem is better than silver and gold (Proverbs 22:1, TLB).

*H*ow would you describe your own reputation? You have one, you know. So does each member of your family. Do you know what *reputation* means? It means "the estimation in which a person or thing is commonly held, whether favorable or not."[1] Sometimes people will say, "What's your estimation of so-and-so?"

Parents can help their children develop their reputation by what they do and say. We see this in 1 Timothy 4:12: "Don't let anyone think little of you because you are young. Be their ideal; let them follow the way you teach and live; be a pattern for them in your love, your faith, and your clean thoughts" (TLB).

Our reputations start early in life. Sometimes children have a reputation by the time they enter school. Right or wrong, once a reputation begins, it tends to be reinforced and perpetuated by other people whether we like it or not. It's important, then, that children learn at an early age to be conscious of how what they say and do will impact other people's perceptions of them. They need to be aware of the opinions people have about them.

Some parents say, "Never forget that you're a Smith [or a MacFarland, or a . . .] ." What they are saying is, "Never shame our family name." There's another family name to be aware of as well: Don't forget that you're a Christian. Other people will check us out to see if we live up to that!

As parents it's OK to be concerned about our children's reputations. But there's another reputation to be more concerned about—your own. That's because it has a direct effect on your children's reputations. Paul urges us to handle ourselves so that "the way you live will always please the Lord and honor him, so that you will always be doing good, kind things for others, while all the time you are learning to know God better and better" (Colossians 1:10, TLB).[2]

September 4

A fool shows his annoyance at once, but a prudent man over-looks an insult" (Proverbs 12:16).

I'm insulted by that comment." We've all felt the sting of an insult. It hurts. It cuts. And it's even worse when it comes from another family member.

The place where life ought to be the safest is often the riskiest—the home. We cut loose at home more than we do elsewhere. All it takes is a bit of sarcasm to unleash a counterattack, and soon it's a matter of who can top who! Why is the home so vulnerable to attack?

First, in the family, you know each other so well that you know where to jab. Children as well as spouses look for targets either to get a reaction or to retaliate. Even when we know there will be retaliation we still do it.

Another reason we attack each other is because we know we can get away with it. You can't resign from your family or fire family members. You're stuck with each other. Sometimes a family member will insult someone and then cover up with, "I was just kidding." Proverbs addresses that, saying, "Like a madman who casts firebrands, arrows, and death, so is the man who deceives his neighbor and then says, Was I not joking?" (Proverbs 26:18,19, AMP).

A third reason the home is so vulnerable is because we live in a society in which humor is built around insults and sarcasm. What do you and your family watch on television? Sitcoms abound with insults, put-downs, and sarcasm. It's easy to imitate what we see, especially if we get a steady diet of it. But Scripture calls us not to be conformed to this world, and that includes humor.

There's a better way to relate as a family, and Peter described it: "You should be like one big happy family, full of sympathy toward each other, loving one another with tender hearts and humble minds. Don't repay evil for evil. Don't snap back at those who say unkind things about you. Instead, pray for God's help for them, for we are to be kind to others, and God will bless us for it" (1 Peter 3:8,9, TLB).[3]

September 5

We have different gifts, according to the grace given us. . . . if it is contributing to the needs of others, let him give generously (Romans 12:6,8).

*G*enerous. Perhaps that's the best word for describing a person with the gift of giving. In the NKJV and NASB translations the verse is translated "he who gives, with liberality." In the original Greek text, the word "give" means "to share a thing with anyone, or to impart." Once again Webster's Dictionary gives us food for thought. There we read that to give is "to be the source, produce; supply; as, cows give milk."[4] A cow cannot *not* give milk. That's their function. And it's the same with a parent or any person who has the gift of giving. They can't help but give. Their whole lifestyle is that of giving. It's a natural, built-in habit.

The concept of giving is a bit foreign to the thinking in our culture today. A person gives by turning over possessions or control of something to another person with no strings attached. There is no cost to the recipient. There is no bartering. The gift is given freely. Givers also will look for ways to give without drawing attention to themselves. And they enjoy giving without the pressure of an appeal. Similarly, parents look for ways to give to their children without the children demanding, expecting, or using some ploy to get what they want.

Giving sets a wonderful example for a child, because it helps them to gain an understanding of how God gives through their parents. And parents should encourage their children not only to give but to express gratitude for what they receive through verbal and written responses. Giving is especially wonderful when the giver is satisfied with whatever he himself has in life, whether a little or a lot.

If neither parent has the gift of giving it's possible to find other people who can become involved with the children so they can be exposed to a wide variety of God's gifts. Also, keep in mind that all gifts have a purpose, and one isn't any better than another. And even if giving isn't our natural gift, we can all learn to give in some way.[5]

September 6

When others are happy, be happy with them. If they are sad, share their sorrow. Work happily together. . . . Never pay back evil for evil. . . . Do things in such a way that everyone can see you are honest clear through. Don't quarrel with anyone. Be at peace with everyone, just as much as possible. Dear friends, never avenge yourselves. Leave that to God, for he has said that he will repay those who deserve it. [Don't take the law into your own hands.] Instead, feed your enemy if he is hungry. If he is thirsty give him something to drink and you will be "heaping coals of fire on his head" (Romans 12:15,17-20, TLB).

*I*f every family lived this out in their daily interactions, what a difference it would make! There are four guidelines here to make your life different.

First, learn to empathize with your family members. Don't pop their balloon when they're happy or joke around with them when they are sad. The writer of Proverbs said, "Being happy-go-lucky around a person whose heart is heavy is as bad as stealing his jacket in cold weather, or rubbing salt in his wounds" (Proverbs 25:20, TLB). Empathy enters into other people's lives so much that you feel what they feel—you walk with them in their shoes. Empathy may call for joy, delight, or sadness, but when you empathize, you are supporting and loving people.

The second guideline is to relate to everyone in the family as well as their friends. You may not naturally enjoy a particular age group, but avoiding a family member's peers, especially if they're different from you, won't make life any easier. Sometimes family members don't like to be seen with other family members. But anyone can learn to tolerate other people.

Third, don't try to get back at someone who hurts you. Let that person's comments or actions slide by. After all, if you retaliate, you become like that person. Is that what you want?

Finally, surprise those who hurt you by giving a gift. In Palestine, homes were heated by wood or charcoal, so if your fire went out, you were in deep trouble. There were no matches or lighters. So if an enemy was in need of live coals and you gave some to him, you were expressing great kindness, as Romans 12:20 says.

So . . . be generous. Be kind. Be different. And you and others will be blessed.[6]

September 7

How dare you tell me, "Flee to the mountains for safety," when I am trusting in the Lord? For the wicked have strung their bows, drawn their arrows tight against the bowstrings, and aimed from ambush at the people of God. "Law and order have collapsed," we are told. "What can the righteous do but flee?" But the Lord is still in his holy temple; he still rules from heaven. He closely watches everything that happens here on earth (Psalm 11:1-4, TLB).

I'm fed up with this neighborhood—the schools, the crime, the smog, the noise, the traffic—I'm out of here."

Millions of Americans move each year for a number of reasons. Some reasons are quite legitimate. Some people move up, some down, some away, and some move only in their minds. It's easy to get fed up with where we are and want a better place. But just because we move to a new environment doesn't mean we'll necessarily experience a difference in our lives. We may move to a different location, but all too often we take our issues and problems with us.

David, the writer of the psalm above, seems to be talking to many of us today. He reminds us that God still rules. Perhaps we need to focus on that fact as much or even more than how bad circumstances are around us.[7] It could make life more livable. Dean Merrill suggests that

> [w]hen we North American Christians get upset with our lot, we need to remember our brothers and sisters in places like the Ukraine. For seventy years Ukrainian believers raised godly offspring in a hostile setting. How did they manage? Every morning they got their children ready for school and said, "Now today you'll be told there is no God, that prayer is a joke, that church is a foolish exercise, that our pastor is a social parasite—but you know better. Hold on to the truth. Greater is he that is in you than he that is in the Soviet system."

The cure for our frustrations is not out there somewhere. It is in the character of God, who loves us and instills within us the fortitude to stand when life appears to be collapsing.[8]

September 8

. . . a time to be born and a time to die, a time to plant and a time to uproot . . . (Ecclesiastes 3:2).

*J*ust wait. Someday it will arrive—the empty nest. Some parents can't wait for it, others dread it.

For some couples, the empty nest is a major loss. It can bring on a mixture of different feelings as expressed in Ecclesiastes 3:1-8: weeping, laughing, mourning, healing, loving, releasing, losing, and relief. The atmosphere of the home changes. There are fewer choices to make, and there is less confusion and noise. Patterns of shopping, cooking, and scheduling will change. New roles must be established, and often new pressures are felt. Needs formerly filled by children will be diverted to other people. Sometimes an additional loss occurs if the parents try too hard to help each other to fill the empty spaces in their lives. They may end up pushing each other away because they're trying too hard, and a feeling of abandonment can result.

If a couple has relied upon the children to hold their relationship together or to preoccupy them, the last child's departure will create an enormous loss within the marital relationship. The mother who has relied upon her role as the primary source of her self-identity may end up feeling abandoned, unloved, uncared for, and depressed. If she also gave up a career to have children, the loss of the last child can elicit resentment.

If a woman's only role is that of a mother, the leaving of the last child is accompanied by the removal of her identity. Such a situation may also reveal that intimacy has been absent in the marriage for many years, for the camouflage is no longer there.

The empty nest also affects fathers. A child who was mother's little girl at age six may have become dad's special pal. When she leaves, he too, could feel devastated.

What will it be like for you? It's not too early to begin thinking and talking about it.[9]

September 9

Without faith it is impossible to please God, because anyone who comes to him must believe that he exists and that he rewards those who earnestly seek him (Hebrews 11:6).

*T*he original meaning of the word *worry* was "to kill a person or animal by compressing the throat; to strangle or choke." Today, *worry* means "joy killer," "to cause distress of mind; to make anxious and ill at ease."[10] Worry is the fear of what might or might not happen.

Is it wrong to worry? Parents worry, don't they? Don't they have good reason to worry in today's world?

Some people say that worry accuses God of being a liar. Those are strong words. But God *has* promised to meet our needs (Philippians 4:19), and worry says, "I don't think so." Worry also questions the sovereignty of God. In Romans 8:28 God promises to use everything that comes into our lives for good, even though we don't understand why or how.

When we worry, sometimes we also feel a bit abandoned by God. Yet Scripture says, "never will I leave you; never will I forsake you" (Hebrews 13:5,6). Worry also tends to erode our faith. But God has yet another promise: "Do not fear, for I am with you; do not be dismayed, for I am your God. I will strengthen you and help you; I will uphold you with my righteous right hand" (Isaiah 41:10).

So what is Scripture saying?

1. Don't fear. Why? Because I, God, am with you.
2. Don't be dismayed. Why? Because I am your God and I will strengthen you, help you, and uphold you.

Did you know that *dismayed* is a word used to describe someone who looks around in bewilderment? Perhaps in the midst of your worry you're unsure of any course of action and you feel helpless.

But look what God does. He strengthens us. *Strengthen* means "to be alert or fortified." The word *help* in biblical Greek means "to surround." You'll be protected on all sides. Finally, *uphold* means "to sustain." So, with all of what God has said He'll do, why worry?

Reading and memorizing the above promises can counteract our tendency to worry. Begin each day by reading them aloud. It's a good reminder.[11]

September 10

Better the little that the righteous have than the wealth of many wicked. . . . The days of the blameless are known to the LORD, *and their inheritance will endure forever. In times of disaster they will not wither; in days of famine they will enjoy plenty. . . . I was young and now I am old, yet I have never seen the righteous forsaken or their children begging bread* (Psalm 7:16,18,19,25).

Parenting, among other things, is *an act of financial faith.* If you were plotting your next twenty years with an eye to accumulate as much money as possible, you would never have kids. Kids are expensive—at least $100,000 apiece by the time you get them launched into adulthood and paying their own way. So if you take up the task of raising one or more children in North America today, you need the above psalm!

Many of us have grown a shade jealous looking at our childless, two-salary neighbors. We think about it: No trips to the pediatrician. No baby-sitter fees. No weekly allowances. No need to own a van. No call for an additional bedroom or two. No orthodontics. No sudden jump in car insurance rates when kids reach sixteen. Most of all, no college tuition, room, board, or books. Meanwhile, lots of quiet, affordable dinners for two, at which the main topic of discussion is planning the next vacation to Hawaii. . . .

But God called us to be *parents.* And his call includes the promises that he will care for us "when times are hard" (verse 19); that he will guide our steps (verse 23); that throughout the years, our children will not go hungry (verse 25). In fact, there's nothing wrong with being godly and having little, says verse 16. It beats quite a number of alternatives.

When shaken by the mounting bills, when discouraged to see no progress in the savings account, when frightened at the thought of college bills ahead, remember the words of the hymn: "Great is thy faithfulness . . . *All I have needed Thy hand hath provided."* And affirm, with David, that children are indeed a blessing in ways no banker can tally.[12]

September 11

*Instead, speaking the truth in love, we will in all things grow
up into him who is the Head, that is, Christ* (Ephesians 4:15).

"Just live and let live" is a motto that many people live by. They say, "Let everyone be who they are the way they are. If you really love people you won't try to change them. You will encourage them to stay the way they are and to fulfill their individual destinies."

Generally, that perspective isn't so bad. We do need to respect the God-given uniqueness the Lord has built into each of us. However, you don't have to read much of the Bible to realize that one of God's primary goals for us as Christians is that we *grow*.

The Bible has a lot to say about growth, change, and becoming mature. While God loves us just the way we are, He also loves us too much to leave us that way. Because He loves us He wants to see us "be conformed to the likeness of his Son" (Romans 8:29). Because He loves us He wants to help us "grow up in all aspects into Him, who is the head, even Christ" (Ephesians 4:15, NASB).

The writer of Hebrews expressed concern that his readers hadn't changed—they hadn't deepened or matured (Hebrews 5:11-14). He begins chapter six by exhorting them to "press on to maturity" (6:1, NASB). He was saying, "Hey, folks. It's time for you to make some changes. It's time for you to grow up."

Our willingness to change, to learn, to grow is God's love language. It tells Him we believe in Him, we trust Him, and we want to be who and what He wants us to be. Openness to change is our way of taking His hand and following Him. He will never give us more than we can handle (1 Corinthians 10:13); He can cause all things to work together for good (Romans 8:28); and He will supply all our needs according to His riches in glory (Philippians 4:19).

When you allow your children to see the growth and changes in your life, they will learn how they can move ahead in life, too. After all, they do believe us more when we live what we say.

September 12

> Israel loved Joseph more than any of his other sons, because he
> had been born to him in his old age; and he made a richly orna-
> mented robe for him. When his brothers saw that their father
> loved him more than any of them, they hated him and could not
> speak a kind word to him. Joseph had a dream, and when he told
> it to his brothers, they hated him all the more (Genesis 37:3-5).

*P*artiality. Favoritism. Think back to when you were a child.
Wasn't there another child who was a favorite—someone
who seemed to get more attention than you and the other kids?
Perhaps it was someone in your family or school or some group.
Perhaps it was someone you didn't like. Or a friend, a sibling,
or . . . even you.

Some children seem to get all the attention and opportunities.
Other children get the leftovers. Some children are always chosen
first for a team. Other children are taken last and reluctantly.

What about your own family? If you have several children, is
there a favorite? Or if you have only one child, have you had
times when you felt it would be a lot easier to love that child if he
or she were just a bit different in some way? If only he or she were
quieter, more talkative, more attentive, less obnoxious. . . .

Children who are easier to love get more attention, smiles, forgiveness, patience, time, and perhaps opportunities. However,
the child who is more difficult to love probably needs more of the
above than his or her more cooperative sibling.

Favoritism can continue when our children marry and we either like or don't like their spouses or their spouses' family.

But let's turn this around. Perhaps you're the one who feels a
bit left out or neglected at times. That can happen to parents, too.
One parent may shower their children with love and attention
while his or her partner is left to starve.

Think about your family. Are there any favorites? Who might
be neglected? Ask God to help all of you balance the attention and
love in your family. Remember to thank God that He doesn't play
favorites. "God treats everyone the same" (Romans 2:11, TLB).

September 13

Here is my servant whom I have chosen, the one I love, in whom I delight (Matthew 12:18).

*I*t's doubtful that you were raised in a home with servants. Not too many of us were. But if so, you remember that those servants had one job to perform—serve.

When you signed on to become a parent, you probably didn't realize that your job description, too, included becoming a servant. Some positions of serving are recognized and appreciated. In others you feel taken for granted. If that's the way you feel at times, remember that someone else who came to serve was unappreciated as well. One of the more than 100 names and titles of Jesus was Servant. This role was a fulfillment of the prophecy in Isaiah 53.

Unfortunately, we live in a world that doesn't value the servant role. We'd rather get than give, take than share, or grasp than release. Children reflect this tendency. We have to teach them to be other-centered. It's all too natural to be self-centered.

All through the New Testament we see that those who had transformed lives were servants. In Romans 1:1, Paul introduced himself as a servant of Jesus Christ. In 2 Peter 1:1, Peter introduced himself as a servant of Jesus Christ. The brother of Jesus, Jude, said the same, as did John in Revelation.

Perhaps we're all afraid of what being a servant might cost us. There are risks. You can focus on the risks involved, or you can focus on service as a privilege and a learning experience.[13]

> Colonel James Irwin, a former astronaut who became a lunar pedestrian, shares that while walking on the moon he realized that when he would return to earth many would consider him an international celebrity. Realizing his role as a Christian, he records: "As I was returning to earth, I realized that I was a servant, not a celebrity. I am here as God's servant on Planet Earth to share what I have experienced that others might know the glory of God."
> If Christ, Lord of the universe, became a Servant for us, can we do any less for Him?[14]

How can each person in your family be more of a servant today? Take a few moments to discuss that now.

September 14

Remember the sabbath day, to keep it holy (Exodus 20:8, NASB).

*B*usy, busy, busy. Does that sound familiar? Especially if you have children. Sometimes parents say, "I've got so much going on and so much to do that I don't even remember what it's like to slow down, let alone stop!" Have you ever had days when you're on the go from dawn to dusk and the only reason you collapse on the bed is because you simply ran out of gas? All parents experience that from time to time. Sometimes the frantic pace is within the home. Other times it's outside the home, and we're going from one activity to another or working 70 hours a week hoping to either pay the basic bills and survive or get that new model car.

It used to be that people looked forward to Sunday as their day of rest and worship. But when was the last time that Sunday, for you, was a day of rest and worship? Sometimes we make Sundays a catch-up day for the leftovers from the week, and soon Sunday blends together with the other days.

Why don't you try to do something different this Sunday? Worship—really worship—and then rest. Look your chores, tasks, and assignments in the eye and say, "You can wait! This is the Lord's day." As Max Lucado puts it,

> It's almost as if activity is a sign of maturity. After all, isn't there a beatitude which reads, "Blessed are the busy?" No, there isn't. But there is a verse which summarizes many lives: "Man is a mere phantom as he goes to and fro: He bustles about, but only in vain; he heaps up wealth, not knowing who will get it" (Luke 4:16).
>
> Does that sound like your life? Are you so seldom in one place that your friends regard you as a phantom? Are you so constantly on the move that your family is beginning to question your existence? Do you take pride in your frenzy at the expense of your faith?
>
> Slow down. If God commanded it, you need it. If Jesus modeled it, you need it. God still provides the manna. Trust him. Take a day to say no to work and yes to worship.[15]

Your week may be much different because of this. After all, it's God's idea.

September 15

As a father has compassion on his children, so the LORD has compassion on those who fear him (Psalm 103:13).

*D*o you ever feel like some of your concerns are too insignificant to bother God with? Did you ever wonder if God really cares about the small details of your life? Perhaps you've looked at the work that's piling up, the kids who need to be chauffeured, and the car that needs a new transmission and you've wondered if God cares about these kinds of details.

Do *children* wonder if God cares about the little things? It doesn't appear so. Listen to their prayers. They're usually simple, basic, trusting, and they include everything from the new pet rabbit to another child liking them at school.

But still we cannot help but wonder if God notices—especially if we're taken for granted by other family members. If no one shows any concern about how hard you work to make a living, why would God be concerned? Why would He be concerned about your anxiety over your sales presentation or the money needed for five new pairs of tennis shoes for your children?

Well, take heart. God is a God of compassion and He's concerned about everything. There are no limits. He is like a gentle, caring father who Joni Eareckson Tada describes so beautifully:

> I remember my father having a kind of intimate, heartfelt compassion with me. Often when my dad would be busy at his easel, I'd sit on the floor at his side with my crayons and coloring book. Even though he was intent on his work, he'd look down at me and smile. And sometimes he'd set his brushes aside, reach down, and lift me into his lap. Then he'd fix my hand on one of his brushes and enfold his larger, stronger hand around mine. Ever so gently, he would guide my hand and the brush, and I would watch in amazement as, together, we made something beautiful. Even these many years later, I find myself warmed by his compassion for me.
> This is the kind of love our God has for us. Father love. The kind, gentle compassion of a dad who deeply cares for his sons and daughters. Maybe you never had a dad like that . . . but you do have such a Father.[16]

September 16

Make my joy complete by being like-minded, having the same love, being one in spirit and purpose (Philippians 2:2).

Most Christian parents would do the right thing if they were sure what the right thing was. But what does a good parent do? Should you try to control your children? Is loving them the same as controlling them? Is controlling them the same as disciplining them? What kind of parents produce the following?

1. Children who have a good self-image and are happy being who they are.

2. Children who conform to the authority of others and have the capacity to get along with their teachers and other authority figures.

3. Children who follow the religious beliefs of their parents, attend the church of their parents.

The two most powerful influences in parenting are control and support. Parental control is defined as the ability to manage a child's behavior. You can coerce your kids through intimidation, verbally batter them into submission, lay a guilt trip on them, or firmly establish boundaries and provide choices.

Parental support is defined as the ability to make a child feel loved. You need to do more than simply tell your child that you love him in order to help him feel loved. You must be physically and emotionally available in such a way that your child *knows* that you love him. Your love comes across in the way you communicate with and touch your child throughout the day.

The best children come from parents who can manage their behavior and communicate their unconditional love. The worst children come from homes where they are controlled but not loved. You may not be able to manage your child's behavior, but by the grace of God you can love him.[17]

That is the way God loves us. He doesn't try to dominate our lives, but draws us to Him through His love.

September 17

The people were soon complaining about all their misfortunes and the Lord heard them (Numbers 11:1, TLB).

Don't grumble about each other, brothers. Are you yourselves above criticism? For see! The great Judge is coming. He is almost here. [Let him do whatever criticizing must be done] (James 5:9, TLB).

Gripe, gripe, gripe. Complain, complain, complain. Some of us are like that. We act like a grumpy bear just coming out of hibernation. Sometimes Sunday mornings can be the worst. Unfortunately, there are some homes where griping and complaining are the norm and cheerfulness is the exception. These homes are anything but healthy. The atmosphere in them breeds pessimism, bitterness, and gloom.

Many years ago there was a comic strip called "L'il Abner." In it was a character who was a grouch. He walked around with a dark rain cloud over his head even though everyone else stood in the sunshine. A family member like that can infect the entire family and be a source of contamination.

Certainly there will be problems, upsets, disappointments, schedule changes, reversals, and illnesses in your family. Those are all a part of life. You can't change what happens, but you *can* change how you respond to your circumstances.

What can you do? Begin each day by finding three reasons to praise and thank the Lord. Write them down, and read your list several times a day. Make a pact with your family that the first four minutes of the morning when you first see everyone and the first four minutes when people come home you will be positive, affirming, and affectionate. By making such a commitment for these key times, you will help set the mood for the day and the evening.

Should someone need to share a gripe or complaint, that's all right. But encourage everyone to share in a way that indicates how something can be different rather than simply criticizing what they don't like.

By the way, all these ideas came from parents who found that they worked. Let them work for you.

September 18

Make sure that nobody pays back wrong for wrong, but always try to be kind to each other and to everyone else (1 Thessalonians 5:15).

*T*he newspaper and television are full of portrayals, reports, and descriptions of violence. It's overwhelming at times, even downright depressing, to focus on all that violence. A California college professor was watching television and heard that "another random act of senseless violence" had taken place in his community. He began to wonder what it would be like to have just the opposite take place—random acts of senseless kindness. So he decided to find out.

In class the next day he gave an unusual assignment. The students were to do something out of the ordinary to help another person and then write a report on the incident. The students liked the idea and responded well to this task. One student bought 20 blankets at a Salvation Army thrift store and gave them to the homeless. Another student was about to park his car in a parking space but instead gave up the space to another driver and parked one-half mile away.

Someone in a local bank heard what was happening and decided to print a batch of bumper stickers that said, "Commit a random act of senseless kindness." They sold for a dollar and the proceeds went to charity. Even the police put the bumper stickers on their cars. Radio programs got behind the idea, as did other teachers and even ministers. Eventually the experiment impacted the entire city. Needless to say, not only was the professor amazed, so were many other people.

Why be amazed at this? Is it so unusual to be kind to one another? Isn't that supposed to be the norm? Somehow random acts of kindness have become seldom and infrequent. How often do we smile and let another car turn in front of us in a jammed parking lot? How often do we stop to help someone pick up a bag of spilled groceries?

What about random acts of kindness in our home? That's the place to begin. When one parent was asked how he was going to be kind to his family, he said, "That's simple. I'm going to speak to my children and speak to my neighbors' children."

September 19

Jesus immediately said to them: "Take courage! It is I. Don't be afraid" (Matthew 14:27).

*W*e're a lot like the disciples, aren't we? We spend time with Jesus, experience His strength, then we forget and become afraid.

Let's look at what happened in Matthew 14. Jesus healed the sick and fed the multitudes. Afterward He told the disciples to go on ahead of Him across the Sea of Galilee, then He went away by Himself to pray. While the disciples were in the boat, a storm arose. In the midst of the thrashing waves and intense wind, Jesus walked toward His friends on the water. They saw Him and thought that He was a ghost. Jesus immediately said, "Take courage! It is I. Don't be afraid." Then Peter, on impulse, got out of the boat, started toward Jesus, realized what he was doing, and panicked.

Carol Kent gives an interesting analysis of what happened and its application for all of us.

1. *Uncertain circumstances*—Almost every time I deal with fear, I face uncertain circumstances—just like the disciples did. My situation seems unfamiliar. My boat is rocking.

2. *Wrong conclusions*—In the middle of my panic, I often look at the obvious instead of the supernatural. Instead of seeing Jesus supernaturally at work in the middle of my storm, I see all kinds of ghosts, represented by my personal fears. Sometimes I voice my fears loudly as the disciples did. Other times I feel angry and powerless. "Where is Jesus when I need Him most?"

3. *Impulsive conduct*—Peter's "jump out of the boat" behavior reminds me of myself. Sometimes I cry, "Lord, if You are *really* here, in the middle of my panic and my frightening situation, prove Yourself supernaturally. I mean, *do* something so I know it's You!"

4. *Desperate call*—When I, like Peter, step out in trust, I sometimes take my eyes off Him and focus on my terrorizing circumstances. The "winds of fear" look much worse than they did before I tried to trust Him. I cry, "Lord, save me!"

5. *Immediate calm*—Without delay He reaches out to me and says, "You of little faith...why did you doubt?" And in the security of His compassionate eye contact and warm, affirming grip, my heart begins the measured, careful journey toward accepting His perfect love.[18]

September 20

He who gives an answer before he hears, it is folly and shame to him (Proverbs 18:13, NASB).

A Letter to a Child About to Be Married

As you look toward your wedding day and a lifetime of marriage, there is one ingredient that will need constant attention for your relationship to flourish. I think you already know what it is—communication. You may think you are communicating now. To a certain degree you are. But the two of you haven't yet learned to really speak one another's language. In some ways each of you is still somewhat of a foreigner to each other. Learn to use your partner's style of thinking and speaking when the two of you interact together. Then you will understand and draw closer.

Remember that communication is not only talking but also silence, a quiet look, a gentle touch.

Discover the best time of the day for each of you to communicate and give each other the gift of your individual attention. Set aside a bit of time each day to sit together, hold hands, and share your heart and your deepest feelings.

But do more than talk. Listen as well. Listen with your mind, heart, ears, and eyes. Practice the principles of God's Word in your listening. "I love the LORD, because He hears my voice and my supplications. Because He has inclined His ear to me, therefore I shall call upon Him as long as I live" (Psalm 116:1,2, NASB).

True listening is total attention, no distractions, and not letting your mind formulate what you are going to say as soon as your partner stops talking. One of the greatest gifts you can give is to listen. Too many discussions end up being dialogues of the deaf! "Let every man be quick to hear [a ready listener]" (James 1:19, AMP).

Above all, remember who it is who never tires of listening to you.

September 21

I will say to the north, "Give them up!" and to the south, "Do not hold them back." Bring my sons from afar and my daughters from the ends of the earth—everyone who is called by my name, whom I created for my glory, whom I formed and made (Isaiah 43:6,7).

Child: I have a question, but by now that shouldn't surprise you.

Parent: No. And since yesterday was Sunday, could it have something to do with church?

Child: It does. The pastor said we were created to glorify God. It was in the Westminster Catechism thing. What does glorify God mean? How do we do it? Why do we have to do it?

Parent: Well, I once taught a lesson about that. In the Bible, *glorify* refers to giving honor, increasing someone's fame, making a person's name great, magnifying someone's reputation, and causing other people to think about someone in a positive way. When we glorify God, we're also thankful for who He is and what He's done.

Why should we glorify Him? The psalmist helps us here: "Great is the LORD and most worthy of praise; his greatness no one can fathom" (145:3). God is worth it. He deserves it.

Another good reason to glorify Him is because you and I exist. He didn't have to create the world. He didn't have to create you or me. And when He did create us, He did a good job. Psalm 8:5 says, "You made [man] a little lower than the heavenly beings and crowned him with glory and honor."

Child: All right, already, I get it. God is really awesome.

Parent: Yes, He is. There's a verse in 1 Peter that says it all: "You are a chosen people, a royal priesthood, a holy nation, a people belonging to God, that you may declare the praises of him who called you out of darkness into his wonderful light" (2:9).[19]

September 22

The tongue is a small part of the body, but it makes great boasts. Consider what a great forest is set on fire by a small spark. The tongue also is a fire, a world of evil among the parts of the body. It corrupts the whole person, sets the whole course of his life on fire, and is itself set on fire by hell. All kinds of animals, birds, reptiles and creatures of the sea are being tamed and have been tamed by man, but no man can tame the tongue. It is a restless evil, full of deadly poison (James 3:5-8).

There is an old African legend about a chief who had to test the wisdom of a young man he had chosen as his successor. So he devised a strange test. "Prepare me two meals, one with the best ingredients available and one with the worst," he said. And so the young man did. The day came and the chief was served a plate of succulent sliced cow tongue with vegetables. It was excellent, and after the meal, the chief asked the young man why he chose tongue. He replied, "The tongue is one of our best parts. It can speak words of truth, bring healing, comfort, give courage, and strengthen another person's integrity. It can speak of love, harmony, and actually hold our village together."

The chief was impressed. He waited eagerly for the next meal. On the day it was to be served, the young man came into the hut and handed the chief a plate full of the exact same food. He ate it, then asked, "Why did you fix the same meal?" Without hesitating, the young man said, "It's true that the tongue can be the best part of us, but it can also be the worst. It can rip people apart, saying words of anger and discouragement. It can spread lies, deceit, slander, and it has the power to destroy our families and our tribe." The old chief sat and thought. He nodded his head. He was now assured he had made the right choice. He had chosen a wise man.

Proverbs talks about the power of our tongues. The book of James does the same. Why? Because it's one of our biggest problems. Ask God to give you the strength to use your tongue for His glory.[20]

September 23

Come to me, all you who are weary and burdened, and I will give you rest (Matthew 11:28).

New babies are miracles. But along with their presence in your life comes another new resident—weariness. The following prayer for a new mother and her trying circumstances can be adapted by you to fit your situation in life. Reflect on this prayer— or your version of it—at the times when you're weary.

O Lord, help me.
I am so tired, so tired.
I love this little child,
but I am physically and emotionally worn out.
Infants are demanding—
late nights,
daybreak mornings,
unpredictable schedules.
I keep waiting for things to get back to normal,
only to realize *this* is now normal.
And I never dreamed how emotionally unstrung
I would feel.
I don't understand why the baby is crying.
The baby doesn't respond to me as a person.
I'm depressed.
I feel alone.
Calm me, Lord.
This will end soon.
Schedules will emerge.
Baby will sleep longer.
I can seek relief—
go shopping some evening,
share my feelings with my husband,
(I have been too proud to admit I don't know)
and I can snatch
every spare moment of rest possible.
Help me relax as I realize
an infant is more than smiles, rosy cheeks,
and affectionate sounds.
But a child, a new baby, is a miracle—
new, ongoing life in your creation.
Thank you.[21]

September 24

As we have opportunity, let us do good to all people, especially to those who belong to the family of believers (Galatians 6:10).

*N*eil Anderson shares some advice one of his students gave to him when he was teaching in a seminary. There are nuggets of wisdom here for the challenges of parenting as well as facing life in general.

People are unreasonable, illogical and self-centered.
Love them anyway.

If you do good, people will accuse you of selfish, ulterior motives.
Do good anyway.

If you are successful, you will win false friends and true enemies.
Succeed anyway.

The good you do today will be forgotten tomorrow.
Do good anyway.

Honesty and frankness make you vulnerable.
Be honest and frank anyway.

The biggest people with the biggest ideas can be shot down by the smallest people with the smallest minds.
Think big anyway.

People favor underdogs but follow only top dogs.
Fight for the underdog anyway.

What you spend years building may be destroyed overnight.
Build anyway.

People really need help, but may attack you if you help them.
Help people anyway.

Give the world the best you've got and you'll get kicked in the teeth.
Give the world the best you've got anyway.[22]

September 25

Pray continually... (1 Thessalonians 5:17).

*M*any parents are now personalizing Scripture to create specific prayers for their children. The following are prayers based upon Scripture for the following topics.

Courage

I pray that when my child passes through the water You will be there and through the rivers, that my child will not be overflowed by them. When my child walks through the fire, that there will be no burning nor scorching. For You are the Lord God (*see* Isaiah 43:2,3).

Faith

I pray that my child will walk by faith and not by sight (*see* 2 Corinthians 5:7).

Peace

I pray that my child, who has been justified by faith, will have peace with You, God, through the Lord Jesus Christ (Romans 5:1)

I pray that the peace of God will rule in my child's heart (Colossians 3:15).

Salvation

I pray, Lord Jesus, that my child will come to understand what You meant when You said, "Whoever confesses Me before men, him I will also confess before My Father who is in heaven" (*see* Matthew 10:32).

Temptation

I pray that You, Lord, know how to deliver my child out of temptations (2 Peter 2:9).

These verses will get you started. You can create other prayers by using a topical index of the Scriptures. Use your children's names when you pray and discover the benefits and joy of praying God's Word for your child.[23]

September 26

Blessed is he whose help is the God of Jacob, whose hope is in the LORD his God (Psalm 146:5).

*D*id you know that happiness is biblical? It is—but Scripture often uses the word "blessed" because the Greek word literally means both "happy" and "blessed." In the beatitudes, for example, you could just as well substitute the word *happy* for blessed.

The word *blessed* does have a unique and special meaning. It tells us that the happiness God gives is special. It's because of how He has blessed us that we can be happy.

But is happiness the same as joy? No, there is a distinction. The word for "joy" is found in both Matthew and Luke, and it can mean "joy" or "delight." In John 15:11 we read about a promise of joy for everyone who believes in Jesus: "These things have I spoken unto you, that my joy might remain in you, and that your joy might be full" (John 15:11, KJV). The source of that joy is our life in Christ.

Joy is also one of the fruits of the Spirit mentioned in Galatians 5:22,23. A person can be happy *and* have joy. A person can also be happy and not have the joy that Scripture talks about. Why is that? Happiness is a transient response. It can come and go. Joy is more long-lasting. It's more a state of being. Joy is also a choice—choosing to focus on who we are in Christ and what He has done for us. Joy has also been called a sense of gladness. It's a chosen attitude, a way of viewing life. And it's the foundation for happiness. The Amplified Bible tells us that joy is not dependent upon circumstances (Proverbs 15:15).

Do your children see the joy in your life? Do they see you happy? Do you see joy in their lives? *Lasting* joy? At the next meal or ride in the car, why don't all of you talk about joy and pray for it. God is waiting to help you discover joy.[24]

September 27

Keep your lives free from the love of money and be content with what you have, because God has said, "Never will I leave you; never will I forsake you" (Hebrews 13:5).

A Christian man heard an urgent news report on his radio that a flash flood was within minutes of entering the peaceful valley where he lived. Immediately he went to his knees and prayed for safety. The words were still on his lips when he became aware that water was gushing under his door. He retreated to the second floor and finally onto the roof of his house.

While he sat on the roof, a helicopter flew by and the pilot asked over the loudspeaker if they could lift him off. "It's not necessary since I have the Lord's protection," he replied.

Moments later the house began to break up and he found himself clinging to a tree. A police boat, braving the waters, approached him for rescue, but he assured them that the Lord would save him. Finally, the tree gave way and the man went to his death.

Standing before the Lord, he asked, "Lord, I'm glad to be here, but why didn't You answer my prayer for safety?"

The Lord responded, "Son, I told you over the radio to get out of there. Then I sent you a helicopter and a motor boat!"[25]

Sometimes we're like the man in the story. We look to the Lord for help but we have our own idea of how He should respond. The answer could be right in front of our eyes and we still won't see it. We're looking for the extraordinary when God often works through the ordinary.

When something spectacular occurs, we tend to think that God was in it. But when it comes to ordinary events, we forget God. The birth of a child is an ordinary occurrence all over the world, but isn't God in that? Isn't He in the conception of a child? Isn't He manifested in the puffy white clouds that transverse the blue sky? God created the universe. There are fixed procedures and laws. He works both within it and beyond it. And much of the time He works in ways that we don't see—probably because we're not looking in the right places. Look around you. Can you discover some new way that God is at work?

September 28

From everlasting to everlasting the LORD's love is with those who fear him, and his righteousness with their children's children (Psalm 103:17).

*L*et's imagine for a moment that you're having a conversation with God. He is going to respond to you in an audible voice with very specific instructions. You ask Him, "God, we know that You have entrusted our children to us. We have certain dreams and goals that we would like to see come to fruition in their lives, but since they are a gift from You, what do *You* want to see happen in their lives?"

God does respond to our prayers. Often His answers are found in Scripture itself. Sometimes we may be surprised that He responds, but that shouldn't be the case because He tells us in Jeremiah 33:3, "Call to me and I will answer you and tell you great and unsearchable things you do not know."

Here is God's response to your prayer about your children . . . in the form of a letter.

Dear Parent,

More than anything I want to see My Son Jesus Christ formed in your children (*see* Galatians 4:19). I want to make sure they don't become entrapped by Satan but are delivered from him (*see* Proverbs 11:21, KJV; Matthew 6:13). I desire that your children will be taught fully about me so that they will know great peace (*see* Isaiah 54:13). I want your children to train themselves to distinguish between good and evil as well as develop a healthy conscience (*see* Hebrews 5:14; 1 Peter 3:21). It's also important for them to put my law in their mind and on their heart (see Hebrews 8:10).

It's important that you help your children choose friends who are wise. Read Proverbs 13:20 and 1 Corinthians 5:11 to discover which companions they should avoid. I want them to remain sexually pure and always call upon Me and My grace to help them keep this commitment (Ephesians 5:3,31-33). I believe you will appreciate My last desire, which Paul mentioned in Ephesians 6:1,2: I want them to honor you at all times.

And remember, I am here to help you. Please always remember the extent of My love for you.

September 29

... how much more shall your Father who is in heaven give what is good to those who ask Him! (Matthew 7:11, NASB).

*D*id you know that your own father has affected the way you perceive God? Think about this for a moment.

If your father was patient, you are more likely to see God as patient and available for you. You feel that you are worth God's time and concern. You feel important to God and that He is personally involved in every aspect of your life.

If your father was kind, you probably see God acting kindly and graciously on your behalf. You feel that you are worth God's help and intervention. You feel God's love for you deeply and you're convinced that He wants to relate to you personally.

If your father was a giving man, you may perceive God as someone who gives to you and supports you. You feel that you are worth God's support and encouragement. You believe that God will give you what is best for you, and you respond by giving of yourself to others.

If your father accepted you, you tend to see God accepting you regardless of what you do. God doesn't dump on you or reject you when you struggle, but understands and encourages you. You are able to accept yourself even when you blow it or don't perform up to your potential.

If your father protected you, you probably perceive God as your protector in life. You feel that you are worthy of being under His care and you rest in His security.

Even though we tend to do so, we cannot base our perceptions of God and our feelings about ourself on how we were treated by our parents. Fathers and mothers are human and fallible—and some of them are even prodigals![26]

Accurate beliefs about God are based on His Word. Knowing who He is and what He is like will help all of us become the parents we want to be and that God wants us to be!

September 30

"I overthrew some of you as I overthrew Sodom and Gomorrah. You were like a burning stick snatched from the fire, yet you have not returned to me," declares the LORD (Amos 4:11).

*I*sn't that a descriptive picture? This statement made by Amos the prophet to the people of Israel describes how God reaches down and saves us. We have been snatched from the consequences of sin. That is why our life has meaning.

In the 1800s there was a famous violinist in Europe whose name was Buckey. People flocked to the concert halls to hear him. Another man, who was a soldier worn out from fighting, also played the violin. But he played on the streets of Vienna for money. Eventually because of his injuries and age he couldn't play anymore and he sat on the street weary and depressed.

A man who happened to be walking by stopped, picked up the soldier's violin, and began to play. As he played, people gathered, and the aged soldier held out his hat. The people filled the hat with coins again and again. They were intrigued by the man playing the violin. The crowds grew and put even more money into the hat. Finally, he stopped playing and left.

"Who was that?" the old soldier asked a man standing close by.

"Didn't you know who was playing for you? That was Buckey the great violinist."

The fact was, he had just taken that man's place, and assumed his poverty, and bore his burden and played his music, and earned his livelihood, and made sacrifice for the poor old man. So the Lord Jesus comes. He finds us in our spiritual penury, and across the broken strings of His own broken heart He strikes a strain of infinite music which wins the attention of earth and heaven. He takes our poverty. He plays our music. He weeps our tears. He dies our death.

All this Christ did for you and me that He might pluck us from the burning.[27]

Spend some time today thinking about the implications of what Christ has done for you.[28]

October 1

He who covers and forgives an offense seeks love, but he who repeats or harps on a matter separates even close friends (Proverbs 17:9, AMP).

Can you say in your own words what's important to you? Better yet, put this book down, go to your children, and ask them what they think is important to you—what they think you value most. Sometimes the way our children respond can be a real eye opener.

A pastor one Sunday told the story of backing his car out of the garage and hearing a snap. He stopped and discovered his favorite fishing pole had been left behind the car. It now was in two pieces.

He walked into the house and asked, "Who was using my fishing pole?"

"I was, Dad," his five-year-old son said.

"Look at it now," he said, holding up the two pieces. "What happened?"

"I was playing with it and set it against the garage door. I forgot to put it away."

The father realized it must have fallen down behind the car. He wasn't pleased, but neither was he going to cry over spilled milk—or broken poles.

"Well, thank you for telling me," he said quietly and went back to the car.

As the pastor told his congregation: "I didn't think much more of it, but two days later, my wife told me that when she and our son were at Sears, he said, 'Mom, I've got to buy Dad a new fishing pole. I broke his other one. Here's my money.' And he handed her his savings of two dollars.

"'That's nice of you to offer,' she said. 'But you don't have to do that.'

"'I want to, Mom,' he said. 'I found out something. I found out that Dad loves me more than he loves his fishing pole.'"[1]

How do you react to your children when they make a mistake? It's easy to remind children of what they did wrong. Sometimes an action on their part becomes so indelibly impressed upon our minds that we end up expecting them to repeat the offense in some way. Unfortunately, such a perception erodes trust and becomes a self-fulfilling prophecy. Maybe that's why the Bible talks so much about love and forgiveness. It's a much better way to live.

October 2

Be subject to one another in the fear of Christ (Ephesians 5:21, NASB).

A Letter to a Child About to Be Married

When you marry, you are giving up your single life and taking on the biblical role of a servant to the person you love. I trust you understand what this means.

To put it simply, your role is to make sure that your partner's needs are met. In a marriage relationship, being a servant is an act of love, a gift to your partner to make his or her life fuller. It is an act of strength and not of weakness. It is a positive action that has been chosen to show your love to each other. The apostle Paul said, "Be subject to one another," not limiting the role of servant-hood to a wife. It's for both of you.

A servant may also be called an "enabler," in the good sense of the word, which means "to make better." As an enabler you are to make life easier for your partner instead of placing restrictive demands upon him or her.

A servant is also someone who edifies another person.

In the New Testament, to edify someone often refers to building up another person. Do you know how you will do this throughout the years of your marriage? Take these verses into your heart and live them out each day:

> Let us then definitely aim for and eagerly pursue what makes for harmony and for mutual upbuilding (edification and development) of one another (Romans 14:19, AMP).

> Let each one of us make it a practice to please (make happy) his neighbor for his good and for his true welfare, to edify him [to strengthen him and build him up spiritually] (Romans 15:2, AMP).

> Encourage one another and build each other up (1 Thessalonians 5:11).

First Corinthians 8:1 sums up the matter of edifying: "Love builds up."

That is your calling—never tear down, don't just maintain, but always build up.

October 3

Call to me and I will answer you and tell you great and unsearchable things you do not know (Jeremiah 33:3).

Can't be done. Tried it. Just won't work. Nope, it's impossible."

Words and phrases such as these bring progress to a roaring halt and deaden the creativity of other people around us. Sometimes we adults rely so much on our years of experience and knowledge that we stifle the learning experiences of our children by failing to let them learn on their own. Some of us seem to have the gift of throwing in the towel. It may be we feel it's a waste of time to try something new. But what would happen if we eliminated those words from our vocabulary and were willing to say, "Let's give it a try"?

A young man recently graduated from high school with a high grade-point average and an outstanding cross-country track record. When his diploma was awarded to him, he couldn't accept it with his hands because he had none. They couldn't tuck it under one of his arms for he had none. He was born without any arms, but by the age of five he had learned to tie his shoes, use scissors, and use a computer. His parents believed he could do it. So did he. The word *impossible* wasn't in their vocabulary.

Earlier in this century someone came up with the bright idea of creating a parachute. Wouldn't you have loved to have been there when the inventor tried to explain his idea for the first time? Can you imagine the facial expressions and comments of the people around him! The inventor, fortunately, was deaf to the word *impossible*. He tried and, yes, there were failures, but he kept at it. He persisted.

So . . . what have you been seeing as impossible in your life? In your children's lives? Have you ever heard the phrase, "The impossible is the untried"? Much of what we experience today in our homes or on the road wouldn't be there if the inventors had listened to people who said, "Impossible!" This isn't a word that God ever uses or calls us to use. Instead, He says the opposite: Try it. Go for it. Let's do it together![2]

October 4

You shall have no other gods before me (Exodus 20:3).

*C*ompetition is a part of our life whether we want it or not. The networks on television compete to capture your attention. They want to be first in the ratings. Family members have been known to compete against each other. Who hasn't heard of sibling rivalry? Your children probably compete for your attention. Household pets compete for their owner's attention. Sometimes married couples compete against each other for their children's time as well. Everyone wants to be number one.

The things that are most important to us are usually those items that we strive for. In a sense, they become number one to us and we don't want anything to keep us from having them. When a person becomes a Christian, however, he or she experiences a value transformation. What was number one in his or her life drops down the rating scale . . . or, at least it's supposed to. Consider Paul's words:

> Whatever was to my profit I now consider loss for the sake of Christ. What is more, I consider everything a loss compared to the surpassing greatness of knowing Christ Jesus my Lord, for whose sake I have lost all things. I consider them rubbish, that I may gain Christ (Philippians 3:7,8).

What do you value the most? If there were a fire in your house and you had five minutes to rescue the things that were the most important to you, what would you take? (Aside from people, that is!) Have you ever made a list of the ten most important possessions in your life? Doing that helps to put life in perspective.

There is a simple message in Paul's words from Philippians. It's this: All the delights of your life and what you value most need a slight adjustment. They need to be moved to second place in your life. Once you became a Christian it's as though you have a parking lot and there's a space reserved for the owner. It's *the* most important spot. It has easy access. God is your owner now. First place is reserved for Him. Not your children, your spouse, your career, your money, your house, but God. He doesn't want to have to compete for it. After all, it belongs to Him. And guess what? He fits in that space better than anything else.

October 5

I am fearfully and wonderfully made (Psalm 139:14, NASB).

*E*motions—feelings—those elusive responses that avoid pre-dictability. Why do they cause us so much trouble? Who needs them? Where did they come from? There's a simple answer. They're a gift—from God. He created you and your children with emotions. Sometimes you may think somebody got an extra dose!

The healthy development of your child's emotional life is vital. The same is true for you.

Dr. Haim G. Ginot says that

> [E]motions are part of our genetic heritage. Fish swim, birds fly, and people feel. Sometimes we are happy, sometimes we are not; but sometimes in our life we are sure to feel anger and fear, sadness and joy, greed and guilt, lust and scorn, delight and disgust. While we are not free to choose the emotions that rise in us, we are free to choose how and when to express them, provided we know what they are.[3]

So, what's the solution? Emotional education. It's actually more important for children to know what they feel than why they feel it. When they do, they are less likely to feel "all mixed up" inside.

If our children are going to have a solid foundation for their emotional expressions later in life, they need to be encouraged to both experience and express a wide range of emotions. That means their emotional experiences must not be limited to pleasant emotions. If they are only allowed to experience one side of their emotions, they will have a limited awareness of who they are and a distorted perspective of others. They will be severely limited in their ability to learn important emotional lessons and become more vulnerable to being controlled by their emotions.

Children should not only be allowed, but enthusiastically encouraged, to experience happiness and sadness, hope and fear, joy and depression, jealousy and compassion.

Perhaps the best way is for them to see a healthy display of emotions in their parents. There are benefits for both you and them.

October 6

Do not conform any longer to the pattern of this world, but be transformed by the renewing of your mind. Then you will be able to test and approve what God's will is—his good, pleasing and perfect will (Romans 12:2).

Christians are people who are called to be exceptions. We are to be different and stand apart from our society. Christian parents want their children to be exceptions as well. Usually they want them to do and be the best they can to the fullest of their ability. But we're not talking so much about grades, awards, or achievements. Performance is important, but too many people base their value and worth on these aspects of their life. What's more important is character. What better schooling can children have than to see their parents exhibit good character qualities? Consider the following qualities for yourself first, and then as positive goals for your children's lives.

If we're not going to be conformed to this world, we need to be people of *integrity*. Our actions need to be consistent with our values. Integrity means we can be depended on, we're trustworthy, we do what is right in accordance with what we believe.

Credibility does tie into performance. It's earned by constantly doing the best, being faithful, and following through. Then others will know they can rely on us. That is so critical in the overall development of a child. If he can't depend on Mom or Dad, then who can he depend on?

Responsibility is a trait we would all love to see in our children. This is reflected by commitment and a willingness to do what needs to be done even when it's out of our arena.

Right along with this is *dependability*—follow-through. Dependable people can be taken at their word, for what they say they will do will get done. They're willing to jump in and act before being asked. They take initiative. This brings us to *tenacity*—tenacious people don't quit; they hang in there. They stay committed.

How are these five character qualities reflected in day-to-day events by each family member? Think about it. Pray about it. Then talk about it as a family. The more it's reflected in your family, the more exceptional you'll be![4]

October 7

"In your anger do not sin": Do not let the sun go down while you are still angry (Ephesians 4:26).

*W*e all want a peaceful child rather than an angry child. Dr. Archibald Hart suggest several ways to make this a reality. These seven helpful principles will help you raise a child who is peaceful instead of angry:

1. *Teach your child to deal with each hurt as it arises.* Allowing hurts to accumulate makes them seem overwhelming—a mountain of hurts that cannot be moved.

2. *Teach your child to take responsibility for his or her own anger.* Your child's anger belongs to him or her; no one else is "making" him or her angry. The anger may or may not be appropriate, but it exists, and it must be reckoned with.

3. *Teach your child to allow other people to have feelings also.* Anger is seldom one-sided. Others have a right to feel angry also. Help your child see *both sides* of the conflict: "If someone has hurt you, it's possible that it's because you have hurt that person yourself."

4. *Listen, receive, and accept your child's anger.* Talking about anger helps to pinpoint its source and also may diffuse some of its intensity. Once your child is aware of where the anger came from, encourage him or her to let the anger go and focus on dealing with the cause of the hurt.

5. *Show your child how to forgive.* Explain why revenge is dangerous. Remind your child of what he or she would want if he or she were in the other person's shoes. And model forgiveness yourself.

6. *Where appropriate, show your child how to face up to the person who is doing the hurting.* This isn't always appropriate or even possible. The person may be too manipulative or reactive, and may even have moved away. But where possible, encourage and support your child in "facing up to the enemy."

7. *Teach your child to seek reconciliation above self-justification.* Reconciliation restores broken relationships. If your child can learn to forgive and be reconciled to those who cause hurt, he or she will have no problem dealing with life's major hurts.[5]

That's good advice for adults, too!

October 8

"Do you hear what these children are saying?" they asked him.
"Yes," replied Jesus, "have you never read, 'From the lips of
children and infants you have ordained praise'?" (Matthew
21:16).

*T*elevision and newspapers regularly tell us about parents who save their children from some disaster. Now and then, however, we hear just the reverse. The parents were saved by a child. Here are two examples:

A three-year-old son of a Maplewood, Missouri police officer told his father, "You forgot this" and handed him his bullet-proof vest as he was leaving to go on duty. The father probably chuckled about it at first, but later on when a burglar shot him in the chest, he was thankful for his child saving his life.

In Canada a father was changing a tire when the jack slipped and he was crushed under the car. His young son called for help; then, using all his strength, he lifted up the car so his dad could breath. Help arrived and his life was saved!

Children also help their parents in less dramatic ways by their fresh perspective and delight in the simple things of life as well as their prayers.

Isaiah talked about a child leading the world (Isaiah 11:6). He was talking about Jesus.

Jesus had a lot to say about children. He said you could learn from them. In fact, if we want to enter the kingdom of heaven we need to believe as they do (*see* Matthew 18:3). That's quite a statement.

What have you learned from your child? What could you learn from your child? What might you need to learn from your child?

Talk about these questions as a family. Your child has something to teach you. Are you willing to listen?[6]

October 9

Pray continually . . . (1 Thessalonians 5:17).

*E*ach day brings with it a multitude of possibilities as well as problems. What a difference it makes when we begin the day by communicating with our heavenly Father and continue this throughout the day. Praying in your own words for your needs as well as using guided prayer from the pens of others is a practice that many people engage in from time to time. Sometimes using the prayers and thoughts of others can assist us in expanding our own prayer life. You can voice aloud those prayers and thoughts in the solitude of your own quiet time.

Thank You, God, for this new day,
for the life you are giving each member of my family:
Thank you for
Blessing each one of us
with the strength and health we need to serve you today,
with the joy we need not to give in to discouragement, anger,
or boredom,
with the protection we need against physical and moral danger,
with the love we need to give hope to those we meet.

Dear God,
I want to respond to everything
beautiful you want to bring to my attention today,
and to transmit my joy to my children.

Like the poet William Blake I want to be able to
"see a world in a grain of sand
And a heaven in a wild flower,
to hold infinity in the palm of my hand
and eternity in an hour."

Anonymous

October 10

He himself is our peace, who has made the two one and has destroyed the barrier, the dividing wall of hostility . . . (Ephesians 2:14).

Fatigue, weariness, exhaustion. These seem to be the built-in companions of parenthood. In fact, whenever a baby is born it seems to bring these companions into the home as uninvited guests. Every parent feels completely worn out at one time or another. That's normal. You're not going to feel at the end of a day like you did in the morning. You gave, you slaved, and juggled demands. It was constant. Some parents never know what it's like *not* to be weary. All types of weariness creep into our lives—physical, emotional, mental, and even spiritual fatigue.

Some days you may want to wave a white flag of surrender and yell, "I give up. I need someone else to take over."

Some days you may get weary of waiting. "I am worn out calling for help; my throat is parched. My eyes fail, looking for my God" (Psalm 69:3).

Some of us may get weary because of criticism and persecution. "I am worn out from groaning; all night long I flood my bed with weeping and drench my couch with tears. My eyes grow weak with sorrow; they fail because of all my foes" (Psalm 6:6,7).

And sometimes this criticism comes from our spouse, parents, in-laws . . . or even ourselves!

Weariness is a sign that you need to rest and refresh. If you don't, you could move easily into the malady we call burnout. Yes, there is such a thing as parental burnout! And you don't recover very quickly from burnout.

God's Word can refresh you. Stop several times a day, quit giving, and start receiving. Take in His Word. Dwell on it and let it refresh you. Take a moment and read Isaiah 40:28-31.

Listen to what Jesus said: "Come to me, all you who are weary and burdened, and I will give you rest" (Matthew 11:28).

Jesus is the one who can give you the rest you need. The more you try to carry everything alone, the more exhausted you'll be. The more you give to Him in prayer (and don't take back), the stronger you'll feel. Try it. What have you got to lose?

October 11

Discipline your son, for in that there is hope; do not be a willing party to his death (Proverbs 19:18).

Frustration, chaos, exhaustion—the three plagues of parenthood. They often seep into our lives when we're trying to control our children. Sometimes our children can act like they are deaf and dumb—at least toward us. To the television or their friends it's a different story. But take heart; you have options. There are a variety of ways you can make your day better, bring out the sunshine again, and give yourself that feeling of once again being back in control.

What can you do to get a child to respond?

You could make a request. A request is a question with a directive in it. It's a question in which we have a prescribed answer that we want. Or as one parent said, "I'd better get it or else!" But a request, in a proper tone of voice, lets a child know that we believe he or she can do what we are asking and that we respect his or her opinion and are willing to consider some alternatives. A request can also point toward the behavior or response we want instead of reinforcing what the child might have been doing wrong. Requests are the most positive options.

Sometimes, though, you may need to state a command. A command tells the child there is no other option, we've run out of time, and if nothing happens there will be consequences. It helps to give the child a choice between doing what you've said and experiencing consequences they will like or not doing what you've said and experiencing consequences they will not care for.

You could also lead your child by verbal instruction or example. Guiding him or her in this way can break down resistance. I'm sure you've heard that it is a lot easier to lead a mule than to try and push it.

One other response is to discipline your child. It's all right to do this. Scripture tells us to. But the discipline needs to fit both the infraction and the person. Discipline that works with one child won't with another. And if it doesn't work, why keep on doing it? Be creative. Be resourceful. Be prayerful. And you will find a way that works.

October 12

The crowds answered, "This is Jesus, the prophet from Nazareth in Galilee" (Matthew 21:11).

*I*f someone claimed to be a prophet today, people would laugh. It would be a joke. But this title given to Jesus in Matthew 21:11 was the highest compliment that could be given to a man in Jesus' day.

There were many prophets in Israel throughout the Old Testament era. These men, who were chosen by God to be His mouthpiece, were called to reveal something about the future or to pass along a message to the people. Each prophet had something distinct to share and added some new insight about God. Each generation could benefit from the new prophet as well as those who had gone before. Consider what God's people learned over a span of hundreds of years:

> *Isaiah*—taught about God's holiness and shared about the coming Messiah.

> *Jeremiah*—taught the people about the importance of their own personal faith.

> *Ezekiel*—in his unique way described God's special relationship with Israel.

> *Daniel*—amidst the stories you probably recall about the lions' den and the fiery furnace, clarified the concept of God's sovereignty.

> *Hosea*—his message must have been welcomed by many with his emphasis upon God's love for the sinner.

Then came another prophet—Jesus. He was different. The other prophets only knew what they shared or had heard before. They didn't know all the truth about God and His will. Jesus did. He was the only one who could give the *complete* revelation of God.

Paul Harvey, a noted newscaster for many years, ends his descriptive stories with the phrase, "And that's the rest of the story." That's what Jesus was: the rest of the story. He was the prophet who brought it all together and gave a full disclosure of God. In addition, He *fulfilled* many of the prophecies that preceded His coming to earth. Remember, Jesus said, "Anyone who has seen me has seen the Father" (John 14:9). Indeed, that's the rest of the story.[7]

October 13

Observe the Sabbath day (Deuteronomy 5:12).

*W*hy is the Sabbath day so special? Some people observe it on Sunday and others do so on Saturday. Whether we choose Saturday or Sunday, what can we do and not do on that day?

Some of you may remember when stores were closed on Sunday. Yes, there was a time when that was true. For some people that was a day for family get-togethers. But for other people from certain backgrounds, the Sabbath day was actually more restrictive, not creative.

Long ago, God set aside one day of the week for rest and worship. He said that in the midst of all the work, turmoil, schedules, and the routines of life, we need to take a break and make one day special—to rest and gather with other believers to focus on Him. Often, however, the reality of getting ready for that special occasion at church can bring some of the most stressful, argumentative, and hassle-filled times of the week.

Before we can worship God, we need to remind ourselves of just what worship is. Jacob said it best after he had spent an entire night alone wrestling with God. Afterwards he said, probably in a soft, awestruck voice, "I saw God face to face" (Genesis 32:30).

Has there ever been a time when during a worship service, during a time of quiet individual prayer, while listening to a praise recording, or while experiencing one of life's momentous events you came away feeling and knowing that you saw God face to face? Can it happen again? Absolutely. How? Perhaps it's summed up best in the words, "Be still, and know that I am God" (Psalm 46:10).

October 14

Give to the Lord the glory due to His name; worship the Lord (Psalm 29:2, AMP).

*L*oss has been mentioned in the pages of this devotional. There's a reason for that. Sometimes life seems as though we are going from one loss to another. The more people there are in your family unit, the more potential there is for losses. Think about it for a minute: Your child will experience the loss of a friend, a pet, an expected grade, not being chosen for a team, dropping an ice cream cone... Go on—you add to the list.

There are numerous ways to handle the losses of life. One of them is worship. Yes, worship. There is a relationship between how we worship and the way we handle losses. Richard Exley describes it well.

> We don't worship God because of our losses, but in spite of them. We don't praise Him for the tragedies, but in them. Like Job, we hear God speak to us out of the storm (Job 38:1). Like the disciples at sea in a small boat, caught in a severe storm, we too see Jesus coming to us in the fourth watch of the night. We hear Him say, "Take courage! It is I. Don't be afraid" (Matthew 14:27).
>
> If you've lived for any length of time, you've probably had opportunity to see the different ways people respond to adversity. The same tragedy can make one person better and another person bitter. What makes the difference? Resources. Inner resources developed across a lifetime through spiritual disciplines. *If you haven't worshiped regularly in the sunshine of your life, you probably won't be able to worship in the darkness.* If you haven't been intimate with God in life's ordinariness, it's not likely that you will know how or where to find Him should life hand you some real hardships. *But by the same token, if you have worshiped often and regularly, then you will undoubtedly worship well in the hour of your greatest need.*[8]

You see, in worship the focus is on God. And that in itself can give us the resources we need to handle the difficulties of life.

October 15

Whoever exalts himself will be humbled, and whoever humbles himself will be exalted (Matthew 23:12).

*I*t's a case of the swelled head, the inflated ego, the over-impressed view of oneself. And whatever swells up or inflates is often popped! You've probably overinflated a balloon and seen it stretch and strain until there's no room left for any more air.

When we surround ourselves with mirrors the only reflection we see is that of ourselves. Remember the mirrors in the old fun houses? They distorted our image and made us look huge or grotesque. That's the way it is with pride. It's an unduly high and exaggerated opinion of oneself. More specifically, pride is conceit.

When you see pride in your children, you want to shake it right out of them. It affects their friendships. But pride affects something else, too, according to Dr. Lloyd Ogilvie.

> Pride takes the place of praise in our hearts. It's the desire to be adequate in our own strength, to be loved by God because we are good enough, and to be admired by people because of our superior performance. The snake is not in the grass—it's in our souls.
>
> Pride pollutes everything it touches. It keeps us from growing spiritually, creates tension in our relationships, and makes us a person difficult for the Lord to bless. It is the basic sin causing separation from God, from our real selves, from others, and from the splendor of living as a spectator of the blessings of God in people and events.
>
> Spiritual pride is the root of all other manifestations of pride. It is Satan's most powerful tool. With it we can miss meeting the Lord, and because of it we can be kept from spiritual growth after we have begun a relationship with Him.
>
> The question that needs careful consideration is how to respond to Christ's promise that those who humble themselves will be exalted. How do we humble ourselves? The way we handle problems is a way to begin. Rather than thinking that given time and our own cleverness we can solve them, we are to admit our inadequacy to find the creative solution. The Lord delights to bless a person like that.[9]

October 16

Blessed is the man who does not walk in the counsel of the wicked or stand in the way of sinners or sit in the seat of mockers (Psalm 1:1).

*W*hat do you want from your children? How do you want them to turn out? What kind of a life do you want them to live? Yes, it's true that sometimes it's all you can do just to keep up with the ordinary, everyday activities, let alone think about the future. But, asking ourselves questions about our children's future can help us to know how we can be shaping their lives today.

One parent responded to the above questions with this answer, "I want my child to live a godly life." That's it. No more words. But *that* says it all. What more could you ask for?

The first three verses of Psalm 1 talk about godly living and what it is. Notice that the person who lives this type of life is "blessed." That doesn't mean too much to us today. Perhaps a better rendition of the word "blessed" is, "Oh, the happiness, many times over..."

Most parents want to know what guidance they can give their children so they will become godly. Let's take a closer look at the psalm.

A godly person doesn't follow the advice of evil men. He or she doesn't imitate wickedness. Keep in mind that it's difficult for children to imitate what they don't see. Some parents laugh at their children's questionable actions. This sends a message. But the message David is sending in Psalm 1 is to steer clear of evil.

"Stand in the way of sinners" can be paraphrased "doesn't hang around with sinners." Who do you spend your time with? Who are your children's closest companions? The influence of other people can either weaken or strengthen your children's lives. "Sit in the seat of mockers" carries the idea of a permanent settling down. It could even mean "permanent dwelling." Scoffers are people who make fun of the things of God. Is anyone in your life like that? Anyone in your children's lives? What do your children read? What do they watch on television?

A pure walk brings happiness. Playing with sin is the first step down a slippery slide. Use Psalm 1:1 as a gauge to measure your family life.

October 17

Now to Him who is able to do exceedingly abundantly above all that we ask or think, according to the power that works in us, to Him be glory (Ephesians 3:20,21, NKJV).

*I*t's fascinating to watch eagles soar. Perhaps you've had the opportunity to see them in the wild. They take off from their perch and use the tremendous power of their wings to gain the height they need. When they hit the fast-moving air currents, they quit flapping, spread their wings, and allow the air currents to help them soar.

God created these creatures in a marvelous, sensitive way. It's not easy to soar. You see, the air currents flow over the upper surface of the wings faster than beneath. So there is less pressure on the top than underneath. There's a purpose in this. It forces the wings up. But there's a delicate balance that has to be maintained. If the angle of the wings is too steep, the eagle loses the lift. When that happens the air stream will break away and the result is turbulence and perhaps stalling. How would you like to stall at 10,000 feet?!

But God created eagles with a set of two small feathers attached to the joint farthest out on each of the eagle's wings. They're called "alulae." These control the air flow over the eagle's wings and give the eagle the balance it needs. With the help of these feathers, an eagle can use the currents to climb higher and higher.

You and I have been given a power through Jesus Christ to stabilize our lives. We're constantly confronted with turbulence. When we allow Jesus Christ to control our imagination, our thought life, and our will, we then have the power we need to soar. Ask Him today to use your imagination to envision what you never dreamed possible. Commit your will to Him for decisions you need to make. We may not have alulae on our wings to help us soar, but we do have the presence of Jesus and His power. Just imagine—how would you like to soar today?[10]

October 18

Wait for the L<small>ORD</small>; be strong and take heart and wait for the L<small>ORD</small> (Psalm 27:14).

*H*ave you ever ached over the disappointment experienced by your child? Parents do that. There is some upsetting event, loss, or even tragedy in your child's life. You wish he or she didn't have to experience that and you wish you could take it all away. Literally your heart and the rest of you aches for him or her. Many times you can't make the situation different for either one of you.

There *is* one step you can take. You can find comfort for yourself and your child by focusing upon God's Word. Reflect upon the following verses several times a day. Let their meaning penetrate to the core of your child's (or your own) area of deepest hurt.

> Show me your ways, O L<small>ORD</small>, teach me your paths; guide me in your truth and teach me, for you are God my Savior, and my hope is in you all day long (Psalm 25:4,5).

> May integrity and uprightness protect me, because my hope is in you (Psalm 25:21).

> Wait for the L<small>ORD</small>; be strong and take heart and wait for the L<small>ORD</small> (Psalm 27:14).

> Be still before the L<small>ORD</small> and wait patiently for him; do not fret when men succeed in their ways, when they carry out their wicked schemes. . . . If the L<small>ORD</small> delights in a man's way, he makes his steps firm; though he stumble, he will not fall, for the L<small>ORD</small> upholds him with his hand (Psalm 37:7,23,24).

> Those who hope in the L<small>ORD</small> will renew their strength. They will soar on wings like eagles; they will run and not grow weary, they will walk and not be faint (Isaiah 40:31).

> Since we are surrounded by such a great cloud of witnesses, let us throw off everything that hinders and the sin that so easily entangles, and let us run with perseverance the race marked out for us (Hebrews 12:1).

> If any of you lacks wisdom, he should ask God, who gives generously to all without finding fault, and it will be given to him (James 1:5).

October 19

Just as you received Christ Jesus as Lord, continue to live in him, rooted and built up in him, strengthened in the faith as you were taught, and overflowing with thankfulness (Colossians 2:6,7).

*I*n school, our children take exams and quizzes. It's been awhile since we've taken a quiz and we miss it terribly, right? Well, whether you do or not, here's an exam for you. Complete the following statements as completely as you can in the next four minutes.

+ I would be more successful if . . .

+ I would be more significant if . . .

+ I would be more fulfilled if . . .

+ I would be more satisfied if . . .

+ I would be happier if . . .

+ I would have more fun if . . .

+ I would be more secure if . . .

+ I would have more peace if . . .

How you finish the above statements reflects your present belief system. That's right—this quiz is a window into the beliefs that are important to you.

What we believe motivates us to seek out what we think will bring us happiness, fulfillment, security, satisfaction, success, fun, peace, and significance. These are actually values. How we function in life—how we behave—is built upon our beliefs. How your children behave is based upon their beliefs.

Some people's behavior is a bit off-base and needs a slight course correction. Is your child's behavior off-base? Check their beliefs. Is there anyone else in your family whose behavior and beliefs need some correction? Do your own behavior and beliefs live up to God's Word? God calls us to a walk of faith that reflects our relationship with Jesus. That's a great foundation![11]

October 20

*H*ave you ever watched a candle maker? His work involves a fascinating process. One of the vital elements is the wick. Without a wick, a candle couldn't perform its function. It's true that the beautiful wax is also important and that's usually what we think of when a candle comes to mind, but the wax won't maintain the flame. It only melts and becomes an unrecognizable blob. The wick holds the fire and burns slowly so the wax can melt gradually and form creative and unusual patterns alongside the candle. After many hours, when the wax is almost gone and the wick has burned away, the candlelight begins to flicker. The flame is on the verge of going out.

As a parent, you may have days when the way you feel is best described by the candle. You may feel as though your wick is smoldering just on the verge of going out. You don't want it to, but you feel beat up, used and bruised, and as much as you try, you can't stop the wax from melting around you.

You may even feel sick with despair and defeat. At times like these you wonder what to do, how to regain your strength, and how much more you can take before that frail flame vanishes altogether.

That's when you want to listen to God. Not only does He say He will not put out a weak flame, but He also is available for you at such a time as this. Jesus said, "It is not the healthy people who need a doctor, but the sick" (Matthew 9:12, New Century Bible). Jesus wants to come to every person, every parent who is struggling and at his or her wit's end. He wants to blow new life into your flame through the gentle wind of the Holy Spirit. Can you sing, "Holy Spirit, fall afresh on me for I need you"? Wick extensions are available. Ask, believe, and receive.

My guilt has overwhelmed me like a burden too heavy to bear (Psalm 38:4).

You know my folly, O God; my guilt is not hidden from you (Psalm 69:5).

*T*here it is again—a tinge—that little irritating feeling that speaks volumes. You know what it is—guilt. It's a feeling of remorse over wrong words or actions or a sense of regret because you failed to speak up or do something when it was needed. You'd like to go back and change what you did but you can't. Neither can you evict that unwelcome tenant called guilt. But there is such a thing as false guilt. That's when you assume the blame for a wrong that someone else did. Parents sometimes carry such a burden for their children.

God knows about guilt. Often we experience it because we have done something against God. In the Old Testament when a person sinned he bought a lamb as a guilt offering. The priest offered it as a sacrifice to atone for the person's sin. Isaiah prophesied that there was coming a Messiah who would became a burnt offering (see Isaiah 53:6,10).

There's a positive side to the guilt felt by you and your children. Guilt tells you when you've done something wrong. But you don't want to wallow in it. Take the next step and follow God's plan. "If we confess our sins, he is faithful and just and will forgive us our sins and purify us from all unrighteousness" (1 John 1:9).

Jesus Christ came to take care of our guilt, which we can't get rid of ourselves. Dr. Edwin Cole says that

> [E]very man must answer for his own actions. And he must answer to God alone. That is why Calvary, where Christ died, is so important. It is the only place in the world where sin can be placed and forgiveness from God received. The only place where guilt can be released.[12]

When someone is bitten by a rattlesnake or takes poison, the doctor usually gives an antidote to counteract the venom or poison. God has done the same for guilt. That antidote is called grace, which means "unmerited favor." When you accept this wonderful gift, the mantle of guilt that you've been wearing turns to dust.

October 22

His mouth is sweetness itself; he is altogether lovely. This is my lover, this my friend, O daughters of Jerusalem (Song of Songs 5:16).

A Letter to a Child About to Be Married

There are many dimensions of love in marriage. One of the most important is friendship. What does friendship love entail? It's an unselfish dedication to your partner's happiness. It's when the fulfillment of his or her needs becomes one of your needs. It's learning to enjoy what your partner enjoys, not just so you can convince him or her you're the right person, but to *develop* the enjoyment yourself as you share the enjoyment together.

Your friendship will mean you can enjoy some aspects of life together, but you're also comfortable with having your own individual interests. Be sure you encourage each other in these endeavors. There needs to be a balance between togetherness and separateness.

Friendship love also involves a certain level of intimacy in which there is openness, vulnerability, and emotional connection. Be sure to share your goals, plans, and dreams, and work together. Never become a stranger to your partner in any area of life.

Remember that marriages that last are marriages that have a husband and wife who are friends. As your friendship develops over the years, you will find that you choose each other for just the joy of the other person's company.

Be sure to practice your friendship. Friendship is part of God's intention for marriage. There is a vow of trust. Don't become selfishly competitive, but wish your partner the best. You should share each other's happiness and rejoice in it almost as much as the other person does.

A friend doesn't automatically approve of everything we do or say, and that's all right. True friends don't attempt to control each other because they respect each other too much. Friends try to understand the other person's preferences. They learn to say, "What do you think?" and, "What do you want to do?" Becoming a friend necessitates changing old habits and beliefs. But that's all right. You'll become a more balanced and mature person. God is going to use your partner to reshape you. Learn to enjoy the improvements.

Carry each other's burdens, and in this way you will fulfill the law of Christ (Galatians 6:2).

*L*ife can be filled with tough times. If you complete your years of parenting without experiencing some type of family crisis or loss, you'll be the exception. Some families handle difficulties well and survive. Others are totally disrupted, and some even disintegrate.

Most of these families are not prepared for life's setbacks. They survive well when life is going well. Some people actually deny that they could have problems.

Second, *family members frequently hurt one another by keeping silent.* It's a challenge, but interaction is vital. Too often, people retreat into their own inner worlds.

Blame is one of the most significant characteristics of families that don't cope well. Sometimes we feel that if we have an explanation for our problems, we can understand and handle them better and feel relieved that someone else was at fault. Statements that start with, "If only you had (or hadn't) . . ." or, "Why didn't you (or did you) . . ." begin to fly from one person to another.

Another common characteristic of families that don't cope well is that they *magnify the seriousness of their problems.* They take problems to the extreme and imagine the worst possible consequences.

Many families, however, make it through their crises. They don't just survive; they grow.

First, *they don't allow themselves to become bitter.* They refuse to live in the past or permit the situation to bring life to a stop.

Second, *they live in the present and have a future perspective.* They seek to learn from what has happened and don't wallow in regrets. They also learn to view the future not as a threat but as an opportunity.

Third, *they learn to manage and resolve their conflicts.* Families that don't do this heap one conflict upon another. And when a new one comes, they respond to it out of the contamination of all the unresolved issues in their reservoir.

Where does your family fit in these characteristics? How are you handling crises? What you learn now will help you in the future.

October 24

Do not conform any longer to the pattern of this world, but be transformed by the renewing of your mind. Then you will be able to test and approve what God's will is—his good, pleasing and perfect will (Romans 12:2).

I just don't fit in. I hate that new school. Everyone is so different. I'm the odd one." These are the laments of a child. But adults experience the same feelings, too. We struggle with possessiveness, cliques at church, jealousy in the office, and favoritism in the higher echelons of the company and wonder, *How can I fit in?*

To fit in, many people compromise, especially in their teens and twenties. In the workplace some people compromise their values to gain a promotion and status. Some become workaholics to get ahead but the price they pay is measured in shallow or nonexisting family relationships.

You may be able to fit in, but first evaluate the cost. Why is it so important? Do you really need what you're working so hard to achieve?

We have actually been called to be aliens in this world—to be different and not fit in. Have you ever given yourself permission *not* to fit into a certain situation? Proclaim that you don't fit in and rejoice over it! Experience the newfound freedom. You're no longer captive to the world. We're called not to fit in.

> *John 1:10*—He was in the world . . . the world did not recognize Him.
>
> *John 14:27*—I do not give to you as the world gives.
>
> *John 18:36*—My kingdom is not of this world.
>
> *1 Corinthians 1:20*—God made foolish the wisdom of the world.

Why let this world tell you how you should be? Wouldn't you rather listen to God?[13]

October 25

Accept one another, then, just as Christ accepted you, in order to bring praise to God (Romans 15:7).

*T*he authors of *Daily in Christ* had some interesting thoughts to share on the subject of acceptance.

There are four concepts we deal with as parents in communicating with our children: authority, accountability, affirmation, and acceptance. We usually line them up this way:

+ We exert our parental authority over them.
+ We demand that they be accountable to us.
+ When they respond to our authority and comply by being accountable, we affirm them.
+ When they put together a positive track record of affirmative behaviors, we convey our love and acceptance.

The reason we have such difficulty communicating with our children is that we have it all backward. Look at God's approach to us as His children. At which end of the list does our heavenly Father start? He starts by expressing His love and acceptance (John 3:16; Romans 5:8). Our children won't care how much we know until they know how much we care. Paul instructs us to "accept one another, just as Christ also accepted us to the glory of God" (Romans 15:7).

When your child shares something personal with you, what is he looking for initially? Not a lecture, not a list of rules he must obey, but acceptance and affirmation. "Tell me I'm all right," he begs. "Give me some love and hope."

When you know that you are unconditionally loved and accepted by God and affirmed in your identity as His child, you voluntarily submit to His authority and hold yourself accountable to Him. Similarly, when your child knows that you love him and accept him regardless of his failures, he will feel safe sharing his problems with you and responding to the direction you give. Children who know they are loved are free to be themselves, free to grow, and free to be the person God wants them to be.[14]

How free do your children feel? How free do you feel? Christ came to set us free.

October 26

The LORD commanded us to observe all these statutes, to fear the LORD our God for our good always and for our survival (Deuteronomy 6:24, NASB).

God never asks something of parents that will bring harm to the home. And it won't weaken the child, it will help that boy or girl ultimately survive. Strong families survive from generation to generation because diligence is applied to the teaching process. And remember, the teaching weaves very naturally and comfortably into the fabric of everyday life. True religion is not something to be forced into or tacked onto life. It should flow through it.

I like the way Charlie Shedd described it in one of his original promises to his tiny son, Peter:[15]

I hope that I will be able to make religion natural to you. It is natural. In fact, I think this relationship with God is the only thing that is one hundred percent natural. We will pray together until it is easy for you to put your arms on the windowsill of heaven and look into the face of God.

Before I put you back in your crib, I want to tell you something Philip said.

We had been out in the country for a ride. It was evening and we ran out of gas. We were walking along after we had been to the farm house, and I was carrying a can of gas. Philip was only four. He was playing along, throwing rocks at the telephone poles, picking flowers, and then, all of a sudden it got dark. Sometimes night comes all at once in the country. Philip came over, put his little hand in mine and said, "Take my hand, Daddy. I might get lost."

Peter, there is a hand reaching to you from the heart of the universe. If you will lay your hand in the hand of God and walk with Him, you will never ever get lost.[16]

By the grace given me I say to every one of you: Do not think of yourself more highly than you ought, but rather think of yourself with sober judgment, in accordance with the measure of faith God has given you (Romans 12:3).

*H*ere is a brief quiz: Who is the most important person in your family? Naturally, the Lord is—that's obvious. But let's consider all the other members of your household: parents, children, even your pet dog or cat. Now, who is the most important and why? What about the one who...

+ makes the money to pay bills?
+ is the most responsive to meeting the needs of other family members?
+ oversees everyone else to make sure they don't forget anything and are on time?
+ brings the most joy and laughter into the house?
+ has the greatest potential for the future?

Those are some choices, aren't they? We all feel at times that we contribute the most and that the family couldn't get along without us. But no doubt the other family members feel the same way about themselves! So, who's the most important? You are. They are. You all are.

Paul tells us in Romans 12:4-6,10:

Just as there are many parts to our bodies, so it is with Christ's body. We are all parts of it, and it takes every one of us to make it complete, for we each have different work to do. So we belong to each other, and each needs all the others. God has given each of us the ability to do certain things well. . . . Love each other with brotherly affection and take delight in honoring each other (TLB).

Is there some family member who is doubting his or her own worth . . . whom you can help feel more important?[17]

October 28

Fathers, do not irritate and provoke your children to anger [do not exasperate them to resentment], but rear them [tenderly] in the training and discipline and the counsel and admonition of the Lord (Ephesians 6:4, AMP).

*I*t's all too easy for children to find their identity wrapped up in performance and appearance. Why? Largely because those are the values their parents and teachers reinforce. Children are applauded if they're cute, if they get straight As, if they say funny jokes, or if they hit home runs. Thanks to the adults in their lives, it doesn't take long for children to internalize and begin to live by three unhealthy principles:

1. If I am physically attractive and others admire me, I will be special.

2. If I perform well and accomplish great things, I will be accepted.

3. If I obtain social status and others recognize me, I will be significant.

But what about the child who isn't cute or entertaining? What about the child who never wins a starring role in the school play or strikes out most of the time in baseball? What if your child is below average academically? Tragically, children like these are often compared, rejected, or ignored by the adults in their lives—including their own parents! They begin to question their identity and doubt their worth. The false values our society promotes can even pervade our Christian homes.

What about you? Children may struggle with identity and self-acceptance because their parents struggle with the same issues. Children who grow up with a false basis for identity and acceptance don't automatically grow out of it when they reach adulthood. As adults they continue to base their identity on these three shaky pillars. They also tend to perpetuate them in their children.

If you are going to help your children realize their identity and acceptance in Christ, lead the way by doing so in your own life. You'll find a better life for yourself in doing so![18]

October 29

My son, keep your father's commands and do not forsake your mother's teaching (Proverbs 6:20).

*P*arents are told, "Someday your children will move out. They'll be on their own, and you'll have to let them go." That's true, but letting go is not a one-time act; it's an ongoing process throughout their lifetime. But what does letting go mean on a daily basis? Chuck Swindoll describes it best.

To let go doesn't mean to stop caring,
    it means I can't do it for someone else.
To let go is not to cut myself off,
    it's the realization that I can't control another.
To let go is not to enable,
    but to allow learning from natural consequences.
To let go is to admit powerlessness,
    which means the outcome is not in my hands.
To let go is not to try to change or blame another,
    I can only change myself.
To let go is not to care for,
    but to care about.
To let go is not to fix,
    but to be supportive.
To let go is not to judge,
    but to allow another to be a human being.
To let go is not to be in the middle arranging all the
        outcomes,
    but to allow others to affect their own outcomes.
To let go is not to be protective;
    it is to permit another to face reality.
To let go is not to deny,
    but to accept.
To let go is not to nag, scold, or argue,
    but to search out my own shortcomings and to correct them.
To let go is not to adjust everything to my desires,
    but to take each day as it comes.
To let go is not to criticize and regulate anyone,
    but to try to become what dream I can be.
To let go is not to regret the past,
    but to grow and live for the future.
To let go is to fear less and love more![19]

October 30

Isn't this the carpenter? (Mark 6:3).

$\mathcal{M}$ost of us don't spend much time thinking about Jesus as a carpenter. It doesn't seem so significant. And yet, maybe it does at that. A carpenter is someone who fashions and creates. Jesus did this both in the expression of His divinity and His humanity. He created the universe. "Through him all things were made; without him nothing was made that has been made" (John 1:3).

But He also fashioned simple pieces of furniture for people. If anyone knew about hard, arduous work it was Jesus. He didn't have a "Home Improvement" set with drills, electric saws, and the latest gadgetry. He had rough tools that were very basic and that required muscle power and produced calluses. His hands were probably covered with numerous bruises and cuts that came from handling wood and His crude tools. You would not believe the amount of time and energy it took to make a simple chair or table.

But what does Jesus' being a carpenter have to do with us? Consider these thoughts from one of the officers in The Salvation Army.

> As the Carpenter, Christ forever sanctified human toil. We are all members of the corporate society. As we derive many benefits, so must we be contributive to the community. Our tasks are given dignity by the One who worked amid the wood shavings at the carpenter's bench for the greater part of His life. His labor enabled the oxen to plow without being chafed by their yokes, children to take delight in the hand-carved toys, families to live in the comfort of a home built by the Carpenter.
>
> Today, the Carpenter of Nazareth who once smoothed yokes in His skillful hands, would take a life that is yielded to Him and fashion it into a beautiful and useful instrument of God's eternal kingdom.[20]

All your effort and toil as a parent has purpose and merit even though you wonder at times if it's worth it. As Jesus is fashioning your life, let Him work through you to fashion your child's life.

> Carpenter of Nazareth, take my life and smooth the coarseness of its grain, work out the flaws and imperfections, make me a worthwhile and useful instrument of the kingdom.[21]

October 31

Finally, brothers, whatever is true, whatever is noble, whatever is right, whatever is pure, whatever is lovely, whatever is admirable—if anything is excellent or praiseworthy—think about such things (Philippians 4:8).

*C*hildren are afraid of monsters, but they also like them. They are usually fascinated by them, read about them, watch them on television, and use them to scare other children. But monsters are just for kids, right? We're too old for that. Well, maybe not.

One woman dreamed she was being pursued by this grotesque, huge, terrifying monster. Wherever she ran it would be right behind her, breathing down her neck. Its teeth were bared and saliva was flying in the wind as it ran. And the noises it emitted were ghastly. The woman ran frantically but couldn't seem to put any distance between her and the beast. In her desperation, she ran down an alley that was a dead end.

All of a sudden she realized, *There's no way out. I'm trapped.* She looked to the left and the right but she was blocked by high walls on all sides. She watched as this hideous monster came closer and closer. It soon came to within inches of her face and she could feel its hot breath. She cried out, "What terrible thing are you going to do with me?" The monster stopped and said, "Hey, lady, that's up to you. It's your dream."

What's your dream? Is it a dream, or more of a nightmare? Some adults do live with monsters pursuing them in their minds. Sometimes our dreams become a portrayal of our thoughts. We give our thoughts and fantasies free rein and the monsters in our minds put on a cloak of reality.

Is there any monster in your life that has been given room to roam? If so, remember that monsters can be tamed. They're only as powerful as our thoughts. God's Word tells us what to do with our thoughts, as we can see in Philippians 4:8. For children, monsters are scary and fun. For adults, they're not fun. Just remember—what your monster does is up to you. It's your dream![22]

November 1

The joy of the LORD is your strength (Nehemiah 8:10).

*M*others and fathers need strength. Lots of it. Your exhaustion will come from too little time for too much to do, restless nights, demands unmatched with your resources, and sudden traumatic events that no one could possibly ever prepare for.

There is a well that never runs dry and will give you the strength of heart and mind that you need. When one of "those days" hits and you feel like you're trying to guide a plow through rocky ground with no one around to help shoulder the load, go to the Scripture. Stop, sit down, take a breath, and read. Silently or out loud. Let the words soak through and saturate you.

> The LORD is my rock, my fortress and my deliverer; my God is my rock, in whom I take refuge. He is my shield and the horn of my salvation, my stronghold (Psalm 18:2).

> The LORD is my light and my salvation—whom shall I fear? The LORD is the stronghold of my life—of whom shall I be afraid? . . . Wait for the LORD; be strong and take heart and wait for the LORD (Psalm 27:1,14).

> Be my rock of refuge, to which I can always go; give the command to save me, for you are my rock and my fortress (Psalm 71:3).

> My soul is weary with sorrow; strengthen me according to your word (Psalm 119:28).

> He who fears the LORD has a secure fortress, and for his children it will be a refuge (Proverbs 14:26).

> Surely God is my salvation; I will trust and not be afraid. The LORD, the LORD, is my strength and my song; he has become my salvation (Isaiah 12:2).

> He gives strength to the weary and increases the power of the weak. . . . but those who hope in the LORD will renew their strength. They will soar on wings like eagles; they will run and not grow weary, they will walk and not be faint (Isaiah 40:29,31).

November 2

The LORD God said, "It is not good for the man to be alone. I will make a helper suitable for him" (Genesis 2:18).

A Letter to a Child About to Be Married

I just wanted to share some random thoughts with you concerning the years ahead in your marriage. Hopefully these will assist you in your journey together. As you grow together in your marriage, there are two roles for each one of you to take. At times you will be a teacher to your partner, but on other occasions you will be the student.

We live in a competitive society. Sometimes that's necessary, but never compete with one another. You will at times disagree. That's normal and healthy, but behaving disagreeably isn't necessary. When there are differences in your relationship your goal is reconciliation, not blame.

Your partner will say or do some things that will bother you. Be sure to tell your spouse what you would *like* him or her to do rather than concentrate on what you don't like.

Remember how you fell in love? You talked, you listened, you did loving acts. You will stay in love by not only continuing to do those very things, but by doing them with a higher level of frequency and intensity than before.

Always be supportive and loyal to one another. Put into practice 1 Corinthians 13:7, "If you love someone you will be loyal to him no matter what the cost. You will always believe in him, always expect the best of him, and always stand your ground in defending him" (TLB).

When conflicts arise, don't avoid them. If you do you will just bury the problem and you'll have buried it alive. Eventually it will rise from its grave and confront you. If you want to get rid of your conflicts, look them squarely in the face, talk about them, and discover creative ways to resolve them. Learn from them. Use them as growth experiences.

A gentle hug or holding one another in silence is an act of love that conveys the message, "You're special. I love you. I understand."

May your marriage be all you want it to be.

November 3

Fathers, do not provoke or irritate or fret your children [do not be hard on them or harass them]; lest they become discouraged and sullen and morose and feel inferior and frustrated. [Do not break their spirit] (Colossians 3:21, AMP).

"That's good enough."

"That's not good enough."

You probably heard these two comments as a child and you probably say them to yourself now. They're both okay, especially the first one, when it comes to being a parent.

Too many parents want to be perfect. Instead, they end up feeling like failures, frustrated over their inability to attain the impossible. Perfectionistic parents also are too demanding of their children. People who can't accept themselves unless they're perfect won't accept the efforts of other people.

But good-enough parents do what they can for the benefit of children. They recognize what they can and can't do and the strengths and limitations of their circumstances. Yes, they'll make mistakes. Yes, they'll disappoint their children. We all do. But good-enough parents are able to give the love and emotional support their children need without being too demanding. They give guidance through word and example. They're able to create a close relationship but also give their children freedom enough to develop their uniqueness and make necessary decisions on their own.

Good-enough parents are students—of themselves, their children, of God, and of good resources about parenting. But they never let technique interfere with being a real person—someone who is approachable, transparent, and admits mistakes.

A single parent can be a good-enough parent; a couple can be good-enough parents, especially when they coparent. Ease up on yourself, strengthen what needs to be strengthened, be available and involved, and above all, relax and enjoy your children.[1]

November 4

Until now you have not asked for anything in my name. Ask and you will receive, and your joy will be complete (John 16:24).

Parent: I can see it on your face. You've got a question.

Child: Uh-huh. You know how we end our prayers, "In Jesus' name"?

Parent: Yes . . .

Child: Well, why do we? Does that mean if we don't say, "In Jesus' name" our prayers are no good or that God doesn't hear us or answer? Who said we have to say, "In Jesus' name" and . . .

Parent: Wait, wait, wait. You have some of the same questions I had when I was your age. Our prayers will still get through to God even if we don't use Jesus' name. The reason we do, however, is because Jesus told us to. When you pray "In Jesus' name" there's more to it than just saying the words. It means that we are willing to be obedient to what He has taught us. And when we are obedient we will be praying what He wants us to pray for. Understand?

Child: I'm trying to . . .

Parent: I guess the big word here is obedience. The more obedient we are to Jesus the more we pray according to His will. Perhaps giving you four purposes of praying in His name will help.

   The first purpose of praying in Jesus' name is to glorify God, not just to get what we want. John 14:3 says, "I will do whatever you ask in my name, so that the Son may bring glory to the Father." Second, praying this way is based only on what Jesus has done, not on us at all. Third, a person who prays in Jesus' name claims to be His representative, so he or she needs to be a true believer. That can be costly today. Finally, when you pray in Jesus' name, you should be trying to pray as Jesus would in the same situation. How's all that for an answer?

Child: So when we use His name, we better know what we're doing. It's pretty serious stuff![2]

November 5

I pray that you may be active in sharing your faith, so that you will have a full understanding of every good thing we have in Christ. . . . I do wish, brother, that I may have some benefit from you in the Lord; refresh my heart in Christ (Philemon 6, 20).

*P*eople joke around about our inability to take possessions with us into heaven. But who would want to? What is there that you would want to take for the duration of eternity aside from your family? Not too many of our possessions would mean that much. Ask your children the same question, and they might say, "My teddy bear" or, "My Nintendo set" or even, "My pet."

Perhaps the question shouldn't be, "*What* would you like to take with you?" but, "Who would you like to take?" Who is it that you want to spend eternity with that doesn't yet know Jesus as his or her Savior? That puts a whole new light on the subject, doesn't it? Do you have a list of the names of people you're praying for so you all can spend eternity together? That's a good place to begin. Once their names are on a list, then your prayers can begin.

God wants us to tell other people about the salvation that we've been given. Of course we want our children, spouse, and other family members to know. But there are other people. What about your postman, grocer, physician, barber, or manicurist? Do they know you're a Christian?

You can tell other people about Christ by the life you live in front of them. You know—the way you drive, talk about others, or respond when an overloaded shopping cart crushes your foot as someone cuts in line at the market. How do you respond to people who mess up your orders or bills or ignore you and take the next person in line? What's your response to the smelly, dirty street person who knocks on your door looking for work or a meal?

Words will tell other people what we believe. But our behavior says volumes more. Let's share who we are, what we have, and who Jesus is.[3]

November 6

Recalling your tears, I long to see you, so that I may be filled with joy (2 Timothy 1:4).

Stubborn, dogged determination. That's what it takes to persevere. Just keep trying again and again and again." That's the message that's been given to children, groups, communities, and even nations: Keep at it.

When Robert the First (1274–1329) was the king of Scotland the English tried to invade his small kingdom. Robert tried to protect Scotland, but a time came when he had to retreat from his castle to avoid capture and death. He escaped to a cave and struggled with depression and the uncertainty of what to do next.

Do you as a parent ever feel uncertain what to do next?

Then the king noticed a very small spider spinning its web. It kept working and working, adding one new strand at a time. Sometimes the spider failed, but it kept at his task, and finally, there was a web inviting some careless fly to come and be captured.

The king observed that the spider's perseverance reflected two qualities—patience and tolerance. The spider never gave thought to giving up. As Robert reflected on the spider, he began to evict his anxious thoughts.

Are there some anxious thoughts that need evicting from your life?

Looking at his problems more objectively and logically, the king saw them in a different light.

Could you take a different perspective of the issues facing you?

The king then made a decision that he would be like the spider and never give up. He came up with some new ideas and put them into practice, kicking the depression out of his life. Finally, in the year 1329, he was successful and the English recognized Scotland's independence.

Do you ever feel that other people conspire against you much like the English did against Robert? Are there obstacles blocking what you would like for your life? Whatever you're facing, instead of hitting it head-on with a direct onslaught, why not go over it, around it, or under it? Try a new approach: calm down, kick out the confusing depressing thoughts—and like the spider—persevere. It's possible with the Lord as your partner.[4]

November 7

"In your anger do not sin": Do not let the sun go down while you are still angry (Ephesians 4:26).

*E*very child gets angry. So does every parent. A child will yell, spit, swear, hold his breath, kick, scream—you could probably add some more expressions of anger. Anger is a natural response; it's a God-created emotion. But children are not born with control over their anger. They have to learn control. Some do, some don't. What can you do to help your children?

Teach your children the cause of their anger. Usually anger is a secondary emotion caused by fear, hurt, or frustration. Teach your children to ask themselves why they are angry.

Let them talk about their anger in a positive way. A five-year-old boy came up to his father and said, "Dad, I'm angry." His father said, "That's great. I bet it feels good to know how you're feeling." After the boy talked about his situation for awhile, he felt better and went outside to play.

If one of your children doesn't talk about his or her anger, you could say, "Honey, I can see you're upset. Do you know what's bothering you? Would you like to talk about it now or later?" Help your children accept the responsibility for their anger. They will tell you that so-and-so made them angry. Kids love to blame. But they need to understand that even when another person may have done something wrong, we are still responsible for how we respond. Help your children choose how they are going to respond. You could suggest to your children the following responses:

+ They could tell three of their friends how angry they are.

+ They could set a timer for 30 minutes, go to their room, and kick and scream.

+ They could write a letter to God and tell Him how they feel.

+ They could tell you how they feel and then you could pray with them.

Give them a choice. By the way, what do you do when you're angry?

November 8

There is a time for everything, and a season for every activity under heaven (Ecclesiastes 3:1).

*L*et's imagine that you've just received a sweepstake letter in the mail that says, "Congratulations, parent. You are a winner. Yes, a winner of $1,440! You can spend the money for anything you want, but there's just one stipulation: You must spend it all within 24 hours. You can't save it nor can you give away any portion of it. It must be spent by you."

What would you do with $1,440? If you're a saver you might want to put it in your savings account, but the letter says you can't do that. Nor can you share it with your children. You must spend it!

So . . . how will you use it? But wait—before you have any visions of a new couch or golf clubs—the $1,440 you are being given isn't really money. It's minutes.

You are given 1,440 minutes to spend during each day of your life, and it can't be saved or given away. How are you using this allotment each day? When you think of a day in terms of 1,440 minutes, it puts a whole new perspective on how you use your time. Too many people look back at their life and wish they had used their time differently.

Some parents who learned about the concept of 1,440 minutes per day started keeping track of their time, discovered the following, and made some adjustments:

> ✦ One father discovered he was using 157 minutes a day just driving back and forth to work.
>
> ✦ A family discovered they were spending 185 minutes a day in front of the TV.
>
> ✦ Another family discovered they spent only 23 minutes together each day.

These families all discovered the truth that once time is gone, it's lost forever. How are you and your family using your time? Are you in charge of it, or is someone or something else dictating its usage? Are you seizing each moment and getting the most out of it? 1,440 minutes—where do they go? How are they used? That's a choice we all have to make.[5]

November 9

Cast all your anxiety on him because he cares for you (1 Peter 5:7).

Nobody likes stress—that feeling of being pulled tight like an overstretched rubber band. An old Anglo-Saxon definition of the word was "to strangle or choke."

Parents battle stress, and so do children. Sometimes parents feel helpless because they're not sure how to help their children learn to cope with stress. There are some basic steps you may already be taking, but it helps to be reminded. Here's what works: Children need parents who care deeply about them and who are available physically, emotionally, and spiritually.

Another help in overcoming stress is the availability of a caring and loving extended family or other adults. These other adults can listen and be a source of support when parents are unavailable. "Adopted" grandparents at your church can provide support for both the child and the senior adult.

It's also essential that children live in an abuse-free environment. Did you know that yelling is classified as emotional abuse? Perhaps we need to watch the volume of our voices more carefully in our homes.

Parents who are involved in their children's school can determine if that environment is helping to cause or reduce stress. It helps to build positive and healthy relationships with your children's teachers.

Also, accept your child for who he or she is. Children who like themselves and can accept their strengths and weaknesses have resilience. They can handle stress better. And there are three ways you can help them (and perhaps help yourself) with acceptance:

+ Keep the competition level in activities to a minimum.

+ Don't overload your children's schedule. Children need time to be children. Allow them time to just "hang out."

+ Let your children know they're valued just for who they are. That will work best if you value who you are, too![6]

November 10

Trust in the LORD with all your heart and lean not on your own understanding (Proverbs 3:5).

Dear God,

I am powerless
and my life is unmanageable
without Your love and guidance.
I come to You today
because I believe that
You can restore and renew me
to meet my needs tomorrow
and to help me meet the needs of my children.

Since I cannot manage my life or affairs,
I have decided to give them to You.
I put my life, my will,
my thoughts,
my desires and ambitions in Your hands.
I give You each of my children.

I know that You will work them out
in accordance with Your plan.

Such as I am,
take and use me in Your service.
Guide and direct my ways
and show me what to do for You.

I cannot control or change my children,
other family members or friends,
so I release them into Your care
for Your loving hands to do with as You will.
Just keep me loving and free from judging them.

If they need changing, God,
You'll have to do it; I can't.
Just make me willing and ready
to be of service to You,
to have my shortcomings removed,
and to do my best.

I am seeking to know You better,
to love You more.
I am seeking the knowledge of Your will for me
and the power to carry it out.

Anonymous[7]

November 11

"Come, follow me," Jesus said. (Matthew 4:19).

*W*hy follow Jesus? Because everything He said and did was in our best interest.

Christ said to follow Him because following anyone or anything else gets us lost.

Christ said to know who we look like because drawing our self-image from any other source but God poisons our souls and spirits.

Christ said to love our neighbor as ourselves because we grow the most when committed to fostering another's growth, not just our own.

Christ said to clean the inside of the cup because that is the only way to develop true character and avoid a shallow existence.

Christ said to stop fitting in with our culture because our culture is sick, and adapting to it will make us sick, too.

Christ said to get real because wearing masks makes our lives empty and our relationships unfulfilling.

Christ said to stop blaming others because taking responsibility for our own problems is essential for true maturity and health.

Christ said to forgive others because unforgiveness is arrogant and hurts others as well as ourselves.

Christ said to live like an heir because to live like an orphan leads to settling for far too little in life.

Christ said to solve paradoxes because it is often that which seems contrary to common sense that is the healthiest route of all.

Christ said to stop worrying because worry only drains us of the energy we need to work on the things that we can do something about.

Christ said to persevere because the fruit of our labor won't ever show up if we grow tired of doing what it takes to bear it.

Everything Christ tells us is in our best interest, and it is critically important to understand that. His counsel wasn't designed to burden us, but to set us free. When He gave His counsel to us, it was aimed at meeting our deepest needs and it will if we follow it.[8]

November 12

Thy hands made me and fashioned me (Psalm 119:73, NASB).

*E*motions! Who needs them? All of us do.

Our emotions influence almost every aspect of our lives. God speaks to us through our emotions. They are like a sixth sense. They help us to monitor our needs, make us aware of good and evil, and provide motivation and energy for growth and change. They give us the vigor, power, and impetus for living.

Sin has led us to respond to our emotions in one of two unhealthy ways. First, we can deny or ignore them. From this perspective, that which is intellectual is considered more important than that which is emotional. In its extreme form, head knowledge is deified and emotions are made suspect. Emotions, at best, are viewed as unimportant and, at worst, considered a mark of immaturity. Unfortunately, when we ignore or minimize the emotional realities of our life we distort our perspective, limit our perception, and lead ourselves to distrust our experiences. We often tend to deny or ignore the very things God wants to use to help us grow.

Second, we can allow ourselves to be controlled by our emotions. This is equally dangerous. This perspective views the intellect as suspect. "If I don't feel it, then I can't trust it," say those who embrace emotions exclusively. But consider the consequences. When Saul allowed his jealousy over David's popularity and success to be in control, he was not able to learn from his mistakes (1 Samuel 18-20). Fear and depression caused Elijah to lose perspective and want to die (1 Kings 19:4).

Whether you deny or ignore your emotions (option #1) or you embrace them and ignore your intellect (option #2), your response is not healthy.

By God's grace, there is a third option. The healthy response is to view our emotions from God's perspective and to bring them into harmony with our mind. Maturity involves the whole person. It is impossible to be spiritually mature and emotionally immature. True maturity involves bringing balance to our heart, head, and will—to our feelings, thoughts, and actions. Each aspect of our lives is important. Each was designed by God for our good. Each is a manifestation of the image of God in us.[9]

November 13

We have different gifts, according to the grace given us. . . . if it is encouraging, let him encourage (Romans 12:6,8).

*A*re you an exhorter? Many people do not truly understand what the gift of exhortation is. Frequently it's equated with preaching, but that's not exactly accurate.

Various versions of the Bible portray this gift differently. For example, the King James version describes this kind of person as "he that exhorteth" (verse 8). In the Berkeley version this person is described as "the admonisher." In the Williams version the person with this gift is described as "one who encourages others." J.B. Philips, in his modern English version, describes this gift as one used in "stimulating" the faith of others. Elsewhere in the New Testament, the concept of exhortation is used to convey the idea of consolation, comfort, and entreaty.

So . . . if a parent has this spiritual gift, he or she will find it very natural to admonish, advise, encourage, and stir up the faith and self-worth of his or her children. When children are in this kind of environment they will feel cheered and uplifted. They will feel fortified because of the parent's noncritical listening as well as his or her belief in the children's capabilities. They will know the parent will be available whenever needed. The gift of exhortation is often manifested by taking the time to explain, amplify, or clarify situations for other people. A balanced exhorter is a person who knows enough not to get so personally involved that it jeopardizes his or her time, knowledge, or finances. He or she also knows not to allow other people to create an unhealthy dependency upon him or her.

Is this your gift? Your spouse's? Your child's? All of us as parents need to be people of encouraging words, for "anxiety in a man's heart weighs it down, but an encouraging word makes it glad" (Proverbs 12:25, AMP).

If exhortation is your gift, it will come naturally. Use it to build up other people and glorify the Lord.[10]

November 14

Do not fret because of evil men or be envious of those who do wrong (Psalm 37:1).

*H*ow can you help your child handle stress? Consider what Archibald Hart says in his excellent book *Stress and Your Child:*

Some stress is inevitable—even necessary—in everyday life. In order to function in the world, your child must stay alert, pay attention, and respond appropriately. He or she must go to school and learn. Certain tasks must be mastered and assignments must be completed. Play, too, involves certain challenges—learning to get along with other children, taking on new physical challenges, stretching mind and body. Every child must, therefore, embrace a certain degree of stress. But the stress problem begins when ordinary stress becomes too much stress.

Think of the human body as a machine. Of course, a human being is more than this, but the analogy is fitting in that the human body, like a machine, was designed to carry out certain tasks in certain ways. And the human body, like every machine, has its certain built-in limitations.

Take an electric motor, for example. If you examine the label on the motor of your washing machine or refrigerator you will notice that the phrase "duty cycle" is stamped on it, followed by a figure that is usually expressed as a percentage. The percentage refers to the amount of time the motor is designed to run. For example, a motor that is rated as "Duty Cycle 20 percent" is supposed to run only 20 percent of the time. If forced to run more than this, it is likely to overheat and suffer increased wear and tear. If used continuously, the motor could burn out.

The human body and mind also have a "duty cycle." Our "motors" are designed for a certain amount of usage—stress, if you will. When the demand placed on the human machine exceeds this usage, the capacity for normal functioning will be exceeded; the result is "overheating" and increased wear and tear. And this overusage is what we commonly call stress. And this damage comes either from severely overloading the machine or from running a moderate overload for an extended period of time.[11]

Does any of that apply to you?

November 15

People were bringing little children to Jesus to have him touch them, but the disciples rebuked them. When Jesus saw this, he was indignant. He said to them, "Let the little children come to me, and do not hinder them, for the kingdom of God belongs to such as these. I tell you the truth, anyone who will not receive the kingdom of God like a little child will never enter it." And he took the children in his arms, put his hands on them and blessed them (Mark 10:13-16).

*T*he ministry of Jesus was marked by touching. He was personally involved with people—all kinds of people. Some of them you wouldn't have wanted to touch. Have you ever had an unkempt, dirty, smelly homeless person approach you for money in a shopping mall? Many of us not only refuse to touch such a person, we also draw back. We're repulsed. And that's understandable.

But have you ever wondered how Jesus would have responded to such people? Perhaps we have a clue from Scripture: "A man with leprosy came to him and begged him on his knees, 'If you are willing, you can make me clean.' Filled with compassion, Jesus reached out his hand and touched the man. 'I am willing,' he said. 'Be clean!' Immediately the leprosy left him and he was cured" (Mark 1:40-42).

This man was covered with leprosy. Probably some of the sores had filthy bandages on them and other sores were open. To touch him was unthinkable. But the purpose of Jesus' ministry shouts loudly to us here: "He was moved with compassion." The leper wasn't the only person Jesus touched. He touched the broken and disabled parts of people's bodies to bring new life to them. He didn't wonder or worry about what other people would think. He wasn't concerned. He knew there was healing in His touch back then . . . and there's healing in His touch today.

The point of all this is a simple question: If Jesus were here, in your presence, for what reason would He need to touch you? How do you need to be touched by your Savior?

November 16

My son, hear the instruction of your father; reject not nor forsake the teaching of your mother (Proverbs 1:8, AMP).

*W*hat can fathers do to be involved with their children in both a unique and lasting way? Here is what some dads do or have done.

+ A father with five children sets aside one hour a week for each of his children. This hour is their time alone. And, the child is the one who decides what they will do, whether it's reading, wrestling, playing games, or going for a snack.

+ One father had his children videotape interviews with their aunts, uncles, and grandparents. The questions asked during the interview all related to the years when their dad was growing up. Not only did the children learn more about their own father, but also the interaction with significant relatives was preserved for the future.

+ Another father tape-recorded the family meal during Thanksgiving and Christmas for a number of years. When each child married, he gave that child a set of the tapes.

+ One father put his children in charge of map-reading and navigation prior to and during their family vacation each year. This also included keeping track of car expenses, figuring out miles per gallon of gasoline, and so on, and keeping this information in a notebook.

+ A father (and mother) worked out both a driving and dating covenant with each of their children prior to the time each of the children began to drive or date.

+ A young father went to several older men in his church and interviewed them with these questions: "What have you done well as a father?" "What do you wish you would have done differently?" "What advice would you give to me?" That was a wise father!

+ Another father met with his family once a month and, during this meeting, everyone shared their upcoming schedules. All the activities were posted on a master calendar that hung in the kitchen. Any changes were not only put on the calendar but were also shared with everyone within 24 hours of the change.

What can you do to enhance the parenting role in your home?

November 17

Jesus said to them, "Surely you will quote this proverb to me: 'Physician, heal yourself!'" (Luke 4:23).

*W*hen you're a parent, a portion of your life is devoted to camping out in doctors' offices. You listen, follow their advice, and in many ways you're dependent on them. But like the rest of us, doctors have limitations, and there are some diseases and problems they cannot cure.

The title of *physician* was given to Jesus by...Jesus Himself. And heal He did! The deplorable conditions we see among the sick today in many poor countries would be overshadowed by what conditions were like during the time of Jesus. Hospitals? No. Clinics? None. Anesthesia? What was that? Sterile conditions? No such thing. But still, Jesus healed. He was the Physician who was caring and compassionate, and He could heal in ways no one else could.

> When evening came, many who were demon-possessed were brought to him, and he drove out the spirits with a word and healed all the sick (Matthew 8:16).

> Great crowds came to him, bringing the lame, the blind, the crippled, the mute and many others, and laid them at his feet; and he healed them. The people were amazed when they saw the mute speaking, the crippled made well, the lame walking and the blind seeing. And they praised the God of Israel (Matthew 15:30,31).

Don't you wish Jesus were here today to lay His hands on people around us or perhaps even on you? If you could ask Jesus to heal you or a family member, what would you want healed? Jesus healed not just the sick in body but also the sick in mind.

Do you know what sets Jesus apart from the other doctors of His time and today? He came as a Physician to heal every single person from a fatal disease called sin. He did this by coming to earth, taking our sins upon Himself, feeling our pain, and putting our suffering upon Himself to make us whole. Yes, our bodies still get old, wear out, break down, and sometimes can't be fixed. But our souls can. The burden of sin has already undergone the Surgeon's knife and is healed. All you have to do is ask for the healing...and it's yours.[12]

November 18

Understand [this], my beloved brethren. Let every man be quick to hear [a ready listener], slow to speak, slow to take offense and to get angry (James 1:19, AMP).

Be a Ready Listener
A Personal Note from a Father

Fathers can have a great impact upon their children—especially a daughter. It's important that you listen carefully to what she is saying and even more carefully to the message behind her words. Treat every opportunity to spend time with your daughter as a unique gift from God—a gift that you'll never experience in exactly the same way again. And allow the time you spend with her to be a gift to her from you.

The times that your daughter wants to be together with you may not always coincide with the times you are available. For example, one time when my daughter was 12 years old, she came home from a piano lesson with the song "Sunrise, Sunset" from *Fiddler on the Roof.* "Daddy, will you play this for me?" she asked. I set aside the book I was reading, rose from my comfortable recliner, and sat down at the piano and played the piece several times—much to my daughter's delight.

After dinner I again settled into my chair to relax and read. "Daddy, will you play the song again?" she begged. My first response, which I did not verbalize aloud, was, "Sheryl, I've already played 'Sunrise, Sunset' enough for one day. I want to read. Play it yourself this time." But I think I heard the Lord saying to me, "You're not too busy. Take time for Sheryl." So I left my chair again and began playing for her. Soon my wife and Sheryl were standing behind me singing the words to the beautiful tune.

Then it hit me: The lyrics describe a father's feelings about his little girl becoming a young woman. I suddenly realized that the words expressed some of my feelings about seeing Sheryl grow up. I played the song several more times as Joyce and Sheryl sang. That became a very important and special time in my relationship with Sheryl—and it cost me less than 15 minutes. But I came so close to missing it by saying, "I'm too busy."

November 19

You have been a refuge for the poor, a refuge for the needy in his distress, a shelter from the storm and a shade from the heat. For the breath of the ruthless is like a storm driving against a wall and like the heat of the desert (Isaiah 25:4).

You're out in the backyard working away. The sun beats down hotter and hotter. You then glance around to see if there's any shade available—if there are any clouds in the sky. If there are, you try to figure out if one will drift by and cast its shadow on you. If and when that does happen, you find relief. The only problem is, shadows don't stand still. They move, so you have to move. Just as you get settled it's time once again to move. Though the relief offered by the cloud is temporary at best, you are grateful because the shadow helped you to cool down.

Some of life's shadows, however, turn up the heat. Everything is going well. The children are doing well in school, there are no illnesses, your finances are all right, and you're excited about an upcoming trip. Then, unexpectedly, something happens that casts a shadow over your life. Something dark drifts into your life and blocks out the sun. Sometimes one of your children become seriously ill, or one of your teens stray away from the Lord for a few years. Unfortunately, these shadows tend to stay for awhile.

How can we handle these shadows? By shifting ourselves underneath another shadow permanently. Yes, permanently. You want a nonshifting, nonchanging shadow, and that comes only from God. "Every good thing bestowed and every perfect gift is from above, coming down from the Father of lights, with whom there is no variation, or shifting shadow" (James 1:17, NASB). God doesn't, never has, and never will change. His shadow overshadows all the other shadows in life! Scripture says, "He who dwells in the shelter of the Most High will rest in the shadow of the Almighty" (Psalm 91:1).

Knowing these promises does wonders not just for parents, but for children, too. Why not learn them together?[13]

November 20

You created my inmost being; you knit me together in my mother's womb (Psalm 139:13).

*A*ren't children a wonder? They can amaze you. Then again, they can frustrate you. They can bring you overwhelming joy or they can break your heart. Above all, they are important—not just to you, but to God.

Children are a product of God's handiwork. Some night when they are asleep, go in and look at them and then read this passage aloud:

> You created my inmost being; you knit me together in my mother's womb. I praise you because I am fearfully and wonderfully made; your works are wonderful, I know that full well. My frame was not hidden from you when I was made in the secret place. When I was woven together in the depths of the earth, your eyes saw my unformed body. All the days ordained for me were written in your book before one of them came to be. How precious to me are your thoughts, O God! How vast is the sum of them! Were I to count them, they would outnumber the grains of sand. When I awake, I am still with you (Psalm 139:13-18).

Your value and your children's just can't be measured. It's so crucial that both you and your children understand how valuable you are.

Your opinion of yourself may fluctuate from time to time, but it probably remains fairly stable. Your children have opinions of themselves, too. Perhaps we could call these opinions a mental picture. And as you know, all sorts of things can happen when we take pictures with a camera. Some of the pictures can be out of focus. Some can be overexposed while others are underexposed.

As a parent, would you say that the picture you have of yourself matches what God says about you in Psalm 139? What about your children? Does their mental image reflect this in-focus picture? If not, you may want to read Psalm 139:13-18 out loud for a number of days. Let its truths soak into your heart and mind so they can refocus your lens. When you have a clear focus of yourself, then your children can have a clearer focus on who they are. Let God's Word be your standard.

November 21

[Jesus] said to them, "Let the little children come to me....and he took the children in his arms, put his hands on them and blessed them" (Mark 10:14,16).

*W*hat is the best way to pray for yourself and your children? That's an important question. Sometimes we can get so busy as a parent that prayer is a last-minute thought, a last resort, or is half-finished because we fall asleep in exhaustion.

Here are some practical suggestions for prayer: First, pray when you're fresh and alert. This will vary because of your metabolism. There is no "best time."

Then, when you pray, be specific. When the blind man came to Jesus he was very direct. "I want to see" was his request (Mark 10:51).

Third, have you ever prayed Scripture passages aloud? Take the promises of God's Word and use them as prayers for yourselves and your children. The Scripture states that "faith comes from hearing the message, and the message is heard through the word of Christ" (Romans 10:17).

Fourth, keep a prayer journal. Don't just list your requests, but write out some of your prayers in detail. Our memories fade in and out, especially when we get older. So when a prayer is answered, go back to the request and write in the date. Some parents give their children the prayer journal they have kept for them when the children graduate from high school. What a gift!

Fifth, remember to ask God what He wants you to pray about for your children.

Finally, remember that some of the prayers you pray for your children are "future or waiting prayers." Are you praying now for the friends that you want God to bring into your children's lives in the next decade? Are you praying for their life's partner? What about their choice of a college or their vocation? You may pray some prayers for 10 to 15 years. That's all right. Just remember this: "Confess your sins to each other and pray for each other so that you may be healed. The prayer of a righteous man is powerful and effective" (James 5:16).

November 22

Become useful and helpful and kind to one another (Ephesians 4:32, AMP).

*T*he boomerang is a weapon used for hunting in Australia. That's where the boomerang was invented. When a skilled person uses it, the boomerang can be thrown for a great distance, and then it circles around and comes back to the hand of the thrower. Amazing? No, not really. That's its purpose. It was constructed to do that.

Our behavior is just like a boomerang. The way we act toward other people will return to us. Most parents begin teaching their children this principle at an early age, especially the boomerang effect of kindness.

Do you remember the fable about the lion and the mouse? A hungry lion caught a mouse, and the mouse said, "I'm not much of a mouthful. You let me go, and someday I may be able to do you a favor." The lion laughed but let him go. Later the lion was caught in a net trap made out of ropes. The mouse came along, gnawed the ropes in two, and the lion was able to get away.

God's Word calls us to be different and reflect the presence of Jesus Christ in our lives. In a world of violence and hatred, being kind and tenderhearted is different! Some people think that only weak people are kind. But a person can be both strong and tenderhearted.

Kindness is a character quality that is never forgotten. Your acts of kindness will return to you like a boomerang. It may take awhile—even months—for your kindness to be returned to you, but be patient. What you do will be remembered. And perhaps someone who doesn't yet know our Lord will ask, "Why are you so kind?" Then you will have an opportunity to tell them about Jesus' work in your life.

November 23

This is what the LORD says: "Let not the wise man boast of his wisdom or the strong man boast of his strength or the rich man boast of his riches, but let him who boasts boast about this: that he understands and knows me, that I am the LORD, who exercises kindness, justice and righteousness on earth, for in these I delight (Jeremiah 9:23,24).

The goal of our life is to understand and know God. And the more that you know Him, the more you're able to praise Him. But did you know that works both ways? The more that you praise Him, the more you will know Him.

Did you know there's a difference between praise and thanksgiving? Think about that for a minute. You thank your children at times. And you praise them, too. Perhaps both of these are mixed together at times. But when it comes to God, there is a distinction between the two. Dr. Lloyd Ogilvie explains:

> Praise would be distinguished from thanksgiving.
> When we give thanks, we glorify God for what He has done; when we praise Him, we glorify Him for what He is in Himself. Praise concentrates on God for Himself rather than His gifts and provisions. And according to His own desires expressed so clearly, He longs for us to glory in the fact that we understand and know Him. The depth of our praise measures the quality of our relationship with Him.
> The psalmist expressed genuine praise when he said,

> > I will praise you, O Lord, with my whole heart; I will tell of Your marvelous works. I will be glad and rejoice in You; I will sing praises to Your name (Psalm 9:1,2).

> In Psalm 63:3-4 the same authentic praise is expressed,

> > Because Your lovingkindness is better than life, my lips shall praise You. Thus I will bless You while I live.

> In both of these verses, the psalmist is riveted on God.[14]

Do you know why it's difficult for some people to praise God? One reason is that it's easier to tell Him what we need. Another reason is pride. When you praise God you're admitting that He is Lord of all. It's always good to remember that God does a better job of being in charge of your life than you do.

November 24

Six days you shall labor, but on the seventh day you shall rest; even during the plowing season and harvest you must rest (Exodus 34:21).

*D*o you have a regular time of rest? Real rest? Parents who are asked this question respond in a variety of ways. They don't say anything, but look at you like you've lost your mind. Or they say, "You've got to be kidding. With three toddlers? Right!" Or, "Not with my schedule. It's impossible!" Or, "I think I did . . . six years ago."

Many people feel that rest is not even possible during the parenting years. But it's got to be there. It's a must both scripturally and physically. It's easy to ignore both the Sabbath and your own needs. Sometimes you don't even know you're ignoring your needs because everything you do is admirable and applauded.

We all have to work at rest. Whether we're a mother, father, executive, schoolteacher, or involved in ministry, we need rest. Dr. Richard Foster describes his battle for rest:

> After a certain amount of immersion in public life, I begin to burn out. And I have noticed that I burn out inwardly long before I do outwardly. Hence, I must be careful not to become a frantic bundle of hollow energy, busy among people but devoid of life. I must learn when to retreat, like Jesus, and experience the recreating power of God. . . . And along our journey we need to discover numerous "tarrying places" where we can receive "heavenly manna."[15]

If someone mentions the word *rest* to you, what's the first thought that comes to mind? Unnecessary, waste, elusive, deserved? The word *rest* is not in the vocabulary of workaholics. Many came from homes that equated rest with laziness. Fortunately, God defines rest differently. He sees rest as necessary; He sees rest as something needed so we can worship Him. If God puts a priority on rest, we'd better listen to Him. After all, it's a gift from Him.

November 25

Give thanks to the LORD, for he is good; his love endures forever (Psalm 107:1).

Let us come before him with thanksgiving and extol him with music and song (Psalm 95:2).

*T*hanksgiving day. Platters of food, mouth-watering aromas, everyone waiting for the first servings—especially the children. Can you imagine what their reaction would be if you gave them a plate with five kernels of corn on it? That's what the pilgrims did when they celebrated the first Thanksgiving. It was done to remind them of the difficult year they had experienced. After prayers of gratitude were offered, then the meal was served.

Think back to the first Thanksgiving you can remember. Try to capture the sights, the sounds, the food, and who was there. Have you ever asked the people at your own Thanksgiving table what they remember about Thanksgivings past? What a great experience it would be for your children (and for you) to talk to someone who experienced Thanksgiving during the depression years or World War II. Ours was a completely different time and culture then.

How can you make your Thanksgiving be both memorable and different this year? How might your family reflect the true meaning of the occasion? Some families make it a point each year to provide for a homeless or less fortunate family as much as they provide for themselves.

Thanksgiving reminds us that we can't run our own lives. We need God. We're dependent upon Him. He desires our gratitude. Perhaps the best way to show thanks is to say "God, thank You for being God. May I be a vessel of gratitude and may I be loving in the way I respond to other people."[16]

November 26

There is now no condemnation for those who are in Christ Jesus. . . . if Christ is in you, your body is dead because of sin, yet your spirit is alive because of righteousness (Romans 8:1,10).

*T*he following prayer from William Barclay reminds us of what Jesus did for us and what He will do for us.

O God, our Father, we thank You that You sent your Son Jesus Christ into this world to be our Savior and our Lord.

We thank You that He took our body and our flesh and blood upon Himself, and so showed us that this body of ours is fit to be Your dwelling place.

We thank You that He did our work, that He earned a living, that He served the public, and so showed us that even the smallest tasks are not beneath Your majesty and can be done for You.

We thank You that He lived in an ordinary home, that He knew the problems of living together, that He experienced the rough and smooth of family life, and so showed us that any home, however humble, can be a place where in the ordinary routine of daily life we can make all life an act of worship to You.

Lord Jesus, come again to us this day.

Come into our hearts, and so cleanse them, that we being pure in heart may see God, our Father.

Come into our minds, and so enlighten and illumine them that we may know You who are the way, the truth, and the life.

Touch our lips, that we may speak no word which would hurt another or grieve You.

Touch our eyes, that they may never linger on any forbidden thing.

Touch our hands, that they may become lovely with service to the needs of others.

Come when we are sad, to comfort us; when we are tired, to refresh us; when we are lonely, to cheer us; when we are tempted, to strengthen us; when we are perplexed, to guide us; when we are happy, to make our joy doubly dear. Amen.[17]

November 27

You, then, why do you judge your brother? Or why do you look down on your brother? For we will all stand before God's judgment seat (Romans 14:10).

Your partner will do some things that bother you or even hurt you. So will your children. What will you do with those behaviors that leave you with a wound? God's word has an antidote to your natural response. It's an interesting concept; in fact, it's reminiscent of the three monkeys "Hear no evil," "See no evil," and "Speak no evil." That's good advice. God's Word adds a fourth suggestion—Think no evil (1 Corinthians 13:5).

Thinking no evil—what a task! It's so easy to think the worst about other people. In fact, we all have a bent toward doing that because we've been marred by original sin. It's not our nature to give other people the benefit of the doubt, but God says it's a better way.

It's not our nature to forgive and let another person off the hook, but God says it's a better way.

Love, as expressed in 1 Corinthians 13, is the better way to live our lives. It's a way that will change our children. Love doesn't think the worst about another person. Rather, love trusts. Love builds up. Love says, "I know you can do better. I know that you can be trustworthy."

When we think evil of another person it becomes an infection that contaminates our view of everything the other person does and makes it appear wrong or bad. What's especially tragic is that when we think the worst of children and express it, they may become so discouraged that they live according to what we think! Aren't we fortunate that God doesn't think evil of us? He's *for* us. Praise God![18]

November 28

Since ancient times no one has heard, no ear has perceived, no eye has seen any God besides you, who acts on behalf of those who wait for him. You come to the help of those who gladly do right, who remember your ways. But when we continued to sin against them, you were angry. How then can we be saved? (Isaiah 64:4,5).

*W*aiting. Some parents feel as though they spend their whole life waiting...for others. Sometimes when we're facing difficult times we feel like we're waiting for God. In fact, sometimes we think He's slow to respond to our needs. Or, we think He's simply absent.

We may not feel that God is doing anything to help us with what we're facing. Why? Because we want help *now*. The instant-solution philosophy of our society often invades a proper perspective of God. We complain about waiting a few days or weeks, but to God a day is as a thousand years, and a thousand years is as an instant. God works in hidden ways, even when you and I are totally frustrated by His apparent lack of response. We are merely unaware that He is active. Remember the words of Isaiah 64.

God has a reason for everything He does and a timetable for when He does it: " 'For I know the plans I have for you,' declares the Lord, 'plans to prosper you and not to harm you, plans to give you hope and a future' " (Jeremiah 29:11). Give yourself permission not to know what, not to know how, and not to know when. Giving yourself permission to wait can give you hope. It is all right for God to ask us to wait for weeks and months and even years. During the time when we do not receive an answer or a solution we think we need, He gives us His presence: The psalmist wrote, "My times are in your hands..." (Psalm 31:15).

November 29

The fruit of the Spirit is love, joy, peace, patience, kindness, goodness, faithfulness . . . (Galatians 5:22).

*I*n the parable of the Prodigal Son, the son came to his father and asked for his share of the inheritance. The father could have simply denied his son's request. He could have given the son a part of his inheritance and saved the rest for later. He could have given his son the money but then somehow kept him from leaving. Or, as so many parents do, he could have gone after his son to save his money and rescue him from his evil friends. There are probably other options he could have chosen, but he didn't.

In dealing with his rebellious son, this father did not throw out his value system, his way of life, or his relationship with the rest of the family. Some people might say that the father was too permissive and he made a mistake giving his son all that money. But let's take a closer look at some of the details in this parable.

First, the father let his son go. Sometimes, parents have to let their children go. Children will make mistakes, they will waste a lot of money, and they may hurt themselves in many ways. But some people only learn "the hard way." The question is, do we as parents value the individuality, autonomy, and responsibility of our children like God values ours? Or must they be carbon copies of us?

The father was patient, too. He was patient enough not to chase after his son when he left. He was patient enough to wait till his son truly came to his senses. In the end he was patient enough not to demand an apology but to wait for his son to demonstrate repentance through changed behavior.

The father was a forgiving person. He had a lot of money as well as time, love, and reputation invested in his son, and now all that investment was gone. Yet the father was forgiving enough to trust his son with the family ring! He could not have trusted his son that much without forgiving him.

This father was faithful to his rebellious son. God's faithfulness to us is a worthy model for the relationships between us and our children.

November 30

Wait for the LORD; be strong and let your heart take courage
(Psalm 27:14, NASB).

*I*t takes courage to handle life today. It takes a lot of courage to be a parent. Why? One reason is because Christian parents have to raise their children in a non-Christian society. We're purposely raising our children to be members of a chosen minority. How does that relate to courage? Look at the definition: "the attitude of facing and dealing with anything recognized as dangerous, difficult or painful instead of withdrawing from it; the courage to do what one thinks is right."[19]

Consider the word of Tim Kimmel on how courage is taught.

> It takes courage to take blame, to admit that we are wrong. It takes courage to swallow our pride, to fork down banquets of crow, and to submit to the consequences. The timid wimps of life stand and fight for their misguided pride and inexcusable actions. They pass the buck and make scapegoats of the innocent.
>
> Life is a network of relationships. The people who crisscross our lives provide more than enough reasons why we need courage. Any relationship, regardless of how deep or how shallow, how weak or strong, how new or old, requires us to make courageous choices. What we do will tell our children everything about who we are.
>
> A courageous person faces those he has wronged and openly admits he let them down. When you admit you are wrong to your three-year-old boy, his eyes may fill with tears. But don't assume they are tears of shame. Far from it! They are tears of pride and confidence in a parent who is not afraid to face personal faults with courage.
>
> When it comes to relationships, courage must work overtime. It takes courage . . .

> . . . to be honest.
>
> . . . to love someone who has hurt you.
>
> . . . to forgive.
>
> . . . to confront someone who is wrong.[20]

God's Word puts it this way: "A man who refuses to admit his mistakes can never be successful. But if he confesses and forsakes them, he gets another chance" (Proverbs 28:13, TLB).

Remember, courage is contagious.

December 1

Happy is he that hath the God of Jacob for his help, whose hope is in the LORD his God (Psalm 146:5, KJV).

I'm bored. I'm not satisfied. I'm not happy." Complaints. Children voice them, and so do adults. Some spouses say, "I'm not happy in my marriage. I deserve to be happy. You don't make me feel that way."

What *is* happiness? If a person tells you he is unhappy, ask him what will make him happy. Put him on the spot. Most people aren't even sure how to answer.

Years ago, there were bumper stickers that said, "Happiness is . . ." with many varied answers. Dr. Archibald Hart wrote a book on the subject and suggested 15 principles of happiness. Here they are. Think about them:

Happiness is relative. What brings happiness to one person in your family may not to another.

Happiness is a choice. Some begin the day with "Today I will be happy no matter what happens."

Happiness is getting your eyes off others. Focus on how God provides for you and what He thinks of you.

Happiness is being able to forgive. Forgiveness is surrendering your right to hurt back.

Happiness is living in the here and now. Don't wait until tomorrow to find happiness.

Happiness is appreciating the little things. Simple pleasures can give more fulfillment than expensive ones.

Happiness is keeping your expectations in check. Where did you get your expectations in the first place?

Happiness is being yourself. Do you delight in the way God designed you?

Happiness is being able to enjoy pleasure. Have you ever invited God to be part of every smile?

Happiness is wanting the right things. What is important to you and your family?

Happiness is something you learn. What have you been learning recently?

Happiness is having the right attitudes. Your attitude toward what happens determines your happiness.

Happiness is praying "Thy will be done." This is the prayer to create maturity.[1]

Happiness is . . . what would you say?

December 2

My command is this: Love each other as I have loved you (John 15:12).

Rosalind Rinker is known for her writings on conversational prayer. In one of her works she penned this meditation for parents to remind us all of how to respond to our children.

1. *My child, I love you.*
   I love you unconditionally.
   I love you, good or bad, with no strings attached.
   I love you like this because I know all about you.
   I have known you ever since you were a child.
   I know what I can do for you.
   I know what I want to do for you.

2. *My child, I accept you.*
   I accept you just as you are.
   You don't need to change yourself. I'll do the changing
       when you are ready.
   I love you just as you are.
   Believe this—for I assure you it is true.

3. *My child, I care about you.*
   I care about every big or little thing which happens
       to you. Believe this.
   I care enough to do something about it. Remember this.
   I will help you when you need me. Ask Me.
   I love you.
   I accept you.
   I care about you.

4. *My child, I forgive you.*
   I forgive you, and my forgiveness is complete.
   Not like humans who forgive but cannot forget.
   I love you. My arms are open with love.
   Please come here! Come here to Me!
   I forgive you.
   Do not carry your guilt another moment.
   I carried it all for you on the cross.
   Believe this. It is true.

Rejoice . . . and be glad![2]

December 3

The LORD God said, "It is not good for the man to be alone. I will make a helper suitable for him" (Genesis 2:18).

A Letter to a Child About to Be Married

Dear Child,

I'd like to tell you about the highest level of intimacy in marriage. It's not the physical relationship, but it can enhance your physical affection. It's the spiritual dimension of your marriage that will keep you fulfilled, close, and married for the rest of your life. You'll know an unbelievable depth of closeness if you learn to pray together.

Prayer is an awareness of the presence of a holy and loving God in your life and an awareness of God's relationship to your partner. Prayer is listening to God, which provides a valuable lesson in learning to listen to one another.

In prayer you will search for anything that hinders you from personally surrendering to God and evaluate your conduct in the quiet of meditation. At times your prayers may be rich with confession and self-humbling, or with renunciation and higher resolve to fulfill God's best. Praying together shuts out the petty elements of daily conflict and anxiety.

Prayer will help you sort out unworthy objects of concern so that you can concentrate on the healthier goals of life and your marriage. No matter what threatens to trouble you, you can find relief in God's presence. If you humble yourselves before God, you will humble yourselves before each other. In this way you will come to a better and more honest estimate of yourselves and your partner. Unbecoming self-assurance and stubborn independence will give way before the recognition of your inadequacy to meet divine standards of life.

Lines open to God are invariably open to your partner, for you cannot be genuinely open to God and closed to each other. Praying together will reduce any sense of competitiveness present in your marriage. The Holy Spirit wants the opportunity to minister to whatever needs you have as a couple. Remember, God fulfills His design for a Christian marriage when the lines of communication are first opened to Him.[3]

December 4

Be quick to hear [a ready listener] (James 1:19, AMP).

One of the greatest gifts you can give to your chid is the gift of listening. As James 1:19 tells us, we are to be ready listeners.

Listening is a gift of spiritual significance that you can learn to give to other people. In Proverbs we read, "The hearing ear and the seeing eye—the Lord has made both of them" (Proverbs 20:12, AMP). When you listen to others, you give them a sense of importance, hope, and love that they may not receive any other way. Through listening, we nurture and validate the feelings of other people, especially when they are experiencing difficulties in life.

Listening is giving sharp attention to what someone else is *sharing* with you. It's more than just hearing what someone else is *saying*. Often what people *share* is more than what they say. We must listen to the total person, not just the words spoken. Listening requires an openness to whatever is being shared: feelings, attitudes, or concerns as well as words. Listening also means putting yourself in a position to respond to whatever is being shared with you.

Listening is an expression of love. It involves caring enough to take seriously what another person is communicating. When you listen lovingly, you invite that person into your life as a guest.

When people know you hear them, they will trust you and feel safe with you. And if you are a good listener, other people will be more apt to invite you into their lives. These same people will also learn through your example to respond openly and lovingly to what you share with them.

As parents, we need to remember that there is a difference between listening and hearing. The goal of hearing is to gain content or information for your own purposes. In hearing, you are concerned about what is going on inside *you* during the conversation. You are tuned in to your own responses, thoughts, and feelings.

With our children, we want to be listeners. We want to care for and empathize with our children. In listening, we want to try to understand the thoughts and feelings of our children. We are listening for their sake, not our own. We shouldn't think about what we will say when they stop talking; rather, we should concentrate on what they are saying.

December 5

Pride goes before destruction, a haughty spirit before a fall (Proverbs 16:18).

*H*ave you ever been around a person who is so taken with his own importance that he is a legend in his own mind? He is full of pride. Whether it's an adult or a child, eventually you get tired of being around him.

Someone once said, "Pride grows like lard on a pig." That's a good description. Those who are proud draw attention to themselves or try to make everyone else's life revolve around them. Dr. Lloyd Ogilvie shares this about pride and how to get rid of it:

There was a frog who envied the ability of geese to fly. One day he convinced two geese to put a strong stick between their beaks. He told them that they could fly in close formation with the stick firmly between them. Then, with his mouth, he firmly grabbed the stick and the geese took off.

The frog was flying! The first to defy the law of gravity. However, when the geese flew over a village, the people looked up in amazement. "What a clever frog!" they exclaimed. "We've never seen a frog fly before. Whoever devised such an ingenious way for a frog to fly?"

The frog could not resist the impulse of pride. He opened his mouth and said, "I did! . . . Ahhhhhh!" Opening his mouth to claim the applause, he let go of his clenched-mouth grip on the stick. Pride went before his fall.

When the actress Sarah Bernhardt performed in Paris, everything was organized around her. After the audiences had jammed the theatre and sat waiting for her performance, the stage manager would go to her dressing room and say with oily solicitousness, "Madam, it will be eight o'clock whenever it suits you."

We think the opposite of pride is humility. And yet how quickly we become proud of being humble. Pride is a poison that pervades our being. It requires a daily antidote. The purging of the antidote is radical. It begins its work when we confess to God that pride is an idol in our hearts. Then comes the surrender of our lives. But finally only Christ can break the power-bind of pride. It's a miracle of His grace. Pride is really trying to fill our emptiness with self-love. When we experience His unqualified love from the cross and the cleansing power of His blood purges us, only then can we let Him throw down and crush the idol of pride.[4]

When we are filled with pride, God ends up in the audience rather than being the producer and director of the play.

December 6

Blessed is the man who trusts in the LORD, whose confidence is in him. He will be like a tree planted by the water that sends out its roots by the stream. It does not fear when heat comes; its leaves are always green. It has no worries in a year of drought and never fails to bear fruit. The heart is deceitful above all things and beyond cure. Who can understand it? I the LORD search the heart and examine the mind, to reward a man according to his conduct, according to what his deeds deserve (Jeremiah 17:7-10).

*T*here is an agony in life that is totally avoidable. It has to do with the feelings that are generated by worry. The word "fret" in Psalm 37:1 can be translated "worry" or "gnaw." When beavers gnaw around a tree eventually it crashes to the ground. Worry has much the same effect on our lives.

Why does the Bible have so many verses about worry? Because of the fall of man we all have a bent toward worry, and God wants to help us overcome it.

With that in mind, go back and read the promise in Jeremiah 17:7-10. Do you understand all that this passage is saying?

A blessed man is one who receives something from God. Here, God is promising stability. He wants to give us a worry-free mindset regardless of what is going on with our children, spouse, school, work, or parents. We can choose to look to God or focus on our circumstances.

The person who is blessed has deep roots. The word "confidence" in Jeremiah 17:7 can be translated "to find refuge." Aren't there days when, after haggling with your preschoolers or teenagers, you'd like to find a refuge miles away? Sometimes we can't leave except to go into the next room and collapse in a chair.

Jeremiah also said that the deceitful heart is beyond cure. Did you know the word "cure" means "terminal"? So our heart can trick us into other schemes to find stability. But God can help us by searching our heart and examining our mind. He can set our feelings and thoughts straight.

Have you experienced this rest and confidence yet? Have your children learned it yet? All of us can![5]

December 7

When it was time for Elizabeth to have her baby, she gave birth to a son (Luke 1:57).

*T*he author of *Devotions for Busy Parents* calls all of us to let God lead us in new directions:

Nine months of silence have taught this father a great deal. In his mind he has replayed his quibbling comment to the angel Gabriel a thousand times. Never again will he hesitate in the face of divine direction; he will do what God wants, *pronto*.

But what about the relatives? They swarm around the newborn babe, oohing and gooing, smiling and suggesting. They are solid traditionalists, followers of Cornford's Law: Nothing should ever be done for the first time.

Family advice can often be a wonderful thing, but it is not inerrant. In this case, God has spoken a different word to Zacharias and his wife, and they single-mindedly proceed to shock the aunts and uncles, the sisters and cousins, with a clear statement:

"His name is John."

It is their first step in fulfilling the dream. God immediately flashes his approval by restoring Zacharias's voice. A marvelous prophecy ensues (verses 67-79), and soon the whole community is talking about what's happening, while any criticism seems to melt away.

What dream is God trying to launch at your house? What bold new venture is he coaxing you to begin? Are you afraid? Would you rather stick with tradition—the way things have always been done by others? Remember, God is not impressed with hesitaters. He wants people who care about what *he* thinks more than what anyone else thinks.

Parenting is more than a matter of common sense. It is a divine calling, and that call often takes on different contours for different parents. Only God, who made your child in the first place, knows what he could do with that special life. Let him name the baby. Let him set the course. Let him chart the future.[6]

December 8

Go out at once into the streets and lanes of the city and bring in here the poor and crippled and blind and lame (Luke 14:21, NASB).

*H*ow do your children respond when they encounter a homeless person? How do you feel when that poorly dressed person or family holds up a ragged piece of cardboard that says, "Will work for food"?

The poor and homeless will always be a part of our lives. Yes, *our* lives. Some people are just one step or one bill away from homelessness. What is our responsibility? Better yet, what is our attitude? What does our heart say? It's easy to judge the homeless and withhold assistance so that we don't encourage them to continue begging. But do we know what we could do to help them? Our calling is not to judge, but to love.

The message in Luke 14 is one of mercy. In what ways does your family show mercy to other people? Perhaps you could pray together the following prayer by Ken Gire.

Dear Lord,

You who had nowhere to lay your head, have mercy on those who have nowhere to lay theirs. Have mercy on those whose only home is the shelter of a cardboard box and whose only possessions are stuffed into a shopping cart.

You who experienced the hunger of the wilderness, be with them in their hunger and in the wilderness they are experiencing. Have mercy on those whose only sustenance comes from the kettle of a soup kitchen or from the kindness of a few strangers on the street.

You who were a man of sorrows, comfort them in theirs. Have mercy on those who look back on their lives with regret and remorse and grief.

As I read your Word, help me to see the landscape of your kingdom in the background. Help me to see that it is sloped toward those whose lives have become ever-widening valleys of hopelessness and despair.

Keep me from being removed from the depths of their suffering or from ever looking down on them, no matter how high I ascend in my social or economic or professional standing. But rather, Lord, melt my heart so I could be a river of mercy in their lives. . . .[7]

December 9

Then he threw his arms around his brother Benjamin and wept, and Benjamin embraced him, weeping. And he kissed all his brothers and wept over them. Afterward his brothers talked with him (Genesis 45:14,15).

*J*oseph knew how to cry. In the family reunions described in Genesis 42–50 we see several instances of crying. Of course, that happens a lot at family reunions, doesn't it?

"Deeply moved at the sight of his brother, Joseph hurried out and looked for a place to weep" (Genesis 43:30). Joseph wept again—uncontrollably—when his brother Judah pleaded for Benjamin not to be kept in Egypt so that Jacob would be spared from any more pain (Genesis 45:2).

We also have the record of Joseph weeping when his father arrived in Egypt (46:29), when his father died seventeen years later (50:1), and when his brothers sent a message to him asking him to forgive them (50:17).

When words fail, tears are the messenger. Tears are God's gift to all of us so we can release our feelings. When Jesus arrived in Bethany following the death of Lazarus, He wept (John 11:35). Ken Gire describes this situation so beautifully in *Incredible Moments with the Savior:*

> On our way to Lazarus' tomb we stumble on still another question. Jesus approaches the gravesite with the full assurance that he will raise his friend from the dead. Why then does the sight of the tomb trouble him?
>
> Maybe the tomb in the garden is too graphic a reminder of Eden gone to seed. Of Paradise lost. And of the cold, dark tomb he would have to enter to regain it.
>
> In any case, it is remarkable that *our* plight could trouble *his* spirit; that *our* pain could summon *his* tears.
>
> The raising of Lazarus is the most daring and dramatic of all the Savior's healings. He courageously went into a den where hostility raged against him to snatch a friend from the jaws of death.
>
> It was an incredible moment.
>
> It revealed that Jesus was who he said he was—the resurrection and the life. But it revealed something else.
>
> The tears of God.
>
> And who's to say which is more incredible—a man who raises the dead . . . or a God who weeps?[8]

December 10

Pray without ceasing . . . (1 Thessalonians 5:17).

*T*here's never enough time for all I have to do, let alone set aside time to pray. Isn't the apostle Paul asking a bit much when he says to pray unceasingly?"

What Paul is really talking about are frequent, brief prayers expressed while we're walking, waiting on a phone call, driving (with eyes open!), or at any time. God is not concerned about the setting but only that we pray.

As parents, we need to pray constantly for our children. What can we pray for? Well, everything, but if you want specifics, here are a few.

Pray for your children's spiritual growth, their character development and any character defects, their views and attitudes about themselves, their ability to say no to temptation, their daily difficulties, the types of friends they will have, protection when they date, and wisdom when they select their future partner. But above all, praise God for each of your children, who they are, and who they will become.

Sometimes parents become discouraged when they pray. Their children still have problems and they feel God isn't answering their requests. Consider how the following parents responded to similar concerns.

> We parents must allow our concept of prayer to be shaped by scriptural reality, for then we will understand that our prayers are not tools with which to manage God. Rather, the opposite is the case, because God uses our prayers to manage us, to bend our will to him and brand our soul with his character. When parents truly pray for their offspring, their prayers bind both their soul and the souls of their children into a mystery that ultimately deepens the life of each.[9]

Often the silence of God is a mute sign of a greater answer. Oswald Chambers explained:

> Some prayers are followed by silence because they are wrong, others because they are bigger than one can understand. It will be a wonderful moment for some of us when we stand before God and find that the prayers we clamored for in early days and imagined were never answered, have been answered in the most amazing way, and that God's silence has been the sign of the answer.[10]

December 11

God said to him, "Since you have asked for this and not for long life or wealth for yourself, nor have asked for the death of your enemies but for discernment in administering justice, I will do what you have asked. I will give you a wise and discerning heart, so that there will never have been anyone like you, nor will there ever be" (1 Kings 3:11,12).

If God said to you, "Ask Me for anything that you want and I'll give it to you," what would you ask for?

Many people would ask for power and control. They believe that will relieve their anxiety. After all, wouldn't we parents like to have more power and control over our teens?

What about money? There never seems to be enough to go around even for those who are wealthy. Part of the tradition in America is the desire to accumulate, but for some people it becomes not an end in itself but a god.

The passage of Scripture quoted above helps us gain perspective. If we ask God for wisdom, with it will come the ability to make right choices. James 1:5 states clearly, "If any of you lacks wisdom, he should ask God, who gives generously to all without finding fault, and it will be given to him."

Wisdom will help you to use power in a positive and healthy way. Wisdom will equip you to evaluate your priorities in a way that enables you to use money and not abuse it.

Wisdom will help you to discern the needs and requests of your children. When your children ask for something, you may want to say, "Let me consider your request for awhile. I want to ask for God's wisdom in making a decision." That may seem like a radical approach, yet it's what God wants from us in all areas of our life.

When we ask God for wisdom, He answers with quite a promise. Take a look again at what He says in 1 Kings 3:12.

December 12

The word of God is living and active. Sharper than any double-edged sword, it penetrates even to dividing soul and spirit, joints and marrow; it judges the thoughts and attitudes of the heart (Hebrews 4:12).

I can't change. I've tried and tried. Heaven only knows it's impossible. I'm stuck." Many people actually believe those words. They're frustrated with their efforts. They try not to yell at the kids, or blow up, or nag them, but they can't seem to change. Yet God's Word says emphatically that we *can* change.

Change is possible for those of us who are believers in Christ Jesus because our faith is an inward transformation, not just an outward conformity. When Paul says, "My little children, of whom I travail in birth again until *Christ be formed in you*" (Galatians 4:19, KJV, emphasis added), he is telling us that we have to let Jesus Christ live *in* and *through* us.

In Ephesians 4:23,24 we are told to "be renewed in the spirit of your mind . . . put on the new man, which after God is created in righteousness and true holiness" (KJV). The new man has to be put on from the inside. We are able to put on the new man because God has placed Jesus Christ within us. We are to let Him work within us. That means we must give Him access to our memory banks and the past experiences that need to be relinquished.

Look again at Hebrews 4:12. The word "active" actually means "energize." God's Word energizes us for change. How? The apostle Paul says, "We demolish arguments and every pretension that sets itself up against the knowledge of God, and we take captive every thought to make it obedient to Christ" (2 Corinthians 10:5).

As a child perhaps you played a game called "Capture the Flag." As adults, we need to engage in capturing our thoughts. Why? Because that is usually where negative feelings begin and communication problems start.

How can we capture our thoughts? By memorizing Scripture. What thoughts would you like to be rid of today? Write them down. Ask God to make you aware of when those thoughts pop into your mind. Write down the thoughts you would like to have in place of the old ones. Read them aloud several times a day. And watch out—that will put you on the road to change!

December 13

Encourage one another and build each other up, just as in fact you are doing (1 Thessalonians 5:11).

*A*ffirmation and encouragement—we can't get enough of them. Lives and relationships are changed by their power. John Trent tells this story from a woman at a conference where he was speaking on affirmation. She said,

"My son has two daughters: one who's five, and one who is in the 'terrible twos.' For several years, he's taken the oldest girl out for a 'date' time, but it wasn't until recently that he'd asked the two-year-old out.

" 'Jenny,' he said, 'I want you to know how much I love you and how special you are to Mom and me. We prayed for you for years, and now that you're here and growing up to be such a wonderful girl, we couldn't be more proud of you.'

"Once he said all this, he stopped talking and reached over for his fork to begin eating, but he never got the fork into his mouth.

"Jenny reached out and laid her little hand on her father's. His eyes went to hers and in a soft, pleading voice she said, 'Longer, Daddy... longer.'

"He put his fork down and told her even more reasons why he and my daughter-in-law loved her. 'You're very kind, nice to your sister, full of energy....' Then, he again reached for his fork only to hear the same words again. A second time... and a third... and a fourth time... and each time he heard the words, 'Longer, Daddy, longer.' "

That father never did get much to eat that morning, but his daughter feasted on words every child longs to hear. His words made such an impression on little Jenny, that a few days later she spontaneously ran up to her mother, jumped in her arms, and said, "I'm a really awesome daughter, Mommy. Daddy told me so!"

A couple of hours. A casual remark or two. Yet, great objects can be moved by small levers. Long years can be warmed or chilled by the lever of small happenings, small comments, and small encounters.

That lever lies in our hand... *in your hand*. The awesome potential of affirmation lies in your grasp.[11]

December 14

Without faith it is impossible to please God, because anyone who comes to him must believe that he exists and that he rewards those who earnestly seek him (Hebrews 11:6).

*T*he life of Wilma Rudolph, the great Olympic sprinter, is a remarkable story of faith. Wilma was born with health problems that left her crippled. She asked her parents, "Will I ever be able to run and play like other children?"

"Honey, you have to believe in God and never give up hope," they responded. "If you believe, God will make it happen." Accepting what her parents said, she painfully struggled to walk. By the time she was 12, to the delight and surprise of many people, Wilma no longer needed braces. She went on to play basketball on her championship high-school team and run for three gold medals in the 1960 Olympics. Her life inspired many other people to higher levels of achievement.

When you hear inspiring stories of faith like Wilma Rudolph's, do you sometimes wonder, *What could I accomplish if I took God at His Word?* Is there something you dream of for yourself or your children yet you also say that it will never happen? Remember, faith is the foundational principle of the Christian life. Believing who God is, what He says, what He has done, and what He will do defines the kingdom of God.

Faith is also the essence of the Christian's day-to-day activity. Paul wrote, "As you therefore have received Christ Jesus as Lord, continue to live in him" (Colossians 2:6, NASB). How did you receive Christ? By faith. How, then, are you to walk in Him? By faith. In Scripture, walking refers to the way you conduct your everyday life. Thus successful Christian living and spiritual maturity are determined by our belief in God.

We tend to think of faith as some kind of mystical quality that belongs only in the realm of the spiritual. But everybody walks by faith. It is the most basic operating principle of life. The question is, in what or whom do you believe? We are challenged to believe in God and take His Word seriously.[12]

Take time to think more about faith today. In what area would you like more faith? In what area do your children need more faith? What could other people do to help you with your faith?

December 15

Praise him, all his angels, praise him, all his heavenly hosts.
Praise him, sun and moon, praise him, all you shining stars
(Psalm 148:2,3).

Child: I've got a question ... and I don't think you're going to be able to answer it.

Parent: If you don't think I can answer it, why are you asking me?

Child: Now, come on. You know what I mean ...

Parent: All right. I do want to hear it ... even if it's tough.

Child: Okay, here it is: Where did angels come from and why were they created?

Parent: (silence)

Child: Did you hear me?

Parent: Yes. I was just formulating my answer. You just happened to ask me something I've been reading about (fortunately!).

When God created the heavens, the earth, the stars, and everything else, He had spectators. They applauded what God did. Job says they "sang together" and "shouted for joy" (Job 38:7). But they were created before the earth was. They had to be created, because the only one who is eternal is God Himself. I think God probably created each one directly and simultaneously. The Bible indicates that angels don't have children (*see* Matthew 22:30) and that they have a higher position than you and I since God created them directly (*see* Hebrews 2:9).

Child: But why did God create them? What do they do?

Parent: They were created for God, plain and simple. You'll notice that in countries like England, where there are kings and queens, there are also fancily dressed guards standing around the palace. They make a statement about the king or queen. Their presence says this person is special and deserves honor, respect, and dignity because of his or her high position. That's the best explanation I can give now. Does that help?

Child: Yes, for now. I'm just glad they exist.

Parent: So am I.

December 16

Moses answered, "What if they do not believe me or listen to me and say, 'The LORD did not appear to you'?"... Moses said to the LORD, "O Lord, I have never been eloquent, neither in the past nor since you have spoken to your servant. I am slow of speech and tongue" (Exodus 4:1,10).

*W*e've all felt like Moses at one time or another. We're asked to do something new or we already have a commitment and we want out. We want to be let off the hook, and we can think of a multitude of excuses just like Moses. Remember, too, that God had already told Moses that He would be with him. Moses had the assurance that he wouldn't be alone, but he was still afraid.

Sometimes at first we believe we can complete the task. Then our mind begins to wander and create worst-case scenarios. These scenarios seem so real that they make us afraid.

Have you ever felt inadequate as a parent? Probably—that's normal. Have you ever felt inadequate as a spouse? Probably—that's normal. Have you ever felt inadequate to take responsibilities at your church? That, too, is normal.

Sometimes, though, it's when we're faced with a new opportunity that our insecurities begin to build and we focus on what can go wrong. It can be anything from taking a new job, climbing the corporate ladder, coaching a Little League team, entertaining 20 people for dinner, or letting your child walk to school without you.

We have three choices available. One is defeat in advance. We can say, "I'll fail. I just know it. I've never been able to do this. Why try? Let's get someone else." Think for a minute. If your child responded to opportunities like that, what would you say?

A second option is to escape in some way. We could plunge into some other activity and become so immersed that we could justifiably say, "I don't have time." That seems like a legitimate excuse.

There is one other option. We could remember what God said in Exodus, "I will be with you," and say, "If God calls me to do something, He will enable me to do it. I'll trust Him and go for it."

By the way, I'm sure you know what happened to Moses later on. After he finally said yes to God, he accomplished a great deal.[13]

December 17

I am not saying this because I am in need, for I have learned to be content whatever the circumstances (Philippians 4:11).

SOMEDAY WHEN THE KIDS ARE GROWN, things are going to be a lot different. The garage won't be full of bikes, electric train tracks on plywood, sawhorses surrounded by chunks of two-by-fours, nails, a hammer and saw, unfinished "experimental projects," and the rabbit cage. I'll be able to park both cars neatly in just the right places, and never again stumble over skateboards, a pile of papers (saved for the school fund drive), or the bag of rabbit food—now split and spilled. Ugh!

SOMEDAY WHEN THE KIDS ARE GROWN, the kitchen will be incredibly neat. The sink will stay free of sticky dishes, the garbage disposal won't get choked on rubber bands or paper cups, the refrigerator won't be clogged with nine bottles of milk, and we won't lose the tops to jelly jars, catsup bottles, the peanut butter, the margarine, or the mustard.

SOMEDAY WHEN THE KIDS ARE GROWN, the instrument called a "telephone" will actually be available. It won't look like it's growing from a teenager's ear. It will simply hang there . . . silently and amazingly available! It will be free of lipstick, human saliva, mayonnaise, corn chip crumbs, and toothpicks stuck in those little holes.

SOMEDAY WHEN THE KIDS ARE GROWN, things are going to be a lot different. One by one they'll leave our nest, and the place will begin to resemble order and maybe even a touch of elegance. The clink of china and silver will be heard on occasion. The crackling of the fireplace will echo through the hallway. The phone will be strangely silent. The house will be

quiet . . . and calm . . .

and always clean . . . and empty . . .

and filled with memories . . . and lonely . . .

and we won't like that at all. And we'll spend our time not looking forward to *Someday* but looking back to *Yesterday*. And thinking, "Maybe we can baby-sit the grandkids and get some *life* back in this place for a change!"

Could it be that the apostle Paul had some of this in mind when he wrote:

. . . I have learned to be content in whatever circumstances I am (Philippians 4:11).

Maybe so. But then again, chances are good Paul never had to clean up many dog messes.[14]

December 18

Now it is God who makes both us and you stand firm in Christ. He anointed us, set his seal of ownership on us, and put his Spirit in our hearts as a deposit, guaranteeing what is to come (2 Corinthians 1:21,22).

*M*ost of us cannot afford to pay cash for a home or even a car. We buy houses and cars on time. However, we still have to save money for the down payment. It's both an exciting and terrifying time when you finally have enough money saved up and you meet with a real estate agent with your check in hand. Once you sign the documents and hand over the check, you're into your home. But it's not paid for yet; you'll have payments for years. You can depend on that!

A down payment has been made for you as a believer. When you accepted the Lord as your Savior, you received a gift—the Holy Spirit. This represents God's down payment to you with the promise that He will make additional payments to you. That's some gift! The Holy Spirit is also a seal of ownership on you. You are owned by God and He promises that you will receive all that comes with salvation. Someday this transaction will be completed—by God. You can depend on that!

When Paul said that the Holy Spirit is a deposit "guaranteeing what is to come," he was talking about your spiritual inheritance. You may have already been the recipient of a material inheritance. Your children will probably receive one (unless you decide to spend all of it first!) Or, perhaps you have never received an inheritance because other people spent it. But you never have to worry about your spiritual inheritance from God being used up. It's guaranteed. You are guaranteed a safe arrival in heaven and your glorification in the presence of God. You can depend on that, too![15]

December 19

You know that we dealt with each of you as a father deals with his own children, encouraging, comforting and urging you to live lives worthy of God (1 Thessalonians 2:11,12).

*W*hat legacy are you leaving as parents? Each of us is creating our own legacy right at this very moment. We have been creating our legacy for many years. As Tim Kimmel says in his excellent book, *Legacy of Love,*

> Your words, your schedule, your choices, your obedience, the way you savor your victories and the way you swallow your defeats all help to define your life. It is this definition that your children rely on most as they seek to chart their own future.[16]

What are other people receiving from you? What are you giving to make your family great? We don't have any option when it comes to leaving a legacy. However, we do have an option as to the *kind* of legacy we leave. What kind will you leave?

In *Legacy of Love,* Tim tells a story about a visit to the Bahamas, where his family came across a graveyard that always has two empty graves. There were some reasons for that. Since the island is on a hard coral platform, it takes several days to dig a grave. And because of limited facilities and refrigeration, bodies cannot be preserved long. So they are buried within a few hours. Should someone die suddenly, the family is usually able to get other people together immediately for a quick funeral.

But in the case of a lingering or terminal illness, the funeral is held in advance!

When people are near death, their family and friends carry them into a church or a house and host a funeral service. Can you imagine hearing your own funeral service? In most cases, doing that worked out quite well because it gave the dying person an opportunity to hear what others had to say about him or her. In some cases though, the dying person recovered. I wonder if hearing the eulogy in advance—whether good or bad—may have encouraged the person to keep on living?

Would you want to hear your eulogy in advance? Do you wonder, like I do, what would be said? What would you want your friends and family to say about you?[17]

December 20

I give them eternal life, and they shall never perish; no one can snatch them out of my hand (John 10:28).

*P*ets can bring a lot of enjoyment to the home . . . as well as some additional work. Most families have at least a dog or a cat.

There are lessons to learn from the presence of an animal in the home. Have you ever noticed how a mother cat carries her kittens? She's not like a kangaroo, who lets her baby ride in a pouch. She's not like a monkey, who makes her baby grasp onto her with his little paws and hold on for dear life. A kitten doesn't have to hang on; the mother grasps the baby by the neck with her teeth and carries it around. A baby monkey's security depends on itself. That's risky. The kitten's security, however, depends on the mother.

What does your security depend upon? What about your child's security? Let's look at your security in your salvation. Does your salvation depend on your ability to hang on like a baby monkey, or does it depend on who God is and what He does? What do you believe? Better yet, what does the Scripture teach? Sometimes we let our childhood and life experiences shape what we believe about salvation rather than Scripture.

Reread the passage for today and consider its truth. God gave you to His Son, and your security is complete in Him. Christ paid the price for your sins . . . in full. Nothing is owed (Ephesians 1:7) and God is satisfied with the payment (Romans 3:25). Jesus is continuing His work for you by constantly praying for you (Hebrews 7:25). How often do you think about that fact? And, when you accepted the Lord, at that moment you were sealed with the Holy Spirit. God owns you (2 Corinthians 1:22).

So, if there is a day when you feel insecure for any reason, remember that your spiritual security in Christ is permanent.[18]

December 21

I tell you the truth, unless a kernel of wheat falls to the ground and dies, it remains only a single seed. But if it dies, it produces many seeds (John 12:24).

*A*s a parent, are you sacrificing for your children or investing in them? Parenting is costly in many ways. Aside from the financial outpouring, parenting can cost you energy, time, privacy, emotional drain, freedom . . . you finish the list.

Some parents tend to concentrate on what they are giving up. They focus on and complain about what they are sacrificing. Some even remind their children of that periodically. "You kids need to remember all that we've sacrificed for you" is a common message. The focus is more upon the parents rather than the children.

Yet some parents don't see children as a sacrifice but rather as an investment or opportunity. When you invest in something you believe that the returns will be of greater value than what you started with. And when you invest in your children you enjoy them, but when you focus on sacrifices you begrudge them. It's true that when you invest in children you still give up some things, but you don't view yourself as someone who is giving up all. Rather, your focus is on the delight of doing something for another person with the expectation that your investment will pay dividends later on.

How do you see your involvement in the lives of your children? As a sacrifice or an investment? Your perspective will affect what you do, how you do it, your attitude, and the final outcome.

Perhaps it's a matter of priorities. If work or recreation are priorities, then you'll view time with your children as a sacrifice.

John 12:24 can be applied to parenting and investments. Could it be that the call to being a parent means dying to what used to be important and coming alive to something new? Like a new opportunity to invest in a life? Energy, time, and money spent on our family is the best investment around. Do you see it that way?[19]

December 22

Now after Jesus was born in Bethlehem of Judea . . . (Matthew 2:1, NASB).

Christmas each year weaves its magic spell upon our hearts. Carols float on the air and there is a surge of love and kindliness not felt at any other time of the year. Creches appear reminding us of the miracle in the manger. In that feeding trough in lowly Bethlehem, a cry from that infant's throat broke the centuries of silence. For the first time God's voice could be heard coming from human vocal cords. C.S. Lewis called that event—the coming of Christ at Christmas—"the greatest rescue mission of history."

During each Christmas season the words of Micah resonate throughout the world. For he was inspired to give the prophecy that named the very birthplace of the Messiah: *But you, Bethlehem Ephrathah, though you are small among the clans of Judah, out of you will come for Me one who will be ruler over Israel, whose origins are from of old, from ancient times* (5:2).

Micah was telling those who were proud and powerful and rich and self-righteous that God's great ruler would not come from their stately and royal environs. He would come forth from the nondescript hamlet of Bethlehem. When over 700 years later the wise men came searching for Him, the scribes had to brush off the dust from the Book of Micah to direct them to the very location where He would be born.

The One who would come is One *whose origins are from of old, from ancient times* (verse 2). This literally means "from days of eternity." It speaks of the eternal existence of Christ. His providence and preeminence are also prophesied as one who *will stand and shepherd His flock and His greatness will reach to the ends of the earth. And He will be their peace* (verses 4-5). What beautiful and precious promises are ours from this plowman who became God's mighty penman.[20]

December 23

God created man in His own image (Genesis 1:27, NKJV).

A baby is born. There's joy and delight... then speculation. Who does he or she look like? The eyes, the nose, the legs... the older a child becomes, the more he or she begins to resemble someone.

We all want our children to resemble us in some way. Some children have been told they resemble their grandfather, uncle, or someone else. Some adopted children have been told they look just like their parents! These resemblances are not just physical qualities.

In the world of plants and flowers, gardeners make certain that new bulbs or seeds are capable of maintaining the same unique characteristics of a plant or flower from generation to generation. Otherwise the plants are worthless. So gardeners are very careful and attentive to their task of maintaining lineages so that bulbs and seeds will perpetuate the exact qualities that were represented in previous generations.

The image that all of us have as believers is Jesus. That's who we resemble. Dr. Larry Crabb, in his book *Understanding People,* suggests that we resemble God in several ways.

We, like our heavenly Father, have a longing for close relationships. "O Jerusalem, Jerusalem, you who kill the prophets and stone those sent to you, how often I have longed to gather your children together, as a hen gathers her chicks under her wings, but you were not willing" (Matthew 23:37).

We were born with a desire to be close to God and people.

We, like God, can experience free will. God does what He wants and so do we. He uses His will to love us, but we have a bent to use our will for our own purposes. Perhaps that's why He says in Philippians 2:13 to allow Him to work through us "to will and to do for His good pleasure."

Like God we experience emotions—Jesus wept, He expressed anger, and He grieved.

Finally, like God, we are spiritual beings. We both have the spiritual dimension.

Who do you resemble? You are God's child. He has joy in that fact. You bear His image![21]

December 24

God so loved the world that he gave his one and only Son, that whoever believes in him shall not perish but have eternal life (John 3:16).

God knows how to give. In fact, He's our model for sacrificial giving.

Take a moment and think about the gifts you've received from people over the years. Can you remember the first gift you ever received? What about the best gift? And, ugh, what about the worst gift? Sometimes families who gather for Christmas or a birthday celebration ask everyone to answer those three questions. That makes for a hilarious but insightful time.

Let's think about the purpose of a gift. A gift is an item that is selected with care and consideration. Its purpose is to bring delight and fulfillment to another person. It is an expression of deep feeling on the part of the giver; usually you put much care and effort into selecting a gift.

When you select a gift, you think about what the recipient would enjoy. What will bring him or her delight? What will bring him or her happiness? What will make his or her day bright and cheery? How will your gift show the person the extent of your feeling for him or her and how much he or she means to you?

If you're like most parents, you put a lot of time, effort, and advance thought into the gifts you give to your children. You plan outings, trips, and look for the latest toys or videos. That's all right. But listen in to a late-night response from a wife to her husband as they were considering what to do for their children:

> Darling, the most important thing you can give your children is the gift of yourself. Long after they have forgotten the gifts you bought them, they will remember and cherish the time you spent with them. I know, because what I remember is not the toys or the dresses my daddy bought me, or even the places we went on vacation, but the things we did together, the time he spent with me.[22]

Gifts that are often appreciated the most are not necessarily those that are the most expensive. They are those which reflect the time you spent considering the desires and wants of the other person and the sacrifice you made to give it.

December 25

The Word became flesh and made his dwelling among us. We have seen his glory, the glory of the One and Only, who came from the Father, full of grace and truth (John 1:14).

*P*erhaps the best way to reflect upon the birth of our Savior is through this prayer.

O God, our Father, we remember at this Christmas time how the eternal Word became flesh and dwelt among us.

We thank you that Jesus took our human body upon him, so that we can never again dare to despise or neglect or misuse the body, since you made it your dwelling-place.

We thank you that Jesus did a day's work like any working-man, that he knew the problem of living together in a family, that he knew the frustration and irritation of serving the public, that he had to earn a living, and to face all the wearing routine of everyday work and life and living, and so clothed each common task with glory.

We thank you that he shared in all happy social occasions, that he was at home at weddings and at dinners and at festivals in the homes of simple ordinary people like ourselves. Grant that we may ever remember that in his unseen risen presence he is a guest in every home.

We thank you that he knew what friendship means, that he had his own circle of those whom he wanted to be with him, that he knew too what it means to be let down, to suffer from disloyalty and from the failure of love. We thank you that he too had to bear unfair criticism, prejudiced opposition, malicious and deliberate misunderstanding.

We thank you that whatever happens to us, he has been there before, and that, because he himself has gone through things, he is able to help those who are going through them.

Help us never forget that he knows life, because he lived life, and that he is with us at all times to enable us to live victoriously.

This we ask for your love's sake. Amen.[23]

December 26

. . . and she smiles at the future (Proverbs 31:25, NASB).

*Y*ou have the power to influence and even control the people around you. And that power is on your face—it's your smile. A smile on your face can be a mood setter and an attitude-change agent. Think about it: Who are you drawn to—people who have a frown and a turned-down mouth, or people who have a smile and a positive outlook? Haven't your spirits ever been lifted by the smile of a friend, someone whose face shakes loose your grip on the difficulties in life and helps you relax? A smile can reach down to the depths of our hearts and release the reasons for delight and joy in our lives.

Your smile reveals your faith in life and your ability to overcome difficulties. By smiling you can become a spreader of joy.

If you want others to be around you, smile. If you want your children to develop a positive outlook on life, smile a lot. Just catching your child's eye and flashing a big smile before he or she stands up to perform conveys your message of confidence: "You can do it. Go for it." A sensitive smile towards your spouse can have as much impact as saying, "I love you."

Smiles are contagious. They can bring a child out of the depths of a bad day and turn his or her gloom into giggles. A smile can disarm the sour disposition of a frazzled friend or a disgruntled customer. Your smile can say to another person, "I'm happy to be here. This can be pleasant. Let's look at the bright side of life."

When you smile, someone may ask you, "What have *you* got to smile about?" And when they do, tell them. What *have* you got to smile about? A lot! As Christians we have a great deal to smile about. Read God's Word and list your blessings.

Your smile is a gift—to you, to other people around you, and for the cause of Christ. When non-Christians ask you the reason for that smile on your face, tell them about Jesus.[24]

December 27

Jesus withdrew with his disciples to the lake, and a large crowd from Galilee followed (Mark 3:7).

*W*hen you listen to a quality band or orchestra, all the parts work together in harmony. The music has balance and rhythm. Without rhythm, the music is awkward and out of sync. It just doesn't flow right.

Have you ever felt like your life isn't flowing right? Like you've lost the rhythm? To have balance and rhythm in your life, four ingredients are necessary: rest, worship, play, and work. Too many of us change and reverse these ingredients and end up with work, work, work, and perhaps a little play.[25]

Did Jesus ever struggle with that problem? Perhaps so. Dr. David McKenna, president of Asbury Seminary, shares an interesting insight.

> Jesus withdraws to the sea with His disciples in order to regain His balance in the rhythm of life. During His ministry in Galilee, the rhythm has been reduced to constant work with little rest, and even less opportunity for worship and play. In fact, when He goes to the synagogues for worship, He meets either human need that requires work or spiritual hardness that requires contest. Worship and work may have become so intermingled that Jesus senses the potential loss of the effective edge in His work and the fine-tuning of His communion with God. In modern terms, He might have been on the borderline of "executive burn-out.". . . His withdrawal to the sea is not cowardice (or laziness), it is a credit to His intuitive sense that the time has come for rest and play.[26]
>
> Work is an activity of high intensity and high production. But as God set the example, even creative work must be balanced by a period of "rest," when physical energies are restored in order to work again. Worship and play, then, must be added to the work/rest cycle in order to fulfill the finer hungers of persons who are created in the image of God.[27]

What needs to be added to your life? To your family's?

December 28

Oh, that I had wings like a dove! For then I would fly away and be at rest. . . . I would hasten my escape (Psalm 55:6,8, NKJV).

*J*ailbreak! This word strikes terror into the local community when prisoners scale the wall and flee into the area. But there are times when we find the idea of a jailbreak appealing: when we want to break out of our own individual prison. When life gets rough and overwhelming, we feel like saying with the psalmist, "If only I could fly away!"

Wings and flight can look inviting on days when you've been through hours of haggling with the kids. Sometimes we want to escape our workplace or the location where we live because circumstances are deteriorating. And we toy with the thought of leaving our church if it's not meeting our spiritual needs. Or, you may have wondered if you are where God wants you to be.

Let's face it. Sometimes we're just worn out and weary. We need a break. Perhaps a change of scenery will make us feel better. But if we can't fly away, we end up feeling stuck and we say, "I'm just hanging in there."

There *is* another alternative: Seek God's guidance to know *where* He wants you and *what* He wants you to be doing. When you make a change in your life, it should be because you see a greater opportunity to serve Him, not because you want to run away.

Are you just plain weary? God has an answer:

Come to me, all you who are weary and burdened, and I will give you rest. Take my yoke upon you and learn from me, for I am gentle and humble in heart, and you will find rest for your souls. For my yoke is easy and my burden is light (Matthew 11:28-30).

The words, "I will give you rest" can be thought of as, "I will refresh or rejuvenate you." That's what we need.[28]

How can we get this rest? Take your every concern to Him in prayer. Don't try to understand your circumstances, make decisions, or take care of problems by yourself. Ask God—and perhaps another person—to help you. That's better than flying away, because when we flee, we tend to take our baggage along with us.

December 29

I am the resurrection and the life. He who believes in me will live, even though he dies (John 11:25).

Throughout the Scriptures, Jesus used the phrase "I am" again and again. He said, "I am . . .

+ the Bread of Life (John 6:35)
+ the Light of the World (John 8:12)
+ the Good Shepherd (John 10:11)
+ the Way (John 14:6)
+ the Truth (John 14:6)
+ the Life (John 14:6)

But the title "Resurrection and Life" is one that shouts out Jesus' authority over life and death. During His ministry, Jesus confronted death directly and broke its hold several times. Remember Jairus' daughter, or the only son of the widow of Nain, or Lazarus, who had been dead four days? Then, on a quiet morning after being buried in His own tomb, Jesus confirmed the words of John 11:25 with His own resurrection.

A favorite story you may have heard comes from England many years ago. The people were anxiously waiting the news from a major battle at Waterloo. They had no phones or radios yet; messages were sent by semaphore signals or flags. The man waiting on the top of Winchester Cathedral saw the signal "Wellington defeated . . ." just as a fog rolled in. Everyone believed their great general had been beaten. Despair settled in. Later in the day, the fog lifted, and the message was repeated. It was the same, but it was followed with two additional words the fog had blotted out before: "Wellington defeated the enemy." Gloom and despair lifted!

The same happened to Jesus' followers. Right after the crucifixion they believed all was lost. But soon the cry, "He is risen" began to ring from gardens, homes, housetops, and whole cities and countries. Now the entire world, from the most remote tribe to the largest city, hears the words, "He is risen."

Jesus wasn't defeated, death was. Jesus wasn't defeated, sin was. Jesus wasn't the victim; He was the victor.

The next time you're feeling down, think about that. It may put everything in perspective.[29]

December 30

The whole Bible was given to us by inspiration from God and is useful to teach us what is true and to make us realize what is wrong in our lives; it straightens us out and helps us do what is right. It is God's way of making us well prepared at every point, fully equipped to good to everyone (2 Timothy 3:16,17, TLB).

*A*DD—Attention Deficit Disorder—is a malady that affects a number of children in our society, usually boys more than girls. It's not a learned response; rather, it is rooted in misfunctioning in the brain. Among the various symptoms is a difficulty in paying attention and staying on track. It's not that the child doesn't hear you. He does. He looks at you, repeats back what you said word for word, and 10 minutes later it's vanished! That frustrates parents and teachers. The predictable response from both is, "Why don't you listen to me?" He did. "Why don't you ever pay attention?" He did. But somehow, even though your words may have registered for the moment, there is little retention of them.

The human race has shown those same symptoms toward God. He created the world with a perfect environment and gave Adam and Eve a few simple, clear instructions. What happened? Man fell into sin. Later God gave the children of Israel the Ten Commandments. They weren't followed. And today we hear sermons preached and we read the Scriptures—we know what to do, but then . . .

Slow learners, all of us. Some of us are even resistant learners. We react with our eyes, listen with our ears, and because of our sin nature, a short circuit gets in the way. But the more you allow God's Word to penetrate your heart and thoughts, the less short-circuiting you'll experience in your life.

Use God's words to correct what you think, say, and do with your family. Consider Solomon's words:

My son, pay attention to what I say; listen closely to my words. Do not let them out of your sight, keep them within your heart; for they are life to those who find them and health to a man's whole body. Above all else, guard your heart, for it is the wellspring of life (Proverbs 4:20-23).

Let God's word renovate your life today. It's possible.

December 31

Though he stumble, he will not fall, for the LORD upholds him with his hand (Psalm 37:24).

*R*emember back when you were in school? You probably raised your hand several times a day to respond to questions, ask questions, or get permission to go to the bathroom. You used your hands all day long then as well as now.

We use our hands for many purposes. We use them to greet each other, to put something together, and to embrace our children. We use them to wipe our children's faces, straighten their hair, or even spank them. Without our hands, life would be difficult. We wouldn't be able to be as affectionate, couldn't work as well, nor communicate as expressively. Life is embraced through our hands.

Are you aware of how often the Bible illustrates God's work through His hands? Scripture says that God lifts up His hands to help the humble (Psalm 10:12); with His hands people know about His works (Psalm 28:4,5); with His fatherly hands we are upheld (Psalm 37:24). God pours out a cup of discipline by His hand (Psalm 75:8). He even fashioned the human race with His hands: "Your hands made me and formed me; give me understanding to learn your commands" (Psalm 119:73).

His hand guided the activities of the early church (Acts 11:12), and it was His hand that brought Paul into his faith in Christ. God is very busy with His hand in supporting, guiding, caring for, loving, and disciplining us.

Perhaps all that God does is described in these ways because we're so dependent upon our hands. Your hands are instruments designed to convey messages of love. Use them in a gentle way to caress, encourage, guide, and lift up another person's spirit. Your hands will express what's in your heart.

How can you use your hands today to further the cause of Christ?[30]

Notes

1. Bruce Narramore. *Parenting with Love and Limits*. The Zondervan Corporation, 1979, pp. 25, 26. Used by permission of Zondervan Publishing House.
2. Original source unknown.
3. Reprinted from John White. *Parents in Pain*. © 1979 by InterVarsity Christian Fellowship of the USA, p. 181. Used by permission of InterVarsity Press, Downers Grove, IL 60515.
4. From *Strike the Original Match* by Charles R. Swindoll. Portland, OR: Multnomah Press, 1980, p. 92.
5. Reprinted from White. *Parents in Pain*, p. 165.
6. *English Ritual*. Collegeville, MN: The Liturgical Press, 1964, pp. 369-70.
7. Lloyd John Ogilvie. *God's Best for My Life*. Eugene, OR: Harvest House Publishers, 1981. Selections from January 4, 10, 14; March 5, 25; April 2, 15, 20; May 3; July 24.
8. Max Lucado. *The Angels Were Silent*. Dallas: Word Inc., 1992, p. 77.
9. Max Lucado. *In the Eye of the Storm*. Dallas: Word, Inc., 1991, pp. 48, 49.
10. James Kennedy. *Your Prodigal Child*. Nashville: Thomas Nelson Publishers, 1988, pp. 42-43, adapted.
11. Ibid., p. 44, adapted.
12. Ibid., p. 45, adapted.
13. Taken from *Encyclopedia of Bible Difficulties* by Gleason L. Archer, p. 253. Copyright ©1982 by The Zondervan Corporation. Used by permission of Zondervan Publishing House.
14. Randy L. Carlson, M.A., president of "Today's Family Life and Parent Talk Radio." *Father Memories*. Copyright © 1992, pp. 201-02.
15. Charles Shedd. *You Can Be a Great Parent*. Dallas: Word, Inc., 1970, pp. 12, 13.
16. Paul and Jeannie McKean. *Leading a Child to Independence*. San Bernardino, CA: Here's Life Publishers, 1986, p. 21.
17. From *Fathering a Son* by Paul Heide Brecht and Jerry Rohrbach. Chicago: Moody Press, 1979, pp. 35, 36.
18. Dr. Ray Guarendi. *Back to the Family*. New York: Villard Books, 1990, p. 83.
19. William L. Coleman. *Before I Give You Away*. Minneapolis: Bethany House Publishers, 1995, pp. 19-21.
20. Lucado. *And the Angels Were Silent*, p. 109.
21. From *On the Anvil* by Max Lucado © 1985, pp. 145-46. Used by permission of Tyndale House Publishers, Inc. All rights reserved.
22. Sheila West. *Beyond Chaos*. Colorado Springs: NavPress, 1991, pp. 142-43, adapted.
23. Gary Smalley and John Trent. *The Blessing*. Nashville: Thomas Nelson Publishers, 1986, adapted from numerous chapters.
24. Pat Hershey Owen. *Seven Styles of Parenting*. Wheaton, IL: Tyndale House Publishers, 1983, pp. 15, 27, 28, adapted.
25. Charles Swindoll. *Living Beyond the Daily Grind*. Dallas: Word, Inc., 1988, p. 203, adapted.
26. Ronda De Sola Chervin. *A Mother's Treasury of Prayers*. Ann Arbor, MI: Servant Publications, 1994, p. 108-09, poem by Lois Donahue, adapted.
27. Swindoll. *Living Beyond*, p. 103, adapted.

February

1. Ken Gire. *Instructive Moments with the Savior*. Grand Rapids, MI: Zondervan Publishers, 1992, pp. 30-31.
2. Sheila West. *Beyond Chaos*. Colorado Springs: NavPress, 1991, pp. 122-23, adapted.
3. *Webster's New Twentieth Century Dictionary, unabridged*.
4. Pat Hershey Owen. *Seven Styles of Parenting*. Wheaton, IL: Tyndale House Publishers, 1983, pp. 48-49, adapted.
5. Tim Kimmel. *Legacy of Love*. Portland, OR: Multnomah Press, 1989, pp. 90-91.
6. "The Risks of Being a Parent" by Anthony Campolo in Jay Kessler, Ron Beers, and LaVonne Neff, eds. *Parents and Children*. Wheaton, IL: Victor Press, 1986, pp. 77-79, adapted.

7. From *What Is a Family?* by Edith Schaeffer. Old Tappan, NJ: Fleming H. Revell Co., 1975, pp. 19, 24.

8. Ibid., p. 117.

9. Patrick Morley. *Two-Part Harmony*. Nashville: Thomas Nelson Publishers, 1994, pp. 202-03.

10. From *What Is a Family?* Schaeffer, pp. 30, 95.

11. Kent and Barbara Hughes. *Common-Sense Parenting*. Wheaton, IL: Tyndale House Publishers, 1995, pp. 117-21, adapted.

12. Archibald Hart. *15 Principles for Achieving Happiness*. Dallas: Word, Inc., 1988, pp. 177-78.

13. Tony and Bart Campolo. *Things We Wish We Had Said*. Dallas: Word, Inc., 1989, pp. 213-14.

14. Morley. *Two-Part Harmony*, pp. 196-97.

15. Henry Gariepy. *100 Portraits of Christ*. Wheaton, IL: Victor Press, 1987, pp. 13-16, adapted.

16. Stu Weber. *Tender Warrior*. Sisters, OR: Questar Publishers, 1993, pp. 166-67.

17. A.W. Tozer. *Knowledge of the Holy*. New York: Harper and Row, 1961, pp. 62-63, adapted.

18. J.I. Packer. *Knowing God*. Downers Grove, IL: InterVarsity Press, 1973, p. 37.

19. H. Norman Wright. *Chosen for Blessing*. Eugene, OR: Harvest House Publishers, 1992, pp. 10, 11.

20. Claire Cloninger. *Postcards from Heaven*. Dallas: Word, Inc., 1992, p. 41, adapted.

21. John Piper. *The Pleasures of God*. Portland, OR: Multnomah Press, 1991, p. 188.

22. Ibid., p. 195.

23. Wright. *Chosen for Blessing*, pp. 13-15, adapted.

24. From *On the Anvil* by Max Lucado © 1985, pp. 91-92. Used by permission of Tyndale House Publishers, Inc. All rights reserved.

25. Archibald D. Hart. *Stress and Your Child*. Dallas: Word, Inc, 1992, p. 142, adapted.

26. William Barclay. *A Barclay Prayer Book*. London: SCM Press Ltd., 1990, pp. 56, 57.

March

1. Richard Exley. *Straight from the Heart for Couples*. Tulsa: Honor Books, 1993, pp. 21, 22, 57, 69, 72.

2. C.S. Lewis. *The Four Loves*. London: Geoffrey Bles, 1960, p. 48.

3. Kent and Barbara Hughes. *Common-Sense Parenting*. Wheaton, IL: Tyndale House Publishers, 1995, pp. 20-22, adapted.

4. *Webster's Ninth New Collegiate Dictionary*. Springfield, MA: Merriam-Webster, Inc., 1991.

5. H. Norman Wright and Gary J. Oliver. *Raising Emotionally Healthy Kids*. Wheaton, IL: Victor Press, 1993, pp. 146-48, adapted.

6. Quin Sherrer and Ruthanne Garlock. *The Spiritual Warrior's Prayer Guide*. Ann Arbor, MI: Servant Publications, 1992, p. 156. Used by permission.

7. Lloyd John Ogilvie. *God's Best for My Life*. Eugene, OR: Harvest House Publishers, 1981, January 10.

8. From *Is the Family Here to Stay?* by David Allan Hubbard. Dallas: Word, Inc., 1971, p. 79.

9. A.W. Tozer. *The Knowledge of the Holy*. New York: Harper and Row, 1961, pp. 55-60, adapted.

10. H. Norman Wright. *Recovering from the Losses of Life*. Grand Rapids, MI: Fleming H. Revell, 1991, pp. 10-11, 19, adapted.

11. Jay Kessler, Ron Beers, and LaVonne Neff, eds. *Parents and Children*. Wheaton, IL: Victor Press, 1986, pp. 109-11.

12. Gary Smalley and John Trent. *The Blessing*. Nashville: Thomas Nelson Publishers, 1986, pp. 36-41, adapted.

13. Dean Merrill. *Wait Quietly, Devotions for Busy Parents*. Wheaton, IL: Tyndale House Publishers, 1994, p. 103, adapted.

14. Wright. *Recovering from the Losses*, pp. 34-35, adapted.

15. Lloyd John Ogilvie. *Twelve Steps to Living Without Fear*. Dallas: Word, Inc., 1987, p. 133.

16. Tozer. *Knowledge of the Holy*, pp. 40-43, adapted.

17. From *On the Anvil* by Max Lucado © 1985. Used by permission of Tyndale House Publishers, Inc., pp. 69-70. All rights reserved.

18. Henry Gariepy. *100 Portraits of Christ*. Wheaton, IL: Victor Press, 1987, pp. 23-24, adapted.

19. Archibald Hart. *15 Principles for Achieving Happiness*. Dallas: Word, Inc., 1988, p. 47.

20. Smalley and Trent. *The Blessing*, pp. 70-72, adapted.

21. Ronda De Sola Chervin. *A Mother's Treasury of Prayers*. Ann Arbor, MI: Servant Publications, 1994, pp. 134-35. Used by permission.
22. Stuart Briscoe. *The Sermon on the Mount*. Wheaton, IL: Harold Shaw Publishers, 1995, pp. 28-33, adapted.
23. Phillip Keller. *Strength of Soul*. Grand Rapids, MI: Kregel Publications, 1993, pp. 172-77, adapted.
24. Ibid., p. 178.
25. *Webster's New World Dictionary*. New York: Prentice Hall, 1994.
26. Pat Hershey Owen. *Seven Styles of Parenting*. Dallas: Word, Inc., 1988, pp. 59-60, adapted.
27. Stuart and Jill Briscoe. *Living Love*. Wheaton, IL: Harold Shaw Publishers, 1993, pp. 60-61, adapted.

April

1. Dennis Rainey. *The Tribute*. Nashville: Thomas Nelson Publishers, 1994, p. 273, adapted.
2. Ibid., pp. 273-74.
3. Phillip Keller. *Strength of Soul*. Grand Rapids, MI: Kregel Publications, 1993, pp. 13-14, adapted.
4. Ibid., pp. 14-15.
5. Richard F. Berg and Christine McCartney. *Depression and the Integrated Life*. New York: Alba House, 1981, p. 34, adapted.
6. "The Promises to Pray with My Wife" by John Yates in Bill McCartney, *What Makes a Man*. Colorado Springs: NavPress, 1992, pp. 72, 73, adapted.
7. Lloyd John Ogilvie. *Discovering God's Will for Your Life*. Eugene, OR: Harvest House Publishers, 1982, p. 136.
8. A.W. Tozer. *The Knowledge of the Holy*. New York: Harper and Row, 1961, pp. 79-82, adapted.
9. Sheila West. *Beyond Chaos*. Colorado Springs: NavPress, 1991, p. 173.
10. Henry Gariepy. *100 Portraits of Christ*. Wheaton, IL: Victor Press, 1987, pp. 31, 32, adapted.
11. Reprinted from *Released from Shame* by Sandra D. Wilson. © 1990 by Sandra D. Wilson, p. 11. Used by permission of InterVarsity Press, Downers Grove, IL 60515.
12. Delores Kuenning. *Helping People Through Grief*. Minneapolis: Bethany House Publishers, 1987, pp. 20, 21.
13. Reprinted from *Where Is God in My Suffering?* by Daniel Simundson, copyright © 1983. Augsburg Publishing House, pp. 28, 29. Used by permission of Augsburg Fortress.
14. Stuart Briscoe. *Sermon on the Mount*. Wheaton, IL: Harold Shaw Publishers, 1995, pp. 139-41, adapted.
15. Ibid., pp. 166-69, adapted.
16. Archibald Hart. *15 Principles for Achieving Happiness*. Dallas: Word, Inc., 1988, pp. 168-69.
17. J.I. Packer and Sangwoo Youtong Chee. "A Bad Trip." *Christianity Today*, March 7, 1986, p. 12.
18. Kevin Lehman. *Measuring Up*. Old Tappan, NJ: Fleming H. Revell Co., 1988, pp. 165-66.
19. Pat Hershey Owen. *Seven Styles of Parenting*. Wheaton, IL: Tyndale House Publishers, 1983, pp. 108-15, adapted.
20. Taken from *The Root of the Righteous* by A.W. Tozer, p. 16. Copyright 1995, 1986 by Lowell Tozer. Published by Christian Publications, Inc. Used by permission.
21. Reprinted from *Parents in Pain* by John White. © 1979 by InterVarsity Christian Fellowship of the USA, p. 164. Used by permission of InterVarsity Press, Downers Grove, IL 60515.
22. Joyce Landorf Heatherly. *Changepoints*. Austin, TX: Balcony Publishing, 1992, p. 124-25.
23. Lloyd John Ogilvie. *God's Best for My Life*. Eugene, OR: Harvest House Publishers, 1981, January 8.
24. Jeanne Zorner. *When I Prayed for Patience, God Let Me Have It!* Wheaton, IL: Harold Shaw Publishers, 1995, pp. 68-72, adapted.

May

1. William L. Coleman. *Before I Give You Away*. Minneapolis: Bethany House Publishers, 1995, pp. 25-28.
2. Dennis Rainey. *The Tribute*. Nashville: Thomas Nelson Publishers, 1994, pp. 276-77.

3. William Barclay. *The Gospel of Matthew*, vol. 1. Westminster: The Westminster Press, 1956, pp. 114-18, adapted.

4. Jeanne Zorner. *When I Prayed for Patience, God Let Me Have It!* Wheaton, IL: Harold Shaw Publishers, 1995, pp. 86-91, adapted.

5. Lloyd John Ogilvie. *God's Best for My Life.* Eugene, OR: Harvest House Publishers, 1981, May 9.

6. Zorner. *When I Prayed*, pp. 105-09, adapted.

7. Ibid., p. 124.

8. Ibid., pp. 120-26, adapted.

9. From *Is the Family Here to Stay?* by David Allan Hubbard. Dallas: Word, Inc., 1971, p. 78.

10. From *What Is a Family?* by Edith Schaeffer. Old Tappan, NJ: Fleming H. Revell Co., 1975, p. 51.

11. Henry Gariepy. *100 Portraits of Christ.* Wheaton, IL: Victor Press, 1987, pp. 43-44, adapted.

12. Kent and Barbara Hughes. *Common-Sense Parenting.* © 1995, p. 85. Used by permission of Tyndale House Publishers, Inc. All rights reserved.

13. Matthew L. Linn and D. Linn. *Healing Memories.* Ramsey, NJ: Paulist Press, 1974, pp. 11, 12.

14. Max Lucado. *The Eye of the Storm.* Dallas: Word, Inc., 1991, p. 29.

15. Dean Merrill. *Wait Quietly, Devotions for Busy Parents,* © 1994, pp. 22-23. Used by permission of Tyndale House Publishers, Inc. All rights reserved.

16. Lloyd John Ogilvie. *Climbing the Rainbow.* Dallas: Word, Inc., 1993, pp. 106-08, adapted.

17. Ibid., pp. 114-19, adapted.

18. Dr. Chris Thurman. *If Christ Were Your Counselor.* Nashville: Thomas Nelson Publishers, 1993, pp. 30-37, adapted.

19. Lloyd John Ogilvie. *Lord of the Loose Ends.* Dallas: Word, Inc., 1991, pp. 43-47, adapted.

20. From *What Is a Family?* Schaeffer, p. 119, adapted.

21. Charles R. Swindoll. *Home, Where Life Makes Up Its Mind.* Portland, OR: Multnomah Press, 1979, p. 13.

22. Ogilvie. *Lord of the Loose Ends*, pp. 53-55, adapted.

23. Ibid., pp. 100-12, adapted.

24. Myron Chartier. "Parenting: A Theological Model." *Journal of Psychology and Theology*, 6:54-61 (1978).

25. Ogilvie. *Lord of the Loose Ends*, pp. 127-32, adapted.

June

1. Ralf Garborg. *The Family Blessing.* Dallas: Word, Inc., 1987, adapted from pp. 11-12.

2. H. Norman Wright. *Chosen for Blessing.* Eugene, OR: Harvest House Publishers, 1992, pp. 23-24, adapted.

3. Mel Krantzler. *Creative Marriage.* New York: McGraw-Hill, 1988, p. 54.

4. James C. Dobson. *Straight Talk to Men and Their Wives.* Waco, TX: Word Books, 1980, p. 136.

5. H. Norman Wright and Gary J. Oliver. *Raising Emotionally Healthy Kids.* Wheaton, IL: Victor Press, 1993, p. 154, adapted.

6. Lloyd John Ogilvie. *Silent Strength for My Life.* Eugene, OR: Harvest House Publishers, 1990, p. 27.

7. Lloyd John Ogilvie. *Lord of the Loose Ends.* Dallas: Word, Inc., 1991, pp. 12-15, adapted.

8. Ogilvie. *Silent Strength*, p. 218.

9. Ibid.

10. Phillip Keller. *Strength of Soul.* Grand Rapids, MI: Kregel Publications, 1993, p. 29.

11. Ogilvie. *Silent Strength*, p. 321, adapted.

12. Stuart Briscoe. *The Sermon on the Mount.* Wheaton, IL: Harold Shaw Publishers, 1995, pp. 9-10, adapted.

13. Sarah Doudney. "The Hardest Time of All" from *The Light of the World: Poems of Faith and Consolation* by Joseph Morris and St. Clair Adams. New York: George Sully and Co., 1928, p. 64.

14. Henry Gariepy. *100 Portraits of Christ.* Wheaton, IL: Victor Press, 1987, pp. 55-56, adapted.

15. *Webster's New World Dictionary, Third College Edition.* New York: Prentice Hall, 1994, adapted.

16. Ogilvie. *Silent Strength*, p. 243, adapted.
17. Lloyd John Ogilvie. *God's Best for My Life*. Eugene, OR: Harvest House Publishers, 1981, June 19.
18. As found in Ronda De La Sola Chervin. *A Mother's Treasury of Prayers*. Ann Arbor, MI: Servant Publications, 1994, p. 181. Adapted from *The Spiritual Warrior's Prayer Guide* by Quin Sherrer and Ruthanne Garlock.
19. Ogilvie. *Silent Strength*, p. 180, adapted.
20. Ibid., p. 180.
21. Dr. Sidney Simon. *Getting Unstuck*. New York: Warner Books, 1988, pp. 175-79, adapted.
22. H. Norman Wright. *Chosen for Blessing*. Eugene, OR: Harvest House Publishers, 1992, pp. 110-11.
23. Jack and Judith Bolswick. *The Dual-Earner Marriage*. Grand Rapids, MI: Fleming H. Revell, 1995, pp. 173-74, 179-80.
24. Carol Kent. *Tame Your Fears*. Colorado Springs: NavPress, 1993, p. 64.
25. Reprinted from *Work, Play and Worship in a Leisure-Oriented Society* by Gordon Dahl, copyright © 1972. Augsburg Publishing House, p. 12. Used by permission of Augsburg Fortress.
26. Paul Walker. *How to Keep Your Joy*. Nashville: Thomas Nelson Publishers, 1987, p. 17.
27. "Celebrate the Temporary" by Clyde Reide, in Bob Benson and Michael W. Benson. *Disciplines for the Inner Life*. Dallas: Word, Inc., 1985, p. 331.

July

1. Taken from *Instructive Moments with the Savior* by Ken Gire. Copyright © 1990 by Ken Gire, p. 60. Used by permission of Zondervan Publishing House.
2. Patrick Morley. *Two-Part Harmony*. Nashville: Thomas Nelson Publishers, 1994, pp. 38, 146-47, 182-83.
3. Pat Hershey Owen. *Seven Styles of Parenting*. Wheaton, IL: Tyndale House Publishers, 1983, pp. 93-99, adapted.
4. Quin Sherrer. *How to Pray for Your Children*. Lynnwood, WA: Aglow Publications, 1986, pp. 17, 18.
5. Henry Gariepy. *100 Portraits of Christ*. Wheaton, IL: Victor Press, 1987, pp. 65-66, adapted.
6. Paul Lewis. *The Five Key Habits of Smart Dads*. Grand Rapids, MI: Zondervan Publishing House, 1994, pp. 65, 73, 75, 87, adapted.
7. J.I. Packer. *Knowing God*. Downers Grove, IL: InterVarsity Press, 1973, pp. 73-80, adapted.
8. Charles Swindoll. *Living Beyond the Daily Grind*, bk. 1. Dallas: Word, Inc., 1988, p. 45.
9. Foster Cline, M.D., and Jim Fay. *Parenting Teens with Love's Logic*. Colorado Springs: Pinon Press, 1992, pp. 30-31, adapted.
10. Kent and Barbara Hughes. *Common-Sense Parenting*. Wheaton, IL: Tyndale House Publishers, 1995, pp. 131-36, adapted.
11. Ronda De Sola Chervin. *A Mother's Treasury of Prayers*. Ann Arbor, MI: Servant Publications, 1994, pp. 89-90. Used by permission.
12. Sherrer. *How to Pray*, p. 76.
13. Phyllis McGinley. *The Promise of the Heart*. New York: Dell Publishers Co., 1959, p. 72.
14. Elton Trueblood. *The Recovery of the Family*. New York: Harper and Row, 1953, p. 94.
15. Hughes and Hughes. *Common-Sense Parenting*, pp. 25-29, adapted.
16. Stormie Omartian. *The Power of a Praying Parent*. Eugene, OR: Harvest House Publishers, 1995, pp. 13-14.
17. Lewis. *Five Key Habits*, pp. 15-16.
18. "Above All Else" by Stormie Omartian. Copyright 1987 by Michael and Stormie Omartian. See This House Music/ASCAP.
19. E. Stanley Jones. *Christian Maturity*. Nashville: Abingdon Press.
20. Reprinted from *Light in a Dark Place* by Henry Gariepy. Wheaton, IL: Victor Press, 1995, pp. 72-73, adapted.
21. Omartian, *Power of a Praying Parent*, pp. 13-14.
22. Ibid., p. 127.
23. "The Importance of Humor" by Tim Hansel. Reprinted from *Parents and Children*, Jay Kessler, Ron Beers, and LaVonne Neff, eds. Victor Press, 1986, pp. 105-06.

August

1. Gary Jackson Oliver and H. Norman Wright. *When Anger Hits Home.* Chicago: Moody Press, 1992, pp. 76-77, adapted.
2. Rudolph Norden. *Each Day with Jesus.* St. Louis: Concordia Publishing House, 1994, p. 150, adapted. Used by permission.
3. Ibid., p. 364.
4. Ibid., adapted.
5. Dennis Rainey. *The Tribute.* Nashville: Thomas Nelson Publishers, 1994, p. 15, adapted.
6. Taken from *Growing Wise in Family Life* by Charles Swindoll, p. 59. Copyright © 1988 by Charles R. Swindoll, Inc. (Retitled: *The Strong Family*). Used by permission of Zondervan Publishing House.
7. Henry Gariepy. *100 Portraits of Christ.* Wheaton, IL: Victor Press, 1987, p. 88.
8. Lloyd John Ogilvie. *Silent Strength for My Life.* Eugene, OR: Harvest House Publishers, 1990, p. 222.
9. Carl Mayhall. *When God Whispers.* Colorado Springs: NavPress, 1994, p. 40.
10. Stormie Omartian. *The Power of a Praying Parent.* Eugene, OR: Harvest House Publishers, 1995, pp. 13-14.
11. Max Lucado. *No Wonder They Call Him the Savior.* Portland, OR: Multnomah Press, 1986, pp. 105-06.
12. H. Norman Wright. *Chosen for Blessing.* Eugene, OR: Harvest House Publishers, 1992, pp. 66-67, adapted.
13. Reprinted from *Forty Ways to Say "I Love You"* by James R. Bjorge. Copyright © 1978 Augsburg Publishing House, pp. 91, 92. Used by permission of Augsburg Fortress.
14. Charles R. Swindoll. *The Grace Awakening.* Dallas: Word, Inc., 1990, pp. 8-9, adapted.
15. Ibid.
16. Tim Kimmel. *Legacy of Love.* Portland, OR: Multnomah Press, 1989, pp. 261-62.
17. Verna Birkey. *Less Stress, More Peace.* Grand Rapids, MI: Fleming H. Revell, 1995, pp. 20-21, adapted.
18. Gariepy. *100 Portraits,* pp. 72-73, adapted.
19. Norden. *Each Day with Jesus,* p. 83.
20. Ibid., adapted.
21. John Mark Templeton. *Discovering the Laws of Life.* New York: Continuum, 1994, pp. 22-23, adapted.
22. Norden. *Each Day with Jesus,* p. 120, adapted.
23. Paul and Jeannie McKean. *Leading a Child to Independence.* San Bernardino, CA: Here's Life Publishers, 1986, pp. 144-45.
24. Tony and Bart Campolo. *Things We Wish We Had Said.* Dallas: Word, Inc., 1989, p. 63.

September

1. *Webster's New World Dictionary, Third College Edition.* New York: Prentice Hall, 1994.
2. Dean Merrill. *Wait Quietly, Devotions for Busy Parents.* Wheaton, IL: Tyndale House Publishers, Inc., 1994, pp. 108-09, adapted.
3. Ibid., p. 42, adapted.
4. *Webster's New Twentieth Century Dictionary, Unabridged.*
5. Pat Hershey Owen. *Seven Styles of Parenting.* Wheaton, IL: Tyndale House Publishers, 1983, pp. 82-89, adapted.
6. Merrill. *Wait Quietly,* pp. 79-80, adapted.
7. Ibid., p. 81, adapted.
8. Ibid., pp. 82-83, adapted.
9. H. Norman Wright. *Recovering from the Losses of Life.* Grand Rapids: Fleming H. Revell, 1993, pp. 148-49.
10. *Oxford Unabridged Dictionary.*
11. James R. Beck and David T. Moore. *Why Worry?* Grand Rapids, MI: Baker Book House, 1994, pp. 18-20, adapted.
12. Merrill. *Wait Quietly,* pp. 216-17.
13. Henry Gariepy. *100 Portraits of Christ.* Wheaton, IL: Victor Press, 1987, pp. 95-96, adapted.
14. Ibid., p. 96.

15. Max Lucado. *The Angels Were Silent*. Dallas: Word, Inc., 1992, p. 42.
16. Joni Eareckson Tada. *Secret Strength for Those Who Search*. Sisters, OR: Multnomah Press, 1994, p. 100.
17. Neil Anderson with Joanne Anderson. *Daily in Christ*. Eugene, OR: Harvest House Publishers, 1993, February 29.
18. Carol Kent. *Tame Your Fears*. Colorado Springs: NavPress, 1993, pp. 28-29.
19. W. Bingham Hunter. *The God Who Hears*. Downers Grove, IL: InterVarsity Press, 1986, pp. 111-14, adapted.
20. John Mark Templeton. *Discovering the Laws of Life*. New York: Continuum, 1994, p. 189, adapted.
21. Ronda De Sola Chervin, *A Mother's Treasury of Prayers*. Poem by Judith Mattison, adapted from *Delight in the Gift*, pp. 103-04. Used by permission.
22. Anderson with Anderson. *Daily in Christ*, May 31.
23. Lee Roberts. *Praying God's Will for My Daughter/Son*. Nashville: Thomas Nelson Publishers, 1993, selected portions adapted.
24. Archibald Hart. *15 Principles for Achieving Happiness*. Dallas: Word, Inc., 1988, p. 24, adapted.
25. Anderson with Anderson. *Daily in Christ*, March 14.
26. H. Norman Wright. *Always Daddy's Girl*. Ventura, CA: Regal Books, 1989, p. 195.
27. Reprinted from *Light in a Dark Place* by Henry Gariepy. Wheaton, IL: Victor Press, 1995, p. 226.
28. Ibid., pp. 226-27, adapted.

October

1. Marshall Shelly. "Helping Those Who Don't Want Help." *Christianity Today* (1968), 65-66, adapted.
2. "The Impossible Is the Untried" by Jim Goodwin in John Mark Templeton. *Discovering the Laws of Life*. New York: Continuum, 1994, pp. 31-32, adapted.
3. Haim G. Ginot. *Between Parent and Child: New Solutions to Old Problems*. New York: Macmillan, 1965, pp. 34-35.
4. Sheila West. *Beyond Chaos*. Colorado Springs: NavPress, 1991, pp. 137-41, adapted.
5. Archibald Hart. *Stress and Your Child*. Dallas: Word, Inc., 1992, p. 224.
6. Rudolph Norden. *Each Day with Jesus*. St. Louis: Concordia Publishing House, 1994, p. 199, adapted. Used by permission.
7. Reprinted from Henry Gariepy. *100 Portraits of Christ*. Wheaton, IL: Victor Press, 1987, pp. 89-90, adapted.
8. Richard Exley. *The Rhythm of Life*. Tulsa: Honor Books, 1987, pp. 127, 137.
9. Lloyd John Ogilvie. *Silent Strength for My Life*. Eugene, OR: Harvest House Publishers, 1990, p. 276.
10. Lloyd John Ogilvie. *Lord of the Loose Ends*. Dallas: Word, Inc., 1991, pp. 55-57, adapted.
11. Neil Anderson with Joanne Anderson. *Daily in Christ*. Eugene, OR: Harvest House Publishers, 1993, February 28, adapted.
12. Edwin Lewis Cole. *Maximized Manhood*. Copyright ©1982, used by permission of the publisher, Whitaker House, 580 Pittsburgh Street, Springdale, PA 15144, pp. 118, 120.
13. Dr. Chris Thurman. *If Christ Were Your Counselor*. Nashville: Thomas Nelson Publishers, 1993, pp. 48-58, adapted.
14. Anderson with Anderson. *Daily in Christ*, March 9.
15. Taken from *Growing Wise in Family Life* by Charles Swindoll, p. 44. Copyright © 1988 by Charles R. Swindoll, Inc. (Retitled: *The Strong Family*). Used by permission of Zondervan Publishing House.
16. Charlie Shedd. *You Can Be a Great Parent* (formerly *Promise to Peter*). Dallas: Word, Inc., 1970, p. 16.
17. Dean Merrill. *Wait Quietly, Devotions for Busy Parents*. Wheaton, IL: Tyndale House Publishers, 1994, pp. 186-87, adapted.
18. Anderson with Anderson. *Daily in Christ*, April 6, adapted.
19. Chuck Swindoll. *The Grace Awakening*. Dallas: Word, Inc., 1990, pp. 146-47.
20. Reprinted from Gariepy. *100 Portraits of Christ*, pp. 78-79.
21. Ibid, p. 79.
22. Templeton. *Discovering the Laws of Life*, pp. 63-64, adapted.

November

1. Jack and Judith Bolswick. *The Dual-Earner Marriage*. Grand Rapids, MI: Fleming H. Revell, 1995, p. 171, adapted.

2. W. Bingham Hunter. *The God Who Hears*. Downers Grove, IL: InterVarsity Press, 1986, pp. 192-98, adapted.

3. Lloyd John Ogilvie. *Silent Strength for My Life*. Eugene, OR: Harvest House Publishers, 1990, p. 233, adapted.

4. John Mark Templeton. *Discovering the Laws of Life*. New York: Continuum, 1994, pp. 74-75, adapted.

5. Ibid., "Fill Every Unforgiving Moment with Sixty Seconds of Distance Run" by Rudyard Kipling, pp. 59-60, adapted.

6. Dr. Archibald Hart. *Stress and Your Child*. Dallas: Word, Inc., 1992, pp. 66-69, adapted.

7. Ronda De Sola Chervin. *A Mother's Treasury of Prayers*. Ann Arbor, MI: Servant Publications, 1994, pp. 34, 35. Used by permission.

8. Dr. Chris Thurman. *If Christ Were Your Counselor*. Nashville: Thomas Nelson Publishers, 1993, p. 134.

9. Gary Jackson Oliver and H. Norman Wright. *When Anger Hits Home*. Chicago: Moody Press, 1992, p. 65, adapted.

10. Pat Hershey Owen. *Seven Styles of Parenting*. Wheaton, IL: Tyndale House Publishers, 1983, pp. 66-77, adapted.

11. Hart. *Stress and Your Child*, pp. 15-16.

12. Henry Gariepy. *100 Portraits of Christ*. Wheaton, IL: Victor Press, 1987, pp. 93-94, adapted.

13. Joni Eareckson Tada. *Secret Strength for Those Who Search*. Sisters, OR: Multnomah Books, 1994, pp. 33-34, adapted.

14. Lloyd John Ogilvie. *Conversations with God*. Eugene, OR: Harvest House Publishers, 1992, pp. 19-20.

15. Richard Foster. *The Freedom of Simplicity*. San Francisco: Harper and Row, 1981, p. 91.

16. Ogilvie. *Silent Strength*, pp. 345-46, adapted.

17. William Barclay. *A Barclay Prayer Book*. London: SCM Press Ltd., 1990, pp. 8, 9.

18. Stuart Briscoe. *Sermon on the Mount*. Wheaton, IL: Harold Shaw Publishers, 1995, pp. 84-85, adapted.

19. *Webster's New World Dictionary, Third College Edition*. New York: Prentice Hall, 1994.

20. Tim Kimmel. *Legacy of Love*. Portland, OR: Multnomah Press, 1989, pp. 139-40.

December

1. Archibald Hart. *15 Principles for Achieving Happiness*. Dallas: Word, Inc., 1988, selected pages, adapted.

2. Rosalind Rinker. Original source unknown.

3. Dwight Small. *After You've Said "I Do."* Westwood, NJ: Fleming H. Revell, 1968, pp. 243-44, adapted.

4. Lloyd John Ogilvie. *Conversations with God*. Eugene, OR: Harvest House Publishers, 1993, pp. 32-33.

5. James R. Beck and David T. Moore. *Why Worry?* Grand Rapids, MI: Baker Book House, 1994, pp. 26-29, adapted.

6. Dean Merrill. *Wait Quietly, Devotions for Busy Parents*. © 1994, pp. 160-61. Used by permission of Tyndale House Publishers, Inc. All rights reserved.

7. Taken from *Instructive Moments with the Savior* by Ken Gire. Copyright © 1990 by Ken Gire, p. 95. Used by permission of Zondervan Publishing House.

8. Taken from *Incredible Moments with the Savior* by Ken Gire. Copyright © 1990 by Ken Gire, pp. 96, 97. Used by permission of Zondervan Publishing House.

9. Kent and Barbara Hughes. *Common-Sense Parenting*. © 1995, p. 91. Used by permission of Tyndale House Publishers, Inc. All rights reserved.

10. Taken from *Daily Thoughts for Disciples* by Oswald Chambers, p. 75. Copyright © 1994 by the Oswald Chambers Publications Assoc. Ltd. Originally published by Zondervan Publishers © 1976. Used by permission of Discovery House Publishers, Grand Rapids, MI 49501. All rights reserved.

11. "The Promises You Make to Worship and Fellowship" by Gary Smalley and John Trent in Bill McCartney, ed., *What Makes a Man.* Colorado Springs: NavPress, 1992, pp. 141-42.
12. Neil Anderson with Joanne Anderson. *Daily in Christ.* Eugene, OR: Harvest House Publishers, 1993, May 31, adapted.
13. Carol Kent. *Tame Your Fears.* Colorado Springs: NavPress, 1993, p. 50, adapted.
14. Taken from *Home, Where Life Makes Up Its Mind* by Chuck Swindoll. Copyright © 1979, 1983 by Charles R. Swindoll, Inc. Used by permission of Zondervan Publishing House.
15. Paul Ennis. *Approaching God.* Chicago: Moody Publishers, 1991, May 18, adapted.
16. Tim Kimmel. *Legacy of Love.* Portland, OR: Multnomah Press, 1989, p. 215.
17. Ibid., pp. 199-200, adapted.
18. Ennis. *Approaching God,* August 15, adapted.
19. "Parenting: Sacrifice or Investment?" by V. Gilbert Beers. Reprinted from *Parents and Children,* Jay Kessler, Ron Beers, LaVonne Neff, eds. Wheaton, IL: Victor Press, 1986, pp. 79, 80, adapted.
20. Reprinted from *Light in a Dark Place* by Henry Gariepy. Wheaton, IL: Victor Press, 1995, pp. 250-51.
21. Dr. Chris Thurman. *If Christ Were Your Counselor.* Nashville: Thomas Nelson Publishers, 1993, pp. 14-20, adapted.
22. Richard Exley. *Straight from the Heart for Couples.* Tulsa: Honor Books, 1993, p. 36.
23. William Barclay. *A Barclay Prayer Book.* London: SCM Press Ltd., 1990, pp. 16, 17.
24. "A Smile Breeds a Smile" by Ted Engstrom in John Mark Templeton, *Discovering the Laws of Life.* New York: Continuum, 1994, pp. 18-19, adapted.
25. Richard Exley. *The Rhythm of Life.* Tulsa: Honor Books, 1987, p. 14, adapted.
26. Ibid., p. 14.
27. David L. McKenna. *The Communicator's Commentary.* Waco, TX: Word, Inc., 1982, p. 77.
28. Lloyd John Ogilvie. *Climbing the Rainbow.* Dallas: Word, Inc., 1993, pp. 103-04, adapted.
29. Reprinted from Henry Gariepy. *100 Portraits of Christ.* Wheaton, IL: Victor Press, 1987, pp. 213-14, adapted.
30. Robert Hicks. *Failure to Scream.* Nashville: Thomas Nelson Publishers, 1993, pp. 621-39, adapted.

Index